COUNTRY LIFE

THE COUNTRY YEAR

A NATURE WATCHER'S CALENDAR AND FIELD GUIDE

GEOFFREY YOUNG

GUILD PUBLISHING
LONDON

CONTENTS

Published in 1989 by
George Philip Limited,
59 Grosvenor Street,
London W1X 9DA

This edition published
1989 by Guild Publishing
by arrangement with
George Philip Limited

CN 3980

Design Teresa Foster
Printed in Italy

INTRODUCTION

This book is for everyone who enjoys the British countryside. It provides a starting point for those who are not merely content to recognize what they see in the countryside, but who wish to understand its place in a constantly changing environment. Month by month, *The Country Year* explains what is happening in the natural world around us, and the complex interactions which lie behind the events we see. It also points out items of interest that we may realistically hope to find, or should look out for, on a country walk.

Each month begins with five introductory aspects of the countryside—five faces of the countryside, if you like.

First, the introduction to the month itself. Over the centuries, natural events have become closely linked with the seemingly unnatural world of human affairs. As well as mentioning some of the highlights of the month that lies ahead, here we also see how nature has become incorporated into human lore and customs.

Understanding the *weather* is, of course, crucial to our understanding of the natural world as a whole, and this is particularly true in Britain, where the weather tends to be so unsettled.

Geography clearly has a strong influence. Situated at the edge of the European mainland and facing the wide expanse of the Atlantic Ocean, Britain has a correspondingly wet (especially so in the hillier west and north) and changeable climate. As weather plays such a vital role in the country year, not only are the anticipated weather patterns analysed for each month, but certain specific aspects of weather are also explored, which are of prime importance to plants and animals. Rain is one of these topics; dew, frost and thunderstorms are others.

However, as the book explains, a local 'microclimate', resulting from such things as aspect and shelter, can have a great impact, making one field very different from another, or even one side of a lane contrast markedly with its opposite. It is important, therefore, that these factors are also taken into account in our understanding.

The countryside today would not be what it is without *farming*, and so, month by month, we gain a glimpse of the work and pleasures which make up the farmer's year. There is, of course, a great difference between hill farming in the Lake District and arable farming in Suffolk, or between Somerset (still a strongly dairy county) and the Shires, for example. However, within these pages we get a bird's-eye view of farm life as a whole.

Primarily, though, the countryside is the home of nature, and this is explored in two ways. Firstly, a key aspect of *natural life* is highlighted and investigated. The secrets of such things as bird song and migration, hibernation, and the special problems which face life on the rocky shore, are revealed. Nor are plants forgotten—for example, we see why some remain green in winter, and examine whether certain plants are able to predict the weather.

Secondly, each month a specific location is visited—a *classic countryside* where something of particular interest is to be seen. In June, for example, the Norfolk Broads are at the height of their beauty, while in September a Chiltern beech wood is much to be enjoyed. The seaside is also considered, with visits to the Farne Islands in April, and the famous Braunton sand dunes in July. A short gazetteer of similar sites is given for each month, chosen to provide interesting trips throughout the country.

The Country Year is also intended to be of practical, everyday use—a helpful reference book to look at before setting out on walks, in order to see and understand fully what may be encountered along the way. For this reason, a field guide is presented for each month. In the course of the year, no less than 600 different species are profiled. These include all the birds likely to be seen in the countryside, and all mammals, amphibians and reptiles, except for the very rare.

A number of fish, both freshwater and marine, may be seen at various times, and these are examined in the appropriate month. Butterflies and other insects and invertebrates are also well covered, as are a good many beautiful wild flowers, shrubs and trees. Toadstools and other fungi figure at their allotted times, too.

The field guides have been divided into five sections for ease of reference: woods and forests; lanes and fields; lakes and rivers; moors and heaths; coasts and estuaries.

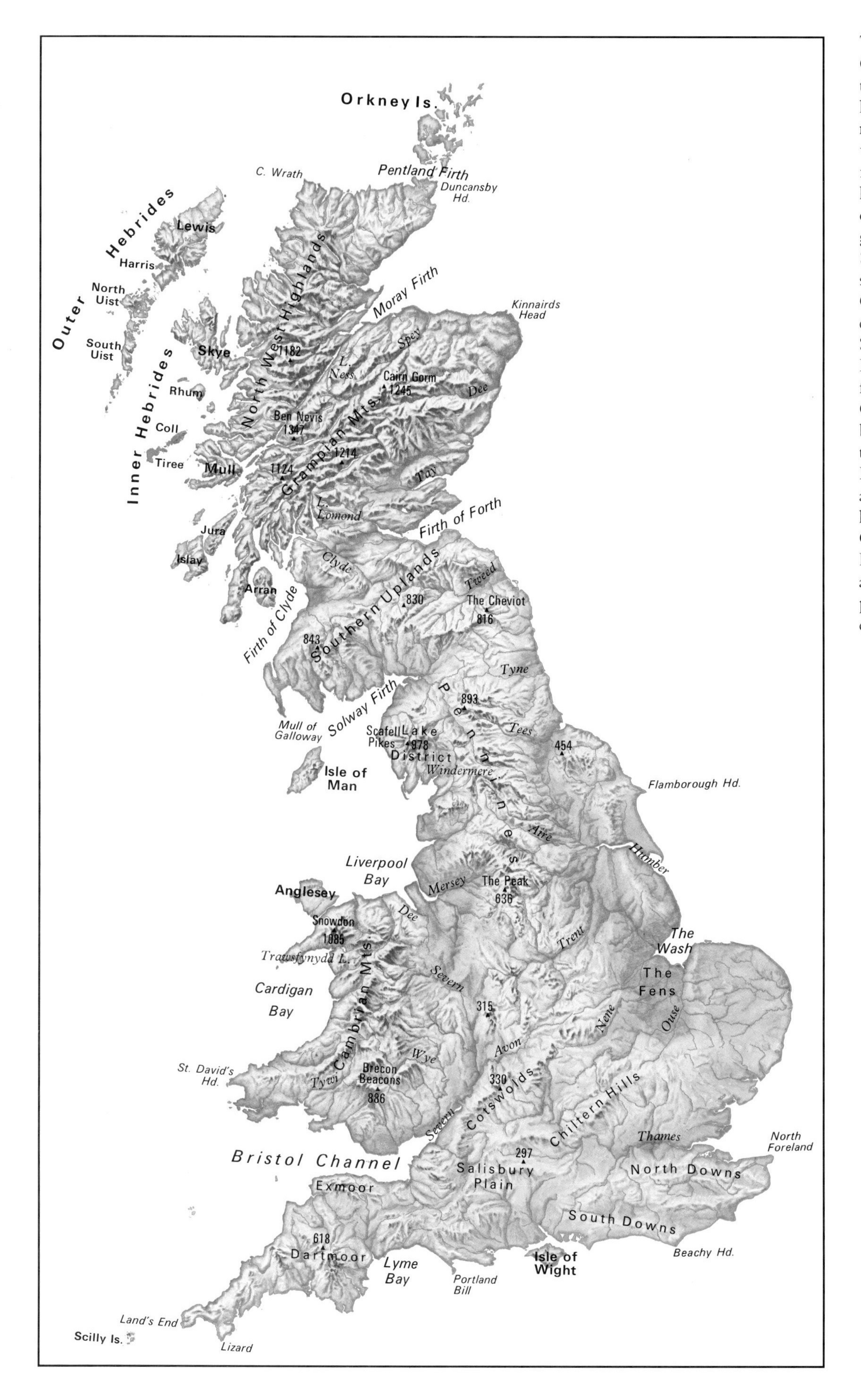

This relief map of Great Britain shows the higher ground lying to the west and north; here there are vast tracts of moorland, while heathlands are located on acid sand or gravel soils in Dorset, Surrey and other southern counties. Chalk downland extends from Salisbury Plain into Dorset and also forms the line of the Chilterns and beyond, as well as the North and South Downs. Limy soils are also provided by limestone in the Cotswolds, the White Peak and some other areas. The valleys and plains usually have clay soils.

However, to understand these five categories, and to make the best use of this book, it is important first to understand the history of the land—for when we walk in today's countryside, we see echoes of very distant times, together with features of today, and a foretaste (in the newly-planted farm woodlands, for example) of tomorrow.

By and large, the rocks that underlie the British landscape are positioned at a slant, which means that the oldest reach the surface in the west and north, sculptured into rugged hills by rivers, and by the glaciers of the Ice Ages. And to set the scene for *The Country Year* we must start when the last Ice Age was waning, about 12,000 years ago.

As the ground unfroze, plants, and in time trees, colonized the land, creating a tangled wildwood in all but the bleakest and wettest sites. Eventually, the rising sea level flooded the English Channel. Soon afterwards, our first farming tribes (New Stone Age) were crossing the country with their livestock. They chose the lighter wooded areas, and cleared fields for their corn while grazing their animals roundabout.

Uncontrolled grazing will, over the course of centuries, destroy woodland; and grazing continued until modern times, maintaining open ground, aided perhaps by climatic changes. This is what we now see as chalk downland, heathland and moorland (tree stumps and pollen found preserved in the peat prove that even the bleak moors were once wooded).

The Stone Age tribes were succeeded by others bringing metal and better ploughs, able to tackle the heavier valley soils. The Romans organized the process (and also began the drainage of many wetlands), and as the population rose over the centuries, the woodland became patchy. In any event, it was no longer true wildwood, but was being cropped as intensively as the fields, supplying timber and 'smallwood' for different uses.

By this time the villages were usually set amidst wide, open ploughland—the open fields of the old manors. But smaller hedged

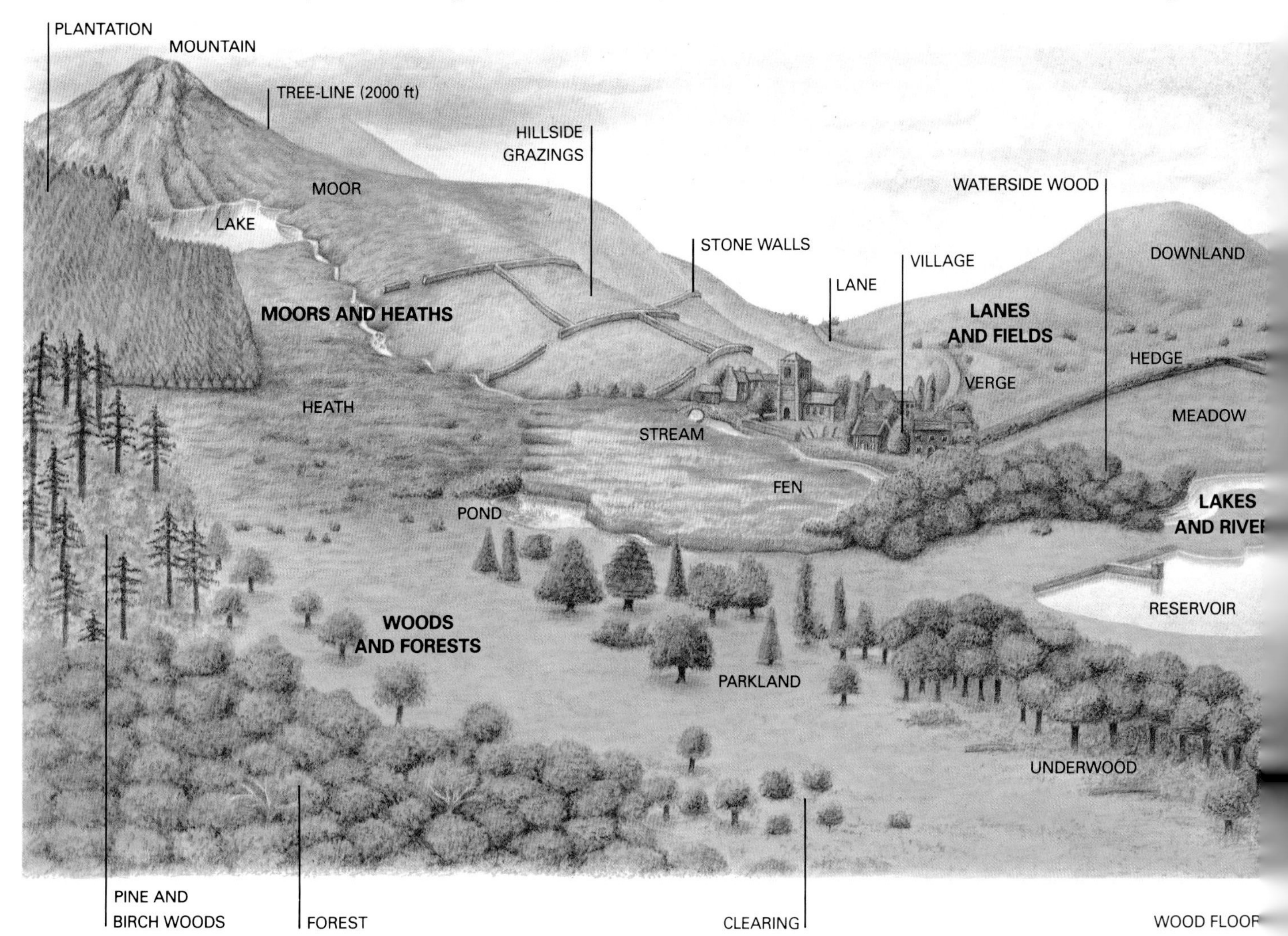

(or walled) fields were already part of the countryside, both in those areas where new ploughland and grazing were still being hacked from the woodland (the 'ancient and ornamental' countryside of parts of the West Country and Essex, for example), and also around the villages. Here cosy fields were hedged or walled to house livestock. Each area has its own detailed field history—in some places, for example, the great abbeys enclosed sheep walks on village lands emptied by the great plagues.

Eventually, smaller fields won the day. In Georgian times almost all that was left of hedgeless lowland countryside, including the open grazing commons and wastes, was enclosed within neatly gridded fields in which new crops and fertilizers, plus new breeds and rotations, could be tested. Farming was even then becoming an industry.

The patchwork fields, both old and new, began to mature. Blowsy hedgerows lapped against stately hedgerow trees, nooky corners abounded, lit by clouds of butterflies, and the bluebell woods and copses rang with bird song. Snipes and lapwings swooped over the meadows that lay alongside rivers, and there were pockets of wetland paradise to be found everywhere—this was the British countryside of everyone's imagination.

In recent decades, however, national policy backed by grant aid has seen hedgerows grubbed up for larger fields, old hay meadows drained and ploughed, and heaths and moors disappearing under the plough or being planted with conifers. Not even ancient oak woods have escaped, for many have been felled and replanted with conifers.

Times are again changing, though. With more food being produced than can be sold, plans are now being laid to take land out of farming, and some of the proposals include new opportunities for wildlife.

Experts recognize up to 30 different kinds of habitats, or living places for wildlife, in Britain's countryside. The illustration below explains how these have been amalgamated into our five key groups to aid identification.

This scene shows how the different habitats are grouped together in the field guide pages. Some of the rather similar habitats which neighbour each other in our scene may share species: the wildlife of a plantation may resemble that of a natural pine wood, which in turn may share some wildlife with forests and woodlands; these will themselves overlap with spinneys and hedges. However, downland and moorland, although both bare, high ground, share few species.

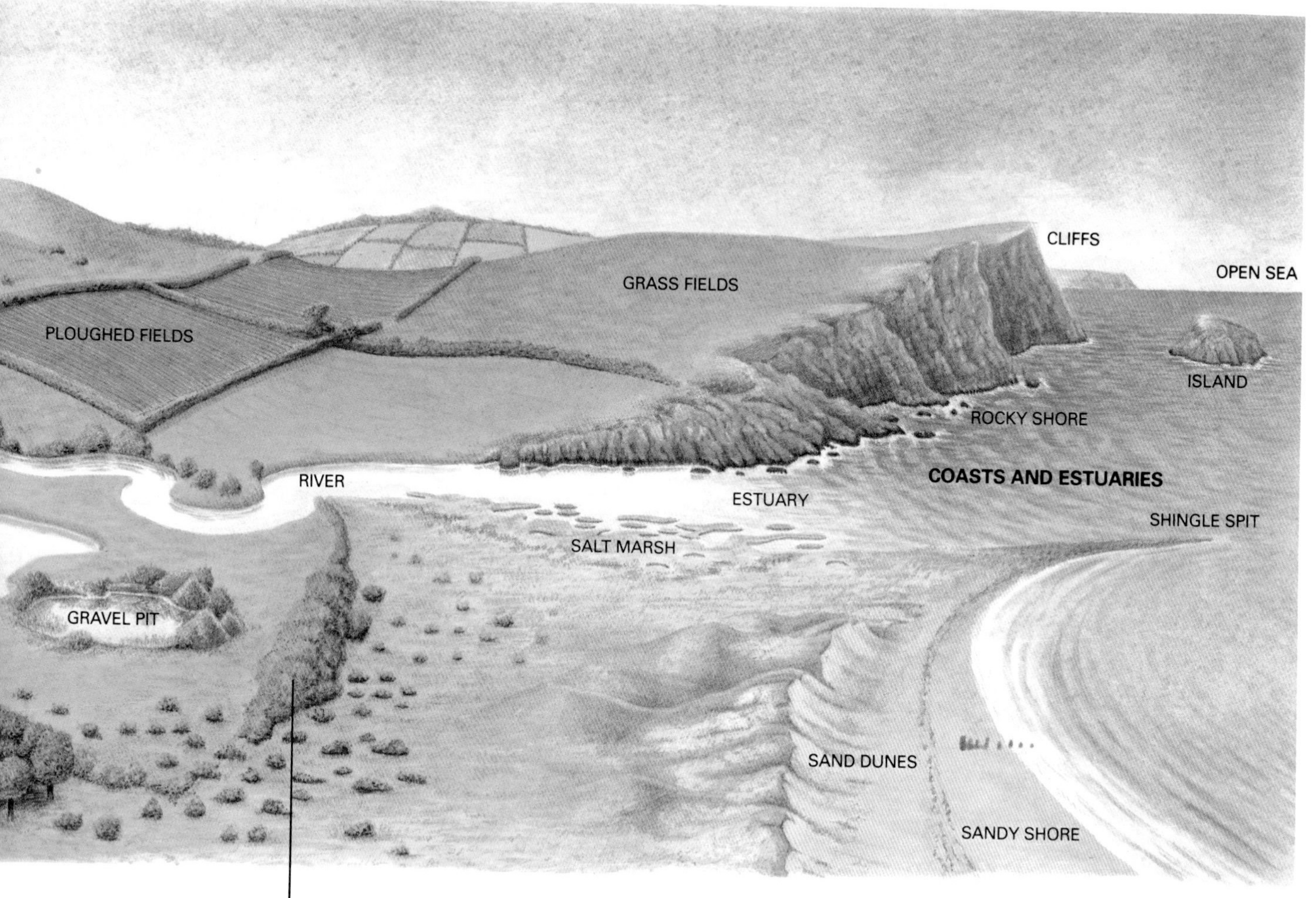

Normally, it is the plants that identify the place. To put it simply, you know you are in a wood because of the trees present, or walking on old downland because of the springy turf and wild flowers growing in it! Some plants have very strong soil links; for example, heather cannot thrive on limy soil, flowering only on acid heaths and moors. Other plants, though, are more widespread and less particular.

Plants also have distribution patterns which largely reflect climate. For many species, Britain is at the end of their natural range. Some are 'Mediterranean': these cannot withstand frost and like warm summers, and so are found only along our southerly shores which experience mild winters (sea holly is one example). Others are 'Atlantic': they, too, prefer wetter winters rather than icy ones, but can cope with cool summers—the bluebell is an Atlantic species, and we have the best bluebell woods in Europe. Small arctic-alpine plants such as mountain avens, able to cope with bitter winters and short cold summers, are found high up on mountains where taller plants cannot grow to overwhelm them.

For butterflies and some other wildlife, Britain is also the frontier, and many butterfly species are more likely to be seen in the south than the north of the country.

The 600 species illustrated have been placed in the type of countryside in which they are most likely to grow (if a plant) or breed (if an animal). Remember, however, that many plants can be found in more than one kind of habitat—several woodland species may also be found in hedgerows, for example.

Again, bear in mind that there are rarely any hard and fast rules in nature. Each species exploits the possibilities in its surroundings. Thus, although some animals are restricted to one particular habitat, many are not. Birds, especially, are seen in a wide range of places outside the nesting season, or on their way to and from their breeding grounds. But while a dormouse is unlikely to be seen out of the woodland habitat, or a water vole far from its waterside burrow, lizards may be found in a variety of dry sunny places—on heathland, but also in sunny grassy areas in woods in the south. In such cases, the more typical habitat has been chosen—where it is *most* likely to be seen.

For the birds, estimated population figures are given for Britain (that is, England, Scotland and Wales), which may help to give an idea of the likelihood of seeing them. Our thanks go to the British Trust for Ornithology for giving us information on which to base these figures. (Where no numbers are quoted, estimates of population figures were unavailable.)

Some bird counts are notoriously difficult, though. For example, 100,000 breeding pairs of lapwings are quoted, but like swifts they are very mobile, and the population may be much higher. The number can also vary year by year—a harsh winter can decimate the population of small birds such as wrens, but numbers will quickly climb back in milder years. The use of the word 'pairs' refers to breeding pairs, but there may also be many non-breeding adult birds. The numbers of birds wintering in Britain or along its coasts are also estimated where appropriate. With some species, the pairs breeding are joined by large numbers of winter visitors.

Wild flowers are usually illustrated in the month in which they first come into flower, although their flowering season often extends to more than one month, while butterflies are usually depicted in the month they are first seen on the wing. In general, the birds, mammals and other wildlife have been placed in a month when something dramatic, appealing or informative can reliably be expected to enliven a country walk.

However, as we ourselves well know, one year is never quite like the next. Over a week, and often by the day, Britain can boast the most changeable weather in the world. This book is therefore organized on *average* sightings, and much of the weather information is based on 30-year records.

In addition, the geographical influence on wildlife must not be overlooked; for example, flowers are seen earlier in the south than the north, and earlier in lowland rather than upland areas, although conditions may vary greatly even within a neighbourhood. A good example is the date of the first appearance of frog spawn, which is usually seen in early February in Cornwall, but not until March or April in Yorkshire.

Other things, such as the famous arrival of the cuckoo, can be more reliably predicted to occur in a particular month. But taking all these factors into consideration, it is sensible to examine the months on either side of the current month in order to get the fullest use from *The Country Year*.

A choice of very varied habitats is always close to hand in our countryside. This view in North Wales offers mountain heights leading down to moorland, while woodland and open fields lie in the foreground. Each carries its own distinct communities of plants and animals, while the river adds those of its own. Just in front of our viewpoint, the lane forms a habitat quite distinct from the fields alongside, with the muddle of boulders creating yet another.

JANUARY

This month can be boisterous with westerly gales, but bitter cold spells with killing frosts frequently arrive from the east to chase away the storms. It is often the coldest month of the year, but by its end we can look forward to the first signs of incoming spring. The season 'late winter and early spring' begins on 20 January, running to the end of March.

Starvation weather for birds often sets in soon after Christmas with the likelihood of freezing spells locking the natural larder. It is not the depth of cold so much as its length which kills, for small birds only have fat reserves for a night or two. Bird-tables are an important lifeline and may attract unexpected visitors as hunger forces vulnerable birds to travel far to new feeding grounds. Many garden birds move to the milder south-west, while European cousins come to Britain. Westerly storms may even bring oceanic little auks inland.

Hares often come into country gardens during extended bleak spells, while hunger will drive rabbits to nibble the unpalatable sedges along a woodland ride or strip the bark from fallen branches. Elder is the only shrub which rabbits regularly reject.

This is the month when the red campions and other hardy flowers, palely trespassing from the previous year, will finally falter. By its end, though, the thin woods look denser as buds begin imperceptibly to fatten and catkins to ripen. Honeysuckle, too, may soon be into leaf. The snowdrop is an early flower and melting snow may disclose it unfolding before it is quite clear of the ground; its stem will then lengthen to raise the flower head.

Drifts of snowdrops may not be as natural as they seem. This plant is not a native, but was introduced from Eurasia into the sheltered gardens of monasteries, from whence it escaped. The warmer microclimate of a wood welcomes it.

All is different in the heart of town, where walls provide shelter and warmth spreads from buildings and traffic to create an artificial microclimate. This lures shrubs into early leaf, and the birds may also react positively, with bursts of song.

However, we must not be misled when rooks enthusiastically inspect their rookeries, for there will be no nest building just yet (although their raven cousins are notoriously early nesters). But in warm spells the activity of birds is certainly increasing. The skylark will sing on sunny days, while in the woods great tits bell noisily and the slighter notes of

Overnight fog and a snap of deep cold have magically decked the branches with rime. Not that the Jersey heifers appreciate this winter paradise—they are more aware of the fact that frozen grass gives hard grazing. The weak January sun cannot make much of an impression here, and the frost has only melted on the occasional bough.

blue tits are also heard. By the end of the month there are snatches of fine chaffinch song. The loudest January song, though, is from the mistle thrush, the 'storm cock'.

In human affairs, the old year traditionally lingered on past New Year's Day. The break was celebrated on Twelfth Night, the night of 6 January, with exuberant wassailing. Much cider was drunk in toasts, and branches were shot from apple trees. It was considered important that all members of the family be present and one would be voted 'Lord of Misrule' to manage the festivities. There is an echo here of the old Roman midwinter Saturnalia, when slaves exchanged places with their masters. Today, it is simply held unlucky to leave Christmas decorations up past this date.

In the past, these first days of the New Year were anxiously watched for omens of the weather to come. Great reliance was placed on special days—the entry for 25 January in a 'Shepherd's Almanack' printed in 1676 ran: 'If sun shines, it betokens a good year; if it rain or snow, indifferent; if misty, it predicts great dearth; if thunder, great winds and death of people that year.' Quaint, perhaps, but in those days poor harvests led to inevitable starvation for many, and villages could be cut off for weeks at a time by floods and snow.

BITTER COLD SPELLS

Mean temperatures can vary considerably from one year to the next, but January is likely to be the coldest month. Traditionally, the 14th is its coldest day: St Hilary's Day. The lowest temperatures are often reached half an hour after sunrise. The coldest low-lying counties are those of the Midlands and East Anglia; here an average daily temperature may be below 3.5°C, compared to just under 5°C and 4°C in December and February respectively.

The uplands are even colder. As a general rule, air temperature decreases by 0.5°C for every gain of 275 ft in height, and so the northern hills frequently carry snow when rain falls on lower ground. The Atlantic Ocean tempers the picture, though, for this is a vast reservoir of relative warmth, fed from the south-west by the North Atlantic Drift, which in turn is spawned by the famous Gulf Stream.

So, while it may be freezing in Kent, in Cornwall the first snowdrops may be opening before the last of the frost-browned rose petals of the year before have fallen. Moving northwards, the ocean's warming influence is strongly underlined, and there is even a subtropical garden at Inverewe on Loch Ewe. The mean daily temperature by the sea on this Scottish west coast can match that of Sussex. Nevertheless, it quickly drops on moving up into the hills just inland.

Exactly what weather arrives where depends on the play between high- and low-pressure systems. During January, marked Atlantic depressions, or lows, frequently approach Britain, bringing wet gales to lash the cliffs and sweep inland. But, in country lore, cold weather is supposed to chase away the storms, and continental anticyclones, or high-pressure areas, are likely to strengthen in January and February, fending off the

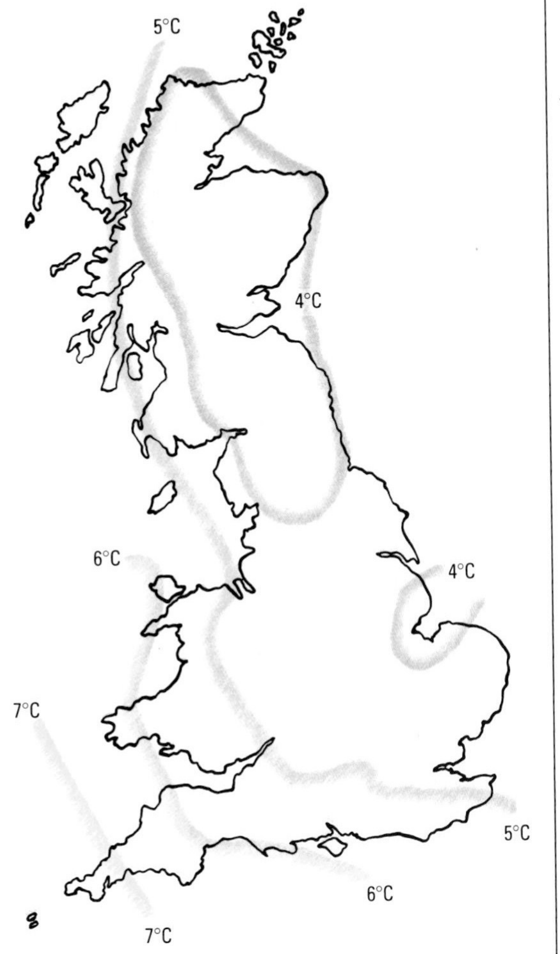

One year can vary markedly from the next, but this map of average January isotherms (lines of equal temperature) clearly shows the influence that the warm Atlantic Ocean has in combating the generally bitter weather reaching us from the east at this time of year. It is, of course, colder in the hills than in the lowlands, and this has been taken into account, with the temperatures adjusted to likely readings if the site was at sea level (using a factor of an increase of 1.8°C per 1000 ft lost in height).

JACK FROST

Jack Frost provides a glimpse of the hidden secrets of weather systems. On window panes, the delicate fern-like pattern of ice crystals illustrates in miniature some of the complex water-ice interactions occurring in the clouds above.

On a freezing day, when drops of water condense on the cold inside surface of a window, it means that the air close to them is saturated and cannot hold any more vapour at that low temperature. The water drops are, in fact, supercooled: although below freezing, they are still liquid. If one of them happens to freeze to form an ice crystal around a speck of dust, you might therefore expect the drop next to it to freeze. But this does not happen directly. Instead, the neighbouring drop vapourizes and then crystallizes as ice directly from the vapour at the edge of the original crystal. In this way, by robbing the water droplets, the initial crystal slowly grows to cover the window with tracery.

Outside in the countryside, frost also holds surprises. It puzzled people in days gone by. In 1789, Gilbert White, one of Britain's first naturalists, wrote in his *Natural History of Selborne* of his amazement in finding that on cold winter nights it was much colder at his depressions and their outriders and (depending on their location) bringing us easterlies of bitter Siberian air and severe cold.

One region may differ markedly from another. If the high lies over Scandinavia, it can draw in cold continental air to bring snow to eastern Scotland while southern counties are enjoying a spell of relative mildness in the central 'warm' sector of a depression. Similarly, easterly winds that arrive when a low moves away eastwards across France can bring snow to Kent, but leave Norfolk free. In general, mild Januaries are those which receive little of the easterly cold continental air. Thus, at this time of year the isotherms, the temperature contours, tend to run not from warmer south to colder north but from warmer west to colder east.

As well as the chill reaching us from the frozen Continent, cold air can also arrive from the north, from the Arctic Ocean, and from the general direction of Greenland. Arctic air has only a short sea passage to warm it up and may bring heavy drifting snow to the north and east.

Hoar frost lying on the grass, and a fox is out busily hunting for his breakfast of voles.

vicarage in the valley than on the down above, and while his trees were scorched by the frost, those up the hill did not lose a leaf.

Frost pockets have long been recognized, as shown by old village names such as Cold Higham. The story is this: cold air, being denser than warm, sinks below it, so that on a still night the air at the valley bottom is chillier than the free air lying above. A frost pocket or hollow is located where the local topography regularly collects a lake of this cold air. On a calm clear night, the ground loses warmth to the air above, and if that air is at freezing point, the ground can also become cold enough to freeze its moisture, resulting in frost. Sandy soils are prone to frost since they tend to be dry and quickly lose heat, whereas damp soils cool more slowly.

Frost is more likely in the uplands of the north and west, for the air temperature tends to decrease by 0.5°C for every 275 ft rise in height. Valleys among these hills are, in effect, exaggerated frost pockets.

Ground frost at the level of the garden lawn is frost which occurs when the air above it is still above freezing point. Ground frosts are about twice as frequent as air frosts, as might be expected from the way that the latter form. If a ground frost sets in early in the night, layers of air above it also become chilled to freezing point until there can be an air frost several feet deep. However, frost coating house and garage roofs (and car roofs) is not proof of an air frost, since ground frost can also form above ground level on metal and other surfaces which quickly lose heat, and so cool to below freezing.

Hoar frost is frozen dew, when the water droplets do not condense until the temperature is below freezing. Sometimes dew supercools without icing at 0°C, but when the temperature falls to −3°C it suddenly crystallizes to give 'white dew'.

Frost can brown the petals of early flowers and curtail the run of scent and pollen. Bees are not attracted to this ignoble blossom and disaster looms for the apple grower. If frost has been light, pollination may take place, but the fruit develops dark 'frost eyes' to make it unmarketable in the shops. Heavy frost, though, can reduce the fruit harvest by as much as 90 per cent. To avoid this, market gardens and orchards are best sited on gentle south-facing slopes with gaps in the hedges below them to let the cold, sinking air flow past without hindrance.

GREEN IN WINTER

Winter threatens plants not only with cold but also with drought, for deep frost locks up the ground water and deprives them of nutrients. Green plants transpire; that is, they utilize the sun's warmth and the breeze to evaporate water from the pores in their leaves. This enables water to be sucked up from the roots, thus transporting those nutrients. While leaves use some of the sun's radiation to produce sugars, the building blocks of life, most of it is used to effect transpiration—hence, leaves remain cool to the touch on even the warmest day.

Deciduous trees shed their leaves in autumn and so avoid the problems of winter drought, whereas conifers reduce water demand by having narrow needle leaves with fewer pores. The leaves of broad-leaved evergreens, such as holly and laurel, have thick waxy skins to cut down water loss, and these evergreens benefit by being able to manufacture sugars in every month of the year.

Holly and ivy are familiar hedgerow evergreens, and in January brambles still keep many of their leaves. On the hedgebanks, the low green rosettes of foxgloves are to be found, while alongside, in the green grass, dandelions, red campions, groundsels and a host of other 'weeds' may still be in flower.

This snow is in fact locking up a natural larder, for tits and other small birds are now unable to search the needles for small hibernating insects.

Surely a contradiction here—are we in the middle of winter or not?

Winter, however, is simply a human shorthand for a time of year when (as with other seasons) a lot is happening in the plant world. Plants adopt various strategies to cope with the demands made by their surroundings at this time of year. For example, broad-leaved trees shed their leaves and become dormant, whereas plants such as bracken and cow parsley die back to a rootstock which will put up new foliage in spring. Coltsfoot flowers from its rootstock before leafing, using food reserves stored the year before. Bulbs are specialized food storage organs that can leaf and flower with some speed when conditions are right.

Some plants opt to spend the cold season as seed. Many are annuals, sprouting in spring, then flowering, setting seed and dying by autumn. Foxgloves are biennials—the first year sees a low rosette of leaves which can survive in the shelter of a wood or hedge, while in the following year the plant grows tall and flowers. A low winter rosette is also adopted by the small-leaved buttercup found in dry chalky grassland; this plant, however, is a *winter* annual, which means that its seeds germinate in autumn and it flowers the following year. Seeds of pink-flowered centaury may germinate either in spring or in autumn.

Sugary sap is a natural antifreeze, and some leaves can survive -4°C without damage, although a single crystal of hoar frost may act as a catalyst to turn the whole into a frozen pulp. A harsh winter could therefore wipe out a colony of small-leaved buttercups from a site where centuary survives, saved by the spring-germinating seeds.

Many buccaneering 'weeds' attempt to live through the winter. What we see on a winter walk is largely the result of the local microclimate of that particular hedge, or wood, or field. If sheltered, some soft green plants may continue in leaf and even in flower from the previous year.

The converse of this is that a 'new year' plant needs a strong cue to recognize that the time is ripe to germinate or to put out new leaves. This can be the *extremes* of winter temperature rather than the averages. The date that coltsfoot flowers reflects the number of days of deep frost in the previous two months. At the protected edge of a wood it could flower in early February, but not until March on an exposed roadside, which could be frozen to a depth of 4 in. (Snow cover would insulate the soil and plant roots against freezing.) Cow parsley needs the cold of winter to cue it to flower the following year, and many seeds need to experience winter's cold before they believe it is spring.

Growth is often triggered when the temperature goes above 6°C for periods, even though it may fall below this at night. Flowering usually depends on a number of internal and external factors, such as the amount of daylight. Snowdrops may already be peeping through a blanket of snow, whereas daffodils develop young flowers in autumn but are held back by the winter cold until warmer times arrive. (They will flower indoors in a bowl by Christmas.) But once the internal switch has been thrown, warmth generally hastens flowering.

Wood meadow-grass is a long-day plant—it only flowers when daylight lasts for more than ten hours each day. Red goosefoot is a short-day plant; it flowers within three weeks if it receives eight hours of light per day. However, if it is given a very long day, it grows taller, but does not flower. For the cereals wheat and rye, it is the *change* of day length from short to long in spring which prompts flowering.

Mistletoe carries its blunt leathery leaves all year. The berries ripen in November and December, and remain until taken by birds.

Groundsel is one of only a handful of plants, very often 'weeds' of waste ground, still in flower in winter.

Evergreen ivy carries leaves of two shapes: those on the straggling non-flowering stems are the lobed 'ivy' shape, as seen here; however, those carried by the flowering stems are oval and unlobed. The leaves may become purple as the winter progresses.

AN EYE TO THE SHEEP

Heavy grazing at this time risks 'poaching' a pasture, when hooves churn it to useless mud. Winter has curtailed grass growth for the last two months or more, and for livestock generally it is the lack of grazing rather than the degree of cold which is the main problem. However, there may be a bite of grass to be found here and there, and on some hill farms the sheep stay out to find it, but even these hardiest of animals may need some extra feed in January.

Down in the lowlands, sheep are often seen munching their way across a field of kale, turnips or swedes, strip-grazing the ground bare up to an electric 'fence' (a wire, in fact) which is moved every couple of days or so.

Sheep can be wintered under cover, for they will get used to dry feed. And if the lambs are due early, it might be sensible to get the ewes in now. However, sheep are prone to catch gut parasites from each other, and wintering them in a confined space puts them at risk of developing pneumonia. But wherever they are, the pregnant ewes need watching. Six weeks from lambing (which usually begins in March, but can be earlier) they will be fed rations of concentrates, containing such things as crushed barley with vitamins and minerals. To build them up, they should also get the best hay.

Diet must always be changed with great care—if a pregnant ewe is quickly moved from fresh grass to dry feed, her metabolism can be upset and she may become comatose. The animal is then quite likely to abort the lamb or even die herself. This can be avoided if dry feeding is started earlier in pregnancy. In the past, before this illness was understood, it was known as 'snow blind', for it struck mysteriously when snow thickly covered the grass. Whatever the weather, though, sheep need plenty of water to drink, which is why they do better while grazing on snow-scattered ground than on a hard, frozen surface in winter.

Winter fodder crops, such as kale and turnips, changed the face of farming a couple of centuries ago. Earlier, the lack of fodder meant that most of the cattle were slaughtered in autumn, while the remainder spent the winter under shelter and were fed on hay. Today, up in the northern hills, you will occasionally still find them snugly stalled in a stone barn, fed with hay from the loft above. But generally times have changed, and in the lowlands in January the milk herd is now under cover in a concrete shed. Here, each day sees a steady routine of feeding, watering and milking, if the cows are still producing milk (the spring calvers are now being dried off in preparation for the calving). But sweet hay and roots form only a small part of their diet.

In winter, their feed nowadays is largely silage—that is, grass cut green in the spring and stored wet and slightly fermented in a clamp (usually nothing more than a walled enclosure). This silage is then covered with black plastic sheets, which are often weighted down with old tyres. Cattle like silage; so much so that the herd's boss cows (usually the older cows that lead the line to the gate) will shove their timid companions out of the way to get at it. Despite this 'bunt order', though, the stockman has to ensure that all his cows get enough feed. This time of year is as crucial for the spring calvers as it is for the sheep; they too need building up and will be weighed to check their response to the rations.

In general, the fields are likely to be grassy green in January. Some of them may well be of grass itself, waiting to be opened up to the livestock in a month or two, but many seemingly 'grass' fields will actually contain the young shoots of winter wheat and barley planted in the autumn. The young plants are perhaps a couple of inches or more tall by now. In the past, sheep might have been let in to graze these fields, but this does not happen so much today because there is a danger of trampling them to mud. If the winter has been mild, the plants may have already started to 'tiller', that is, put out side shoots, each of which will produce a head of grain.

A bare ploughed field is usually left to its own devices as the ground is too muddy to work with the tractor. In fact, for the arable farmer with no animals, January is a rather slack month altogether, thus allowing the farmer to catch up on various odd jobs around the farm. There could be some maintenance to be done, such as clearing ditches, which may be done by hand or with a mechanical scoop. Perhaps some of the farm roads will be repaired at the same time, hardened up with loads of gravel. It is also a good month for overhauling and repairing farm machinery.

January is certainly never counted as the first month of the farming year (rather, it is October). It is more a time for seeing the accountant and ordering fertilizer, or perhaps even reading a book or two!

The hungry sheep wander far across the bleak moors in search of a bite. Many breeds of hill sheep have a strong 'hefting' instinct which keeps them to the slopes they were born to. Even so, the fell farmer must cover a great deal of ground to check on his flock.

THE DEE ESTUARY

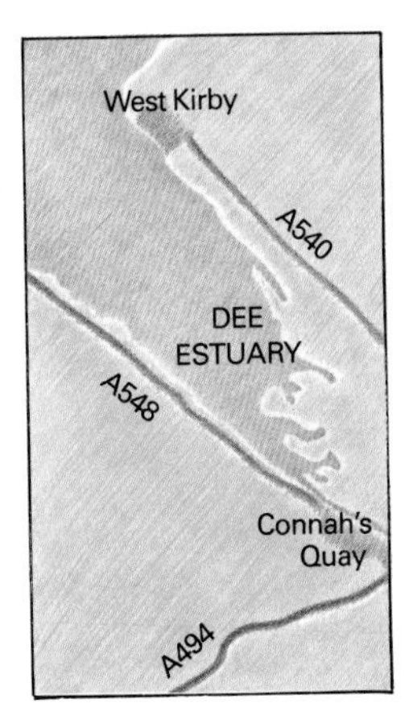

The Dee Estuary, Clywd, comprises 32,000 acres in all, and wintering birds feed from the inner reaches out to gutters around the Hilbre Islands. A good viewing place is the shore between West Kirby and Red Rocks. There are also large numbers of birds around the Point of Air.

The sombre winter estuary of the River Dee breaks into exciting life as the high tide advances. Vast wheeling flocks of waders approach in its vanguard, performing spectacular massed aerial evolutions, flickering black and white against the sky.

Out of reach of the sea, they quickly drop to land. The shore fills, with orange-billed oystercatchers at the tide's edge and longer-legged godwits in the shallows. Vocal dunlins crowd in thousands on the drier sand alongside close-packed masses of knots, both species wintering here from breeding grounds within the Arctic Circle. Parties of sanderlings tirelessly patrol the tide-line, chasing the lapping waves with clockwork energy. In some places, groups of redshanks concentrate.

Food is the key to the presence of these massed flocks of wintering waders, which are regularly 100,000 strong. When the tide turns, they will follow it out on to the exposed mud. The featureless mud-flats teem with shellfish and other invertebrates which live off nutrients drained from the river systems. Unpolluted estuary mud is twice as productive as the best farmland, and 50 times as rich as the open sea. True, not all seashore invertebrate species can adapt themselves to the changes when fresh water mixes with salt water, but those that can are present in enormous numbers.

There can be up to 2000 ragworms in a square yard, while the tiny spire snail, *Hydrobia ulvae*, no more than a quarter of an inch long, can be massed at around 12,000 to the square yard in the top of the mud. Cockles are also within reach of the birds' bills. However, only the longer-billed godwits and redshanks will be able to dig down to reach the tellins buried deeper in the mud. Appetites are enormous. In spite of their name, oystercatchers feed on cockles and mussels, and account for perhaps as many as 300 cockles a day each, the equivalent of their own body weight in food.

Clearly, during a single winter these flocks may make considerable inroads into the estuary's reserves. Such feeding grounds are vital to the survival of the birds—nowhere else can provide winter food in this bulk. Thus, the barrages planned for other estuaries, such as the Mersey, Severn, Humber and Cardiff Bay, will keep the mud-flats covered and lead inevitably to the death of great numbers of waders, some of which are a significant part of the total world population.

The feeding of these birds is controlled by the twice-daily tides. While in autumn they can usually afford to feed only by daylight, now in the short winter days of January they may be forced to feed at night also, and by touch rather than sight. Winter roosting takes place, night or day, when the mud is covered. And although the mud, bathed by a mixture of salt sea and fresh river water, may freeze in very cold spells, preventing feeding, protracted gales bringing in breakers to cover the feeding grounds are often the greater threat.

The Dee Estuary serves an equally important role for huge numbers of passing migrant birds in spring, and again in autumn. These come to rest and feed on the long haul between Africa and their breeding grounds in the summer Arctic tundra. The numbers of wintering species are swelled when the migrants arrive—for example, the hundreds of wintering sanderlings may be joined by up to 5000 cousins.

This spring migration is always a hasty one, the birds feeding frenziedly, eager to be away to benefit from the short northern summer. Their return is more leisurely. And as the adults leave the Arctic before the juveniles, the Dee Estuary in August teems with birds still splendid in their breeding plumages—knots and godwits brick-red, sanderlings with rusty backs and breasts, and dunlins with black belly patches. Their duller offspring will arrive in September.

Perhaps as many as 10,000 of these grey plovers (*Pluvialis squatarola*) winter on coastal mud-flats in Britain. They are often seen scattered across the shore, with a typically 'hunched', neckless posture. The grey plover has an unmistakably mournful three-part call, 'tee-oo-ee', which sounds rather like a boy's whistle.

BRITAIN'S ESTUARIES
Many of these wintering estuaries will also delight the birdwatcher in other seasons (NR = nature reserve):
1 Firth of Forth (Skinflats NR, Lothian).
2 River Nith (Caerlaverock NR, Dumfries and Galloway).
3 Morecambe Bay (NR), Lancashire. Home to some of the biggest wintering populations of waders in Europe, with over 250,000 at times.
4 River Humber (Spurn Peninsula NR, Humberside).
5 Dovey Estuary (Ynys-hir NR, Dyfed).
6 The Wash. One of Europe's most important locations for wildfowl in winter.
7 River Ore, Suffolk.
8 The Swale (NR), Faversham, Kent.
9 Bridgwater Bay (NR), Somerset.
10 Exe Estuary, Devon.
11 Poole Harbour (Arne NR, Dorset).
12 Langstone Harbour (NR), Hampshire.
***Dee Estuary**, Clywd.

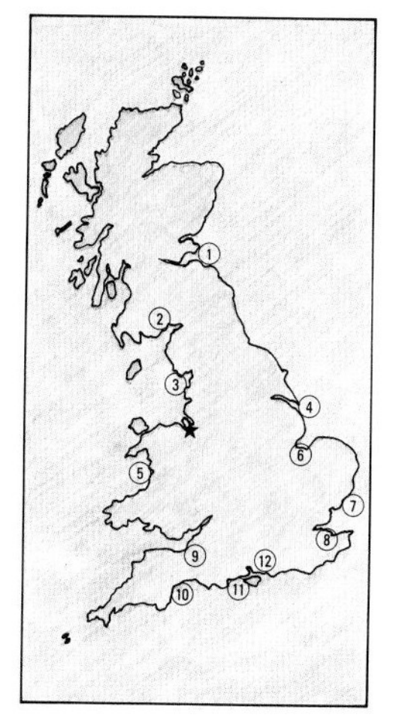

A flock of knots flies in to search the muddy foreshore of the Dee Estuary. The flocks of wintering waders on estuaries such as this are the closest we in Britain get to the vast numbers of grazing animals of the African game parks.

SNOWDROP *Galanthus nivalis* Flowering early (January–March), scatterings of snowdrops may now be seen, appearing like ice crystals in the frozen wood. A snowdrop will even push its way up through snow, for the flower is well protected by a leafy sheath; the stalk then lengthens to raise the flower head tall. Though perhaps native on the Welsh borders, elsewhere in Britain it is usually an escapee from gardens (monastery gardens were its likely origin).

JAY *Garrulus glandarius* 150,000+ pairs resident. This wary bird is usually glimpsed flying away, but its raucous calls echo through the empty January woods. Last autumn it buried acorns, beech mast and berries, and may now be seen reclaiming them. Mating gatherings take place in the spring, but jays are usually seen singly or in pairs.

LICHENS Three main groups are (left to right): shrubby lichens (e.g. *Usnea subfloridana*); crusty lichens, which look like miniature crazy paving (e.g. *Lecanora conizaeoides*); leafy lichens, which resemble a rosette (e.g. *Parmelia subrudecta*). They are composite forms, representing a co-operative between a green alga and a fungus. Rootless, they rely on nutrients brought by rainfall, and are at risk from acid rain (which contains sulphur dioxide, released by burning coal, oil and other fuels). Lichens therefore act as air pollution indicators. For example, if all three groups are seen, the air is pure; slight pollution will kill the shrubby species, while heavier pollution also destroys leafy varieties. Really severe pollution will kill even the toughest crusty lichens, making a 'lichen desert' of bark and stone.

GREAT TIT *Parus major* 2,000,000 pairs resident. Its loud, ringing, see-sawing 'tee-cha' call echoes in the woods, but it has a great variety of notes, such as a repeated 'pee-too'. It is noisiest between the last week in January and early May.

DRONE FLY *Eristalis tenax* Unlike other hover-flies, this may be seen now on sunny days, for it flies throughout the year. Its larva is the rat-tailed maggot found in the liquid of manure heaps or foul ponds.

MOTTLED UMBER *Erannis defoliaria* The male moth is seen flying from November to March, but the female is wingless. Regarded as a minor pest, its caterpillars can defoliate trees in spring.

COMMON HAZEL *Corylus avellana* On the bare twigs, male catkins now hang (January–March) as 'lamb's tails'; the female flowers resemble the leaf buds, but tipped with red hairs. This shrub is often seen in the underwood, filling the space between trees in an oak wood. The nuts are ripe in September or October, and are collected by squirrels, mice, and birds such as nuthatches.

BLUE TIT *Parus caeruleus* 3,500,000 pairs resident. Like the great tit, it is familiar at bird-tables. Research with ringed birds has shown that 'regular' winter garden visitors may change by the day, with individual birds always on the move. This reflects natural behaviour, for roving flocks of tits visit 'feeding stations' in the woods as a means of tapping all possible sources of food. When nesting, blue tits will share the wood with great tits, hunting in the leafy canopy while the latter search the lower branches.

WINTER ACONITE *Eranthis hyemalis* This is now in flower (January–March), prior to the appearance of its leaves. A garden flower from southern Europe, it is remarkably sensitive to temperature, refusing to open when the day is below 10°C, and so has become naturalized only in woods where it is cosseted by the local microclimate.

GREY SQUIRREL *Sciurus carolinensis* Its coat is now silvery-grey in colour, with a brownish tint running down the back (in summer, it has chestnut flanks and paws). Although normally solitary animals, courtship chases are seen in early spring. A second courtship (and brood) may also occur in the summer if there is enough food. A ball-like 'drey' of sticks, built on boughs, serves as both home and nursery. The grey squirrel buries nuts, but has no real memory of the caches' locations; it will now make frustrated scrapes in the ground. Introduced last century, it is most commonly a lowland species.

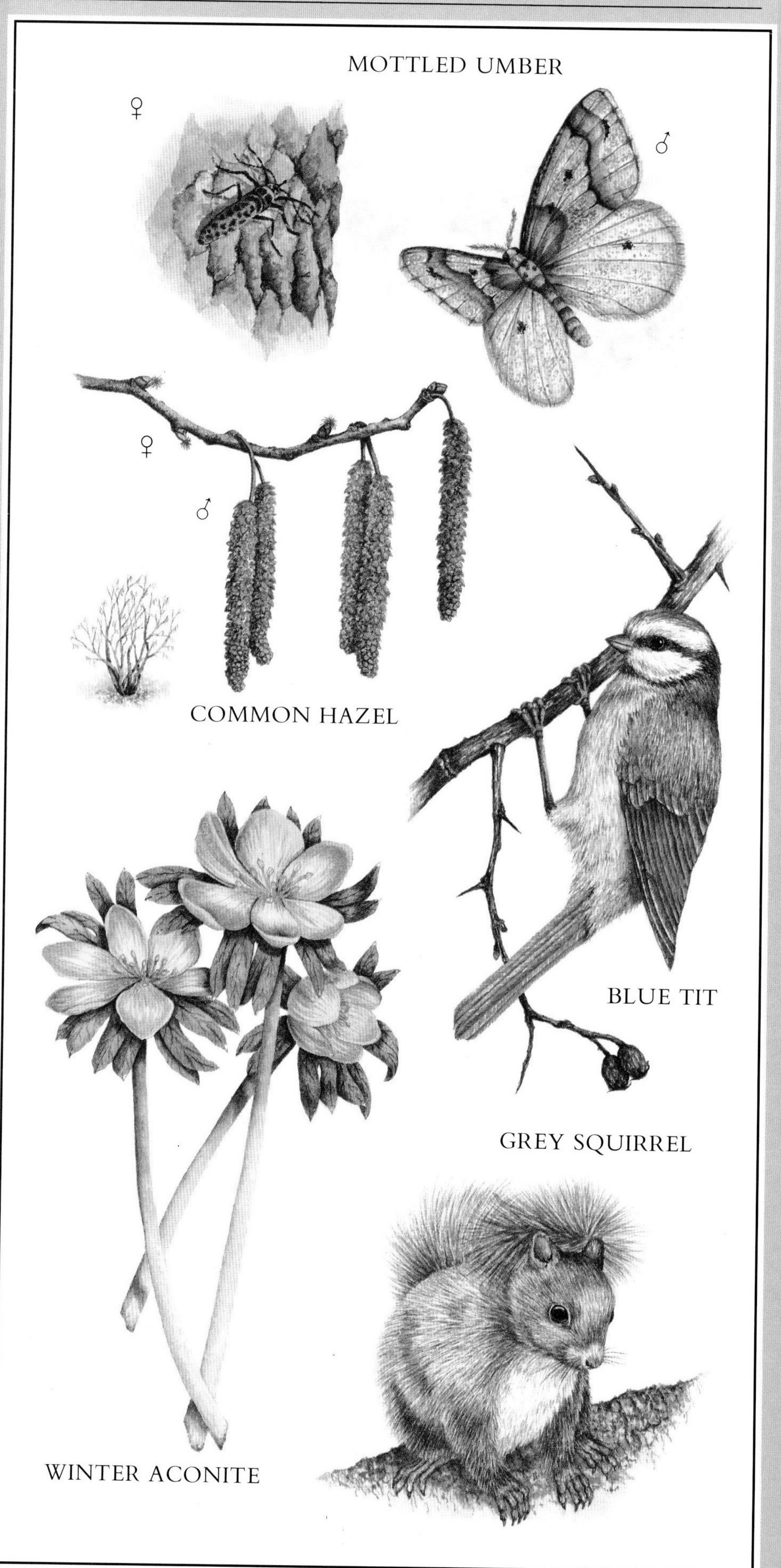

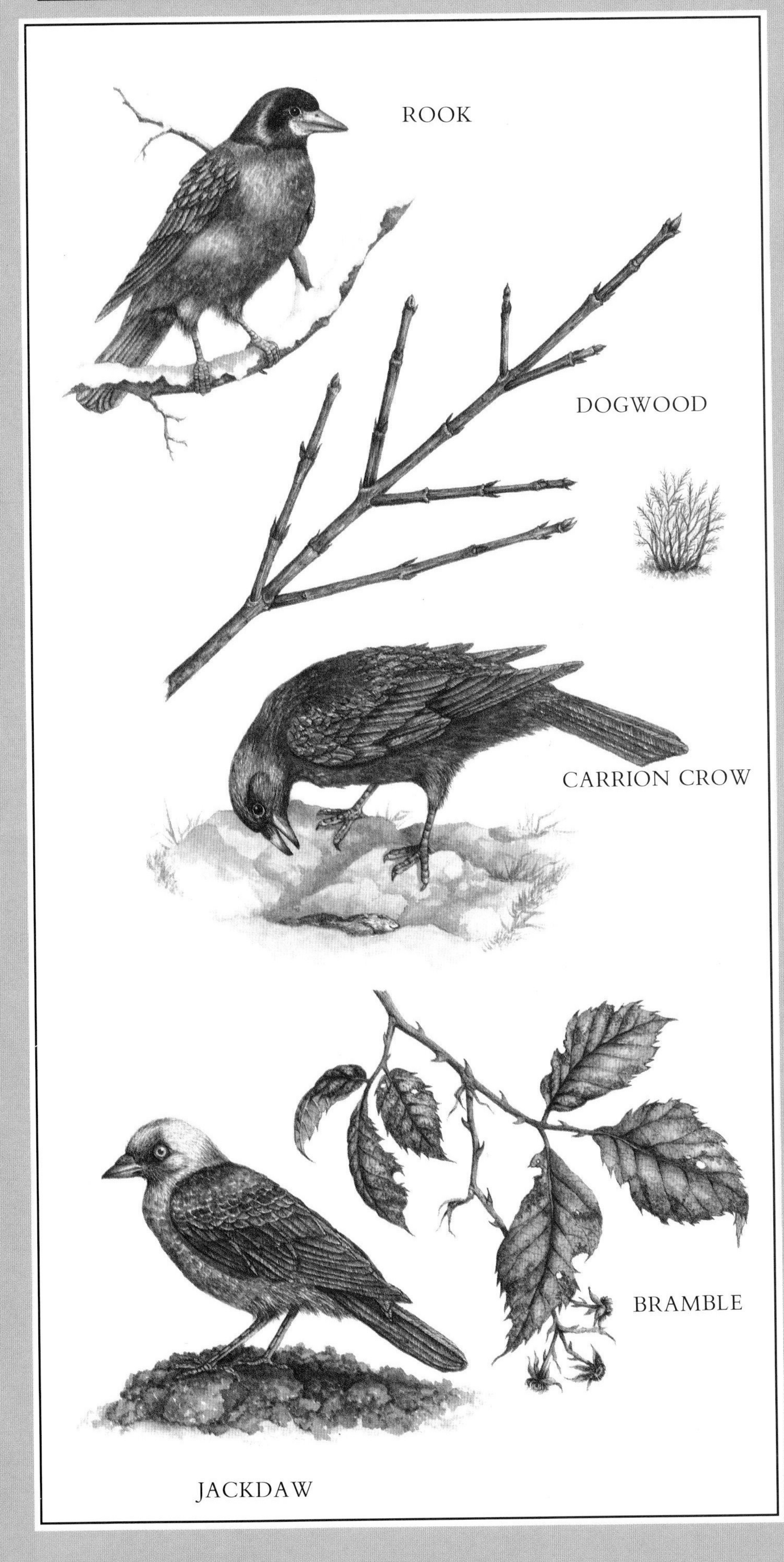

ROOK *Corvus frugilegus* 800,000+ pairs resident. Although starvation weather may lie ahead, an early augur of the spring to come is the sight of rooks high in the trees, before the buds show any signs of bursting, noisily inspecting their bulky nests. They may begin to thieve sticks and quarrel—rook parliaments can also be seen, with the colony collecting together to upbraid an outsider. The rook begins to breed early, perhaps starting in February, but as it is a ground feeder it will rely on (and wait for) an early supply of plump worms and other invertebrates to feed its young. Its loud cawing is one of the most familiar sounds of the countryside. Adult rooks have a bare white patch at the base of the bill and feathery 'trousers' (the carrion crow has sleeker legs).

DOGWOOD *Cornus sanguinea* With blood-red twigs, the dogwood now stands out handsomely in the bare hedges. It carries heavy heads of white blossom from May to July.

CARRION CROW *Corvus corone corone* 500,000 pairs resident. Its harsh triple croak is a familiar call on late January dawns when the bird makes an investigative circuit of its territory. Sorely persecuted for its theft of game-bird eggs, its original habitat tastes have now been forgotten, and this wily bird survives even in towns, scavenging rubbish. It is found all over Britain, except in the far north-west. Nesting later than rooks, and less gregarious, the carrion crow often chooses isolated tall trees.

JACKDAW *Corvus monedula* 300,000+ pairs resident. These birds are now, before breeding has begun, often seen flocking and feeding in the fields with rooks. Jackdaws also nest in colonies, but prefer chimney-stacks and tree holes. In the autumn, European cousins may arrive to swell numbers.

BRAMBLE (or BLACKBERRY) *Rubus fruticosus* There is a large clan of similar microspecies, differing slightly in flowers (usually May–September), prickles, and fruit (sometimes already ripe in August, but often lingering). Some leaves persist in winter (these will provide iron rations for deer in woodlands).

WILD PRIVET *Ligustrum vulgare* This plant has narrower leaves than its garden kin, but equally heady-scented blossom (June–July). Semi-evergreen, it is notable in January's bare hedges, especially on limy soil.

MISTLE THRUSH *Turdus viscivorus* 300,000 pairs resident. Known as the 'storm cock', it will sing its fluty far-reaching notes even through winter storms, perched on a high branch. A notable early nester, it is heard every month except July and August—its song begins to peak in mid-January, but starts to fade in April when other songbirds are gamely proclaiming their home patch.

FOX *Vulpes vulpes* With an appetite for almost anything edible, including voles, rabbits, dead lambs, and even fruit (the cubs will also eat beetles), the fox is found from mountains to suburbs, where it scavenges among yards and dustbins. Its coat is still at its winter finest in January (foxes moult untidily during the summer), and the vixen now begins to call for a mate, shattering the quiet of night with her unearthly shrieks. Short triple barks, with a touch of a howl, are also heard. In March, she will bear her cubs in an 'earth' (which may now be cleaned out). The dog fox feeds her at this time, and food scraps often litter the area surrounding the den. The cubs usually remain together until autumn, when they disperse voluntarily or are chased off by the parents.

HOODED CROW *Corvus corone cornix* Seen along the east coast of Britain in winter, it is now returning to its breeding grounds in northern Scotland—it may breed with carrion crows where their ranges overlap.

HOUSE MOUSE *Mus musculus* Strongly reliant on human activity, this mouse lives close to its food store, but if supplies run out it will soon move. It leaves droppings and a stale smell as clues to its presence. Most spend the winter indoors, but some live outside in hedges during the summer. Breeding over five litters a year means peak numbers in autumn, but winter mortality (plus catches by predators) accounts for 90 per cent of the population.

REDPOLL *Acanthis flammea* 140,000 pairs breed; 500,000 birds in winter. This small, active bird is now often seen by the riverside in alder and birch woods, sometimes in the company of other species. With an undulating flight, it flits from tree to tree. A distinctive 'chi-chi-chi-chi' flight call is heard; later on, when breeding, trills are added, and the cock carries out a looping, weaving display flight. The redpoll is one of the birds that have benefited from the blanket plantings of conifers in recent years.

COMMON ALDER *Alnus glutinosa* Very plentiful in the wetlands of former times, the alder is still seen today on stream banks and also in wet woodlands. At this time of year, last year's dark cones and the unopened catkins make the crown dense and lend it a purplish tint. The hanging catkins and smaller female flowers will open (in February) before the leaves appear.

WATER VOLE *Arvicola terrestris* Despite being known as the 'water rat', the water vole is in fact only distantly related to rats. Although it is more active during the day than at night, this charming animal is usually first heard rather than seen on a winter's walk, as it jumps into the water with a 'plop' when footsteps approach. While eating, it untidily crops a 'lawn' in the streamside vegetation (leaving many morsels discarded), but will also feed on such things as worms and water snails. Preferring clean, slow-moving water, a male holds over 300 ft of bank as its territory. The burrow system has entrances above and below water, but in marshy areas it may make its nest among the rushes.

MOSS *Brachythecium plumosum* Mosses are simple evergreen plants that are rootless, but with a stem carrying leaves and spore capsules, which are seen in winter or spring. They are found in damp sites, such as ditches, watersides and woodlands; like ferns, their male sperm needs a film of water to swim through to reach the female egg-cells. The fronds of some species are loose, while others form tight cushions. Despite their seeming fragility, mosses manage to survive January's deep frosts.

COYPU *Myocastor coypus* Originally introduced from South America to be bred for its underfur, this large animal escaped to flourish in fenny East Anglia, eating reeds as well as crops, such as sugar beet and carrots, in the fields alongside. It burrowed into the fragile river banks, and became such a nuisance that a large-scale eradication programme was put in hand, which was deemed a success in 1988 (though some may have survived). Cold winters leave it at a loss, for it cannot feed on frozen vegetation and is unable to cope with ice.

REEDMACE (or 'BULRUSH') *Typha latifolia* Though commonly known as the 'bulrush', this handsome plant is in fact the reedmace; it acquired its more popular name in Victorian times when the artist Alma-Tadema chose it to add drama to his famous painting of 'Moses in the Bulrushes'. (The true bulrush has a less conspicuous flower head.) In January, reedmace 'sausages' are still to be seen on slacks and backwaters, or even roadside ditches, but will soon disintegrate and shed their seeds.

WATER BOATMAN (or BACKSWIMMER) *Notonecta glauca* Able to swim, dive and fly, this insect is active all year (and may even now be mating). It is a carnivorous bug, armed with a piercing, sucking beak, which can inflict a sharp bite on an intruding finger, especially at this (hungry) time of year.

WINTER HELIOTROPE *Petasites fragrans* This is an unexpected flower (December–March) now seen on the winter river bank. It was introduced from south-west Europe, but is now colonizing damp places and wasteland.

CORMORANT *Phalacrocorax carbo* 6200 pairs resident. Cormorants nest in colonies, sometimes large, at coastal sites, but in winter they are frequently seen on lakes and reservoirs inland. Their practice of shallow fishing suits such habitats (the shag, though, which fishes in deeper water, is rarely seen inland). They are often seen perched with wings akimbo—to help them dry out perhaps, although their plumage is not noticeably less waterproofed than that of other water birds.

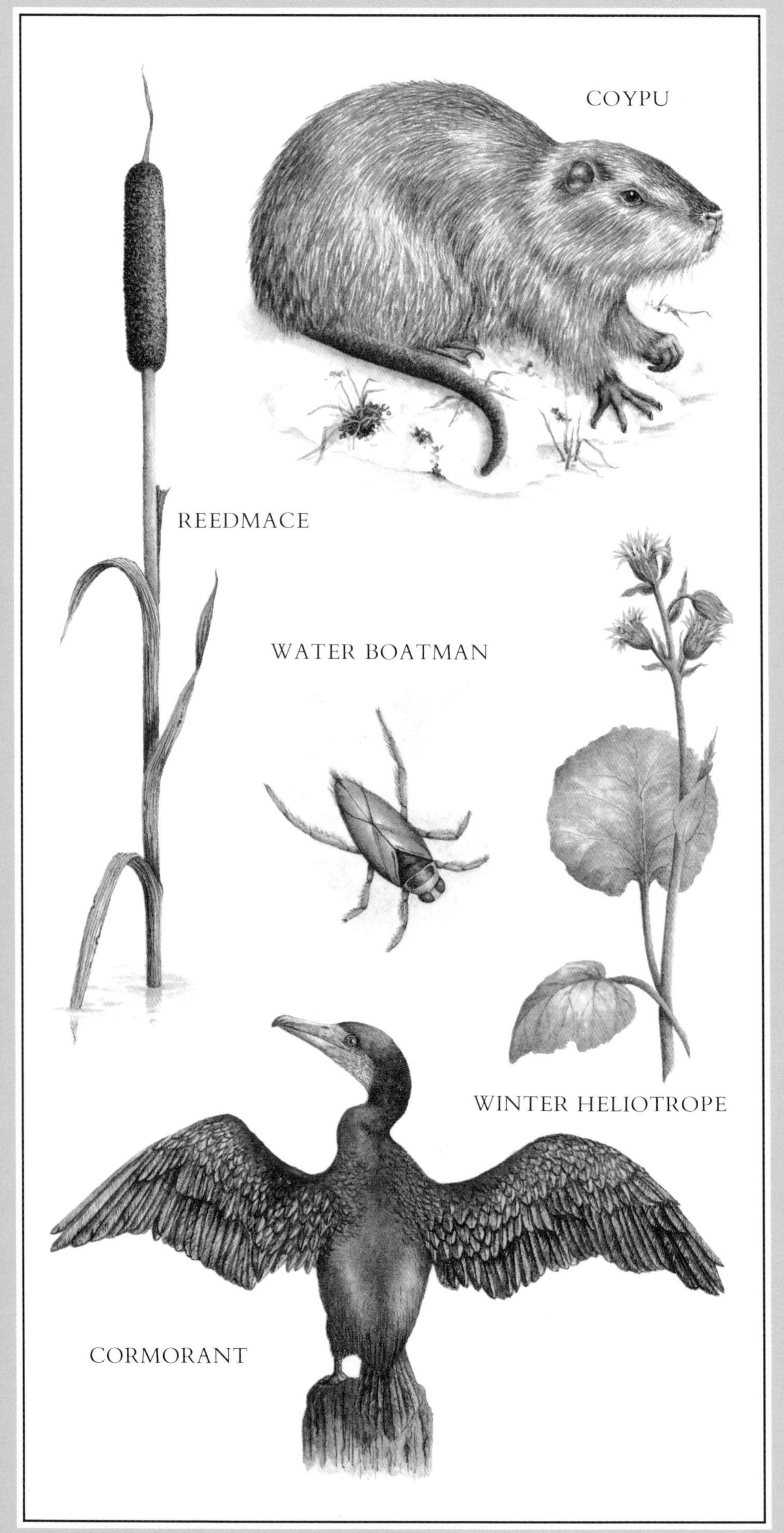

COMMON GORSE *Ulex europaeus* Its bright-yellow pea flowers warm the eye in January, for it may now be flowering strongly, particularly in the south-west (though its usual peak is in April). Although appearing to be quite hardy, common gorse can be badly damaged by heavy frost. Its pod was the emblem of the Plantagenet kings.

RAVEN *Corvus corax* 4000 pairs resident. This is one of our earliest breeding birds, laying its eggs in February, so this month it is active around its craggy nest site (the nest may have been started a month ago). In flight, ravens make masterful use of the air currents around their cliffs, especially in courtship and display flights which are now seen. They are scavengers, but also kill rabbits and small birds.

SCOTS PINE *Pinus sylvestris* Now in its full glory, this tree is handsome with heavy needles and orange-barked upper boughs. It is our only native pine—when the land warmed up at the end of the last Ice Age, the Scots pine created forests over much of the country, before being invaded and overshadowed by oaks and other broad-leaved trees. However, pine forests remained on poor soils in Scotland, and relics can still be seen there today. Pollination between the male and female cones takes place in May, whereupon the scales swell to seal the female cone, which soon hangs down from the twig. It turns green and is about $\frac{1}{2}$ in. long at the end of the first year, growing again the following spring to over 2 in.; it then becomes woody and brownish by the autumn. In the winter and spring, its winged seeds are released when the cone scales gape apart in spells of good weather. Popular for amenity as well as timber, Scots pines can now be found planted in all parts of Britain.

HERDWICK SHEEP *Ovis* (domestic) Although domesticated, these sheep are now so much a part of the Lakeland fells that they all but count as wildlife. Our hardiest sheep, they are left to forage for themselves even in winter—and with safety, for they will not stray from the familiar area in which they were born. Their intensive grazing helps keep the fells free from scrub.

COWBERRY *Vaccinium vitis-idaea* A denizen of moorland pine woods in the north, the cowberry keeps its leaves in winter, unlike its cousin, the bilberry. It flowers from May to August.

BRAMBLING *Fringilla montifringilla* 50,000–200,000 birds in winter. Present from October to April, this winter visitor comes to Britain in larger numbers when the seed harvest at its breeding grounds in Scandinavia and Russia has been poor. Though it will visit remote plantations for the seed crop, this bird is often seen in winter beech woods, flocking with chaffinches and greenfinches for the fallen mast.

WILD CAT *Felis sylvestris* Larger than the family pet and with a blunt-tipped tail (though crossbreeding can and does occur), the wild cat is restricted to the Scottish Highlands, where it holes up in a den among remote rocks or in the depths of a forest (plantations may have aided its spread). It is most likely to be glimpsed at dusk or dawn, crossing the open moors. In winter, it often has to travel far to find its prey, and will take anything below the size of a lamb or hare.

COMMON WINTERGREEN *Pyrola minor* Evergreen as its name suggests, this plant is seen in pine woods, and on moors and dunes with acid soils. It flowers from June to August. Valued in the past for its healing properties, today's embrocations use factory-manufactured oil.

SISKIN *Carduelis spinus* 20,000 pairs breed; 100,000 birds in winter. Upland conifer plantations have benefited siskins; these birds rely on spruce (and pine) seeds for food, taking them when the cone scales gape open to release them on dry days in winter and spring. At this time of year, they flock not only in plantations but also in alder woods—and are found all over Britain, for winter mobility added to winter visitors from Europe means that they may be seen anywhere. They now also visit bird-tables, but will retire to hills, heaths and moors to nest. During this month, they utter a high, rather squeaky note, but the sweetly musical nesting song will brighten the plantations in spring.

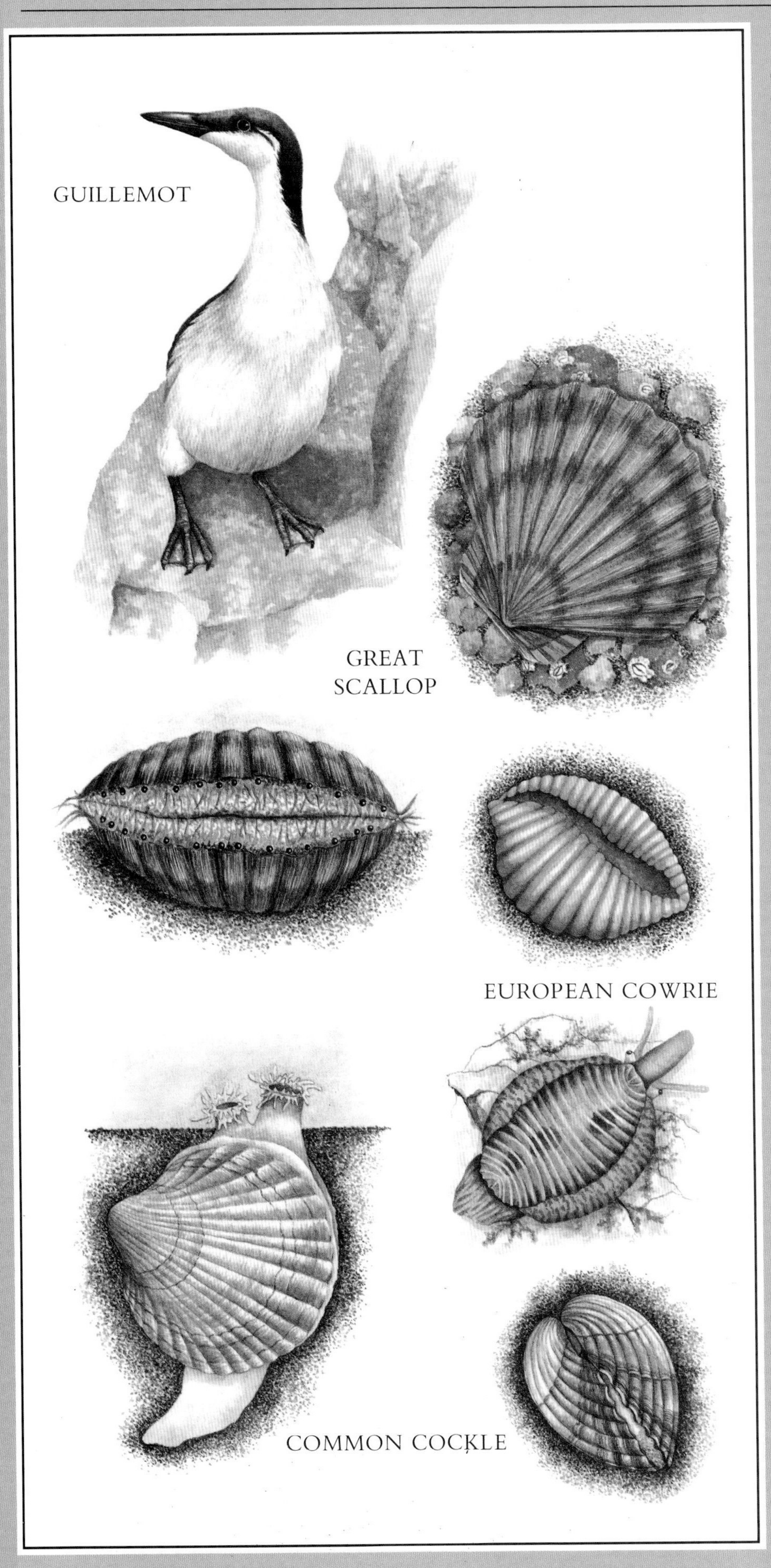

GUILLEMOT *Uria aalge* 500,000 pairs resident. This bird breeds on isolated rock pillars and islands, such as the Farne Islands, nesting on ledges in colonies. After breeding (when it becomes whiter around the throat as part of its winter plumage) it tends to disperse to sea, swimming for much of the time as it finds flying tiring with its short wings. However, this puts it at risk from oil slicks, and one of the saddest sights of winter is that of sea birds, oiled and dying, washed up on a beach, guillemots among them. Sea birds (and waterfowl) gain buoyancy from tiny air bubbles trapped in the feather fronds; oil glues these and destroys both buoyancy and the insulation they give against cold. The bird also sickens from swallowing the noxious stuff while trying to clean its feathers. Nursing such an oiled bird is a job for an expert; light oil may be removed with detergent, but the bird will then need time to preen its feathers back to a waterproof state.

GREAT SCALLOP *Pecten maximus* Dredged from deeper waters, this bivalve is highly prized as a food. Its empty shells are often seen littering stormbound beaches in winter. (Other smaller scallops may also be found, such as the variegated scallop, *Chlamys varia*, which has unequal 'ears' protruding from its shell.)

EUROPEAN COWRIE *Trivia monacha* Found in rock pools, this shell is far more modest than the handsome tropical cowries, for it grows to only $\frac{1}{3}$ in. long, with 20 or more 'ribs'. The growing shell is snail-like at first, but then the outer whorl grows out over the inner, to give the adult its unmistakable cowrie shape.

COMMON (or EDIBLE) COCKLE *Cerastoderma edule* Occurring in vast beds at tidal estuaries and shores, these cockles are sometimes packed at 10,000 to the square yard near the surface of the sand or mud. When covered with water, they extend a pair of siphons which suck in the gritty water and filter off the suspended food particles. (Before being cooked, they have to be kept in clean sea water for several hours while this grit is discharged. For waders, though, this is no deterrent, for grit aids their digestion.)

BALTIC TELLIN *Macoma balthica* This tellin's name is derived from its abundance around the Baltic Sea. It has siphons, but, unlike the cockle, is a deposit feeder: the siphons hoover the surface of the sand around it. Tellins are able to tolerate the low salinity of estuaries.

RAZORBILL *Alca torda* 100,000 pairs resident. As with guillemots, so too will razorbills often be found oiled and beached in winter. Great care is needed when handling these birds, as the heavy bill suggests. These birds breed in colonies alongside guillemots, but will choose more sheltered crevices for the nest. Their throat and cheeks become dark while breeding.

EDIBLE OYSTER *Ostrea edulis* This is found in both natural and cultivated beds, with one shell cemented to the bottom for security. Oysters are traditionally eaten in the months which have an 'r' in their name.

RAZOR SHELL *Ensis ensis* The disjointed shell is frequently to be found on winter beaches when the tide ebbs, although the live animal is rarely seen. It is evolved for rapid burrowing and is almost impossible to dig up—even the long-billed waders rarely manage to take it. Warned by vibrations in the sand, it extends a muscular foot downwards, which is then swelled with blood to act as an anchor; other muscles then contract to draw the shell down.

OYSTERCATCHER *Haematopus ostralegus* 30,000 pairs breed; 200,000 birds in winter. In January, this bird is usually seen in piping flocks on sandy shores and estuaries, where cockles, mussels, shrimps and worms (but rarely oysters) are plentiful. It opens the bivalves either by hammering or by stabbing through the linking muscle—and the young (which are unusual among waders in that they are fed by the parents) seem to adopt their parents' method. Later on, the flocks will break up for breeding—from April in the south to June in the far north. They make a simple scrape of a nest on shingly or grassy shores, and may also nest inland, alongside water on northern moorlands and pastures.

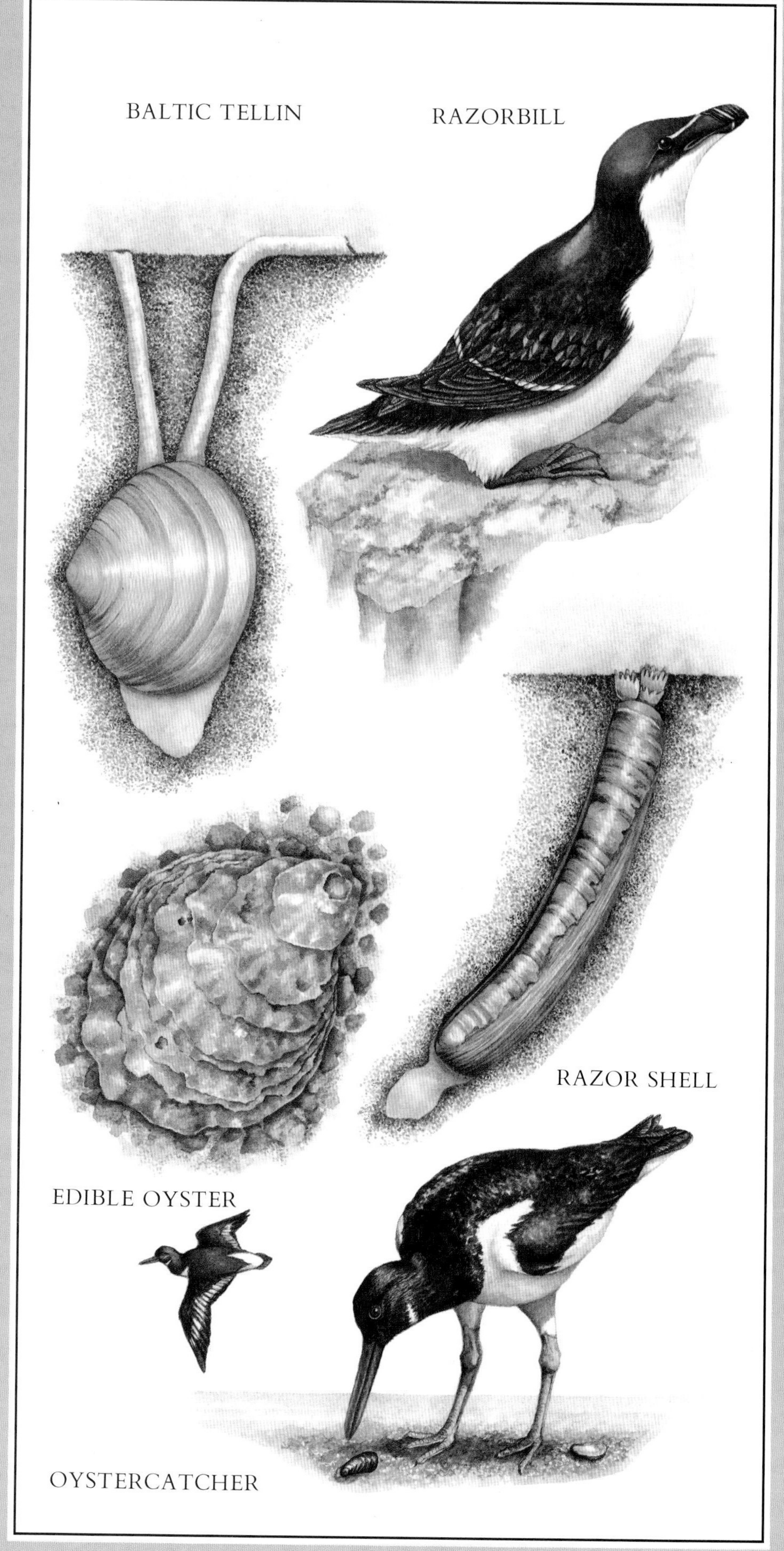

FEBRUARY

In rural almanacs, February is celebrated as a milestone month, for the days again begin to feel longer. It can bring the worst of the winter's weather, but deep winter rarely lingers long, and the month may also bring those delightful first springlike days to tempt out hibernating butterflies.

Although February is largely still wintry, the first true flowers of spring may appear alongside the tattered, obstinate loiterers from the year before. This is especially true in the south-west, which is strongly influenced by the Atlantic. The weather that comes from the ocean is often chilly, but it is not as cold as that which strikes from the east.

Primroses and violets flower first in the sunken lanes of Cornwall and Devon. Less noticeable, but a true sign of approaching spring nevertheless, are the leaves of cuckoo pint and other April flowers, now to be seen in the hedgerows.

In the south-west, frog spawn is a likely sighting at this time. Indeed, the progress of spring across Britain can be charted by its first appearance. (By early April, frog spawn will have been seen in all parts of Britain.) Frogs today find refuge in garden pools, for most field ponds have been filled in.

February, therefore, can be expected to dust the countryside with green. Generally, the sap has yet to rise, but buds of the sallow show silver—and it seems to flower twice, so conspicuous are both its buds and catkins.

Birds will still make extensive journeys to new feeding grounds in bleak spells. Many wintering ducks now leave the estuaries and reservoirs to make the best use of the short summer in their Arctic breeding grounds.

Although the month is still wintry, the dog violet, one of the first true flowers of spring, can sometimes be seen in the sunken lanes of the West Country before the grass itself shows new growth.

Bird song also increases, and the full song of the blackbird, heard towards the end of the month, is a sign that pairs are being formed, and even nesting begun. Ominously for these early birds, though, February sees 'crow marriages' or mate-selection meetings among the magpies. These pirates will take eggs and nestlings of thrushes, blackbirds and other species nesting in the still-bare hedges.

Animals generally are more active, and moths such as the dullish-coloured spring usher and mottled umber come to lighted windows. Bumble-bees are also seen.

Many farms arrange to have some lambing now, as the lambs will be just weaned in good time to make the best of the spring grass to come. These first lambs of the year may well be born to sheep with Dorset-breed blood. Such sheep can lamb in any month, but are usually managed so that they do so in February or March, and again in August or September. (Alternatively, they can produce lambs in July, December, and April the following year, thus giving three crops within two years.)

In fact, the old Celtic lambing feast of Imbolc fell at this time of year; it later became incorporated into Candlemas, 2 February, which is somewhat early for today's lambs. This Christian festival celebrates the purification of the Virgin Mary, and snowdrops were once picked in celebration.

A notable day in February is of course St Valentine's Day, the 14th. This day, though, has no connection with St Valentine, but is instead a descendant of the Lupercalia, the fertility feast of the Roman Pan. The country belief (described by Chaucer) was that birds chose their mates on this day, and most Valentine traditions were means by which girls discovered their husbands-to-be. This lovers' festival is celebrated today by sending Valentine cards or messages.

The spells of weather now coming from the Atlantic can be relatively mild, in temperature if not in power, for in February our coasts can experience some of the fiercest storms of the winter. Here we see a rough sea thundering against a Cornish cape, the waves primed by their long fetch across the ocean.

FREEZING PATCHES

Filldyke is an old traditional epithet for February, but a misleading one, for this month is in general drier than its neighbours. Over central and southern England, for example, 6 per cent of the year's rain falls in February, compared with 9–10 per cent in January and 7 per cent in March. The drop is even more marked in western areas: 10–11 per cent of the year's rain falls during January in Cornwall but only 7–8 per cent in February.

Towards the end of the month, the temperature of the Atlantic waters off the west coast drop towards their coldest of the year, down to 9°C off Cornwall. The incoming westerly air, often a source of rain, is cooled by this cold Atlantic water. As a result of this fall in temperature, its vapour-holding capacity also decreases, and this means that it gives less rain (or snow) when it reaches the land.

This air is not bitingly cold, however. It is, in fact, comparatively warm: in Cornwall, the farmer's growing season is reckoned to begin on 20 February and last until 8 January the following year. This is the period when the 1 ft soil temperature remains above 6°C, and grass can grow. Cornwall's growing-season start date compares with 20 March in Dyfed and 28 March in Lancashire, both of which are affected by the Irish Sea. Other seas are also plummeting to their lowest temperatures in February.

Like January, February can have spells of both cold and stormy weather, but generally it is a quieter month. Cold in February arrives by the same routes as in January, but it can be particularly biting when the air comes straight from the Arctic. February in the Arctic is colder than January, and so these northerly winds bring Highland valleys their lowest temperatures of the year, with perhaps sharp snowfalls on lower ground.

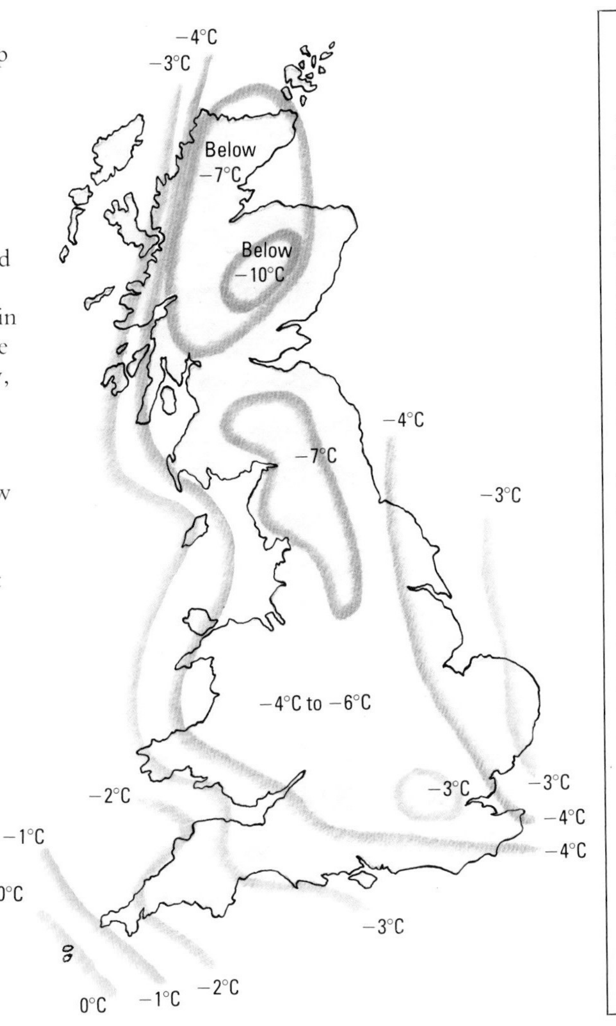

Based on Met. Office data, this map shows the average minimum temperatures for February. The readings were generally taken at weather stations sited near towns and villages rather than in remote places, so the extreme cold of, say, Dartmoor or the Pennines does not register. The map does, however, show us how chilly February can be. Remember also that local microclimates have a strong influence on minimum and maximum temperatures.

ICE

In the winter of 1683–4, the River Thames froze over to a depth of many feet, and Charles II had it swept and decorated as a pleasure ground. Even the giant bonfires that were lit did not thaw the ice. Other 'Frost Fairs' were held in 1795 and 1814, but there have been none since. However, in 1963, the Thames above Kingston Bridge froze over, while in Yorkshire cascading waterfalls were transformed into curtains of ice.

Those were unusual years, but ice is regularly seen in most parts of Britain, especially during cold spells in February.

When the air temperature above a pond or lake drops, the water also cools, losing warmth to the air. Thus, when the temperature of this air is at or below 0°C, the water gradually cools to 0°C and begins to freeze. But before this happens, something unusual occurs, which is important to aquatic life.

Gases and liquids normally become denser as they become colder. However, fresh water is densest not at 0°C, when it changes state to form ice, but at 4°C. When the temperature of the pond surface reaches 4°C, the top layer of water sinks to be replaced with warmer water from below, which itself then cools and sinks. Slowly, in this way, the whole pond reaches

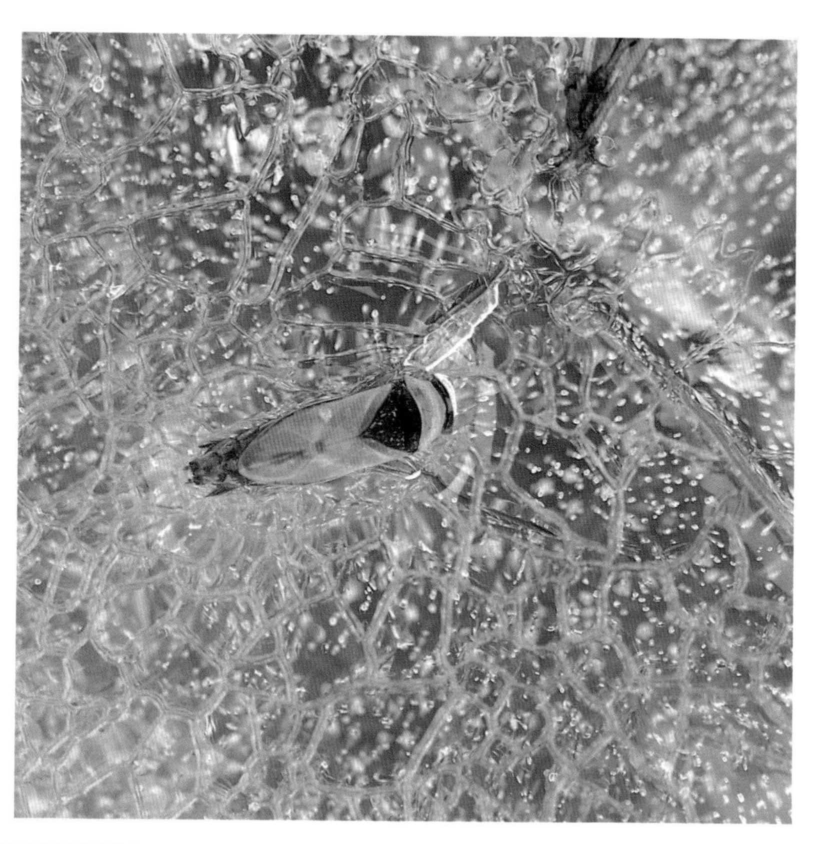

Above An unlucky backswimmer lies frozen into the ice on a woodland pool. Its struggles to escape have created a small, ice-free hollow.

Above left A young heron stands disconsolately at the edge of a hole in the ice. These birds are endangered when long, hard spells keep the ponds and streams frozen.

4°C. If the air then cools further to 0°C, ice forms on the surface and floats there; but the body of water below the ice remains above freezing and, although chilly, aquatic plants and animals have no problems surviving.

Ice forms most quickly on shallow, still water, especially where rocks or reed stems break the surface to give it a starting hold. If the air is cold enough, it will also form in the more sheltered bays of the rapid trout-becks in the hills; spray may build a roof of ice over the moving water.

Both dippers and kingfishers can feed below ice if a patch of open water allows them access. Although dippers will attempt to remain in their territories, in hard winters kingfishers move to brackish coastal waters which are slower to freeze. During such times, many herons starve; they fish standing at the waterside, and it is the water below the bank which freezes first.

Winter winds can keep lakes ice-free by whipping up waves large enough to mix the surface water. When small streams and ponds are frozen, their resident waterfowl have to move elsewhere, and the larger reservoirs often attract considerable numbers.

In really cold spells, sea water sometimes freezes as floes and land-fast ice, while in estuaries the exposed mud can freeze at low tide. If this occurs, the waders and other birds lose precious feeding time. But ice poses another threat to sea birds: gulls, splashed when making low passes over waves in bitter weather, have been known to fall with iced-up feathers.

Ice can also make life difficult for birds of the open countryside, as they too need to drink. In addition, glazed ice is a serious threat to those feeding in trees and on the ground. It occurs during a temperature inversion, when the ground is wrapped by a blanket of air below freezing while warmer air rests on top of it. When rain falls, it freezes where it splashes, forming an icy coating on twigs and pine needles. Tits and other birds starve, for they cannot now feed on the insects lying dormant in the bark and between the needles. The ground, of course, is also covered in this way, and birds such as starlings (which push their bills down into the soil) and blackbirds may go hungry. Such episodes will lead to large dispersal flights to find ice-free feeding grounds.

Freezing fog can also coat branches with a dusting of minute ice crystals, known as rime.

ANIMAL TRACKS

Birds and butterflies press themselves on our attention. They sing, sport and display themselves before our eyes. But a faint scream from the grass may be all that is revealed of an angry encounter between two shrews. A flash of tan coat will be all that is seen of a roe deer buck alerted by a breaking twig underfoot, and now bounding away through the trees. Even the familiar grey squirrels are comparatively secretive animals.

Added to this, many mammals are only active in darkness. For mice, this gives them a better chance to escape predators, although the hearing and night-sight of the tawny owl are acute. For the larger animals, nocturnal activity may be due not to ancestral intuition, but simply caution. It is known that badgers, for example, are often active in daylight in hidden, rarely-visited coastal combes.

Nevertheless, animals cannot avoid leaving signs of their activities. February is a good month to look for these, with snow and a low sun setting off the shadows of hoof and paw prints. Even such simple things yield insights into the complex, hidden lives of wildlife.

The easily-recognized track of a hopping rabbit may lead not to the rambling communal burrow, but to a recent excavation instead. A few days before giving birth, the doe digs out a separate, blind burrow or 'stop' for her offspring. As her breeding season can extend from January to August, there is a chance that this year's new excavations will now be seen.

The snow can also reveal hare tracks, which may be distinguished from those of a rabbit by the greater distance between each footprint in a group of tracks. The males are in breeding condition from January to June, and the site of the scrambled mating chases may occasionally be seen in the snow. The favourite food of both hares and rabbits is grass, and in thick snow cover it is interesting to see which substitutes are preferred.

Feathers are the classic sign of nature in the raw. Hawks leave a ring of feathers below a perch, having plucked their prey before eating. If it manages to catch a bird, a badger will eat it on the spot, leaving a scatter of feathers, whereas a trail of feathers could point out the path back to a fox's earth.

This earth or den is at the hub of the fox's wide-ranging territory. At this time of year, the vixen fills the winter nights with ghostly shrieks and howls to attract her mate. They will hunt and travel together for three weeks, but then begin to forage alone. The entrance to the earth is often messy with the feathers

Below right This unusual trail was left by a squirrel.

Below Here the snow preserves the tracks of a capercaillie, with the bird's wing marks impressed into the snow at take-off.

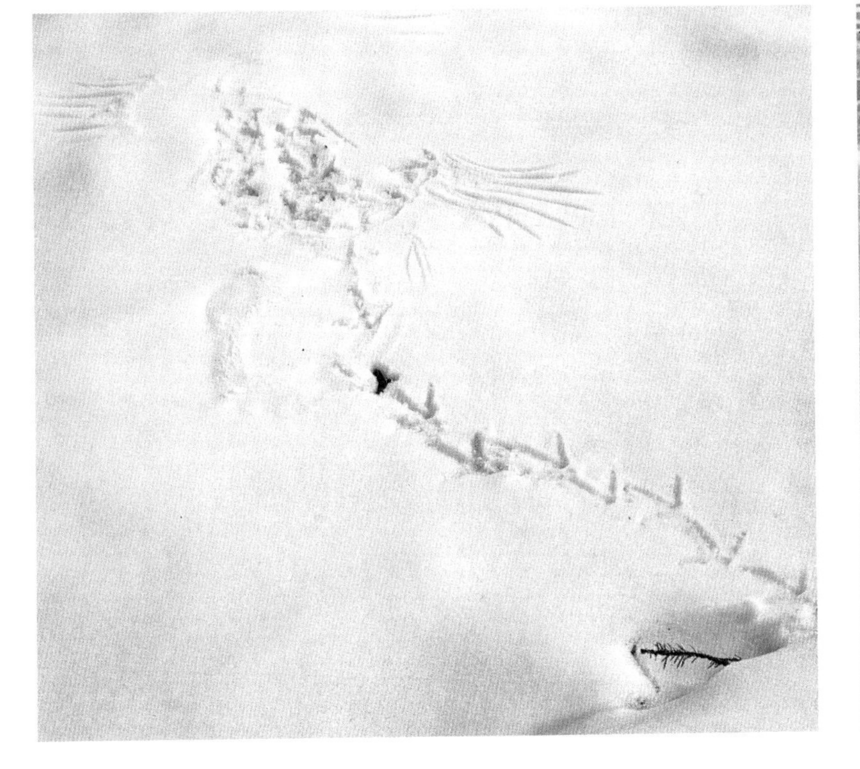

and bones of prey which the fox brings back to devour.

Badgers are neatly mannered in comparison. Not only do they use regular dung pits, but the entrances to the set—clearly visible at this time of year through the bare shrubs—are often piled high with soil dumped from scraping the burrow clean; old bedding grass is often mixed in with this soil. Well-worn patrol paths radiate out from the set, and along these the badgers' distinctive hairs may be found snared on low twigs and barbed-wire fences. (Some say that these paths were man's ancestral footpaths through the dense prehistoric wildwood.) The territories of neighbouring sets can overlap.

Earthworms form part of the diet of badgers, and their diggings in search of the worms can be seen, with the snow having been brushed aside to expose the warm soil below. (Later in the year, badgers may even dig down to reach defenceless young rabbits in their stop.) Warm spells may also enliven grey squirrels to dig for the nuts they buried the year before, although it is clear from the many scrapes that they do not have an exact memory of the locations of their hoards.

In Britain, the classic wildlife sighting is that of the otter, now sadly gone from many lowland rivers. The paw prints are a clue, although these are difficult to identify. But a decisive sighting is the animal's spraints: these are easily-recognized, tarry-looking droppings, 2 in. long, glistening with fish-bones and not unpleasant smelling. They are left as a territory marker on rocks or hard surfaces such as bridgeworks at the water's edge. (Foul waterside droppings are likely to be those of mink, escaped from fur farms and now living wild.) After a fish kill, the otter leaves a cleaned spine and skull, with the skin neatly concertinaed.

Otters hunt a stretch of water for a night or two before moving on. Their whole territory may encompass several square miles and many streams and rivers. They prefer slow-moving water to that which flows fast. Otters are solitary except when mating, which can occur at any time of the year. The cubs are lively animals and love games, sliding down slippery icy banks to splash into the water. Such playgrounds are something to look out for on a snowy walk.

A mountain hare lies all but hidden by the snow—an excellent camouflage technique.

Nose deep in a drift, this fox is hunting voles. Snow is a very good insulator, and small rodents may still be active in their tunnels and trackways through the grass below.

THE SPRING SOWING

During February, some of the wheat harvested the previous year may be found surplus to requirements and be sold off (if this has not already been done). In the past, Candlemas Day, 2 February, was counted the mid-point of winter, and a date by which the canny farmer still had half his hay in store to see the animals through to spring. In those days, too, the ground was often still unworkable with horse-drawn ploughs, but powerful machinery enables more to be done today.

We may now see a burst of activity in the ploughed fields, with the tractors out on Sundays too, as is usual during peak periods in the farming year. However, the weather still holds the key and work may come to a complete standstill. February, often one of the drier months of the year, can be bleak and frozen hard for days at a time, so that frost scorches the blades of the winter barley and wheat planted in the autumn. But there is an equal chance of mild weather.

If the weather allows, sowing the spring wheat and barley can be one of the jobs now tackled. The field may already have been rough-ploughed in the autumn, the plough leaving clods which the frost will have subsequently shattered. The task is now to create a perfect seedbed with fine, even tilth. There is skill in this, for when making passes across the field it is very easy to 'puddle' and compact the ground.

As well as giving a good grip, the tractor's large tyres spread the load which is an advantage. On a clay soil, heavily-loaded narrow wheels would soon create paths of unbaked brick.

One of several designs of harrow may be used, dragged by the tractor. Some are simply a grid of metal prongs which tear into the surface, while others have small sharp discs or curved and sprung tines. Some expensive models have the tines vibrated under power from the tractor. A cultivator may be used, with tines which are dragged deeper into the soil. Or perhaps a roller will be brought in to firm up the surface. The choice is dictated by the type of soil and the condition it is in—the aim of the farmer is to get away with as few passes as possible, for time costs money in farming as it does in anything else.

The fields need fertilizer. 'Muck'—that potent, well-trodden mix of dung and straw from the livestock sheds—could be spread before ploughing. Of course, many farms do not keep cattle, but in any event, it is quite usual nowadays to use a factory-made inorganic fertilizer. This comes either as a liquid to be sprayed from a crossbar behind the tractor, or in the form of granules. These granules are spread over the ground with a broadcaster, consisting of a cone, bolted on behind the tractor cab, which holds the granules, with a spinner below the cone to fan out the granules to each side. The grass fields—the pastures and leys—may now be given their first nitrogen of the year in this way. The winter wheat and barley (which at this time of year also look like grass) can be sprayed. Without nitrogen, their hungry young green leaves will falter and become tinged with yellow.

Fertilizing at this time means that the growing plants gain early nourishment, for the soil will not naturally provide much nitrogen until the ground temperature is regularly above 7°C or so, when the soil bacteria become active. For full growth, the crops will need feeding again in the coming months up until July.

However, the farmer may choose to feed

Getting the soil of the ploughlands into good heart, ready for the seed, lies at the heart of good farming. But what is done depends on the field, for no two fields have quite the same soil.

the fertilizer granules along with the seed when it is sown, and this will usually be a compound fertilizer including potash and phosphate.

In early times, sowing was carried out by hand, the peasant flinging the grains to either side as he walked up and down his field, much to the delight of the pigeons and rooks, no doubt. Seed 'fiddles' were in use a couple of centuries ago, with the 'bow' turning a wheel to spin the grain out. This was basically a hand-held version of the modern fertilizer broadcaster, and in fact the broadcaster is useful when seeding difficult corners.

Today, sowing is generally highly mechanized and accurate. The seed drill is another piece of equipment towed and powered by the tractor. It is a wheeled, narrow box, as much as 20 ft wide, fitted with an array of pipes and trawls. As it moves along, slits are cut in the soil, seed is dropped into them (with perhaps fertilizer also), and then the soil is raked back over. In addition, on flinty ground, the soil may now be rolled to push down the flints, avoiding the risk of catching the combine blades with them later in the year.

In a mild year, another urgent February task is the spraying of the autumn-sown crops against mildew and other diseases. The winter wheat and barley may also need rolling to firm up the soil loosened by frost.

THE CAIRNGORMS

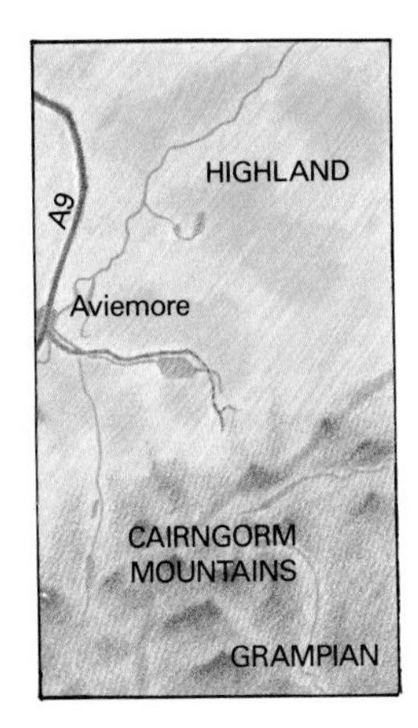

The Cairngorm Mountains fall across the boundary between the Highland and Grampian regions. From the ski centre at Aviemore, visitors pass along the ski road to use the chairlifts which then carry them to the summits, where conditions can be arctic even in midsummer. Relics of old pine woods survive in nearby Glen More National Forest Park.

The Cairngorms present us with 160 square miles of rolling plateau, the widest tract of high ground to be found in the Scottish Highlands, and indeed anywhere in Britain. The general height is over 3000 ft above sea level.

This sprawling, bleak terrain, never tamed by man, rather resembles the tundra, the cold open plains of the Arctic Circle. But it is also a relic landscape, of a kind once seen in lowland Britain when glaciers and ice gripped the land during the Ice Age. It was only when this drew to an end some 12,000 years ago that shrubs and trees could begin to invade this open ground.

In the Cairngorms, it is height which maintains this ancient open scenery, rather than the northern location. This is clear when the area is compared with the Scottish west coast, not so far away, where the winter in some places can be as mild as in Cornwall.

Quite heavy snow falls on the Cairngorm hills. It can be scant in December and January in some years, but there is usually enough snow in February to provide reasonable skiing. The chairlifts near Aviemore enable even non-skiers to visit these wintry heights to sample the Arctic for themselves, and they run also in the summer.

The skiing relies not so much on widespread snow cover, but on long-lived snow beds, drifted into sheltered areas. There can be considerable drifting in the high winds.

The snow is generally at its deepest by the end of April; it then begins to thaw, but melting may not be complete even by August. This summer thaw, especially during dry June, feeds the River Dee, and also the River Spey, one of Britain's fastest rivers.

Now in winter, the red deer have moved up to 20 miles away to find lower grazings which suit them. But, intriguingly, there are often reindeer grazing on the Glen More slopes—the herd of Swedish and Norwegian stock was introduced in 1952. Reindeer were once a native species, but went the way of the wolf; records show that they were still living in Caithness in the 12th century. Today's herd is domesticated, although they still closely resemble their wild ancestors. Their favourite diet is a ground lichen, 'reindeer moss', which they reach by scraping away the snow cover. Unusually for deer, both sexes carry antlers, although the bulls shed theirs in December, to grow them again in late spring.

Ptarmigan can be seen on the tops of the Cairngorms, and sometimes come to feed on skiers' snack crumbs. They are extremely hardy birds and can survive at high altitude even in winter. Their feet carry feathers, which not only insulate them but also make useful snow-shoes. These birds moult in stages from mottled brown to white to suit their surroundings, and once moulted they are at risk from marauding golden eagles if their camouflage fails through lack of snow or an early widespread thaw. They maintain white wings and breasts in the summer, and will remain on the hilltops to breed, their breeding being cued by the melting of the snow in May.

This melt reveals a terrain littered with shattered granite rocks. There are mossy heaths, rushes and bogs in some places, with saxifrages and cushions of moss campions, dotted with pink flowers, in others. Such gems would be seen on most Welsh and Lakeland mountains were it not for the sheep, but sheep are not grazed on the Cairngorms.

The melt brings up other birds to breed alongside the ptarmigan. The dotterel is one, choosing to nest on bare whale-back hummocks (the ptarmigan prefers rocky ground). A few snow buntings also breed here.

Paradoxically, patches of late snow help them all. As the valleys below warm up, flushes of insects emerge, and are frequently wafted up the slopes to be stranded on the snow, from where they are easily picked off by the birds.

The last native reindeer (*Rangifer tarandus*) lived in Caithness 800 years ago. Hunting and firing of the forests wiped them out, but in 1952 a small number, resembling their wild ancestors, were reintroduced into the Cairngorms. Other stock was later added, and a healthy herd can now be seen.

BRITAIN'S MOUNTAINS
Nothing can match the Scottish peaks for true arctic conditions but they are usually only reached after long, hard hikes. These heights may be easier to attain:
1 Pass of Glencoe, Highland.
2 Ben Lomond, near Loch Lomond, Central.
3 Helvellyn, Cumbria.
4–7 The Pennine Way. This 250-mile walk covers many summits: at **Edale**[4], Derbyshire, it crosses 2000 ft ground; then, to the north, **Pen-y-ghent**[5] (2273 ft) near Settle, North Yorkshire, **Cross Fell**[6] (2930 ft) near Penrith, Cumbria, and **Windy Gyle**[7] (2032 ft) in the Cheviots.
8 The Cleveland Way. This reaches high summits on the North York Moors.
9 Snowdon, Gwynedd. There is a railway to the top.
10 Butser Hill, near Petersfield, Hampshire.
11 Haytor, Devon. The most accessible of Dartmoor's tors.
***Cairngorm Mountains**, Grampian/Highland.

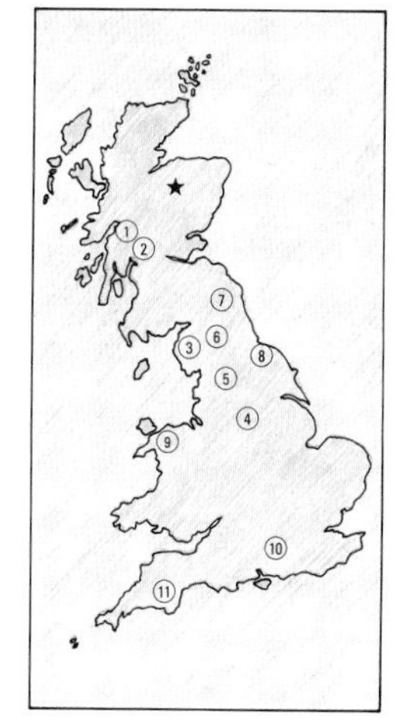

The massive snowbound flanks and shoulders of the Cairngorms form the background to this scene. They look—and ecologically they are—a world apart.

GREAT SPOTTED (or PIED) WOODPECKER *Dendrocopos major* 30,000 pairs resident. An evocative sound of the season is the drumming of a woodpecker. Usually it is this bird which is heard, drumming from late February well into April, raining ten blows a second with its bill on a resonant dead branch. This drumming is a territorial warning, the equivalent of the song of other birds, and it may be heard at any time of the day as rivals answer each other like echoes. Well-developed skull muscles cushion its effects and prevent damage to the bird's brain. The bird will also be heard hammering its way below the bark to extract grubs and other insects, and a nest hole will be excavated high on the tree trunk by both the male and female using this method.

LESSER SPOTTED WOODPECKER *Dendrocopos minor* 5000 pairs resident. Less common than the great spotted woodpecker, this bird is only found south of the Scottish border. It also drums at this time of year, but rather more rapidly and less loudly. Both birds also call—the great spotted with a harsh 'tchik', the lesser spotted with a shrill 'keek-keek'.

WINTER GNAT *Trichocera relegationis* This non-biting gnat looks like a small crane-fly. It is seen dancing in swarms on winter afternoons, even (unusually) soon after a fall of snow.

SWEET VIOLET *Viola odorata* One of the first true flowers of spring (February–May), this violet is now beginning to appear along woodland edges. Britain has several species of wild violets, but this is the only one to carry a scent. However, its fragrance seems to last only a moment, for one of the essences in the sweet scent dulls the sensitivity of the nose. For this reason, these violets (whose flowers may often be white) were once strewn on church floors to counter the musty smell.

STINKING HELLEBORE *Helleborus foetidus* This plant is often grown in gardens, but it is also a native species, and makes an exciting and uncommon sighting when found growing wild. The evil-smelling flowers (February–April) attract early bees.

SPRING USHER *Erannis leucophaeria* This is one of the first moths on the wing in spring, seen now in February or March. The males fly at night and come to lighted windows (the females are wingless). Though rather drab, they are still a happy augur of approaching spring.

CHAFFINCH *Fringilla coelebs* 5,000,000 pairs resident. One of our commonest birds, the chaffinch's loud, dashing, energetic song may already have been heard in early winter, but it is becoming more frequent during this month; it will be lessening by late May. It is one of the easiest of bird songs to recognize, starting slowly but then hastening to end with a 'kiss-me-dear' flourish. Experts have even identified local dialects of note sequences in it. As with other seed-eating birds, the chaffinch has quite a broad bill, but it also takes insects which it feeds to its nestlings to provide the protein their fast-growing bodies require.

BARREN STRAWBERRY *Potentilla sterilis* This plant is now in flower (February–May). Though, at first glance, very similar to the wild strawberry, notice the gaps between the petals, and the small, bluish-green leaves. In addition, its fruits do not swell but remain hard and dry.

TAWNY OWL *Strix aluco* 50,000 pairs resident. The hooting of this owl is frequently heard in February. It is one of the most familiar of all calls, yet what is often described as 'tu-whit, tu-whoo' is usually *two* separate calls: a quavering territorial hoot from the male and a sharp 'ker-wick' from his mate. The hooting is usually heard for some time after dusk and again before dawn. The tawny owl will drop soundlessly from a perch to catch its prey of small rodents (sometimes small birds), its excellent night (and binocular) vision aiding its acute hearing. But, like other nocturnal predators, hunger may force it to continue hunting by day if the weather turns severe, as it often does in February. If caught unawares by day, this owl may be mobbed by small birds, and even magpies will attack it. It nests in a hole in a tree trunk or in similar cover.

COLTSFOOT *Tussilago farfara* This rather bleak month has few sights as welcome as the cheery flowering of coltsfoot. Moreover, it can brighten even the most forbidding of waste ground, for its roots will delve deep in search of nourishment. Flowering ends in April, to be followed by the appearance of the large leaves.

GREEN WOODPECKER *Picus viridis* 10,000 pairs resident. A shy bird, but now beginning to make itself known with its demonic 'yaffle'—a fast 'plew-plew-plew' call mostly heard between now and June. The green woodpecker likes a mix of old trees (for nesting) and open spaces, for it is largely a ground feeder, lapping up ants and other insects with its long tongue. It will dig itself a nest hole in a tree trunk, but it rarely drums.

BUMBLE-BEE *Bombus terrestris* Bumble-bees first appear when warm days guarantee that the sallow catkins are ripe with pollen and nectar. First seen are the queens, while the workers fly from May onwards. More active than hive bees, they start early in the morning, snug in their furry coats, using every hour of daylight, flying even in drizzle.

SMALL TORTOISESHELL *Aglais urticae* Hibernating butterflies are apparently easily misled by a few days of warmth into believing that spring has arrived. If such weather occurs, this butterfly may now be seen, but it is likely to be weak and is doomed if it cannot find nourishment from the nectar of dandelions or other flowers. Pairing in early spring, new generations fly in June and again in August and September (these will hibernate, seen again next spring).

BLACKBIRD *Turdus merula* 4,000,000 pairs resident. Its glorious liquid song usually becomes full in late February or early March, but by June it begins to fall silent during the day, and will soon cease greeting the dawn. Tunelessly noisy from October onwards, it will clatter loudly at dusk in winter. Its famous liking for worms is ill-served when February brings days of frozen soil, and blackbirds are often reduced to scant pickings among the leaf litter.

DUNNOCK (or HEDGE SPARROW). *Prunella modularis* 2,000,000 pairs resident. Despite the latter name, this is not of the sparrow clan. It is a dainty ground feeder, and is rarely seen on a bird-table. It has a wren-like warbling call, heard mostly between now and July.

KESTREL *Falco tinnunculus* 30,000+ pairs resident. A common sighting throughout the year, this is now our most widespread bird of prey, perhaps best known for hovering above motorway verges. It catches voles and other small mammals in the long grass below. Natural nest sites are tree holes, but it will also nest on buildings.

ENGLISH ELM *Ulmus procera* This tree flowers early (February–March), before the leaves appear. Sadly, all but a few elms have been killed by 'Dutch elm disease', a fungus (carried by bark beetles) which grows to block the sap tubes. Thin-barked saplings may survive, but if they are infected their green leaves will turn brown in June and die.

MOLE *Talpa europaea* Life for a mole is made up of a continuous patrol of its tunnels, snapping up worms and other small creatures that have wriggled through the walls of its burrow system. As soil is an excellent insulator, worms (and hence moles) can remain active throughout the year. In February, 'molehills' (the excavated soil from new runs) may poke through scatters of snow, as can shallow surface tunnels themselves. These new systems sometimes appear on low-lying pastures, where they are almost certain to be flooded in the coming months. Except when briefly mating once a year, moles are solitary animals.

BLACK-HEADED GULL *Larus ridibundus* 100,000+ pairs resident. This bird's head may now start becoming patchily dark, and in March it will have gained the full 'executioner's hood'. (It will lose it again in winter, except for a dark spot behind the eye.) Though a seagull, it is often seen following the plough, and a sign of spring is its disappearance from farmland and playing fields to breeding sites, which are often beside inland waters rather than on the coast.

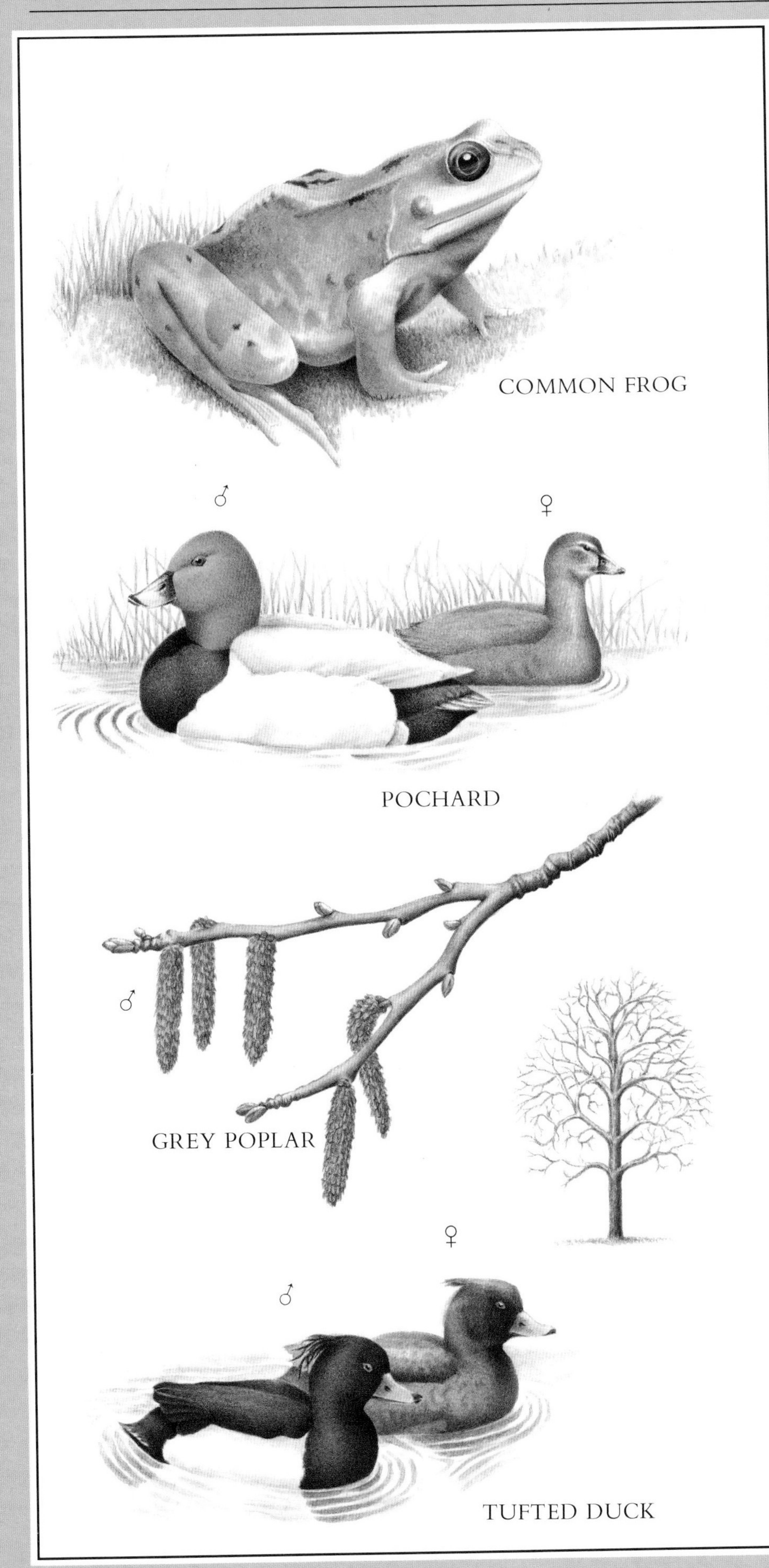

COMMON FROG *Rana temporaria* On awakening from its winter hibernation, this frog starts to move towards water. Courtship and spawning will follow, during which time many males compete to lay hold of a female to fertilize the eggs. (Spawning may be delayed if the female is waiting for her own biological trigger, such as the growth of green algae which will feed the tadpoles.) After mating, frogs remain waterbound until April; they then hide away in beds of young nettles and other damp places, where they will remain until hibernation in the autumn, living on a diet of small flies and worms. As for the spawn: a fortnight after laying, the tadpoles wriggle out of the eggs and soon begin grazing on green slimes. By the time the hind legs have grown, the young frog is omnivorous, eating small animals for protein. In ten weeks, all the legs are grown and it is gulping air; the gills, followed by the tail, then disappear. Young frogs leave the water in midsummer.

POCHARD *Aythya ferina* 200 pairs breed; 50,000 birds in winter. With spring on its way, pochards now engage in communal courtship, the drakes swimming around a duck, head down on the water's surface with neck feathers raised, accompanied by 'heavy breathing'. Pochards are often seen with their more numerous cousins, tufted ducks; and like tufted ducks, pochards also nest in reedbeds, but have less liking for gravel pits.

GREY POPLAR *Populus canescens* Now starting to appear, the reddish male and green female catkins grow on different trees. The young leaves can be seen quite early in spring, with a pale, withered appearance.

TUFTED DUCK *Aythya fuligula* 7000 pairs breed; 60,000 birds in winter. Feeding mainly on food such as small fish and molluscs, this species does not compete unduly when it mingles in 'rafts' with pochards, which prefer a diet of aquatic vegetation. Tufted ducks are now our most common diving duck, familiar even on city ponds, and they have greatly benefited from the large number of flooded gravel diggings and reservoirs.

GREY HERON *Ardea cinerea* 6500 pairs resident. In February, these elegant birds are vociferously refurbishing their nests, which are lodged conspicuously in colonies, in traditional heronries situated high in trees not too far away from a stream or river. Herons may starve if February freezes the ponds and streams, for they fish in the shallows, either from the bank itself or standing in the water, remaining motionless for hours waiting for a tell-tale ripple. Ice, freezing first from the shallows outwards, quickly baffles them. At courtship time, when bowing and neck flexing are to be seen, the birds' legs and bills are bright pink in colour, becoming yellow again when the eggs have been laid. Off-duty birds may occupy 'standing grounds' near the heronry—such places will also attract April's youngsters.

GREAT CRESTED NEWT *Triturus cristatus* and COMMON NEWT *T. vulgaris* These newts usually hibernate on land and move to breeding pools quite early in spring. There is now an elaborate 'dancing' courtship at the bottom of the pond, and each egg is separately wrapped in waterweed by the female. (In both species, the female lacks the crest seen on the male in the breeding season.) After about seven days, the carnivorous newt tadpoles appear. They are more slender than other tadpoles, and keep their tails. At the end of August, when fully formed, these young newts will leave the water. Numbers of the great crested newt are now declining and it is becoming quite rare.

PINTAIL *Anas acuta* 30 pairs breed; 30,000 birds in winter. This elegant duck, long-necked and rakish in build, is typically a surface feeder, but may be seen up-ending in its quest to reach deeper water vegetation.

SALMON *Salmo salar* A migratory fish, the salmon is now starting to arrive at spring-fish rivers (summer-fish rivers have an autumn run). As they move upstream, the fish will often have to overcome obstacles such as sluices and waterfalls on their journey to the spawning grounds in the headwaters, frequently resulting in spectacular leaps.

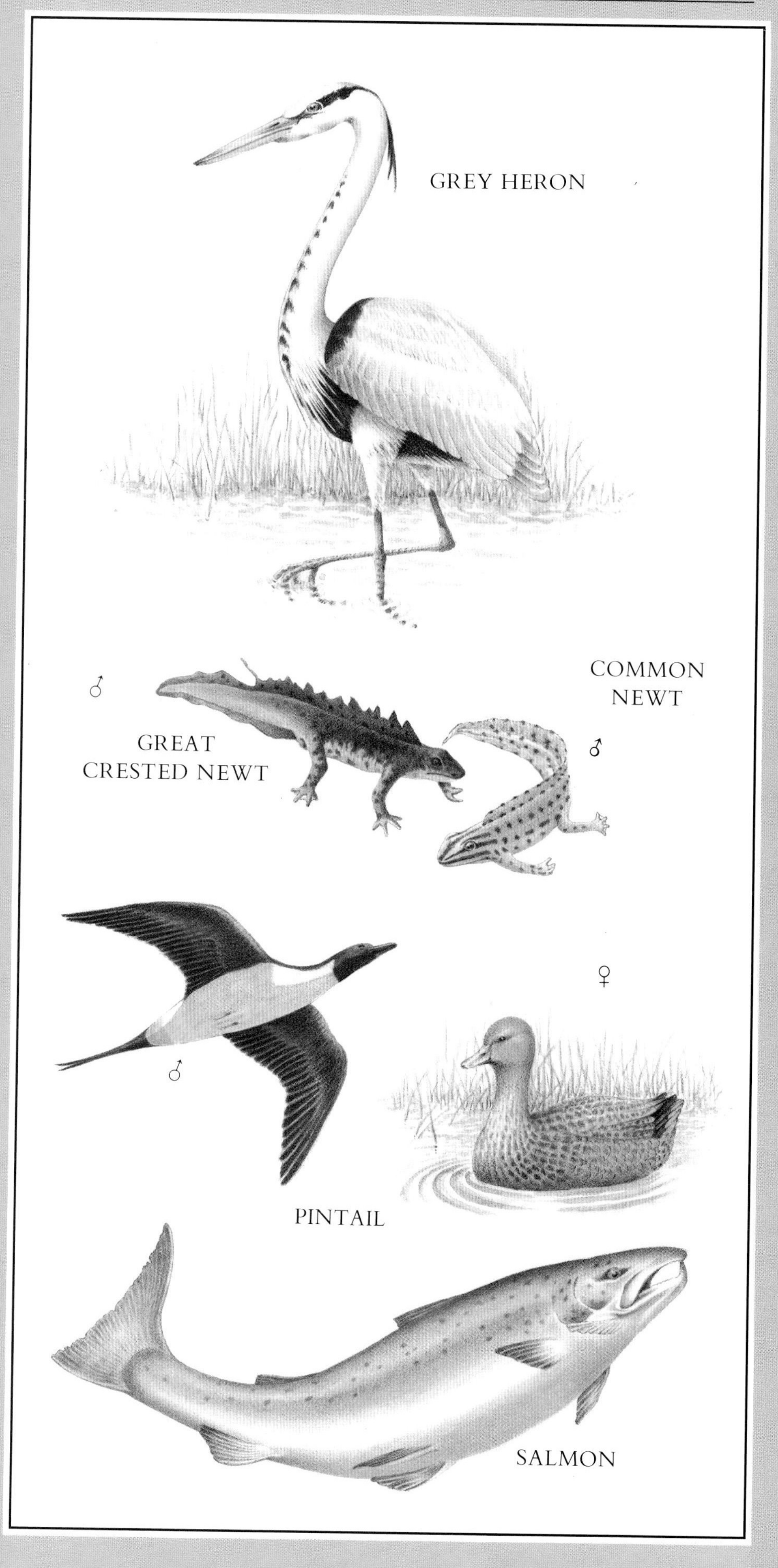

SILVER BIRCH *Betula pendula* The budding catkins now give a purplish haze to the bare profile of this tree. After pollination, the female catkins ripen in September to scatter their seeds widely on the wind when the leaves turn (it is one of the earliest trees to change colour in the autumn). This generous seeding enables birches to colonize open heaths and moors.

DIPPER *Cinclus cinclus* 20,000 pairs resident. The plump dipper winters in its territory, a mile-long stretch of rushing stream in the west or north of Britain. It will greet a sunny day, even in February, with a rippling song, heard above the noise of the water. (Indeed, parts of July and August are the only times of year when this bird is not heard.) It gathers food by walking into the torrent and along the bottom of the riverbed, steadying itself against the current with its broad back, searching for small invertebrates. The bird's nest may be behind a waterfall or under a rocky overhang.

FERAL GOAT *Capra* (domestic) Small herds are seen in mountainous areas, though in winter they often descend to graze in the valleys. Originally of domestic stock, they started running wild many centuries ago, and with the absence of forced inbreeding the goats began to assume the diverse shaggy coats seen today. Moving in small tribes, the nannies are joined by one or two billies for the autumn rut. Some early kids may be seen now in February (though most are born in March).

WOLF SPIDER *Pardosa amentata* On sunny days, this spider, one of the earliest of the year, can be seen chasing across walls and along the ground. It spins no web, but catches its prey by jumping on it. Mating (in spring) is hazardous for the male, and he 'dances' to soothe his hungry mate. The female will later be seen carrying her cocoon of eggs around with her.

COAL TIT *Parus ater* 400,000 pairs resident. Although they often winter in mixed flocks, parties of three or more of these birds may now be heard answering each other with quick, ringing exchanges among the conifers or other woodland trees.

CROSSBILL *Loxia curvirostra* 5000 pairs resident. The seeds of many conifers are now ripe, providing a rich larder for birds able to tackle the unopened cones. With its strange bill, the crossbill is ideally equipped for this, and so these birds now begin to breed in groups high in the trees. A brood may consume up to 100,000 seeds. Feeding acrobatically among the branches, spruce, larch and fir cones fall to common crossbills, whereas the heavier-billed parrot crossbill can tackle pines. Conifers do not produce heavy seed crops every year, and birds bred in good years may face starvation in the poorer ones. If so, they may 'irrupt', that is, travel far in search of food, returning only after a year or two. Britain often receives irruptions of Scandinavian crossbills.

STOAT *Mustela erminea* In the autumn, stoats of the far north rapidly moult to clad themselves in a white coat (ermine) which may still be seen in February—the tail retains its black tip. Those in the south also moult a thicker coat, but remain brown in colour. In the spring, there is another, slower, moult. Unlike most camouflages, ermine is probably not for protection against predators, but a disguising aid when approaching prey.

ALPINE CLUBMOSS *Lycopodium alpinum* In spite of their lowly appearance, clubmosses are interesting plants to look out for on mountains and moors. They are a relic form of vegetation, for although flowering plants now dominate our world today, during the age of the coal swamps giant clubmosses were among the plants which held sway. Yellow spore-carrying cones are seen in the summer.

RED KITE *Milvus milvus* 30 pairs resident. Persecuted almost to extinction by gamekeepers, the kite's small resident population now centres in remote Wales, where it is perhaps most easily spotted across open ground in winter (some Scandinavian birds come to south-east England in winter). Its characteristic hovering gave its name to the children's toy. Often a carrion scavenger, it was common on the filthy streets of medieval London. Nowadays, though, it nests in hillside oak woods.

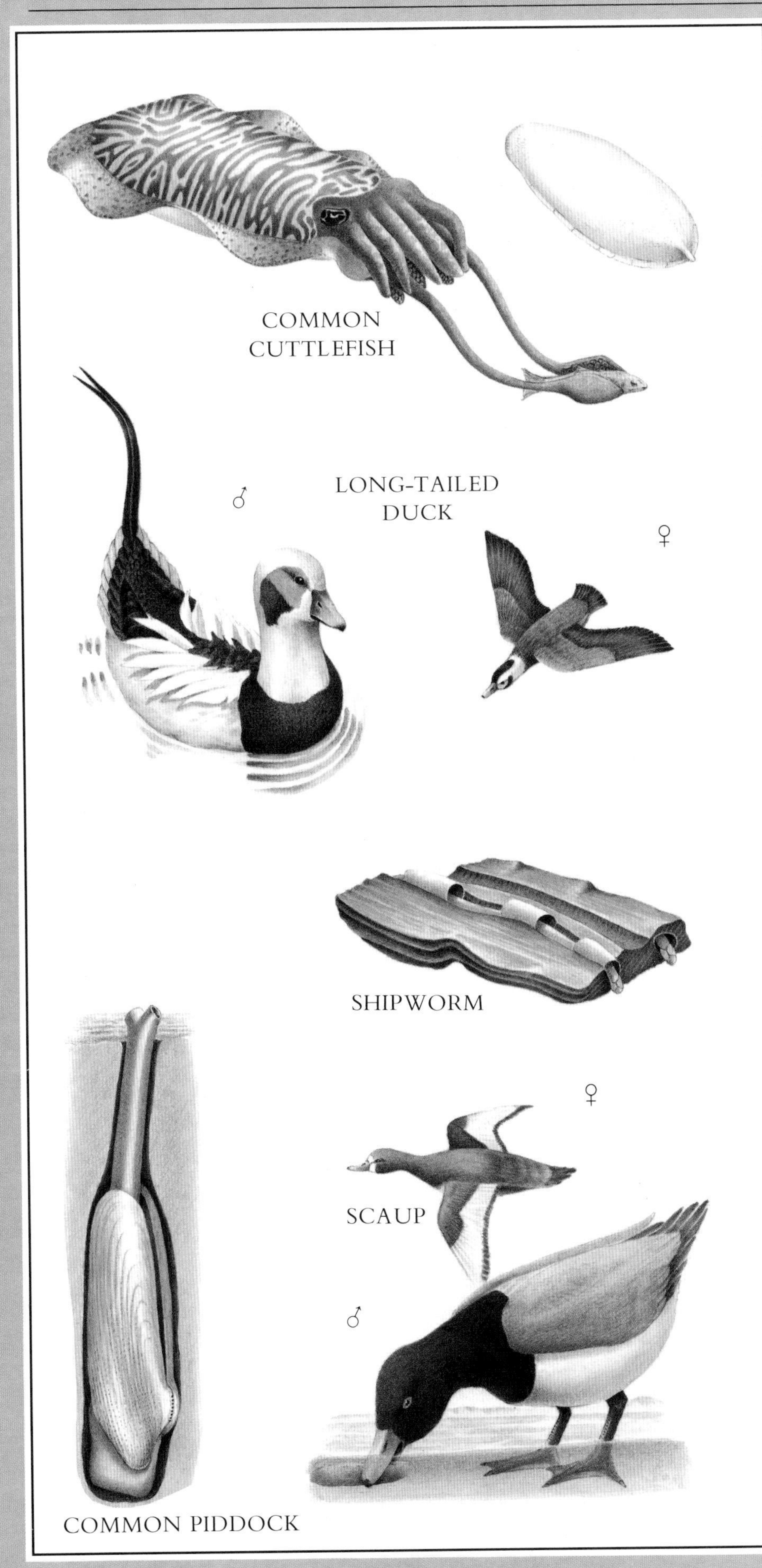

COMMON CUTTLEFISH *Sepia officinalis* Winter storms now bring in a wide variety of items for the beachcomber, including the brilliantly white cuttlebone. This was the internal skeleton of the common cuttlefish, which also gave the creature its buoyancy. Together with squids and octopuses, cuttlefish are cousins to shellfish, the muscular foot evolved into tentacles. Cuttlefish hunt small fish, prawns and shrimps, and eject clouds of 'ink' to confuse predators.

LONG-TAILED DUCK *Clangula hyemalis* 10,000 birds in winter. This is a diving duck, usually remaining offshore in northerly areas. Courtship now begins, prior to the ducks' departure in March or April for their far-northern breeding grounds, and the birds may be seen jostling near the shore. They will begin to return in September.

SHIPWORM *Teredo navalis* A true shellfish, despite its worm-like body, this animal actually digests the wood it bores into (unlike the piddock); the two halves of its shell have been reduced to function as a 'drill bit'. Shipworm caused many maritime disasters in past centuries (men-of-war were often 'copper-bottomed' to protect them against its attack). Today, it can still affect the timbers of jetties and may sometimes be found in floating timber brought in by storms.

COMMON PIDDOCK *Pholas dactylus* The holes bored by the piddock can be found in rocks or stiff clay exposed at low tide, and sometimes also in timber washed ashore by the sea. The toothed edges of both halves of the shell are used as chisels, see-sawing to make a round hole which can become 6 in. deep. This animal sifts sea water for food; when dead, its shell remains embedded in the hole that has been created.

SCAUP *Aythya marila* 5000 birds in winter. A typical sighting from October onwards, these birds are seen on estuaries and inlets, such as the Firth of Forth, which provide beds of mussels for which they have a taste. Here they often congregate in large flocks. A few may remain past March to breed on islands in lakes.

GOOSE BARNACLE *Lepas anatifera* This stalked barnacle is found attached to driftwood brought up by storms and currents from the warmer waters of the southern Atlantic. In medieval days, and later still, barnacle geese were believed to hatch from these crustaceans—this idea may have arisen from the barnacle's feather-like 'cirri', which strain food from the water. The advantage of this mistaken belief was that, as these geese were supposed to be of marine origin, they could be regarded as fish and were thus suitable for eating on Fridays and during Lent!

COMMON WHELK *Buccinum undatum* The shells of this mollusc are often found cast up on winter beaches, encrusted with limy worm tubes. (Empty whelk shells are a favourite refuge for hermit crabs.) The egg-cases may also be found on beaches.

SHELDUCK *Tadorna tadorna* 15,000 pairs breed; 60,000 birds in winter. These handsome birds are now being seen in their colourful breeding plumage after some months of dull 'eclipse' plumage. (This eclipse is assumed during a 'moult migration': in late July, the adult birds begin to congregate off the north coast of Germany, and some also gather in Bridgwater Bay, Somerset, to moult.) The shelduck's nest is often deep in an empty rabbit burrow, on sand dunes for example. The flightless young remain together in crèches of several broods, supervised by a few adults. The birds feed heavily on the small spire shell *Hydrobia ulvae*, found in estuary mud, but this larder is locked up in winter if a freeze ices the exposed mud, leaving the birds to go hungry. However, they have an advantage over waders in that they can up-end to feed below the surface when the tide comes in to cover and unfreeze the mud.

COMMON RAGWORM *Nereis diversicolor* Its name comes from the way it hangs limply when pulled from the mud. Anglers may now be seen digging it up at low tide from estuaries and harbours to use as bait. It burrows, but it may also live sheltered beneath stones. Swimming with the aid of numerous 'paddles', ragworms are both predators and scavengers.

March

This can be a blustery month as well as being cold. The spring equinox, on or about 21 March, is traditionally counted the first day of spring, but this is often premature. Nevertheless, winter is in its death throes. Nothing can disguise the fact that birds are now heartily singing. Clocks are put forward on a convenient Sunday towards the end of the month, so that daylight extends well into the evening hours.

'Spring sets in with its accustomed severity'—that joke is already 300 years old. March has the reputation for being a stormy month, at least at its start, and there is still a risk of frost.

However, longer periods above 6°C trigger grass into growth. And not only grass, for the month is also marked by many flowery portents, such as daffodils and primroses, both as yellow as the plump ripe catkins. According to an old saying, you know spring is really here when you can cover five daisies with your shoe. In the milder south-west, as many as 50 different species may now be in flower, and the first spiders' webs will be seen. Brimstone butterflies are also starting to emerge, and it is the vivid, butter-yellow male (the female is paler) which is thought to have given the name 'butterfly' to all species of these insects.

With the temperature fluctuating around the crucial level, there are usually differences to be noted even between the two sides of a country lane. Sloe can be a sensitive indicator, flowering on bare twigs on one side, but with a touch of green leaf on the other.

Frog spawn is now eagerly being sought in many parts of Britain. The dates of the first sightings advance from south-west to north-east.

Blackbirds and song thrushes also reflect local spring. They are now singing along with other birds, and they can lay early, a few days after the temperature nudges past 4°C for longish periods. This early nesting can prove costly, though, for the eggs and young are clearly visible in the thin hedges and are much pirated by magpies, crows and jays.

The arrival of the first of the summer visitors is heartening. The date of the first sighting is not, of course, a guarantee of spring, for the birds can arrive in the middle of a bleak spell, but it is a reliable augur of things to come.

The song of the chiffchaff, now heard for

the first time, is easily recognized. Woodpeckers are also heard drumming. For the expert, though, the arrival of the wheatear in March and that of the sand martin are indubitable signs of spring.

The famed dawn chorus thus begins to strengthen. To the delight of blackbirds and others, earthworms often now make journeys across the soil surface, and at dawn they are frequently trapped, mapless, on gravel paths and concrete standings. The worms' dispersal activity will continue in April and then fade.

Easter, the most movable of festivals, can fall in March. Its earliest possible date is 22 March, while the latest is 25 April. It is calculated with Byzantine complexity as the first Sunday after the first full moon on or after the spring equinox. If this day happens to be a Sunday, then Easter falls a week later. The introduction of the moon suggests that the church took over earlier customs as was its habit. In fact, the name comes from Oestre or Eastre, the Great Goddess of the Saxons.

The word 'Lent', the 40 days before Easter, has the same root as the word 'lengthen', which the days now noticeably do. It is preceded by Shrove Tuesday, which was celebrated with tugs-of-war and such battles in the past; their origin is perhaps symbolic of the struggle between winter and spring.

Although a mixed month, March often brings as its gift new sunshine falling from a crystal-clear sky—the first really warm weather of the year. Here in the Lake District, the welcome warmth counters the snow; the bright light heightens the muted tones of the old year's bracken and strengthens the lines of the land.

COLD AND GUSTY

The effect of cold airstreams lingering from February may be tempered by the stronger sun of March as the days lengthen. But although the sky can be tantalizingly blue with scampering clouds and pleasantly warm temperatures for the first time in the year, there are many setbacks in this varied, gusty month. Many of the flowers which welcome the spring arrive late, though some may also arrive early.

The trigger for them is the average daily temperature. At about 6°C, green plants can put on nourishing growth, but, as already mentioned, it is the soil temperature to a depth of 1 ft which is the important criterion. The temperature of the soil generally follows that of the air, which is regularly measured at all kinds of weather stations. In March, the average daily maximum and minimum air temperatures both take a jump up from those of December, January and February. At Bodiam in East Sussex, for example, the average maximum reaches 10°C from 7°C, while the minimum rises to 2°C from 1°C—the crucial soil average of 6°C is therefore likely to be reached. In a severe winter, a lower figure is averaged, but in mild winters the average is well above 6°C.

These swings around the critical temperature explain why spring may be early or late, and why the buds break at different dates even within a small area. Microclimates, or local weather areas, which regularly produce pockets of warm (or cold) air, now make a great deal of difference. (For example, gardeners know that brick walls give early growth below them—they offer shelter from cold winds and also capture and store warmth for the plants growing at their base.) In addition, microclimates are created not only by woods, hedges and suchlike, but also by larger areas of hill and valley topography.

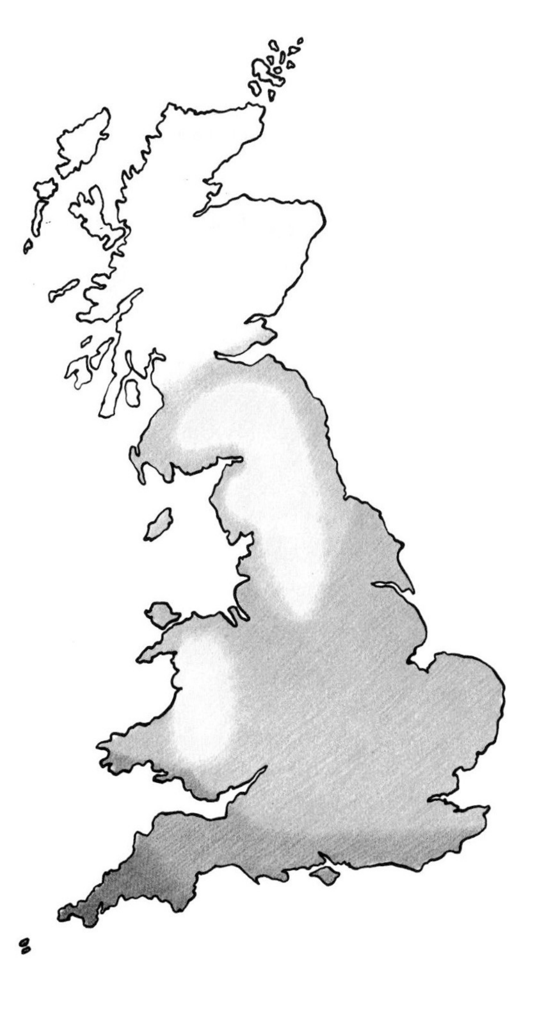

Grass starts into growth when the temperature 1 ft deep in the soil passes 6°C—grazing in the open fields usually begins about a week later. Other plants also put on a spurt of growth, with leaf buds starting to swell and flowers to open. Local microclimates can, of course, hasten or retard the arrival of spring; for example, exposed pastures can be well behind valley fields situated only a mile or two away. This map, showing the start of the growing season across Britain, clearly illustrates the advance of spring.

WINDS AND GALES

'March enters like a lion and goes out like a lamb', according to the old country saying. While gales can occur at any time of the year around Britain's coasts, they are most frequent inland between November and March. March sees these out.

A gale is defined as a wind in excess of 25 knots (around 31 mph), or above force 7 on the Beaufort scale, which is strong enough to make whole trees sway. Strong gales of force 8 will break off twigs, and force 10 (above 55 mph) will uproot trees and even (if the root systems are entangled) entire woods.

Gales—and even milder winds—therefore represent considerable energy. The origin of this energy is the sun. About half of its radiation passes straight through the Earth's atmosphere to be soaked up by the sea and land, which become warmed by it. Much of this warmth is then radiated back, heating the air above. As warm air is less dense than cold air, it rises and pressure is reduced. When this mass of air subsequently cools and sinks, high pressure is the result. In order to even the balance, air moves from high-pressure towards low-pressure areas in the form of winds.

In general, however, in many parts of Britain the growing season really begins in March, and the grazing season too, although this is necessarily later to allow the grass to get some height behind it. The growing season begins in the west of Dorset on 21 March, while its grazing season starts on 1 April, which is about the same as for Norfolk. The dates for the Lancashire coast are 23 March and 28 March, respectively.

The winter's continental highs are now starting to lose their potency, but an anticyclone over Scandinavia can still confront the westerly weather and stagnate movement over Britain. This gives dry, warmish spells.

However, British weather is justly famous for its variety. March's 'lambing storms' are spells of Arctic air bringing snow showers to eastern Scotland and (sometimes) down the country into Kent. Although snow blizzards can still strike in the Scottish Highlands, they are now rather a surprise at similar heights in the Lake District and Wales, in particular.

Stormy seas led in by gales typify the often unruly, gusty weather of this variable month.

The global wind pattern at all altitudes is affected by the rotation of the Earth. In the northern hemisphere, when air masses sink, thus increasing the air pressure, they spiral out *clockwise* to create a high or 'anticyclone'. However, around a low or 'depression', the air spirals in an *anticlockwise* direction before rising. (To illustrate this, for example, when standing with one's back to the wind, the low must lie somewhere off towards the left.)

Daily weather maps picture the positions of lows (and troughs of low pressure linked to them) and highs (with ridges of high pressure running from them). They are shown by isobars, which are contours of equal air pressure, and winds blow generally along the line of the isobars. The closer the isobars lie together, the steeper is the pressure gradient, and so the winds are stronger.

On a daily average, well over half the winds of England and Wales arrive from the west or south-west, 20 per cent come from the north or east, 10 per cent of the days are calm, while the remainder blow from the south and east. Scotland's winds are rather more frequently north-easterlies.

Winds are most strongly felt when they strike the land from a sea fetch or are met directly, high on the hills. Friction against the sculptured surface of the plain with its hedges, trees, villages and farmsteads can reduce the force and speed of a wind by as much as two-thirds and break it into gusts and lulls. This is noticed particularly on a gusty March day, where although it is gusty near the ground, the clouds are seen to race freely overhead.

Localized winds also occur. One example is the 'helm' wind, which in westerly weather can blow down the sheltered east side of the Pennines with some force. Lee slopes are normally less windy places.

Another, much gentler, local breeze is sometimes felt along the foot of hills on tranquil summer evenings. As the sun sets, the slopes cool and cease warming the air above them. As it cools, this air becomes denser and sinks, to be felt as a light breeze.

In August, sea breezes often make many eastern seaside resorts bracing; how they do so is described on page 153.

Fortunately, a gale seldom persists for more than a day, because the system of lows which spawn it are usually moving with such speed that they pass by during that period. Prolonged gales occur where perhaps a whole series of depressions pass one after the other.

BIRD SONG

Birds are excited in spring. Clarion calls and bursts of sweet song are broken by amorous chases, when suitors sport down the hedgerows or swoop low over the fields in display.

Many and various are the courtships now taking place. Male house sparrows build a nest and advertise it by cheeping nearby. For the past month, great crested grebes have enacted a complicated watery dance ending with the ritualized present-giving of a gift of weed. Cock snipe plunge down to their mates, the air vibrating over their tail feathers to create a distinctive humming sound. And for many bird species, song has a vital role in breeding.

Apart from alarm and warning calls, songbirds have a particularly elaborate vocabulary of notes for courtship and beyond. For them, the nest is not simply a nursery for their young; it is also the central point of their territory which must provide food for them and their nestlings. Once mated, the birds will sing, often from a prominent song post near the nest, to warn intruders away. Where the notes fade with distance, another bird can stake his claim. Thus, they spread themselves through a wood, or down a hedgerow, or across the back gardens of a leafy suburb.

The territory is always being tested by rivals. If the occupier falls prey to a cat, a replacement soon appears. And territories may become squeezed under pressure—blackbirds, remembering the rich pickings of winter bird-tables, will nest more closely to one another in garden areas than they do in their natural woodland home.

The result of the song is to deter rival birds of the same species. By and large, a bird of one kind does not pose a territorial threat to a bird of another, for each searches for its own food in its own way—for example, great tits hunt among the lower branches of trees and on the ground, while blue tits roam the tree canopy. Thus, many species of bird can sing happily alongside each other, as demonstrated by the wonderful dawn chorus.

In woods and gardens, the blackbird usually starts this chorus 40 minutes before sunrise (although he may be delayed by fog or wind). He is joined at intervals by the song thrush, wood-pigeon, robin, mistle thrush,

Right As the robin holds territory all year long, its pure, sweet, but (to our ears) rather melancholy song is heard in all months, except perhaps July, when it is usually moulting.

Far right The sweet, rippling, warbling song of the dipper echoes the sound of the tumbling streams along which this bird nests.

willow warbler (our commonest summer visitor) and wren, usually in that order. The chiffchaff joins in, and later, in mid-April, the newly-arrived cuckoo adds his descant; this note is not a territorial call, but a location appeal from male to female—she replies with a slighter, rather bubbling note.

Strong at dawn, the chorus gradually fades while the birds go about their daily business of foraging for incubating mate or brood. Blackbirds and thrushes sing regularly again towards dusk, but pigeons, and indeed many birds, often repeat odd bursts of song during the day.

Doggerel phrases can catch the rhythm of a bird's song, if not its sound. The song thrush has a repetitive chortle: 'get-up-get-up-get-up; run-along-run-along-run-along; time-for-tea-time-for-tea-time-for-tea; tea-tea-tea; don't-be-late-don't-be-late-don't-be-late!'

'A-little-bit-of-bread-and-no-o-o-o-cheese', laments the yellowhammer, while the chaffinch sings 'will'o-will'o-will'o-will-you-kiss-me-dear'—a delightfully dashing ending.

Much bird song is beautiful to the human ear, and seems full of musical meaning. However, it is unlikely that any detailed message is involved—a blackbird will sing through the noise of a pneumatic drill or the thunder of heavy traffic, when communication is presumably impossible. Musical notation cannot capture the birds' notes with accuracy, but sonograms can be obtained, using an instrument known as a sound spectrograph, and analysed.

The blackbird makes a good example, for now in March it is rivalling the famed nightingale in fluency. Its story begins the previous autumn when the pair breaks up, although the hen bird seems to linger at the nest site. The cock birds irritate the winter dusk with noisy 'chinking', and sometimes voice their rattling alarm call. They are pulling rank on each other, establishing their superiority to attract hen birds, and may be paired by the New Year.

Their intimate courtship is celebrated by singing sets of soft, if rather unsure, notes; a subsong which can only be heard nearby. But as the sonograms show, these notes in fact act as the dictionary for the voluptuous full song.

This is being fluted by early March, when the nest site has been chosen. The sonograms show (and this can be tested with a home tape recorder) that the blackbird uses as many as 20 different phrases which are repeated. These change over a number of weeks, during which time notes and trills are added and subtracted.

Left The wren is a very small bird with a very big song! Its song is surprisingly loud, with up to five rather similar phrases hurled out at the world around.

Far left The yellowhammer's song consists of a run of some half-dozen shrillish notes, followed by one long, drawn-out 'a-little-bit-of-bread-and-no-o-o-o-cheese', as it is sometimes written.

LAMBING TIME

The tasks begun in February continue into March, dancing to the weather's tune. In country folklore, 'a peck of dust in March is worth a king's ransom', for a dry (and hence dusty) spell is good for finishing the sowing. The British climate means that the spring-sown grain has to be in bed as early as possible to give the longest growing period. Barley is usually the main crop sown in spring, while in autumn it is wheat.

Many new-born lambs are seen in March. It is not the weather which determines their appearance, of course, but the date on which the ewes were tupped or mated the previous autumn. The gestation period is 147 days—nearly five months. Mountain sheep are mated later than the lowland breeds to allow for the delayed start of hill grass: the length of growing season, which starts when the soil temperature passes the crucial 6°C, decreases by between five and six days for every 100 ft increase in altitude in Wales and the north. But the start of the *grazing* season must wait still longer, until there is some appreciable grass growth on the pastures. Rain is a factor, but in the north-west a farmer can expect to lose 10–12 days for every 100 ft increase in height.

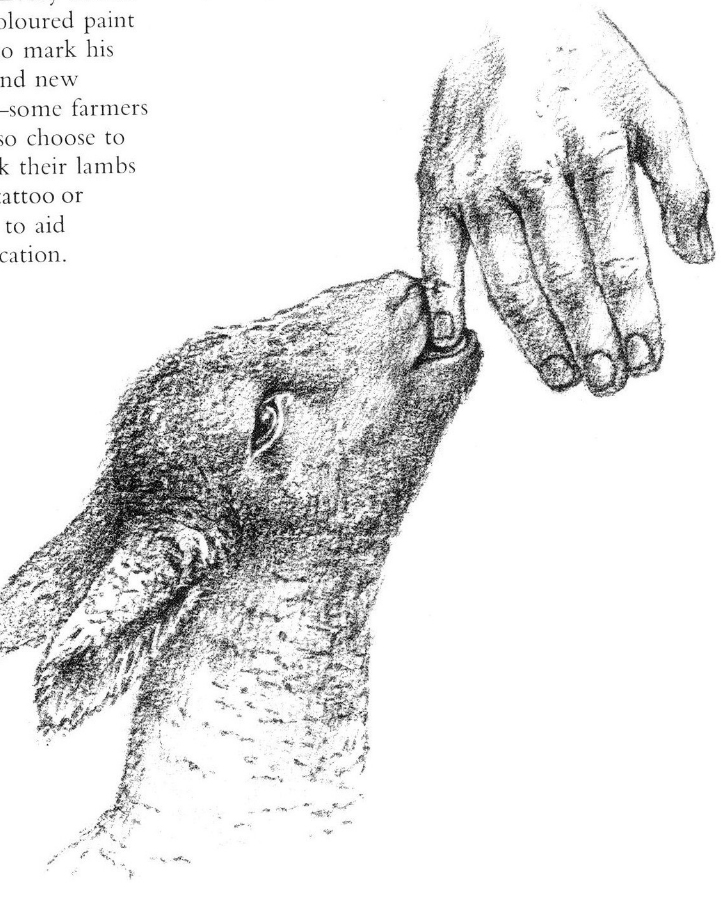

Orphaned lambs frequently need to be reared by hand, and may need coaxing to accept a bottle of milk or glucose and water. Every farmer has a coloured paint brand to mark his sheep and new lambs—some farmers may also choose to earmark their lambs with a tattoo or ear-tag to aid identification.

Lowland farmers with large holdings often stagger the tupping, in order to get small flocks due to lamb at different dates. This makes it possible for at least some of the lambing to avoid likely foul weather when March gales splatter the ground with sleet, while there is an equal chance that some will coincide with the first flush of new grass. This is very rich in protein and is ideal for the ewes in milk.

Staggering the lambing also spreads the work of the shepherd, for although most sheep can cope out in the open, or with a simple shelter made up of no more than a few bales of straw, perhaps one in ten will have to be brought in as a precaution. For this reason, the lambing fields are usually sited close by the farmstead to make supervision easier.

The shepherd may be one of the farm workers, or hired help. On small hill farms, the farmer tends to take on the job himself, but full-time shepherds are usually employed to handle the large flocks of Scotland. All are likely to use the traditional shepherd's crook—this is wielded to catch a leg and hold the sheep for closer inspection.

The lamb in the womb puts on a spurt of growth during the last six weeks, and so the mother will have been 'steamed up' with mashes of oats, sugar beet and ground nuts, carried out to feeding troughs in the field; she will also be fed some good hay. To prime the lamb against disorders, the ewe will be injected with serum at this time.

When she is due to give birth, the ewe usually wanders restlessly away from the flock, lies down and points her head up towards the sky in a characteristic manner. The lamb is born a short while later. It is in danger of getting chilled if it remains wet, but quickly responds to the mother's licking massage and is suckling within a quarter of an hour. Dry and with a good stomach of milk, the lamb is a tough little creature. It does, however, need to keep a full stomach to survive, and must therefore suckle regularly for the first few weeks of its life.

Twins are usually smaller than single lambs, and some breeds bear smaller lambs than others. However, all lambs will put on

quick growth for the first 10–12 weeks.

Upland sheep breeds usually have singles, which is perhaps an inherent precaution of nature as the scant hill grazing provides less milk. Lowland crossbreeds, though, often have twins or even triplets, which are of course twice or three times as profitable if they can be safely reared. But a sheep has only two teats, and although triplets may share in rotation, there is a danger of at least one lamb failing.

Occasionally, a ewe will reject the second of her twins, and some ewes may die in labour. Thus, there will be lambs which are likely to need fostering on to a ewe which, in turn, has lost her own lambs. Although they can be hand-fed with milk or glucose and water four times a day, this is an emergency measure, and successful adoption, though requiring a bit of patience, is greatly preferred.

As a ewe will smell and then reject any lamb which is not hers, she must be misled into believing it is her offspring. It has long been the custom, still tried today, to skin the dead lamb and tie the fleece around the orphan. Alternatively, the lamb may be rubbed with afterbirth cleansings from the ewe, or the ewe's nostrils and the lamb sprayed with scent. Another trick is to stall the ewe tightly, so that she cannot turn and butt away the suckling lambs. After some days, she becomes used to them and can safely be released. However, the mothering instinct of sheep is easily upset, and if even the friendliest dog is allowed to run loose among a flock in spring, scattering the sheep, disaster may well follow, with lambs abandoned.

After a short while, the lambs are moved with their mothers to fresh grazing, to be stocked at perhaps six to the acre. During these early days, their tails are docked and the males are castrated. At the age of four weeks, the lambs will be beginning to nibble grass.

It takes hard-won skill to handle a sheep without causing fright or harm. With this expertise, the shepherd has to cast the ewe to judge her well-being after the birth of her lamb.

THE RIVER WYE

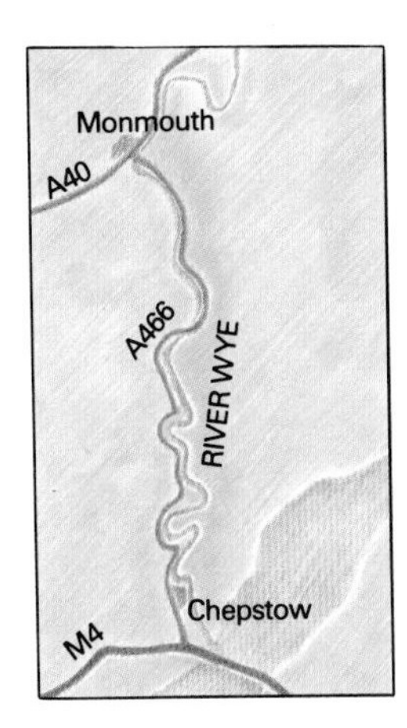

The River Wye forms the boundary of several counties, but it is the lower reaches which yield the more spectacular views, such as at Symonds Yat, near Monmouth, and at Wyndcliffe, two miles north of Chepstow.

As it winds its way down the boundary between England and Wales, the Wye provides some of the finest river views in the country, shouldering steep slopes on one side, holding meadows in a close embrace on the opposite bank. It is well worth climbing up to the vertiginous heights of the 'Eagle's Nest' at Wyndcliffe, a couple of miles north of Chepstow, to view the meanders far below. Symonds Yat, just to the north of Monmouth, is also (and justly) famous, for it is here that the river twists in a whiplash coil.

However, the Wye is renowned also for its spring run of salmon. Indeed, it is one of the rivers where very large fish may still be glimpsed (and perhaps caught), although netting, pollution and other hazards mean that present-day records may never match those of past years. (Other rivers, such as the Tweed, are noted for finer fish on the later summer-to-autumn run.)

The spring run on the Wye takes place between early January and late May. During this time, the sleek, supple salmon arrive back to begin the journey upstream to their spawning grounds. These are the fast-flowing, gravel-bedded tributary streams, perhaps the very same in which they themselves hatched from the egg. Spawning will take place in the autumn. Swollen and heavy, they congregate in headwaters cool enough to satisfy their instincts (they seek water of between 2°C and 6°C).

With vigorous twists of her body, the female digs a 'redd', or hollow, in the gravel, in which she and her mate lie side by side to shed eggs and milt. Emptied, the female then moves upstream, and again, by twists and turns, dislodges gravel to cover the now-fertilizing eggs. There may be as many as 15,000 eggs in a single redd.

In March or April, these eggs hatch into small 'alevins' which feed from their yolk sacs, but when this supply is exhausted they begin to emerge from the gravel to feed, being called 'fry' until they reach a finger's length. From then until about 6 in. long, a year old, they are known as 'parr', hungrily taking small crustaceans and other food. After a year or two, these parr prepare for the ocean; their tails become forked and powerful, and their skins turn silver. This done, as 'smolts' they now begin to swim down to the sea, feeding voraciously along the way. Once the salt water has been reached, they then set off for their new feeding grounds, many swimming 2000 miles to the waters off Greenland, covering up to 30 miles a day.

Growing rapidly, they will stay a year, or perhaps longer, before beginning the return journey. Tagging suggests that they return to their birth-river, but how they 'remember' it is not known. What is certain is that they enter it well-fed and strong, in order to combat the river current, and predatory anglers. They rest in holding pools between fast runs up the rapid stretches, but on their way up many higher waters they may also have to leap waterfalls to regain their childhood nursery, and are often seen massing in the plunge pool below, waiting their turn.

When spawning is over they are drained and exhausted. These 'kelts' are too weak to fight the current and will gradually drift downstream. Bruised and lacerated, most die from disease, but some survive to regain the sea and, in time, reach those renewing feeding grounds. These will return, to spawn again. Growth rings on their scales can be used to determine the age of the fish and a recent survey showed that around 7 per cent of Wye salmon had spawned twice. Very rarely will there be a third journey.

The life story of this fish illustrates just how complex may be the fit of an animal to its habitat and the season.

Salmon apart, the Wye is also notable for the rich woodlands which clothe its steeper flanks. There is a yew wood at Wyndcliffe, for example, with many fine old trees.

The extremely complex and fascinating life story of the salmon (*Salmo salar*)—the king of fish—is described in detail here. During spawning, it should be noted that the male's heavy underjaw develops a distinctive upturned hook, or 'kype'. When spawning is over, this kype will gradually disappear.

BRITAIN'S FISHING RIVERS
These are splendid unpolluted rivers, noted for their salmon, trout and other wildlife:
1 River Spey, Grampian.
2 River Tweed, Northumberland. An autumn salmon river.
3 River Eden, Cumbria.
4 River Lune, Lancashire.
5 River Derwent, Humberside. From its source in North Yorkshire, to its confluence with the River Ouse, this river is of great wildlife interest.
6 River Dee, Clwyd.
7 River Dove, Derbyshire. Starting near Buxton, Derbyshire, it joins the River Trent in Staffordshire.
8 River Towy, Dyfed. Coracle fishermen may be seen netting salmon.
9 River Test, Hampshire. A famous trout river.
10 River Avon, Dorset.
11 River Taw and River Torridge, Devon.
12 River Dart, Devon.
***River Wye**, Gloucestershire.

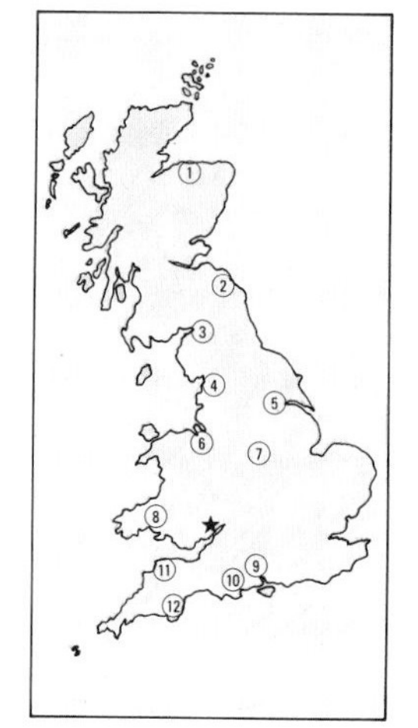

The River Wye looking upstream from Fairview Rock towards Symonds Yat, a famous viewpoint. Notice how the river has cut itself a sharp slope on the outside of the bend which is thickly wooded; on the inside of the bend are one or two flat fields.

CHIFFCHAFF *Phylloscopus collybita* 400,000 pairs visit. Heralding winter's end, the song of this bird is an unmistakable 'tsip-tsap-tsap-tsip', voiced from a high song post. It sings for longer than any other visitor, from late March well into October, and it will often sing in July when most birds fall silent. Nesting in cover, such as brambles, its diet consists almost entirely of insects. (The chiffchaff's twin is the willow warbler, *P. trochilus*—2,500,000 pairs summer here—but this bird offers a sweet waterfall of notes, heard mainly during April and May. It arrives later and leaves earlier than the chiffchaff, but chooses much the same habitat.)

PRIMROSE *Primula vulgaris* Its name means 'first rose' and it now begins to brighten woods and hedgebanks (March–June), heralding the arrival of spring with a violet-like scent in spells of hot sunshine. It may also be seen flowering in autumn in damp western areas, but is rarely seen on dry soils.

LONG-TAILED TIT *Aegithalos caudatus* 200,000 pairs resident. An early breeder, this tit makes a remarkable nest of moss and cobwebs, sadly often conspicuous and at risk in the leafless hedges. Family parties stay together, and are seen roaming the trees in single file with many a 'tsi-tsi' call. Mortality can be high in winter due to a high rate of heat loss.

LESSER CELANDINE *Ranunculus ficaria* This is one of the first plants to respond to the warmth of spring. The flower usually has eight or nine petals, but there may be more. By May or June, though, all is withered away, leaving only the green leaves.

COMMON (or HAZEL) DORMOUSE *Muscardinus avellanarius* This tiny animal is probably awake by now—the cue is a temperature of around 6°C. It likes good cover in woodland or hedgerow, and reveals its presence by removing honeysuckle bark for its summer nest, taking thin strips from 3–8 ft above the ground. As the dormouse is nocturnal, and usually arboreal, the population is hard to estimate. The winter nest is built on the ground; hibernation begins in September or October.

WOOD ANEMONE *Anemone nemorosa* Shooting at the end of February, this plant's lovely white flowers appear a short time later (March–April). It is also known as the 'windflower', from the way the wind sets it nodding in the wood. Although it will only flower if there is enough light, this anemone may be seen loosely carpeting areas of woodland before the tree leaves break.

WOODCOCK *Scolopax rusticola* 10,000 pairs resident. This bird is a wader, with a bill adapted to probe for worms in soft soil, and so prefers rather damp woodlands where it nests on the ground. Its odd display flight, or 'roding', now begins to be seen at dusk (it is largely a night bird), during which it circuits the treetops with slow-beating wings (though its flight is quite fast), uttering a shrill call. At man's approach, however, woodcocks will take off swiftly with a clatter.

SPECKLED WOOD *Pararge aegeria* This butterfly is seen flitting with a weak, erratic flight across woodland rides and glades, or occasionally along shady lanes, especially to the south and west. It is often early on the wing, having overwintered as a chrysalis. Others, from hibernating caterpillars, are seen in April and May. A second brood will be flying from August well into October.

DOG'S MERCURY *Mercurialis perennis* Having pushed its way up through the soil in February (or even January), this rather dull-looking plant is now in flower—the male and female flowers often grow in separate patches. It is one of the few regular plants of beech woods, and also carpets many old-established oak woodlands. The stems and leaves will remain upright until the autumn.

MARSH TIT *Parus palustris* 100,000 pairs resident. Despite its name, the marsh tit prefers drier woods with existing holes for nesting, and may be identified by its voice, which includes a 'pitchew' call. (Easily confused with the marsh tit is its twin the willow tit, *P. montanus*—50,000 pairs resident—which voices a loud 'tchay' cry. This tit chooses damper woods with rotting timber to excavate its nest hole.)

BRIMSTONE *Gonepteryx rhamni* This early herald of incoming spring awakens from hibernation to fly strongly down the hedges (it will be seen flying from now until June). The male's bright colour gave us the word 'butterfly' (the female is paler). The eggs are laid on buckthorn bushes, and another brood will fly from August until the first frosts force them to seek the shelter of ivy or other evergreens.

BLACKTHORN (or SLOE) *Prunus spinosa* Its white blossom now decks the hedgerows (March–May), though it may be seen as early as February in some places and years. The blossom is the snow of 'blackthorn winter', for bleak days are still common even though spring is now well on its way. The berries (sloes) are ripe in August and September, and are much favoured by blackbirds.

YELLOWHAMMER *Emberiza citrinella* 1,500,000 pairs resident. The yellowhammer's song, 'chiz-iz-iz-iz-iz-iz-zee', can now be heard. The refrain is repeated about six times a minute with six-second intervals, and may continue for a good length of time. This early song has been known to start even in February in some years, continuing well into August, and is one of the few bird voices heard across the harvest fields at the end of July. It likes open areas with some rough cover and a few trees, and builds its nest on the ground or in low bushes.

BROWN HARE *Lepus capensis* The brown hare lives a solitary life out on open ground, or even moorland up to 2000 ft. It feeds mainly at dusk and dawn on grass and crops (and tree bark when hunger strikes deep). Otherwise, much time is spent lying belly-flat against the ground in order to remain unseen (hares are perhaps most frequently noticed among the short, yellow stubble after harvesting). The resting place is often a shallow depression, or 'form', which, when protected by vegetation, may be noticeably snugger than the surrounding open ground. 'Mad March hares' mark the main breeding period. Now (and in April) they are often seen in pairs or even groups, the females up on their hind legs, boxing away the larger males.

RABBIT *Oryctolagus cuniculus* Bred for meat and fur in Plantagenet times, rabbits only became common a few centuries ago. Then, in the 1950s, numbers were seriously hit by the disease myxomatosis. Today, though, they are again common. Social animals, rabbits dig quite complicated burrow systems with many exits; the deeper chambers are for winter, with shallower ones for summer. The young are born in a separate blind burrow, or 'stop'. Rabbits usually feed at dawn and dusk (but all day in quiet places), relying for safety on a rapid dash back to the burrow. The feeding areas become grazed short, and they will strip bark when very hungry, though elder is rejected. Droppings are left on ant-hills or other slight rises, probably as territory markers.

PEACOCK *Inachis io* Seen emerging from hollow trees, ivy or garden sheds on warm days in early March, this butterfly will fly well into June. It is a strong, cross-country flier. The eggs are laid on nettles; this brood will emerge in the summer to fly until late autumn, visiting the garden before hibernating.

LAPWING *Vanellus vanellus* 100,000+ pairs resident. Other names for this bird are 'peewit' after its call, or 'green plover' after its breeding plumage. This elegant bird is now back on its nesting fields and moorlands, swooping and diving exuberantly in display, issuing a strange bubbling note heard only at this time of year. It moves regularly in winter when the ground freezes and locks up its larder, and snaps of frost in spring may force flocks back to milder south-westerly areas. Lapwings are waders—the young feed themselves from the soil.

BUTTERBUR *Petasites hybridus* Its exotic flowers (March–May) are seen where the lane crosses a stream or other damp ground. Large green leaves grow (up to perhaps 2 ft across) after the flowers have died.

COMMON EARTHWORM *Lumbricus terrestris* This species, which plugs its burrow with leaves, is now seen crossing paths at dawn. On damp days in late summer, with the 'saddle' noticeable, they will emerge to breed.

COMMON TOAD *Bufo bufo* This amphibian makes an epic springtime journey when the temperature in March (or early April) regularly reaches 7°C. Led perhaps by ancestral memories, hundreds of toads may make for a breeding pond, a migration which can be over a mile long and take up to ten days. On the way, obstacles will be climbed and roads crossed (at which time some conservation groups even operate toad-lollipop wardens). Toads require deeper water than frogs (though both may breed in the same pool), and a struggling mass of males will be seen, trying to scramble on to the back of a female to fertilize her eggs. Once breeding is over, the toads return to land, to be followed some three months later by the youngsters.

GREAT CRESTED GREBE *Podiceps cristatus* 3500 pairs resident. These birds are now returning to lakes and gravel pits (but not in the Highlands) where they are seen in breeding plumage with marked head tufts and ruff. The quaint courtship display may even start as early as February in some years, in which they headshake and present each other with waterweeds while posturing high out of the water. The female may 'trumpet' and the male dive beneath her. Also charming is the way they often carry the young on their backs.

KINGCUP (or MARSH-MARIGOLD) *Caltha palustris* Though less common today due to the 'improvement' of river banks and widescale drainage, this plant may now be found in glorious flower (March–May), growing sturdily.

REED BUNTING *Emberiza schoeniclus* 400,000 pairs resident. Now starting to reoccupy nest sites, the reed bunting chooses not only reedbeds and waterside cover, but also dry scrub and even plantations. Its song cannot be mistaken—three notes followed by a whistle: 'tcheep-tcheep-tcheep-tchizzup'.

DACE *Leuciscus leuciscus* Preferring clear, fairly fast-flowing water, the dace is now spawning, from February to May, and at this time it moves to gravelly or stony shallows. It is a shoaling, surface-living fish.

REDSHANK *Tringa totanus* 40,000 pairs breed, plus large numbers in winter. The 'sentinel of the marshes' is now seen at its breeding sites in damp grassy places, and also on moorland and hill pastures. Rapid, shallow wingbeats mark its display flight. Like other waders, the young feed for themselves, and are led to areas of damp soft soil when they leave the nest—hard ground in a dry spring is thus a hazard. They flock on estuary mud-flats from late July onwards and are noisy birds, piping alarm notes hysterically at any intruder—but they also have a fluting call.

GOAT (or PUSSY) WILLOW *Salix caprea* The twigs with their catkins are picked as 'palm' to decorate the Easter church. Their nectar and pollen attract early insects, and tiny seeds are released in midsummer.

GARGANEY *Anas querquedula* 50 pairs visit. It is uncommon, and unusual too, in being the only duck to summer rather than winter here (this it does further south). As a dabbling duck, it chooses shallow pools.

BROWN TROUT *Salmo trutta fario* Needing clear water, rich in oxygen, which is also cool (26°C will kill it), the brown trout chooses either fast-flowing streams or cold, deep lakes. Patterning itself to its surroundings, a river fish usually has a yellowish underside and red-spotted sides (white flesh); lake fish tend to be more silvery (with pink flesh). When spawning (October–February), the river fish move further upstream while lake fish move into the rivers, the eggs being laid in gravel reaches. The close season for trout usually ends on 1 March.

EEL *Anguilla anguilla* Swarms of young eels (elvers) are now arriving after a 3000-mile journey from spawning grounds across the Atlantic. They gather, for example, in Bridgwater Bay, Somerset, and when the water is warm enough they swarm up the rivers. They can also wriggle overland to other streams or ponds, to grow as 'yellow eels', inactive in winter when food is scarce. After perhaps 18 years, they stop feeding and turn silvery; these 'silver eels' return to the ocean to breed.

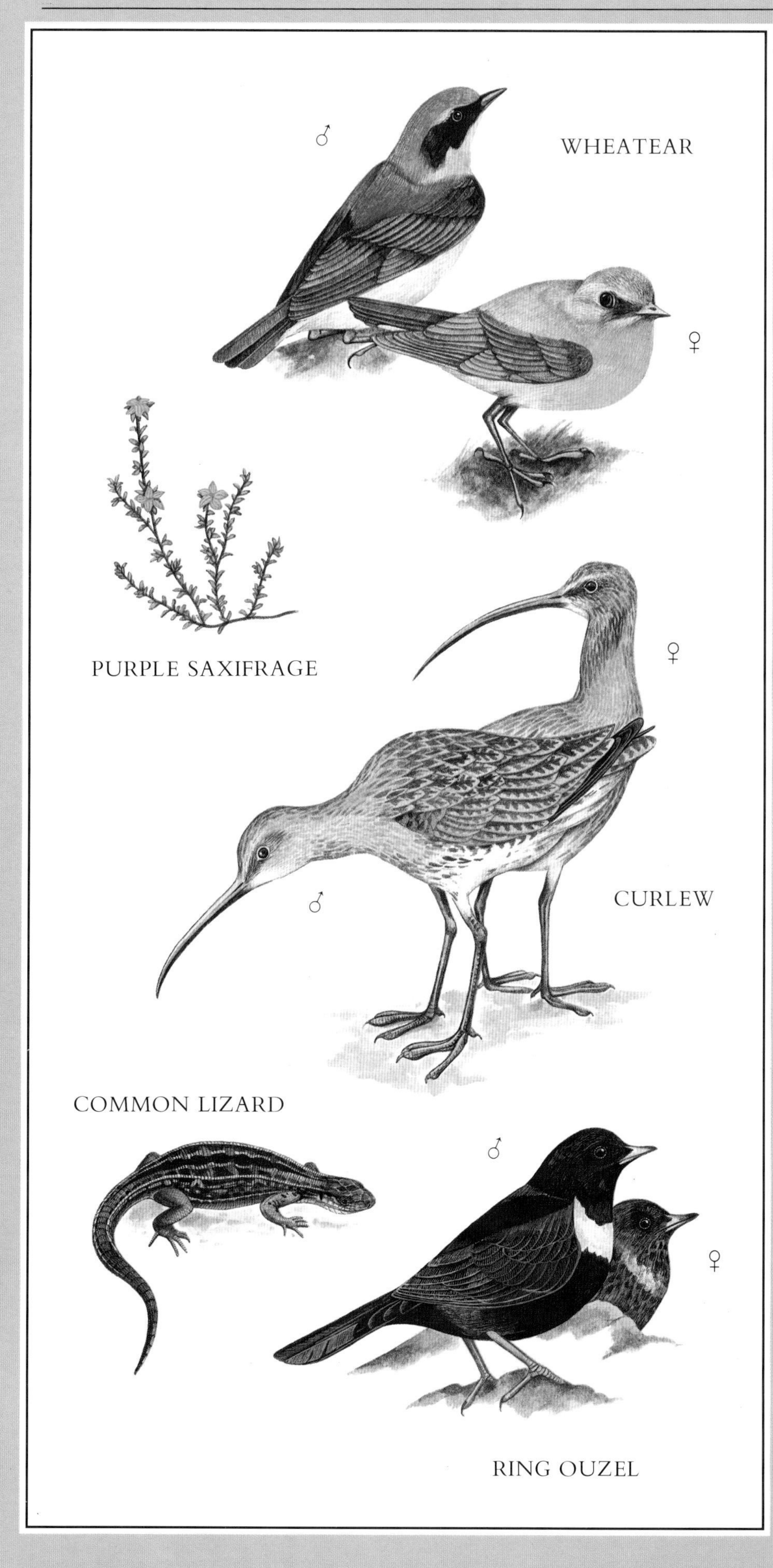

WHEATEAR *Oenanthe oenanthe* 40,000 pairs visit. A true harbinger of spring is the early arrival on moors and hillside pastures of this bird. Easily recognized when it shows its white rump while flitting over the ground, it voices its spirited song with skylark-like warbling and harsher discords—often from the ground. It nests in crevices, and sometimes in dry-stone walls. Return migration begins at the end of July, when southbound birds may be seen unexpectedly on golf courses, for example.

PURPLE SAXIFRAGE *Saxifraga oppositifolia* This flower is often the first seen in mountainous areas (March–May), though it also grows at sea level in northern Scotland. With much of our uplands grazed by sheep, it is only likely to be found on streamside cliffs or rocky ledges.

CURLEW *Numenius arquata* 40,000 pairs resident. Its plaintive 'coor-lee' cry is now starting to be heard on its breeding moors and marshes. The birds space themselves out (a good number would be four pairs per 100 acres) and beat the bounds of their territories, uttering a bubbling song. In March they also fly in courtship display, rising steeply with quick-beating wings, calling all the while, to glide down with notes dying away. The nest is in the shelter of rough grass. In autumn they will return to coastal salt marshes and flats.

COMMON LIZARD *Lacerta vivipara* Although occasionally seen on warm winter days, this lizard usually hibernates from October until now. Numbers may be seen together in the breeding period from April to May; the female retains the fertilized eggs, and the young are 'born alive'. A lizard's diet consists mainly of spiders, flies, beetles and caterpillars.

RING OUZEL *Turdus torquatus* 8000 pairs visit. The 'mountain blackbird' arrives now in remote upland areas. It is shyer than its cousin (and with a much simpler voice) and is usually only glimpsed from afar. But when nesting it is more aggressive and may fly at an intruder. It is also seen feeding in lowland areas when the return migration is under way.

SLOW-WORM *Anguis fragilis*
Although resembling a snake, this is in fact a legless lizard. It is not a very speedy predator, however, and worms and slugs form its diet. But it can move quickly enough when found out of hibernation, basking on sunny March days. This is a vital sun-soak, for reptiles are cold-blooded, with muscles and senses only fully active at 25°C+. It gains warmth from direct sunshine or from the walls of its burrows in which much time is spent. The eggs are held within the female's body until hatching time, during July and August. Slow-worms retire to hibernate again in October.

GREY WAGTAIL *Motacilla cinerea*
20,000 pairs resident. This bird is seen along the rushing becks of the hills, tail constantly twitching. It may also nest by slower lowland streams (where it is often seen in winter), or even quarries, lured by suitable nesting crevices. Now in March, the male with black breeding bib is displaying, flying slowly from one perch to another, with tail fanned out and feathers plumped up.

MINING BEE *Andrena* species. Early on the wing, these solitary bees are useful for pollinating fruit trees. They are also harmless, for their sting is too weak to pierce skin. Their burrow holes are often found on sandy banks.

GOLDEN EAGLE *Aquila chrysaetos*
400 pairs resident. On sunny days in early spring, these magnificent birds display with alternating swoops and glides. They are impressive fliers, calmly riding the thermals above their territories in the Scottish Highlands (and occasionally the Lake District). Breeding begins in March, in huge nests in remote eyries on crags. Often seen hunting in pairs, one behind the other, they will take carrion and perhaps lambs, as well as hares and grouse.

MINOTAUR BEETLE *Typhaeus typhoeus* This beetle may now be seen crawling across the bare soil of a heath. It quarries beneath cowpats or other droppings, laying its eggs in rolls of dung, which the grubs later eat. (The female has much shorter spikes on her thorax than the male's horns.)

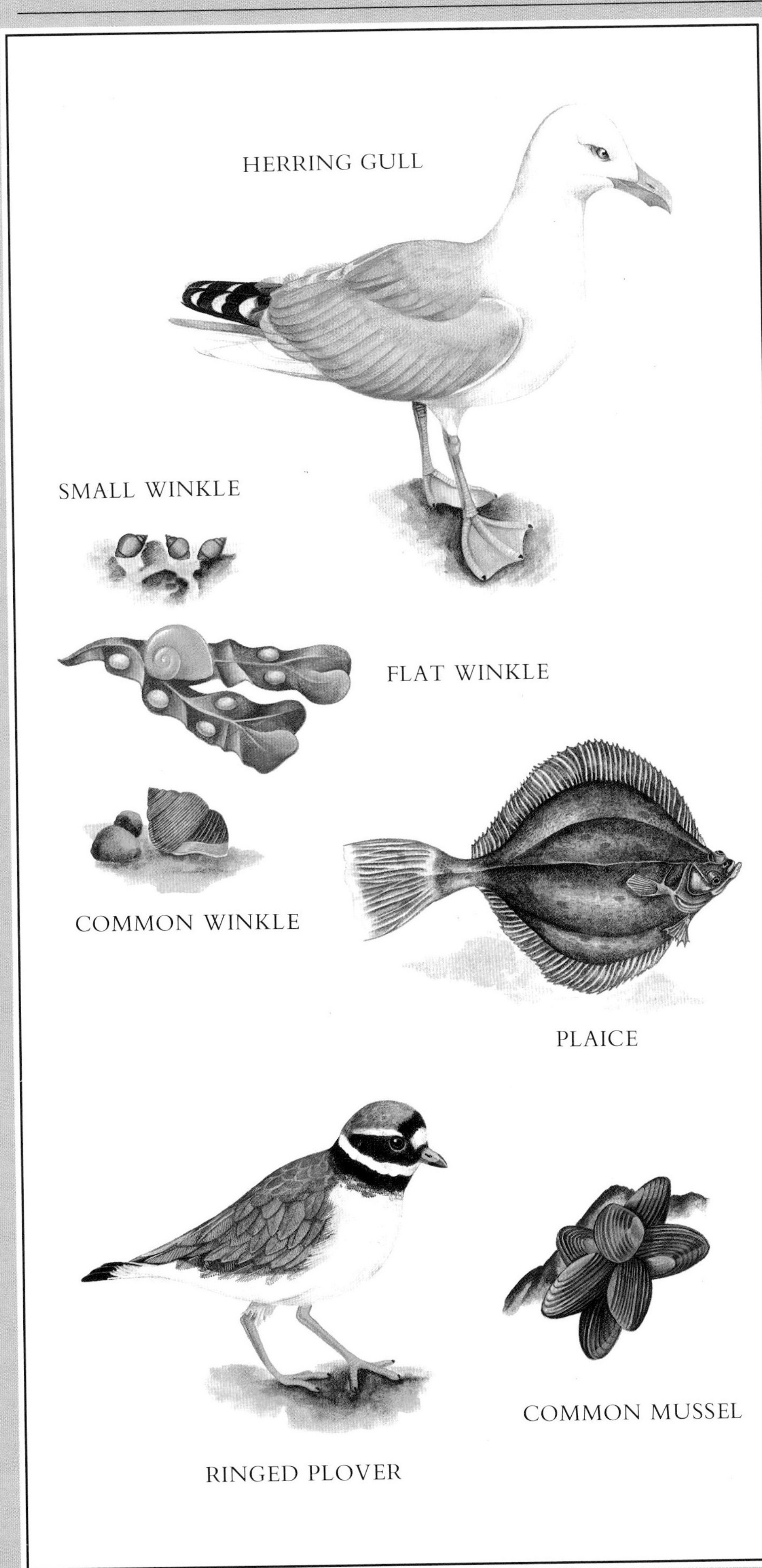

HERRING GULL *Larus argentatus* 300,000 pairs resident. A piratical scavenger (its name is a misnomer), the beady-eyed herring gull is seen at rubbish tips and may even breed inland, but in March it is found mainly on the coast, nesting colonially not only on natural cliffs, but also on roofs. Nestlings will peck at the red beak spot on the parent's bill to provoke a regurgitated meal. The gull's narrow wings enable it to manipulate its flight quickly and exactly to ride the shifting breezes bouncing back from the waves below; it is equally agile at the cliffs.

WINKLES The distribution of the species depends on their tolerance to exposure by the tide: small winkles (*Littorina neritoides*) live in crevices above the high-water mark; flat winkles (*L. obtusata*) are seen on bladder wrack; common winkles (*L. littorea*), eaten by birds as well as man, are seen in pools at low tide.

PLAICE *Pleuronectes platessa* Living in shallow coastal waters, adults stay close inshore until January before moving offshore to spawn, returning between April and June, depending on the water temperature (the young remain inshore for four years before moving to deeper waters). The best catches from the shore are made from April to October, when the plaice loses its appetite for winter's duration.

RINGED PLOVER *Charadrius hiaticula* 5000 pairs breed; 10,000 birds in winter. The eggs of this bird, lying in their simple scrape of a nest, are a classic example of camouflage (as are the chicks)—which puts them at risk from heedless holiday-makers, for they nest on shingle shores. The female may feign a broken wing to lure intruders away from the nest. Their 'pattering' of the tidal mud with their feet—to get a response from their prey of small shellfish and worms—is also typical.

COMMON MUSSEL *Mytilus edulis* This bivalve grows attached to rocks and timbers, but in sheltered areas it may form packed beds on the mud between high- and low-tide levels, to the benefit of many birds. Mussels higher up the shore remain small, for they can only feed when the tide is in.

TOPSHELLS The flat (or purple) topshell (*Gibbula umbilicalis*) is found high on the shore, while the common (or painted) topshell (*Calliostoma zizyphinum*) is seen at the lower tide level.

OTTER *Lutra lutra* This animal is now beginning to be seen along the coasts of western Scotland, returning to the shore after spending winter on the salmon rivers. Here, active by day, it is frequently seen. But elsewhere in lowland Britain a sighting is now sadly rare, for in these areas it is nocturnal, and its distribution is patchy and decreasing, due to disease, pollution, destruction of dens or 'holts', plus competition from feral minks (fortunately, otter hunting is now illegal). Otters prefer to hunt eels and slower-moving coarse fish. They mark their river-bank territories with tarry-looking 'spraints' that often glisten with fish-bones. The dog and bitch only unite for mating; the cubs may be born in any month.

COMMON ACORN BARNACLE *Balanus balanoides* This highly-adapted crustacean, living cemented upside down on the rocks, extends feathery feeding hairs through the hole in its shell top to catch food particles. Coating the rocks from low tide even to the splash zone above the high-tide mark, it is most numerous on exposed coasts.

LESSER BLACK-BACKED GULL *Larus fuscus* 50,000 pairs on coasts. Mainly a summer visitor, this gull returns to its breeding sites later than the herring gull. They are, in fact, closely related, being two of several distinct races of the one species found around the Atlantic; they may interbreed, but rarely do. However, though closely similar in habit, this gull is less partial to rubbish tips and, given the choice, prefers flat ground for nesting.

DAB *Limanda limanda* Larger dabs are usually spawning in deeper water by now, but by August they will return to rejoin smaller brethren in sandy shallows to feed and recover their strength. Anglers fishing in inshore waters frequently catch these fish, particularly on the east coast.

APRIL

Weatherwise, April can vary greatly from year to year. Warm springs may see Surrey catching up with Cornwall in the early growth of bluebells. But April, the month of the cuckoo, can just as easily be cruel everywhere, promising much and giving tantalizingly little. The season 'spring and early summer' is reckoned to begin on 1 April, lasting until 17 June.

The first cuckoo is often to be heard welcoming the spring under a brilliant blue sky, dotted with puffy white clouds—a typical April sky, if any weather can be counted as such. But, 'When the cuckoo sings on an open bough, keep your hay and sell your cow', it signals a late spring, with little new grass yet to graze.

In spite of the appearance of warmish April showers, it is also a rather dry month. So much so, that the black fenland soils are sometimes blown up in April dust storms.

The familiar cry of the migrant cuckoo is now to be heard echoing loudly through the woods and countryside, indicating that summer will soon be here.

There is no doubt that the countryside is greening, although the north still lags behind the south. Local geography also plays a part—trees are delayed in those valleys and hollows which collect cold night air: the frost hollows. Indeed, if a severe frost does strike after leafing, the trees affected may be defoliated and will have to bud anew and grow another crop of leaves.

There is an old saying that, 'Ash before oak, look for a soak, oak before ash, look for a splash', but an ash tree will leaf later than a close-neighbouring oak, by as much as three weeks. A fairly regular occurrence is the 'blackthorn winter': while the hedges are heavily laden with snowy-white sloe blossom, the weather turns bitter, and in this changeable month, a day or two of such weather is extremely likely.

With the advance of spring, flowers of diverse hues appear. The deep lanes in the forward West Country are now patriotically decked with the colours red, white and blue—of campion, stitchwort and bluebell.

The pond is also becoming a lively place, and frog spawn may be expected over much of the country by now. This is the month of

the adder on many moors, while on the coast the summering terns are starting to arrive.

Generally, the explosion of plant life is accompanied by flushes of insects. These feed the arriving summer visitors. The swallow is now seen and the chiffchaff is widely heard; but many summer songbirds slip back unnoticed to join the chorus when their mates arrive (males and females often arrive at different times) and when pairs are formed.

The first nightingales are heard towards the end of the month. The full song reaches its peak around midnight, although the bird will also sing in the daytime (and not all the birds that sing at night are nightingales).

Why the cuckoo, of all the birds, should be the one chosen for gusty rustic humour is not hard to guess. A 'cuckold' is the husband of an unfaithful wife, and is a word that has been in use since medieval times. The bird's notes are, like the innuendoes, simple and unmistakable. What has been forgotten is that counties had 'cuckoo days' of practical joking—Surrey's was held on 14 April.

Something of this is retained in April Fool's Day, the first day of April. Or rather it is half a day, as the joke rebounds on the player past midday. The sport is to catch the victim unawares (perhaps the joke that spring plays on unsuspecting winter).

Here we see April on the banks of Yorkshire's River Wharfe. Some trees are already into leaf, while for others the joyous green force of spring has yet to break their buds. At this time of year, local topography plays a part, and one side of a valley can be noticeably later into leaf than the other.

PASSING SHOWERS

As well as a good deal of sunshine at this time, there may well be those famous gentle April showers. In weather lore, it only needs an occasional coincidence to renew a popular belief. Generally, however, April can be a rather dry month with rainfall much as it was in March—7 per cent or less of the year's total falls in central and southern England. In May, it will increase to 9 per cent.

There may be westerly weather, but there is also the strong possibility that a high may develop somewhere over northern Europe. This draws in winds from the north-east or easterly directions, and in April these can be as frequent as from the south-west and west.

The sun is now strengthening, and in the lowlands there is less likelihood of a freezing day, although night frost can still be severe, especially in valleys sheltered from wind. There is the chance of an odd snowfall in the lowlands of Scotland, but further south this is likely to be merely a light scattering of snow across the ground which quickly melts.

Coastal regions now tend to be cooler than those inland, for the warm sun heats the ground while the Atlantic, Irish Sea and North Sea remain cold.

Overall, it is a characteristic of April that although it is a changeable month, and long spells of settled weather are less likely, differences between north and south become increasingly marked.

In fact, the temperature isotherms, which in January ranged north–south (between warmer west and colder east), now range east–west, from warmer south to colder north—a pattern which will remain until early winter. Spring has definitely arrived in most of the southern region, and the soft, moist growing season now begins even in central and northern Wales. However, it is still likely to be delayed in Scotland.

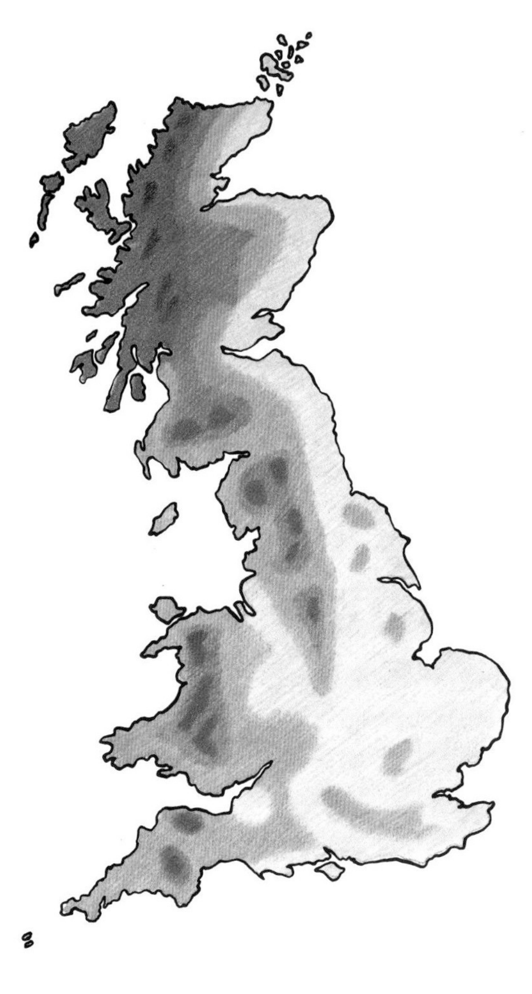

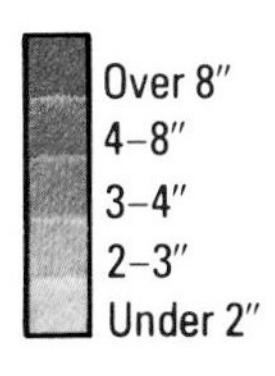

April showers fall gently in comparison to the storm-driven rains of winter. This map of April's average rainfall, based on 30-year averages, might almost be a map of landforms, so closely does it echo the contouring of hills and lowlands. This pattern is seen in rainfall maps for all months of the year, but the variation from one year to the next, or from one village to another, can be very marked. In Surrey alone, April's rainfall may average 1.78 in. in one place, but be 2.20 in. elsewhere, not too far away.

CLOUDS

Clouds are weather made visible, and now in April there is usually a good variety to see. They gather, move and disappear in answer to unseen motions in the atmosphere, obeying natural laws that we cannot sense.

The amount of moisture held by the air varies with its temperature, with warm air able to hold more than cold. Air becomes saturated when it holds as much water vapour as it can for its temperature. If it is then cooled, it must release some of it. At this 'dewpoint', the excess water condenses in the form of very small droplets. (Action nuclei, such as small particles of dust, smoke or minute salt crystals, are required, otherwise the air becomes supersaturated.)

Although these droplets are much larger than the molecules of water vapour, they are well under a thousandth of the size of a raindrop. Nevertheless, we can see them easily as cloud (or, if at ground level, mist or fog). However, if the temperature is very low, as it often is at altitude, the cloud droplets freeze to become minute ice crystals.

Three families of clouds can be seen: stratus lies in a level sheet at the height at which its dewpoint is reached; cumulus is a lumpy cloud, bulging above its flat dewpoint base;

Above Here we see altocumulus, which often resembles a layer of cotton-wool balls. Below this lies some ragged cumulus, the noticeably flat base-line marking the height where the rising air reaches its dewpoint and begins to condense.

Above left Wispy cirrus clouds—these high-level clouds consist of fine ice crystals.

and cirrus has a wispy appearance.

Alternatively, their base height may be used to define them. High-level clouds exist from around 3–8 miles overhead, and include cirrus (wispy 'mare's tails'), cirrocumulus (small 'cauliflowers' ordered in groups or lines), and cirrostratus (a uniform hazy layer). Medium-height clouds, which form $1\frac{1}{4}$–3 miles above ground, are altocumulus (rounded masses in groups or lines), altostratus (a veil through which the sun may weakly shine), and nimbostratus (dense grey rain-clouds). 'Nimbus' is the Latin word for 'rain'. Stratus is a lower-lying cloud, rather like a fog, which sometimes gives drizzle.

There are also cumulus and cumulonimbus clouds. These are 'heaped' and may rise tall above their base level. Cumulonimbus, which often develops from cumulus, is the prince of the clouds, stately and possibly dangerous. It is the towering, anvil-headed storm cloud of a summer's day.

Clouds reflect the weather, and can be read to analyse what is invisibly occurring in the sky above. For example, on a warm summer's day, cumulus clouds often form over land, while the sky over the sea remains clear. The reason for this lies in the fact that the atmosphere itself absorbs very little of the sun's heat directly. However, the sea and the land do absorb it, and when they are themselves heated, they reradiate it to warm the air above. The sea takes longer to warm than the land; therefore, in summer sunshine, the air over the land is likely to rise as warm bubbles, which cool into white cumulus.

On the other hand, dark rainy nimbostratus is often seen along the fronts between air masses when a chisel of colder air forces the warmer air to rise up over it.

Not all clouds bring rain—where and when it rains depends on the total weather system. Cumulonimbus can bring rain—and lots of it: 2 in. an hour, compared to nimbostratus which brings $\frac{1}{2}$ in. per day. But the rising turbulent air that creates cumulonimbus may be powerful enough to toss its contents up thousands of feet in minutes. Eventually, hailstones will be created, while the electric charges generated by this agitation will be released as strokes of lightning.

Day to day, clouds have little direct effect on wildlife, although the rain and snow they bring certainly does. Migrating birds can be blinded by cloud, but often winds have more effect, carrying the travellers far off course.

THE WATER MARGIN

The river water-crowfoot, which may flower at the end of April, decking swift-flowing streams with white, is clearly closely related to the yellow buttercups of the fields—perhaps the aquatic world is not as foreign as it might at first seem to be. Many water plants are now spurting into growth.

The many and varied freshwater habitats add delight to the countryside. Hills gather the rain into tumbling streams and unite them into bubbling young rivers. Where these reach the plains they take on the majesty of age, winding slowly to the sea. Sometimes the water pools itself into mysteriously deep lochs and tarns in the hills, or reedy meres in the valleys. The winter storms replenish disused gravel pits, and in clay country quickly bring streams to turbulent flood. On the chalk, this lashing rain soaks away to reappear as springs below the flanks of the downs. Running from their underground reservoir, these chalk streams rarely cross their banks, maintaining their level all year round.

The natural life of these waters closely reflects the conditions. Trout will be found in cool, highly-oxygenated, clear waters where they feed by sight. Coarse fish, though, inhabit slow, warm and turbid flows, feeding by touch and smell. Dragonflies will hover over pools and ponds later in the year, while the dainty mayflies will soon be flitting over running water. And while the arrowhead may grace the edges of streams, the bulrush will only grow in slack or still water.

Most of Britain's aquatic plants are land plants by ancestry, having colonized their new habitat at some time in the distant past. These terrestrial forebears have been lost for the water-lily, but the link is clear for the water-crowfoot, despite having had to adapt for the new environment. Like many submerged plants, it has forsaken a rigid stem for pliability, and sways without resistance to the changing flows of the current. Yet although its leaves trail on and below the surface, it must, like the water-lily, flower and pollinate in the air.

One general characteristic of aquatic plants, however, is that they more frequently rely on spreading without flowers. For example, duckweed, one of our smallest flowering plants, can bud one leaf from

Below right (top) The male common newt is seen here in his breeding colours and crest.

Below right (bottom) The raft spider will run out over the surface of the pool to attack its prey.

Below These feeding tadpoles show different stages in development.

another to cover a pond in a few weeks in early summer, while reeds grow from roots which range as widely as those of nettles.

Winter ice, though, will quickly crush even the sturdiest of stems. To avoid this, water-lilies and reeds die back to the submerged rootstock in the way of many land plants, but new strategies have been adopted by others to withstand winter's severity. In autumn, some duckweeds bud off leaves which sink, heavy with starch reserves. However, by spring, these reserves have been consumed and the plants are now rising to greet the new season. The water soldier sinks its leaves by encrusting them with lime; the spring leaves lack this, so the plant becomes lighter overall, and rises.

Although the surface of the winter pond is bare, evergreen submerged plants can continue photosynthesis below the ice. If it is less than 2 in. thick, and free of snow, enough light will reach them, and they can gain the gases they need from supplies in the water. Moreover, the ice is a good insulator against bitterly freezing weather, although it will, of course, itself thicken downwards if the cold spell is prolonged.

Only a token part of the animal life will reveal itself to a casual glance down into the water. The majority of aquatic animals are small and only become active at night. Many of these are the immature stages of insects, but warm, settled weather conditions will soon prompt them to leave the water, shuck their larval skins and fly free.

As with plants, so too with animals—many freshwater aquatic species seem to have had land-roaming ancestors; the humble water snails make a good example. The freshwater winkle has gills and is presumably directly descended from sea-living ancestors, while the pond snail has lungs and clearly was once land-based; it has to surface from time to time to breathe.

Prolonged ice in winter may put pond snails at risk, although they can reduce their demands by becoming torpid. Water spiders and water beetles also have to surface regularly to breathe. The immature stages of these beetles breathe air as well—now active in April, they are among the more voracious of the water's inhabitants and will take the now-sizeable tadpoles, and sometimes even small fish.

For much of this water life, winter is a time of hibernation. Those that do remain active are still somewhat lethargic. Spring, however, brings the release of new energy, and at this time of year the pond is a busy place, often frantically so.

Hawker dragonflies are among our most dramatic insects. This, the club-tailed dragonfly, breeds in sluggish streams and rivers in the south, but like others of its kind it is often seen hunting far from water. Hawkers are expert fliers, taking their prey while on the wing.

COWS TO PASTURE

In the north, April is the main cereal-sowing month. Potatoes may also now be planted everywhere in good fertile soil. A special planter is used for this task, hitched to the tractor. It has a row of ridging ploughs to create a set of furrows, into each of which a rotating wheel drops the seed potatoes, one at a time. A second set of ploughs then pushes the ridges up over the potatoes. It is important that this is done well (and maintained), for if the growing potato crop is exposed to light they turn green. However, if an early crop is wanted, the seed potatoes are given a bit of light so that they start bearing sprouts or 'chits' before planting. But as these damage easily, farm workers will often sit behind the tractor, feeding these potatoes into the planting wheels by hand.

In April, lambs are being born in the hills, while the January lambs (reared in shelter, the flock having been fed hay and concentrates) are now at the butcher's in time for Easter

when lamb prices are at a premium. Lowland ewes still need to be closely watched—they give good milk with lush grass but this may strain their metabolism, and they may suffer comas of 'grass sickness' as a result.

Cattle can be as delicate and suffer from a 'bloat', a violent indigestion which blocks breathing and can kill. Urgent drenching, the forced drinking of a reliever, is necessary to effect a cure. Cows may also suffer from various other complaints, such as 'grass staggers'. This occurs if the new grass is low in magnesium (a mineral which aids muscle control) and can be a quick killer.

The cows are now appearing back on the pastures from their winter sheds, with their diet becoming adjusted back to grass. Cattle are far better than sheep at converting British grass into meat and milk. Beef and milk production are usually separate enterprises for the farmer, each with its own calendar and cash flow. A dairy cow brings in a monthly milk cheque, but beef cattle are a longer-term investment, in the same way that wheat and barley are, in that they represent money tied up until sold.

The cattle most commonly seen nowadays are the black-and-white Friesian breed, producing abundant milk. They can be bred with their own bulls to produce high-yielding milker progeny, but it is quite usual to cross a Friesian cow with a beef-breed bull, with the bullocks (castrated bull calves) being reared for beef. Such a cross is sometimes easy to recognize—for example, a calf from a Friesian mother and Hereford father has the patchy coat of the mother, but the broad white face of its massive father.

Cows have a nine-month gestation period and can be mated in any month, but this is usually timed so that beef calves are born in the spring. They will then be taking milk from suckler cows at their most productive time, before themselves beginning to graze the new grass. However, many are artificially reared, being housed and fed a concentrate-rich diet.

Calves may be born out in the fields where, in some pain, the mother will uneasily leave the herd and choose a site against the hedge or fence. The birth can take six hours or more. Colostrum, the first milk produced after calving, is vital to the newly-born animals, for not only is it rich in protein, but it also contains vitamins and antibodies to prevent disease. It is the staff of life. Within a couple of days, though, they can safely be reared by bucket, being fed with milk substitutes.

In the dairy herd, calving usually takes place in the autumn. The calves are soon removed from their mothers, who give milk that can be sold—calving at this time means they can produce milk throughout the winter months. Even a dairy cow calving in spring and grazing the best grass would not be able to support her calf and, at the same time, profitably produce milk for sale.

The growing grass means that grazing beef calves quickly put on weight. Many small farmers now begin a process of buying in animals, fattening them on their fields and then selling them on, perhaps to a butcher. At weekly auctions up and down the country, farmers must rely on their own wits and experience to get into profit.

The traditional system of grazing is known as set-stocking, where the cattle have free access to an allocation of pasture, but today the fields may also be strip-grazed, corridored by an electric fence, or paddock-grazed, where the grazing area is divided up with fencing. A few farms practice zero-grazing, which entails cutting the grass and feeding it to yarded cattle.

Some late-April fields may be caustic yellow in colour, with musky-scented oilseed rape coming into flower; bees are attracted, although the honey is rather bland. It is often planted as a break crop—that is, a crop sown and harvested between the highly-profitable wheat or barley years, allowing the soil to regain its natural vigour after their intensive cultivation. A break crop is also a barrier to grain-crop diseases; without a host, they die out in the soil.

Although the spring may be uncertain, the land has now certainly cast off the chains of winter. It is a happy day when the cattle are led back to the pastures for the first time in the new year.

THE FARNE ISLANDS

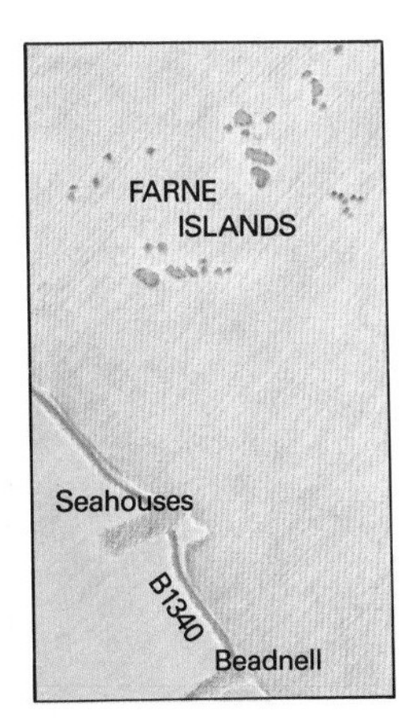

Visits by boat to the Farne Islands, off the coast of Northumberland, can be arranged from Seahouses, though they depend on the weather. Landings may be made on Longstone, Staple Island and Inner Farne. Some of the islands belong to the National Trust.

These islands, off the coast of Northumberland, are treeless. Some of them rise rocky and bare from the pewter North Sea, but even here spring is welcomed with snatches of fresh green wherever roots can cling. Others have a depth of turfed soil. That these islands are here at all on this softer coast of Britain is due to a layer of hard volcanic rock, the famous Whin Sill, which nudges above the waves. Its columnar structure betrays its origin, and its fractured planes and faces offer innumerable nesting sites for birds.

Now, in April, these cliffs are busy. Not that they are ever really quiet, but spring and autumn see 'falls' of linnets, skylarks, redwings and other exhausted migrants, with perhaps a peregrine or two hunting for them. Grey seals also breed here, the pups being born between September and December; mortality is heavy, though, and gulls haunt the beaches to pick clean the sad corpses.

Some of the islands are the strongholds of herring gulls and lesser black-backed gulls, which harry other species and pirate their eggs and nestlings. At nesting time, their close presence can only be tolerated by equally-belligerent cormorants. Fulmars also hold their own; they defend their nests by spitting foul liquid at an approaching gull.

Many other sea birds find security on the islands, such as puffins, razorbills, guillemots and kittiwakes. In addition, eiders, ringed plovers and terns will make their choice of island for nesting.

At this time of year, the birds are scouting out their nest sites. Terns fiercely defend their nests by dive-bombing intruders and can inflict deep cuts with their beaks. Access to the islands is restricted from 15 May to 15 July during the birds' breeding season, but even boat spectators observing the colonies from afar are advised to wear strong headgear.

Not only do the nesting birds exercise a choice of island, but they also 'zone' themselves on the island of their choice. Thus, although shags would choose the same sites as cormorants, they avoid the islands where these nest. For both of these species, the nest is a heap of seaweed, often sheltered by a boulder. Guillemots and razorbills are more cliff dwellers, perching on ledges in the case of the former, and in cracks and caves or on scree in the case of the latter. The guillemot egg is acutely conical to stop it rolling off, and is also glued to its ledge with a paste of droppings for added security.

Further up the cliff, on high ledges, kittiwakes make nests of seaweed, cemented with droppings. Fulmars also nest at this level. There is considerable overlap if all the birds share the same cliff, but these broad preferences tend to ration out the ledges and avoid quarrels at this busy time. Over the top of the cliff, puffins are found; these handsome birds nest in burrows and so need a depth of soil. Terns nest on open ground.

Behaviour matches situation. Exposed to marauding gulls, guillemot and razorbill chicks are persuaded by their parents to parachute down to the sea when only half grown, where they can be safely tended.

Sea birds do not have private feeding territories, sharing instead the bounties of the wide ocean, but the food supply is important and lies behind the timing of their nesting. The 'blooming' of the plankton in the sea as it warms is crucial; these minute organisms are heavily plundered by other creatures, which in turn are consumed by the sizeable fish on which the birds feed.

This blooming is little affected by cold spells in the air above, and so the breeding of sea birds is less influenced by changeable weather than that of land birds, although the puffin's breeding cycle may be delayed if the ground is waterlogged. Gales affect sea birds to a greater extent, while cold is generally less harmful for them. The shag, for example, feeds on fish seen from the surface, and storm-tossed waters make fishing difficult.

Up to 500,000 kittiwakes (*Rissa tridactyla*) breed in Britain, but only along the coast; this gull is rarely, if ever, seen inland, and spends much of its time out to sea. The colonies nest on small ledges on the steepest cliffs, safe from rats and other four-legged predators. Its rather strident call gave the bird its name.

Puffins on a rocky outcrop of the Farne Islands. Nesting in burrows, they will seek less stark islands for breeding. Some of the Farnes, such as Brownsman and Staple Island, have sufficient depth of soil for them.

BRITAIN'S ISLANDS AND CLIFFS

Other well-known islands and cliffs, famous for their sea birds, include:

1 Noup Head, Westray, Orkney. One of the largest sea-bird sites in Britain.
2 Fowlsheugh, south of Stonehaven, Grampian.
3 Isle of Man (NR), Fife. Migratory songbirds are also attracted here.
4 Bass Rock, Lothian.
5 St Abb's Head, Borders.
6 St Bees Head, Cumbria. A well-populated cliff.
7 Bempton Cliffs, Humberside. Home to England's largest colony of cliff birds, notably kittiwakes.
8 South Stack, Holy Island, Anglesey.
9 Bardsey Island, Gwynedd. Noted for its shearwaters.
10 Skomer Island (plus Gateholm Island and other islands off the Dyfed coast).
11 Durlston Country Park, Swanage, Dorset.
12 Lundy Island. Situated 19 miles off the coast of Devon.
***Farne Islands**, Northumberland.

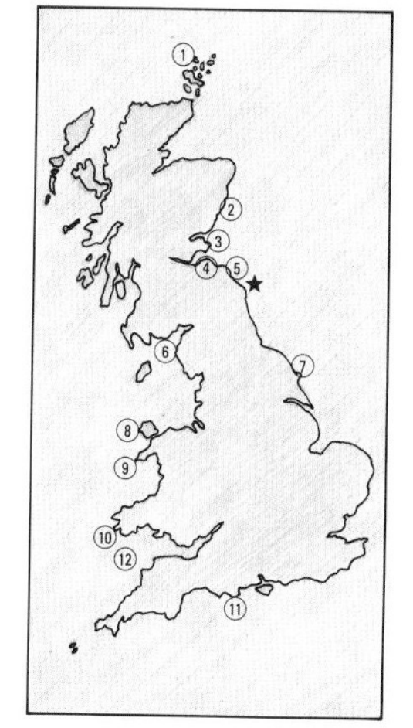

BLUEBELL *Endymion non-scriptus* Although the bayonets of its leaves were very strong in March, the eye is now caught by the bluebell coming into flower (April–June). Once open, its flowers fill the wood with a heady scent. The bluebell is a typical 'Atlantic' species, thriving in a mild damp climate, and we have the best bluebell woods in Europe (in oak woods, it is often succeeded by bracken, dying as the fern fronds unfurl). In the wetter west (and even elsewhere), it will also be seen along hedgebanks and perhaps out on grassland. (Bluebells are known as 'wild hyacinths' in Scotland.)

WILD STRAWBERRY *Fragaria vesca* This now begins its long flowering season (April–October), with the luscious fruit also available for long periods in summer. It prefers dry, limy soil and has long, arching runners to root new plants.

NIGHTINGALE *Luscinia megarhynchos* 3000 pairs visit, nesting south of a line from the Severn to the Humber. Mid-April is a good time for the first nightingale to be heard, but it has a short song season, rarely being heard after the second week of June, although the birds stay longer. Singing as often by day as by night, it is better heard at night when the woods are quiet, and on calm nights its voice can carry far. It has a very rich, powerful and varied song, consisting of a series of short phrases and fluid notes. This bird is rarely seen in the deep woodland cover where it nests—it likes dense low cover and will desert a wood which becomes too leggy.

LAWYER'S WIG (or SHAGGY INK CAP) *Coprinus comatus* This fungus is often now seen; the cap gradually blackens with age.

WOOD WARBLER *Phylloscopus sibilatrix* 10,000 pairs visit. Arriving in April, this warbler is usually to be heard in rather open woods. Its wonderful song is partly a sequence of single notes which blur into a shimmering trill, and partly a repetition of a plaintive tone, often given when the male spirals down to his mate. The birds start to leave for equatorial Africa in late July.

NUT WEEVIL *Curculio nucum* With spring under way, there is now an explosion of insect life, with many leaf, flower and seed eaters to be seen. The nut weevil may be observed on leafing hazel bushes—as soon as the young nut has set, the female bores a hole in it with her long rostrum (snout) in order to lay an egg within. The grub will then feed on the growing kernel and later eat itself out (leaving a small hole in the nutshell).

RAMSONS (or WILD GARLIC) *Allium ursinum* This fills damp woods and shady places with a spectacular carpet of white flowers from April to June, carrying a drifting scent of garlic. (Its broad leaves rather resemble those of lily-of-the-valley.) Ramsons may be found anywhere in Britain, but in the north it sometimes flowers on more open ground.

REDSTART *Phoenicurus phoenicurus* 100,000 pairs visit (numbers have declined in recent years). This handsome bird now arrives, and you may be lucky enough to glimpse it singing from a perch, shimmering its fiery tail ('start' comes from the Anglo-Saxon word for tail). The nest is in thick cover or a suitable hole usually in spacious (but not beech) woodland, but it may be built in a stone wall in open country, for example. Its song is a brief warble ending in a rattle. These birds leave in the autumn.

WOOD-SORREL *Oxalis acetosella* Flowering across Britain (April–May), this plant is typical of some beech woods. Its clover-like leaves make it one of the claimants to be the shamrock, used by St Patrick as a symbol of the Trinity; the leaves fold down at night, and often droop in rain. Its nectar attracts bees, but seeding fails; then, in late summer, a lower flower bud appears (rarely opening), which fertilizes itself for seed. The green leaves are thus held all through the summer.

WILD CHERRY (or GEAN) *Prunus avium* This tree's first flowers now begin to appear, mainly in southern areas, just before the leaves open. In July, the red fruits look like small garden cherries.

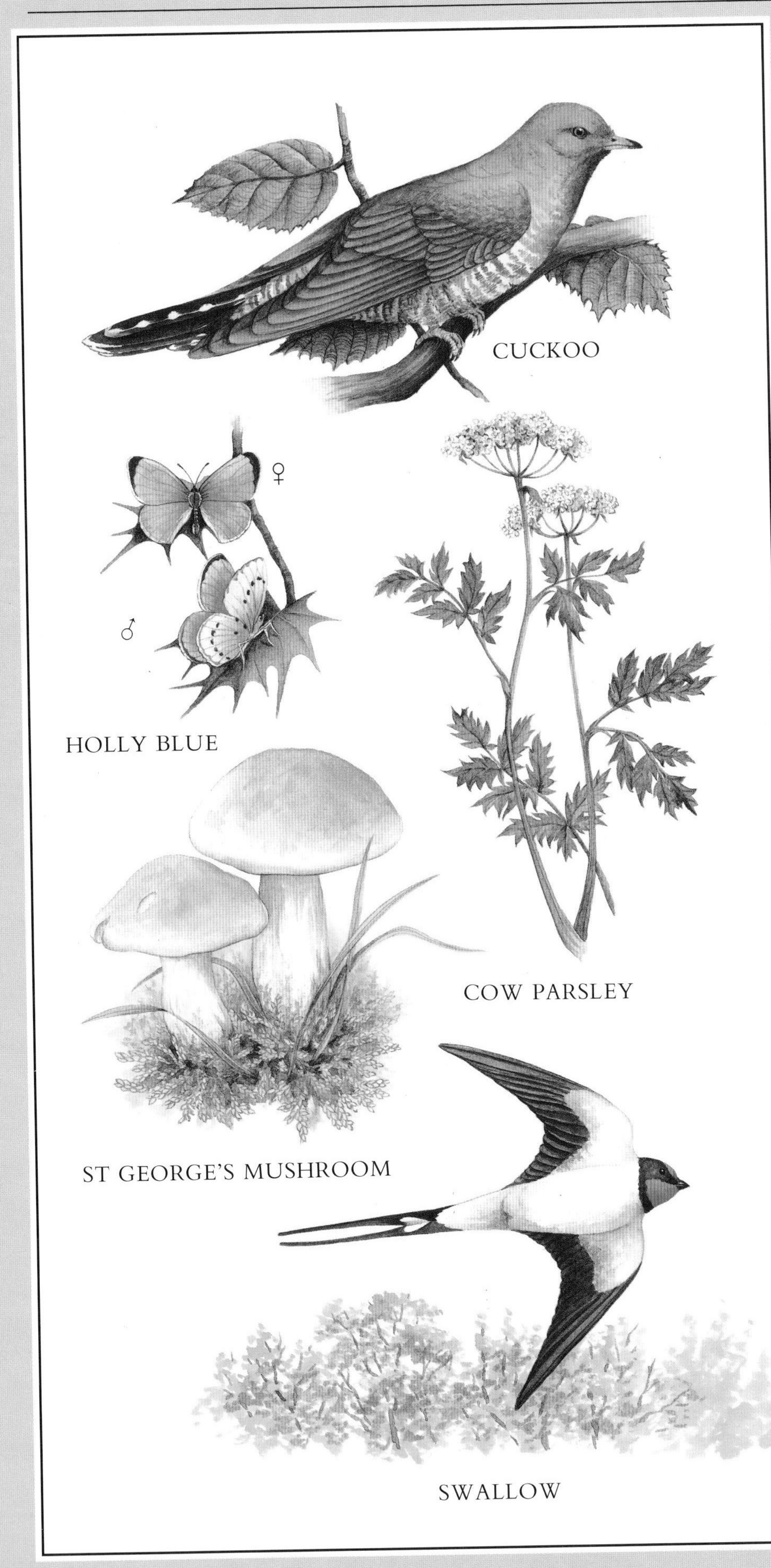

CUCKOO *Cuculus canorus* 20,000 pairs visit. The classic call of spring is that of the cuckoo, usually first heard in the second or third week of April, though some birds may arrive before then. The male calls 'cuckoo' from a high branch; the female has an odd bubbling note. The birds seem rather hawklike in flight, moving fast with shallow wingbeats. After waiting for a nearby dunnock, reed warbler or meadow pipit to lay, the female will lay her own egg, which can resemble those of the host, in the nest. Newly-hatched, the young cuckoo ejects the other eggs from the nest and takes all the food its step-parents can fetch.

HOLLY BLUE *Celastrina argiolus* Often seen now in parks and gardens, mainly in the south, this butterfly lays its eggs on holly in the spring; the brood from these eggs will fly in August, to lay their own eggs on ivy. It hibernates in the chrysalis stage.

COW PARSLEY *Anthriscus sylvestris* Now coming into flower on roadsides (April–June), this plant has hollow stems. It seems to flower for a long period, but what is in fact seen is a succession of rather similar cousins. The flowers, seeds and leaves of these various roadside umbellifers differ.

ST GEORGE'S MUSHROOM *Tricholoma gambosum* This large edible mushroom is seen on old grassland in the spring.

SWALLOW *Hirundo rustica* 500,000 pairs visit. As is usual with incoming migrants, first arrivals are followed over the weeks by the bulk of the clan. The first arrive from South Africa in early April, but favourable tail winds may bring them earlier. Adults seem to return to the previous locality, even to the same nest site, generally within a shed or other building. They may land, but only to gather mud for the nest (they feed on flying insects and sip water while swooping across the surface). Towards the end of August, they gather in large numbers, joining with cousins from northern Europe. Sudden departure can follow, but it is not unknown to see a swallow in November, or even December, tracking a lonely route down a river.

COWSLIP *Primula veris* A favourite spring flower (April–May), the cowslip's nodding heads are now seen rising from a rosette of rather wrinkled leaves. It prefers limy soils, and was much commoner in the past, growing on most 'unimproved' pastures (although it was less common in the north). This situation is now changing, though, for some have been planted on motorway embankments.

MOREL *Morchella esculenta* Distinctive with its honeycombed cap, this is one of the fungi seen now in spring. It grows on open grassland, as well as along shady hedgebanks and in woods.

HOUSE MARTIN *Delichon urbica* 300,000 pairs visit. These birds arrive somewhat later than swallows, perhaps congregating to feed over reservoirs before separating to their colonies. Built outside buildings, the nests are more familiar than those of swallows. The birds build with mud collected from pond edges and so may be disadvantaged in drought. There are often two or three broods, and a late one can delay departure. Even though these youngsters may be fed by earlier broods as well as by the parents, their chances of surviving the flight to Africa are slim.

LADYBIRDS The seven-spot ladybird (*Coccinella 7-punctata*) is one of the more familiar species, as is the two-spot ladybird (*Adalia 2-punctata*), which is variable in colouring. Although they can be lured out by earlier warm spells, these small beetles are usually seen now, with a hunger for greenfly and other aphids (now also appearing). Ladybird grubs are also voracious feeders, consuming as many as 50 aphids each day.

LORDS AND LADIES *Arum maculatum* Apart from this name, it has a host of lusty local names, such as 'cuckoo pint', believed to be from the word 'cuckold'. Its shiny green leaves have been apparent since March, but the unusual flower now appears (April–May). Midges, lured by the foetid smell of the upright spadix, become caught within the bulb of the spathe to fertilize the hidden cluster of flowers, which will develop into the glossy red berries seen in September.

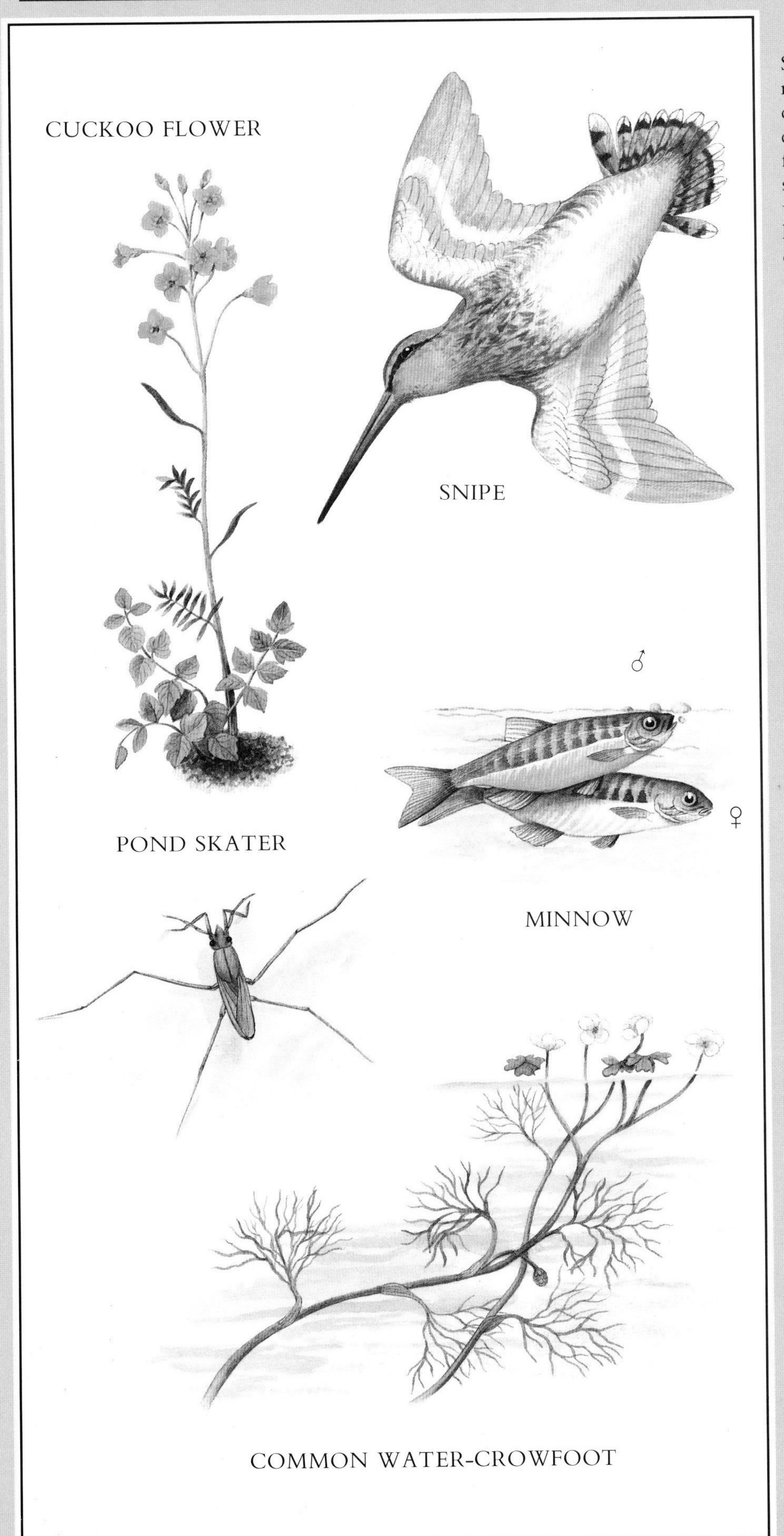

SNIPE *Gallinago gallinago* 10,000 pairs resident. The snipe now begins its odd courtship display. It climbs and then enters a shallow dive with outer tail feathers extended; these vibrate in the slipstream and with the quivering wings create a resonant bleating known as 'drumming'. One run complete, the bird climbs again with quickly beating wings to repeat the performance. Snipe are attracted to soft ground, probing for worms and other food with their very long bills. When disturbed they twist away with a harsh alarm call, a challenge for wildfowlers (there has, however, been a great depletion in snipe numbers in recent years, probably due to the drainage of wetlands for arable use). Rather solitary birds, they may gather in groups towards the end of the year.

CUCKOO FLOWER (or LADY'S SMOCK) *Cardamine pratensis* Now, at the time of the cuckoo's call, this plant is coming into flower (April–June) on wet ground, streamsides, and even some damp verges.

MINNOW *Phoxinus phoxinus* These fish prefer clean, slower-flowing streams than the trout-becks, but with some gravel on which they will spawn (they are found everywhere, except the northern Highlands). With the water now warming, minnows feed in shoals near the surface. The male is assuming breeding colours, and before spawning (most actively in early May) these fish will swarm in the shallows.

POND SKATER *Gerris lacustris* After hibernating ashore, this insect is now seen again, usually in numbers rowing the surface of a pond or a quiet bay in a stream, searching for prey trapped on the water's surface. This they can see, but they also sense surface vibrations. They will mate in spring, and a new generation is seen from July onwards.

COMMON WATER-CROWFOOT *Ranunculus aquitilis* This begins to flower at the end of April, and will generally continue through to September. Cousin to the buttercup, it has evolved two types of leaf shape to suit its habitat: rounded floaters, and divided submerged fronds, which are able to sway with the current.

GRASS (or RINGED) SNAKE *Natrix natrix* This, our largest snake, emerges from hibernation in late March or April, just before breeding, and may now be seen basking in the sun. Damp places are its usual habitat, and it is often seen swimming sinuously, searching for frogs, newts and other prey. Its eggs are laid in piles of dead leaves or rotting compost (supplying the warmth for incubation); hundreds are laid, and 'plagues' of small snakes often emerge in late summer. If threatened, a grass snake may feign death, lolling with its tongue out (many predators ignore their prey if presumed dead).

FRITILLARY *Fritillaria meleagris* This handsome wild flower (April–May) is a nostalgic relic of the traditional British countryside. Although grown in gardens, it is now sadly restricted in the wild to a handful of meadow nature reserves in southern counties.

THREE-SPINED STICKLEBACK *Gasterosteus aculeatus* Found in a wide variety of waters throughout Britain, in April the males leave the shoal, stake out their territory, and build a tunnel nest. They take on breeding colouration (red undersides) and court any female swimming within range. With the eggs laid, the female is chased away (though others may yet be enticed). The male will then guard the eggs, wafting fresh water over them with his fins.

WHIRLIGIG BEETLE *Gyrinus natator* This insect is often seen gyrating in groups on the water surface, though it will quickly dive in alarm. Feeding on matter held by the water's surface tension, it now becomes active and will remain so until October.

SAND MARTIN *Riparia riparia* 200,000 pairs visit. Now most often seen, although the first sightings may be as early as March, these birds nest in tunnels (excavated with their feet) in the natural cliffs of river banks and sand hills. Gravel workings may also offer opportunities for colonies. Liking a crowd, these birds feed together over water. In late July (when house martins are still nesting), they begin gathering to roost communally prior to migration.

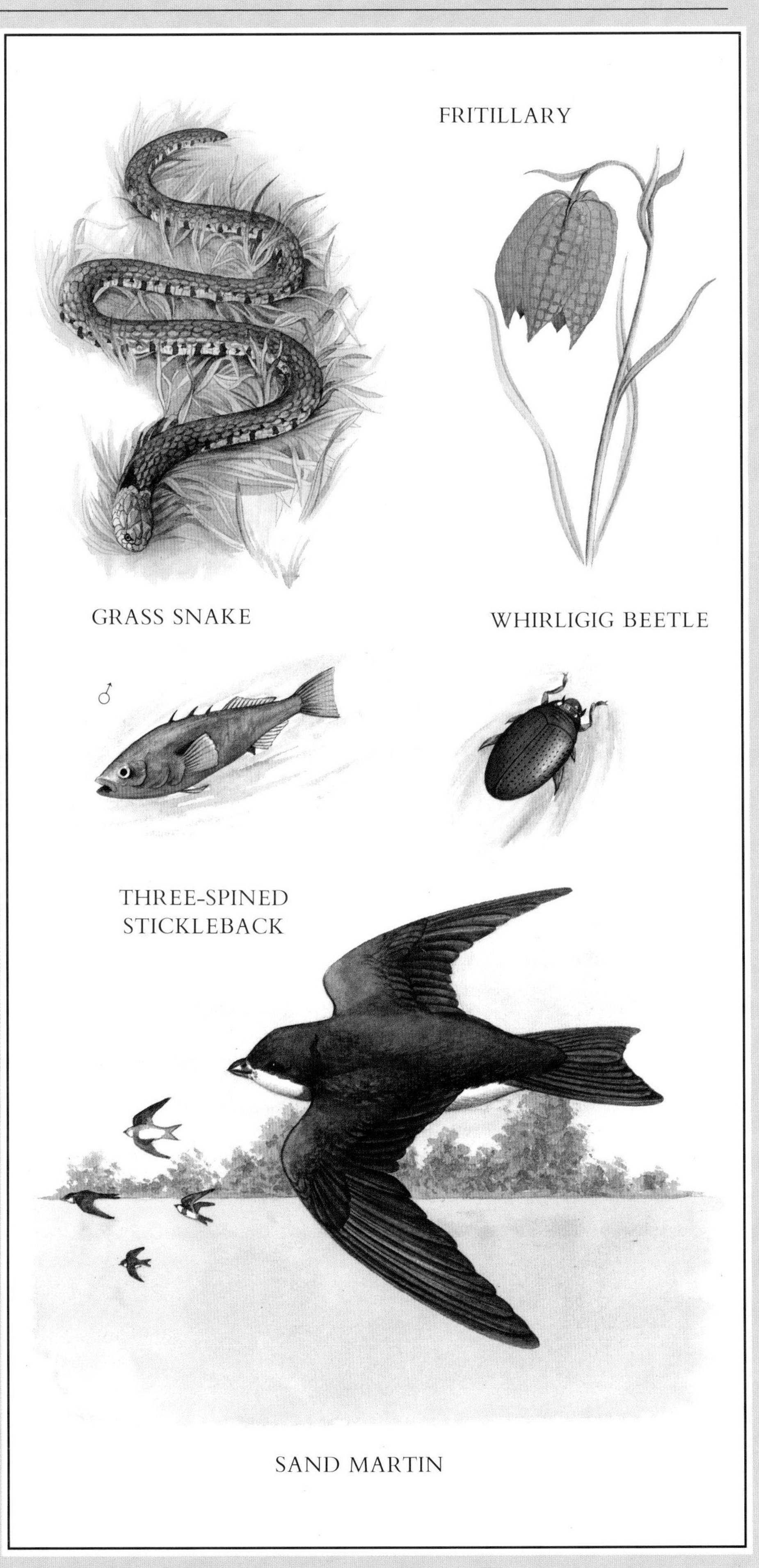

MEADOW PIPIT *Anthus pratensis* 1,000,000 pairs resident. On the moors, look out for the charming song flight of the meadow pipit. The male flutters steeply and slowly with thin calls, then spirals or glides down with a stronger outburst of song. It is usually numerous on moorland, but is also seen on downland, sand dunes and other open lowlands. In Scotland, the breeding grounds are occupied as soon as the snow begins to clear, but the clutch is smaller on higher terrains. Its nests are a favourite goal of cuckoos, and only the later broods in July are safe when the cuckoos begin to leave.

EMPEROR MOTH *Saturnia pavonia* This is one of our most spectacular moths. The male is now seen flying fast by day over heathery moors and heaths, looking for a mate (she flies only by night). The caterpillar, newly-hatched in May or June, feeds on heather or bramble, and despite its bright-green overall colouring is remarkably well camouflaged. The brown silk cocoon, in which the insect will winter in its pupal stage, is created in August and found empty in spring.

LOUSEWORT *Pedicularis sylvatica* A plant of damp moors and heaths, this is now attractively in flower (April–July).

COMMON SANDPIPER *Actitis hypoleucos* 50,000 pairs visit. Arriving in early April, this bird moves to the rocky shores of upland streams to nest on the ground. There is a fine courtship display, with the male circling higher, trilling the while. They feed in the mud of shallows and watersides. In August, they may be seen during migration at coastal freshwaters with continental cousins. A few may even remain in winter.

MARSH HORSETAIL *Equisetum palustre* This (like the alpine clubmoss) is a relic member of a once-great family of plants which dominated the coal swamps. With a rather primitive appearance, horsetails are found in a variety of damp habitats; this particular species inhabits heaths and acid, boggy ground. Two different types of stem are produced: one is sterile, while the other carries a cone.

PALMATE NEWT *Triturus helveticus* This small newt is seen in upland as well as lowland pools. Now in spring, the males have a smooth crest along the back, webbed hind feet, and a filament on the tail.

EUROPEAN LARCH *Larix decidua* A favourite garden and plantation tree since Victorian times, this conifer is often seen in full maturity. Deciduous, in spring it begins to bear tufts of bright-green needles—but just before this, now in April, the tree bears clusters of yellowish male cones and pink female 'larch roses', which will develop into ripe seed cones.

GOLDEN PLOVER *Pluvialis apricaria* 30,000 pairs breed; 300,000 birds in winter. The calls of this bird include a beautiful liquid 'klew-ee', and a musical 'koo-roo'. Now on its moorland breeding haunts, the male especially may show some black below (there are races with slight differences in summer plumage). After breeding they will be seen on lowland grazings and arable fields, and on the coast.

BOG MYRTLE *Myrica gale* Found mainly in the hills, in boggy landscapes, this shrub has resinously fragrant leaves. Its catkins are now seen (April–May), before the leaves appear.

ADDER (or VIPER) *Vipera berus* With a population estimated at 100,000–500,000, this is Britain's commonest reptile. The males emerge from hibernation in March, with the females a short time later, and in April the courtship is at its height (males may be seen confronting each other and wrestling). Contrary to its bad reputation, however, this is a shy snake, preferring not to be seen, and it usually slithers away when approached. Although it immobilizes small mammals with a bite, adders have in fact killed only 14 people in Britain in the last 100 years. A bite is only likely if the comatose snake is angered in spring, or a mother is disturbed with her young. (Unlike the grass snake, the eggs are held within her body and the young are 'born alive' in August and September.) Adders will hibernate again in October, in a suitable den.

LITTLE TERN *Sterna albifrons* 2000 pairs visit. The season is marked by the arrival of the 'sea swallows', the terns, which make lively watching as they pause to hover before diving for fish. Among these arrivals are the little terns, which choose coastal shingle and sand spits for their noisy breeding colonies. The eggs, laid in the simple scrape of a nest, are well camouflaged, but the birds suffer acutely from human disturbance and predation by gulls. (Arctic terns, *S. paradisaea*, are noted for massing together to mob and strike the heads of intruders—other coastal nesting birds even join their colony to gain this protection.)

SAND EELS These slim, eel-like fish shoal over sandy bottoms and are a favourite food of terns and other sea birds. Some feed at dawn for a few hours before retiring to a sand burrow, while at other times they swim near the surface. The lesser sand eel (*Ammodytes tobianus*) is more common than the greater (*Hyperoplus lanceolatus*), which has a black spot on either side of its snout.

BOTTLE-NOSED DOLPHIN *Tursiops truncatus* This intelligent mammal may now occasionally be seen near the coast. (At the time of writing, a family group had been resident in Cardigan Bay, Dyfed, for three years, but sadly the youngsters have been found dead, weakened by toxins accumulated from their food.) The Greek scholar Aristotle wrote of the squeaks and groans made by dolphins, but recently we have learned that they use a natural sonar system to locate fish, emitting clicks and other sounds which echo back to be caught in an 'echo chamber' in the forehead.

ALEXANDERS *Smyrnium olusatrum* A sturdy, celery-smelling plant with shiny foliage, alexanders is now beginning to flower (April–June). Its distribution ranges from Norfolk southwards, around to North Wales. Not only is it found on the coast, but also, rather strangely, within a mile or so of it (for example, along lanes). The reason may be that it was introduced, spreading first along its preferred coastal habitat, and then moving gradually inland, but without sufficient time yet to reach far in this direction.

BASKING SHARK *Cetorhinus maximus* A positive sighting can lend excitement to a swim off the Scottish west coast from April onwards (as well as Cornwall and the Channel Islands). It is usually seen in calm weather, swimming slowly near the surface, with its large fin protruding above the water; it may even come in to scratch itself against the rocks. However, despite appearances to the contrary, it is harmless, and feeds by straining plankton through a sieve of gill rakers.

GREAT BLACK-BACKED GULL *Larus marinus* 20,000 pairs resident. This huge gull with fierce pale eyes is even more piratical than other gulls now that its breeding season is under way. It will take wounded sea birds and raid their nesting colonies for young and eggs. Though not as common as other gulls, it has been culled in some places where predation has been heavy. It sometimes nests in colonies, on islands or cliff stacks safe from foxes and rats. When easy prey is not available, it reverts to scavenging.

THRIFT (or SEA PINK) *Armeria maritima* Forming cushions from which the delicate flowers arise (April–August), this plant often decks large areas of salt marsh and cliffs. It may also be found high up on mountain ledges in northern England and Scotland, but not in habitats which lie between coast and mountain. The reason is probably that these two habitats were the only ones never to become covered by scrub or forest when the land warmed up at the end of the Ice Age.

COMMON DOLPHIN *Delphinus delphis* This is the dolphin of the Mediterranean, but it also inhabits warmer Atlantic waters, and schools may occasionally be seen leaping off southern and western coasts. Schools have even been known to enter rivers, presumably in pursuit of fish, and become stranded as a result.

SPRING SQUILL *Scilla verna* A pretty, starlike flower (April–May), this is found growing in cliff-top turf along the west coast, from south Devon to the Hebrides, and at some places on north-eastern coasts. Its long leaves remain after flowering.

MAY

The first of the month, May Day, is a date evoking gaiety, the threshold of an exuberant month of bursting green, fertility and warmth. Shakespeare's 'darling buds of May' are now everywhere to be seen. Yet caution is not amiss—the traditional saying 'ne'er cast a clout till May be out' meant, in other words, keep your vest on, but it is unclear whether this referred to the hawthorn in the hedge or to the month itself.

May can have cold spells with even a late snowfall. The children's song tells of 'gathering nuts in May, on a cold and frosty morning'; the nuts here are not those of hazel, nor chestnut, which ripen in the autumn, but the tubers of pignut, a relative of cow parsley found in unploughed grasslands.

Certainly, frost is on every gardener's mind. Local frosts can brown the young bracken in a tide-line along the sides of a frost hollow, and more importantly scorch the apple blossom and congeal the nectar and pollen so that bees fly elsewhere.

A newly-hatched mayfly: the nymphs shuck their skins and break the surface as net-winged adults. As mayflies need unpolluted, highly-oxygenated water, their presence indicates that a stream is clean.

The flowers in field and hedgerow ring quickening changes. The dandelions are now blowballs, but the fields retain their yellow colour as buttercups replace them, while along the lanes, cow parsley breaks into white. Sheets of bluebells still strongly scent the woods, their colour slowly darkening as they age. On the heaths, broom comes into vivid yellow flower, while the sea cliffs become spangled rock gardens.

Among the birds, most of the summer visitors have now arrived, although the numbers of each are swelled weekly by new arrivals. Swifts scream overhead; the turtle dove is also a late arrival, first seen during this month. Bird song reaches its peak at the end of the month and beyond.

In the streams, the pent-up hatch of mayflies awaits the trigger of a settled warm spell. Anglers should grab their rods at this time, for this hatch activates the trout.

The may, the hawthorn blossom, cascades down the hedges by the latter half of the month. At one time, it came into flower at the start of the month, which was too early to

signal the end of the cold spells. But in 1752 the calendar was reformed, dragging the year forward by 11 days. This became necessary because the old Julian calendar, adopted in the sixth century, had made inaccurate allowance for leap years. Pope Gregory introduced the new calendar in 1582, but it was not adopted by Protestant countries until 1752. In Britain, it was greeted with rioting, for people believed that it stole 11 days from their lives.

May is a nice example of the often long history of our names. In classical mythology, Maia was one of seven heavenly sisters, the brightest of the seven stars of the Pleiades. But her name probably originated in the older Sanskrit 'mah', meaning 'to grow'.

In olden days, lads and lasses went 'a · maying' on May Day, greeting the dawn and returning with fresh green sprays of may to decorate their doors. On this day, the 'Green Man', a villager decked in foliage, danced through the village demanding bread and cheese from everyone he met—a token sacrifice. In addition, there was dancing round the village maypole, with a May King and Queen; the pole was originally a young sapling. The May Queen survives often as a Rose Queen in parish festivals, especially in the north of England, but is not restricted solely to the month of May.

Hawthorn blossom in the hedgerows, together with cow parsley, marks this heady month. At one time, hedgerow hawthorn welcomed the start of the month (and was thus called 'may'), but since the reform of the calendar in 1752, it now flowers about a fortnight later. The flowers have a sweet, sickly scent.

SUNSHINE AND FOG

Frost may still be a strong possibility on clear nights during this month. At this time of year, though, it is a localized event and geographical location plays a part—for example, while the last frosts in Cornwall occur on average in early April, those of the Vale of York are in early May. Cambridge can have from 40 to 80 nights of frost a year, or Kew between 14 to 60.

The Azores high, which is responsible for drawing in much of our westerly weather, may be moving northwards, but Arctic air can still reach Britain and bring snow showers to low ground in Scotland. However, the growing season has now begun high in the Pennines and further north.

May sees the start of one local kind of weather which can, unfortunately, ruin many holiday days. Between mid-May and September, easterly breezes bring rather damp air from the Continent to cross the North Sea. As this water is relatively cold, the air passing over it may be cooled so much that some of its moisture is condensed out to create fog. The coolest stretches lie between the Humber and Aberdeen, and it is along these more northerly coasts that the fog may be long-lasting, although it generally clears as the day warms up. This fog is such a regular feature that it has its own traditional names: 'haar' in Scotland, 'sea fret' further south, and 'roke' in Yorkshire and Humberside.

On the other hand, a high over Germany with a low to the south-west over the Atlantic can generate air movements up from southern Europe, with the arrival of south-easterly winds and high temperatures.

Some consider that the onset of the warm spells of early summer is heralded by two or more days with maximum temperatures of 21°C. At Kew, these occur on average around the middle of May.

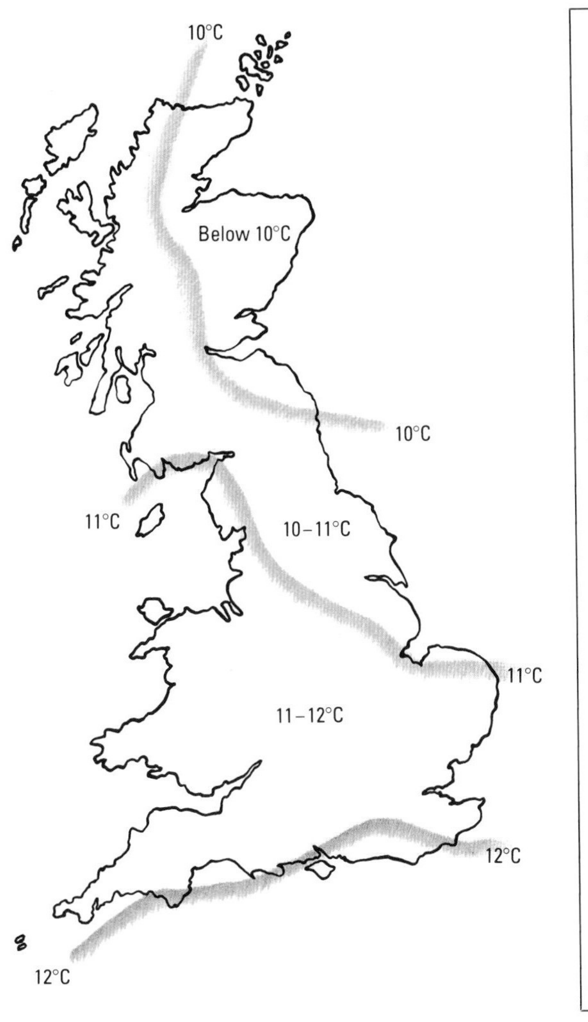

The map shows the average mean daily temperatures for May. The word 'average' signifies that the readings given are the average of readings taken over many years, while 'mean' indicates that the figure is the average of maximum and minimum daily temperatures. Of course, these readings refer to the actual site where the recordings were taken, and it must be noted that neighbourhood geography will affect local temperature. But the map does show that generally May can be a rather chilly month.

FRONTS AND DEPRESSIONS

Unlike parts of Africa where, for example, spells of weather stagnate for long periods, Britain's weather is wonderfully changeable. This is partly because it is influenced by different air masses. Two dissimilar masses meet along a front, and an important one for the British Isles is the polar front, between cold, dry, Arctic polar air and warmer, wet, tropical air moving generally up from the south-west. The colder, denser polar air tends to undercut the warmer, lighter air.

A disturbance to the front will often trigger the genesis of a depression, or low. If a tongue of warm air bulges into the cold domain and rises, it will cause a drop in pressure, destined to become the centre of the depression. Polar air swings round anticlockwise to replace the rising warm air. Some 20 hours after the start, a distinct bulge of cold air has circled around, chiselling below the warm. Where this rises, it cools and clouds form, bringing rain (or snow). This is a *cold front*.

As a result, ahead of it to the east or north-east, the warm air is also being swung anticlockwise over the cold air confronting it. This *warm front* is also marked by clouds and rain (or snow). Cold air is thus chasing warm air anticlockwise around the centre of the

Clouds are weather made visible. Here the difference between the temperature and humidity of adjacent air masses is clearly demonstrated. Note, however, that a front can be expected to have a much more complex cloud pattern than this.

depression. The polar front as a whole tends to move sideways from west to east, and the depression also moves, at perhaps 15 mph. And as it moves, the weather dances to its tune.

The sight of high, wispy cirrus clouds towards the horizon may be the first clue that a warm front is approaching. These are followed by thicker and lower cloud, and the pressure, measured by a barometer, drops. The wind strengthens and heavy rain (or snow) falls. The precipitation continues until the warm front has passed, whereupon the pressure stops falling and the temperature rises. The rain may turn to drizzle, but this is likely to stop when the warm sector of the depression arrives. It becomes calmer and warmer, and indeed the sun may be strong enough to dry out much of the cloud.

The advance of the pursuing cold front is marked again by a fall in pressure, strong gusty winds, and banks of cloud bringing heavy showers of rain (or snow). The temperature drops as the cold front moves away, but the sky can clear dramatically, with occasional clouds marching across a deep-blue sky.

The cold front is more violent than the warm. It is moving faster, and will eventually reach the warm front and 'catch its own tail'. Cold air now merges with cold at lower levels, while the original warm air rests like a reservoir above, marked by a belt of cloud along a single, rainy *occluded front*. After this, the depression will lose its energy and fade away.

However, another is soon on the way. Sometimes, a series of such depressions cross once every two or three days, although one is never quite like the next, with both the speed and path varying as well as the kind of cloud they bring.

Many depressions pass north-eastwards, between Iceland and Scotland, while the troughs of low pressure, which often extend from them, sweep rainy weather across Britain. The appearance also of secondary depressions, together with Atlantic troughs and depressions, moving past Britain to the south, certainly make forecasters work for their money.

Polar air is, of course, colder in winter, and the contrasts are sharper, with the polar front more marked. The depressions, too, are usually deeper, bringing the stormier, wetter winter weather.

EGGS IN THE NEST

The nest of the long-tailed tit is one of the masterpieces of the natural world—its lining of feathers alone may take 2000 journeys to collect, and the finished dome is elegantly encrusted on the outside with camouflaging lichens. Where air pollution has killed the lichens, this industrious bird uses instead scraps of paper or even fragments of expanded polystyrene.

For many birds, making a nest is not a task undertaken lightly. Swifts must catch wind-blown grass on the wing, for they cannot land to pick it. (If they do inadvertently ground themselves while collecting, they cannot easily fly off again; if found, they must be gently tossed back into the air.)

Even without a fine finish, the structure of a nest can be a feat of ingenuity and skill. The perched nests of house martins have always caused amazement—as Shakespeare put it in Macbeth: 'no jutty, frieze, buttress, nor coign of vantage, but this bird hath made his pendant bed and procreant cradle'. Traditionally, before houses, they nested on riverside or mountain cliffs, and there are still a few cliff colonies to be found.

The reed warbler's nest is woven around a handful of reed stems in the form of a deep cup, relying only on friction to keep it in place when the reedbeds sway violently in gusts of wind. Many other birds adopt holes in trees or even simply large crevices in the bark, but the nuthatch intuitively narrows the entrance of its chosen hole with mud to prevent the entry of other birds.

The intricately-woven nest of the long-tailed tit is one of the marvels of the natural world. It is camouflaged with lichens.

Sometimes both the male and female share the nest building, but for the hen this extra activity means energy spent, or food used up, at what is a crucial time for her and the future of her species.

Breeding, as a whole, seems to be triggered when glands react to the increased daylight hours brought by the lengthening days of spring. Cold weather has no effect on this, and so nature cleverly introduces a second cue, namely the amount of food available to the hen bird. This is usually directly linked with the temperature, and thus with the warm spells of weather that the spring brings in—when spring warms the countryside, it is greeted by a flush of insects which hatch from eggs or emerge from hibernation. Cold spells will delay this hatch, however, and songbirds will also postpone egg-laying. For blue and great tits, laying seems to begin about four days after the start of a warm spell. If the weather then turns colder, further laying will be delayed.

The great tit hunts for weevils and caterpillars on the young leaves of the lower branches, while the blue tit, hunting in the canopy, tends to rely on the hatching caterpillars of the winter moth and other moth species. In the case of the great tit, the hen needs enough food to lay her own weight in eggs over the course of a few days.

There is some advantage in getting an early start. The supply of caterpillars will dwindle as the weeks pass—they begin to pupate, and of course many are taken by wasps and other predators than birds. The strategy adopted by the great tit, therefore, is to lay a large clutch of ten or more eggs at once.

An apparent contradiction is that a mild winter and warm spring, bringing a population explosion of caterpillars, holds hidden dangers for birdlife. If they quickly defoliate the trees of their young leaves, the caterpillars will themselves starve, die, and drop to the ground. For the birds, the larder will thus be emptied, to the hazard of the growing, ever-hungry nestlings later on.

Cold weather reduces the number of eggs laid by these birds. Cold may also result in thinner-shelled eggs or even smaller eggs, for with less food available the hen bird cannot gain sufficient calcium and other minerals necessary for large eggs. For example, meadow pipits lay smaller clutches when nesting up in the hills than in the valleys.

Blackbirds, by comparison, lay a series of smaller clutches. The first are clearly sighted through the thin spring foliage and are often raided by magpies, but the later clutches are better hidden. If the eggs are destroyed, the birds will lay again, but usually fewer eggs.

Lapwings and mallards are examples of birds which have adopted another strategy. Their skimpy nests are soon deserted, with the newly-hatched chicks foraging on their own account, relying on their mother only for daytime protection against predators and for night-time warmth.

On the face of it, sea birds nesting on the exposed cliffs should be the birds most strongly affected by the weather, but in fact the opposite is true. Their nests are adapted to withstand buffeting from storms (even eggs are shaped to roll in a tight circle on the rocky ledges) and their food supply is reliable, with the birds breeding when the minute plankton in the warming seas bloom and multiply at the start of their food chain.

Very young mallard ducklings—they will soon be feeding for themselves under their mother's watchful eye.

A handsome turtle dove with two youngsters. Like other young pigeons, they are covered with very coarse down.

Left The wide gape of these young starlings' mouths triggers the instincts of their parents to feed them. The nestlings compete with each other, sheer hunger forcing the struggle.

Far left Even the narrowest ledge will suit the guillemot. Its single egg, seen here lodged against the rock, is tapered so that it rolls in a tight circle, reducing the risk of it falling over the edge.

CUTTING THE SILAGE

The fields of oilseed rape are now in full gaudy yellow flower and make themselves visible for miles. The grain fields no longer look like grass, and some of the grass fields are now being closely mown, leaving them pale yellow in colour. It is silage which is now being cut here, and the clatter of the mower is a common sound of May.

Silage is a rather modern crop. Grass itself, on the modern farm, is a crop much like all the others. This is quite a change from older traditional farming, when wet fields that were difficult to plough were permanently set aside for grass, which was grazed or cut for hay. Over the last couple of centuries, though, more and more of these fields, in many parts of Britain, have been made ploughable by drying them out. This can easily be done, for example, by inserting rows of clay pipes or tunnels of tiles through the soil. These fields are then taken into the arable system, although grass is also regularly sown alongside the other crops.

Sown grass can be grazed directly in the field, and with the exception of some beef calves, most livestock should now be out doing just that. (Incidentally, all stock at grass will need dosing for internal parasites every three weeks.) Alternatively, the sown grass can be cut and stored for winter fodder as part of the overall strategy for the year. Special hybrid grasses give lush growth to convert into greater milk yields and heavier animals.

These short-term grass fields are known as leys. The two types of grass most commonly sown are Italian rye grass and perennial rye grass, but cock's-foot and timothy may also be grown. The expert can tell them apart by their leaf, but if they come into flower head they are easier to distinguish—timothy has a head like a miniature bulrush.

The choice will reflect the soil and how long the field is to be under grass. Timothy and perennial rye grass are often planted

In May, the lush growth in the silage fields keeps the clattering mowers busy. The newly-cut grass is left lying on the ground for a while before being gathered up and taken to the silage clamp.

together for a long ley of seven or more years, while Italian rye grass is grown in two-year leys because it is quicker to form a dense turf but soon dies off. Clover is also often sown in longer leys, for it needs time to establish itself. As well as giving green fodder, this plant adds nitrogen to the soil when the bacteria in its root nodules get to work.

Hay can be made from these ley fields in June, but it is more usual to cut them in May, for silage. The grass is usually left to wilt after mowing, before a special forage harvester is towed across the field which picks, gathers and chops the cut grass and blows it through a curved spout into a trailer pulled alongside.

This chopped grass can be stored in a silo, but is more commonly dumped and kept in a simple clamp—a walled enclosure. It is usually sprayed with an additive to encourage the fermentation required, and is covered by heavy plastic sheeting to exclude all light. This sheeting is then weighted down with old tyres to keep out the air. Not the prettiest part of the country view, but functional, nevertheless. Large black sacks are sometimes used as an alternative.

The fermented silage pickles itself; good silage has a pleasant smell, but it can be extremely pungent. Kale leaves, pea stalks and leaves, and other greenery also make good silage.

In May, grass is at the height of its productivity. Unlike hay, silage is thus being cut when it is at its richest. The grass will continue to grow, of course, and have another spurt in July. One more crop of silage could be cut then, or the field grazed, depending on the needs of the stock now and in the coming winter.

The February lambs may now be sold to the butcher; after ten weeks they can weigh 80 lb. This is just about right, for extra quick weight now means more fat than is liked in today's market.

An eye must always be kept on the cereals. They need rain for growth, and a drought now could be very damaging. If it has been a slow cold spring, the spring-sown barley may have sprouted unevenly, giving a ragged field that may delay the harvest. As there is also the threat of fungus and other diseases, the tractor will perhaps be out spraying. To avoid more damage than necessary, the tractor follows 'tramlines', now clearly marked in the growing crop. However, it makes sense to heed the weather forecasts (and the farmers' programmes on the radio) for there is little point in spraying if rain showers are soon going to wash the leaves clear, or high winds cause drift.

At the end of May, the elegant heads of wild oat (a crop weed) can appear above the wheat and barley. It cannot be removed by spraying as it is a cereal cousin; it ripens early, and by harvest the seeds have dropped to the soil. It can only be cleared when a break crop brings a new regime. The same goes for couch grass, another hated weed, although this can (expensively) be killed with a pre-emergence spray or at the two-leaf stage.

Stored under light-proof polythene sheeting, the silage will ferment, retaining its nourishment. The cattle are sometimes allowed to feed themselves from this store; the restraining rope will be moved each day.

EBERNOE COMMON

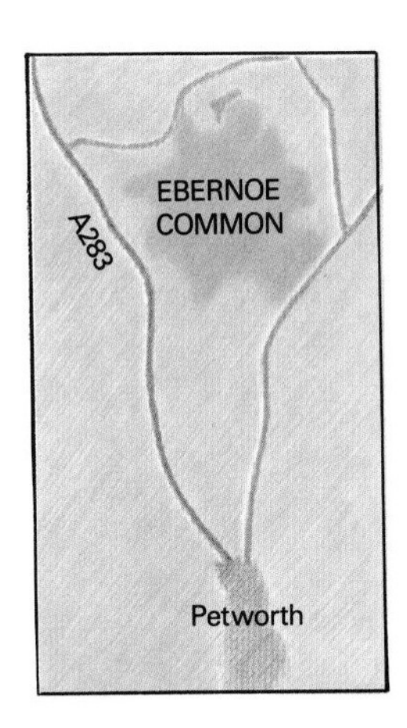

Ebernoe Common, West Sussex, is a 170-acre nature reserve in the care of the Sussex Trust for Nature Conservation; it is open to the public along the paths. While in the area, it is worth visiting the very different landscape of Petworth Park, which was given a 'natural' look by Capability Brown in the 18th century.

Carpets of bluebells fill the senses with both colour and heady scent. They are usually at their best in May, and here in Britain, with our 'Atlantic' climate of comparatively mild, wet winters, they make an outstanding botanical spectacle. They do not grow far into Europe where the climate becomes 'continental' with cold dry winters, nor are they found in Scandinavia. However, they are common in Scotland where, at low levels, the Atlantic often tempers the effects of the northerly latitude. In fact, so well do bluebells respond to Atlantic conditions that, in the West Country, carpets of the flowers can be found growing out on open grassland where this is not grazed.

Bluebells bow out the spring and herald the summer. When they flower in woodlands such as Ebernoe Common, West Sussex, the dawn chorus of the songbirds is peaking. Oak and beech are coming into full leaf, while cascades of hawthorn can be seen along some of the woodland paths.

However, bluebells can also be read in another way. Together with many other natural clues now to be seen, they can often help us to date a wood. Many of our woods are old, in the sense that they have never been anything other than woodland. In the past they were 'coppiced', with the underwood being cut for smallwood. This regularly opened up the floor of the wood to sunshine, and succoured the bluebells and other flowers growing there.

Clearly, other plants slow to establish themselves and sensitive to disturbance can be further clues to an old wood. Early purple orchid is one, as are patches of wood anemone somewhat earlier in spring. Wood-sorrel, yellow archangel, and the unusual flower of herb paris are similar clues, each growing on the soil they prefer. Even the seemingly ubiquitous dog's mercury may mean that the wood is as old as the village church nearby.

Woodland shrubs are similar indicators. In coppiced woods, hazel was encouraged or even planted as it was so useful for fencing and other jobs. Hawthorn grows in Ebernoe and is a common woodland shrub; if this is the Midland hawthorn, with a broader-lobed leaf, that too would be a clue to antiquity. The wild service tree is another indicator of old woodland, as is the small-leaved lime—like its hybrid cousin of town streets and parks, this tree flowers in July, but now in May its leaves are seen to be only half the size of its cousin. The tree is usually found only in woods which documents show are old.

Nightingales sing their rich song in Ebernoe at this time of year. Like many migrant songbirds, they like good low cover, and coppicing has helped them here by producing a thick undergrowth. In fact, between three and six years after the cut suits them best, for they will not return when it grows tall and leggy.

Parts of Ebernoe have now become, through the course of time, a splendid high forest woodland. As well as oaks, there are many beeches here, which were probably planted to replace oak timber trees that had been felled. The age of the tall timber woodland trees can be roughly estimated by measuring the girth at about 5 ft from the ground. Every half inch counts for one year of age (for a tree standing in the open, count an inch for one year). Of course, whether these trees have been planted or not, a wood may be far older than the trees in it.

Later in the year, especially in July, an authentic old woodland such as this will produce some splendid butterflies, one example being the purple emperor; the males, in particular, fly at the level of the tops of the tall trees. White admirals fly in sunny glades, but seek honeysuckle shaded by tall trees to lay their eggs. The silver-washed fritillary is also on the wing here in July. These lovely insects are never seen in the ranked conifer plantations.

When the delightful bloom of the early purple orchid (*Orchis mascula*) appears, it can herald more than spring (it flowers from April to June). Although it can be seen on grassland, it is most often found in woodland—and if seen growing in the same wood as bluebells and wood anemones, this is a sign of an old wood.

BRITAIN'S ANCIENT WOODLANDS
Many ancient oak woods in the south were severely damaged in the 1988 'hurricane':
1 Dinnet Oak Wood, near Ballater, Grampian. One of the few scraps of Highland oak wood.
2 Forge Valley Woods, near Scarborough, North Yorkshire.
3 Coombes Valley, Leek, Staffordshire.
4 Sherwood Forest Country Park, near Ollerton, Nottinghamshire.
5 Pengelli Forest, south-west of Cardigan, Dyfed.
6 Forest of Dean, Gloucestershire. Now coniferized, but with areas of older oaks.
7 Shotover Country Park, Oxfordshire.
8 Wyre Forest, near Bewdley, Hereford and Worcester.
9 Bradfield Woods, near Bury St Edmunds, Suffolk.
10 Northward Hill, near Rochester, Kent.
11 New Forest, Hampshire.
12 Ebbor Gorge, near Wells, Somerset.
***Ebernoe Common**, West Sussex.

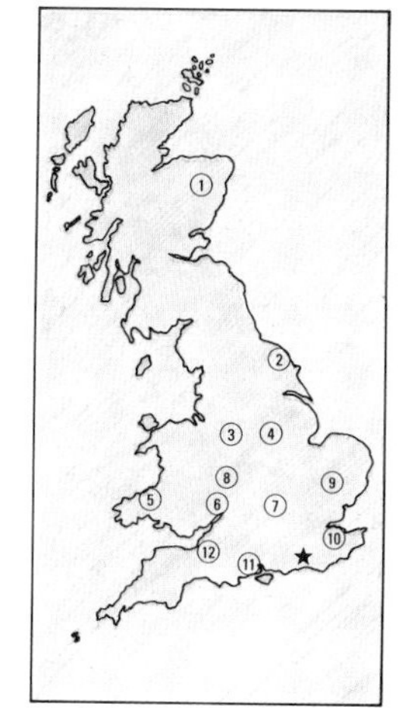

Scatters of bluebells can be found in the woodland of Ebernoe Common, and the approach roads afford many glimpses of other fine bluebell woods.

WILD RHODODENDRON *Rhododendron ponticum* With almost tropical gaiety, this evergreen shrub is now bursting into flower (May–June). A native of southern Europe today, it was in fact growing in Britain before the Ice Age, but during the last century or so it has been widely planted as cover for pheasants, as well as for its ornamental flowers. Spreading rapidly on acid, sandy or peaty soils (it is a cousin of heather), this plant now rampages through many woodlands. It is even considered a scourge in some places (such as Snowdonia, where it occupies large areas of hillsides), for it blocks the light and prevents the growth of young woodland trees.

MAY BUG (or COCKCHAFER) *Melolontha melolontha* This beetle's diet consists of oak leaves and the foliage of other deciduous trees. Flying during the evening and at night, it is often attracted to lighted windows (in fact, its bumbling arrival is a sign of the season for any house within reach of an oak wood). This insect seems active for only a short while, before mating and then dying. Its grubs will live for two or three years in the soil before reaching maturity.

COMMON ASH *Fraxinus excelsior* The graceful ash cohabits with oak, but may form its own woods in limestone areas; it is also a field tree. It carries flower clusters (April–May); the bunches of 'keys' (seeds) ripen in late summer, and are very noticeable festooning the bare autumn branches.

BLACKCAP *Sylvia atricapilla* 800,000 pairs visit. This bird is often first seen in April, but the majority usually follow in May. A shy bird, the blackcap is now in full song, which is beautifully varied and pure throughout, with no harsh notes; voiced in snatches of up to five seconds, with matching pauses, it is sung with all the abandon of the skylark. The nest is in cover, often deep in a bramble patch. It will cease singing in July and (unlike some other birds) moult completely before starting its departure for Africa in August. Its diet will change from insects to blackberries and other fruit before leaving.

GARDEN WARBLER *Sylvia borin* 200,000 pairs visit. Arriving now and nesting in thick cover, this bird, which is even shyer than its blackcap cousin, rarely visits gardens. Also, it usually remains hidden while singing, unlike the blackcap. It has a melodic far-reaching song, less varied than that of its cousin and with rather longer phrases. It leaves at the same time as the blackcap, but delays its moulting until after arriving in Africa.

LILY-OF-THE-VALLEY *Convallaria majalis* This flower (May–June) is worth looking out for in dry woods on limy or sandy soils. Though a 'garden' plant, it is a native species.

NEW FOREST PONY *Equus* (domestic) Half-wild herds of ponies still remain in the New Forest, Hampshire, and foals might now be seen. Originally, they were small, stocky, hardy animals, rounded up in the autumn 'drift' for pack animals or for duty in the mines, but during the last century the stock was improved with Arab blood; today many ponies are a good two hands (8 in.) taller and more slender, but less hardy. They graze mainly in the valley bottoms and may 'haunt' (an old Forest word) an area about four miles across.

ENGLISH (or PEDUNCULATE) OAK *Quercus robur* This is the oak of the lowlands with heavy clay soils. It is now in flower (April–May) and coming into leaf, though a frost pocket can retard it. Various kinds of galls are often seen on the catkins and new leaves; these occur when the irritation of a gall wasp larva within the oak's living tissues leads to the proliferation of pithy cells which the grub consumes—later in the year, the exit hole of the insect can be seen in the now-hard, brown marble gall. The acorns, on long stalks, ripen in September. (The sessile or durmast oak, Q. *petraea*, is identified by its different leaves, which are on long stalks, and stalk-less acorns; hybrids of mixed character may also occur.)

SANICLE *Sanicula europaea* Its flowers may now lightly carpet beech woods on chalky soils (May–August). The small fruit, seen in autumn, is covered with hooked bristles.

SWIFT *Apus apus* 50,000 pairs visit. This bird feeds on the 'soup' of flying insects carried up by pockets of warm rising air, but cold wet spells with few such insects pose hardship and it will make long journeys to better areas, even while nesting. It is also unsettled by thunderstorms. Living more or less on the wing, it feeds, snatches nest material from wind-blown grass and scoops up water, all without touching ground. It can grip the edges of its nest below a roof, but if accidentally grounded cannot raise or relaunch itself. Swifts are often seen in screaming parties. In July they move slowly south, although most remain here during August before leaving for tropical Africa.

CREEPING BUTTERCUP *Ranunculus repens* This is now in flower (May–September), replacing the dandelion in gilding the meadows—but this buttercup is also commonly seen in gardens, spreading its runners quickly across unweeded vegetable beds. Creeping buttercups like damp soil (as do meadow buttercups, *R. acris*, while bulbous buttercups, *R. bulbosus*, prefer dry ground).

ST MARK'S FLY *Bibio marci* Once believed to appear first on St Mark's Day (25 April), the males now swarm on sunny days, sluggishly flying up and down with legs dangling. When the females fly up from the grass below, they are seized and mated.

GRASSHOPPER WARBLER *Locustella naevia* 10,000 pairs visit. The song of this shy, skulking bird is heard from deep cover at any time of day from now into July. It is like no other song, consisting of a high-pitched whirr rather like the reeling in of a fishing line (or the noise made by some grasshoppers).

BROWN ARGUS *Aricia agestis* Despite its brown colour, this butterfly is in fact a 'blue'. It can be seen in Scotland, but is only fairly common south of Yorkshire. It is now actively on the wing over dry, limy grasslands, and a second brood will fly from late July to September. When ready to lay her eggs, the female searches for rock-rose or storksbill, on which the caterpillars will later feed.

MIDLAND HAWTHORN *Crataegus laevigata* This is the less familiar cousin of the common hawthorn (or may) of the hedgerows, and is usually seen in old woodlands (but not only in the Midlands). It flowers somewhat earlier than the common hawthorn (*C. monogyna*), which comes into flower usually well past the start of the month. Hawthorn blossom, which is occasionally pinkish, is sweetly scented, attracting bees, but also has a sour tang which attracts flies. In autumn, some leaves may turn brilliant red to match the crimson of the ripe berries, or 'haws'. Birds prefer these softened by frost, and will sometimes be seen stripping the bushes.

CORN BUNTING *Emberiza calandra* 100,000 pairs resident. The male sings a jingling song, rather like the rattling of a bunch of keys, from a fence post or other such perch. When displaying to its mate, it has the odd habit of flying with its legs dangling clumsily, and it may be seen flying in this fashion at any time during the breeding season. A bird of the open fields, it flocks with others when breeding is over.

WEASEL *Mustela nivalis* Although hunting mainly at night—by scent rather than sight—this small predator is often seen bounding across a country lane. Hunger is the spur: a weasel needs to eat a third of its weight each day, and will take any animal, or even carrion, though voles are the main prey. It will stand on its haunches to smell out the surroundings. At this time of year, family parties of mother and young are sometimes seen. (Unlike stoats, weasels never become white in winter.)

OX-EYE DAISY *Leucanthemum vulgare* Once seen everywhere, this is now an indicator of unimproved meadows (May–September); however, it may sometimes be seeded on to motorway banks and verges.

TURTLE DOVE *Streptopelia turtur* 100,000 pairs visit. This small dove is one of the last summer arrivals, and it will not have spread much across England before the end of May. Its soft purr adds langour to the days of high summer. In August, these birds will begin to return to Africa.

ORANGE-TIP *Anthocharis cardamines* Signalling the arrival of warmer weather, this striking butterfly is a hardy regular throughout May, ranging across waterside meadows and elsewhere. Though the female lacks the orange wingtips of the male, both sexes are easily recognized. The eggs are laid singly on the cuckoo flower, which grows in damp places, and on other wayside flowers.

SEDGE WARBLER *Acrocephalus schoenobaenus* 200,000 pairs visit. Arriving from late April onwards, the sedge warbler is an opportunist in seeking a nest site. Not only does it choose waterside reed- and osier-beds, but also young conifer plantations, for dense low cover seems more important to its instincts than wet surroundings. It will also nest among reeds in damp sand-dune 'slacks'. A shy bird, it is more likely to be heard than seen, and has a hurried, jumbled song. It leaves in September, having perhaps doubled its weight with excess fat to burn off in a single hop across the Mediterranean and Sahara.

LARGE RED DAMSELFLY *Pyrrhosoma nymphula* Many colourful damselflies are seen on the wing over water between May and August (their nymphs are aquatic), and the adults are often seen mating 'in tandem'. Unlike their dragonfly cousins, damselflies rest with their wings folded back, and despite their fragile appearance, they are in fact fierce predators of smaller insects.

YELLOW FLAG (or WILD IRIS) *Iris pseudacorus* With its bright colour and sturdy leaves, this is one of our most stately wild flowers, now seen alongside rivers and on marshy ground (May–July). It is believed to be the origin of the heraldic fleur-de-lis, decorating royal coats of arms. The petals later fall to reveal glossy green capsules, which will ripen and split to shed the seed.

COMMON (or BRONZE) BREAM *Abramis brama* This fish is found everywhere in Britain, except in the south-west counties. Spawning now begins, which is often accompanied by much threshing and leaping in the shallows.

RAGGED ROBIN *Lychnis flos-cuculi* The classic wild flower of wet places is now seen everywhere (May–June), even in wet habitats up to 2000 ft (the height of the tree-line) in Scotland.

MOORHEN *Gallinula chloropus* 200,000 pairs resident. Now, in the middle of its long breeding season (March–August), the moorhen is as aggressive as the coot in defence of its territory. Even after breeding, in the winter months it often defends a 'core' territory despite feeding outside it. It wanders further from water than the coot, and can even be seen alongside roads, perhaps nesting in ditches. It swims with a jerky head action, and its long toes enable it to stride on floating vegetation.

FOUR-SPOTTED DARTER *Libellula quadrimaculata* Now hatched from their aquatic nymph stage and flying (some may migrate here from Europe), these darters will rest on waterside leaves or twigs to await the passage of insect prey; they then dart out in attack. These dragonflies lay eggs by 'kissing' the pond surface with the abdomen.

MAYFLY *Ephemera danica* Mayfly nymphs live in clean, often running water, but they will now rise to the surface in large numbers (unless delayed by cold weather); here their skin splits, and the adult shucks itself free. However, this dull 'dun' is not quite mature—it must again moult to become the gleaming, net-winged, mature insect, which does not feed but simply flies in ceaseless courtship. After a day or so, their duty done and the eggs fertilized and laid, these mayflies die, falling to the waiting trout.

COOT *Fulica atra* 50,000 pairs resident. The males are renowned for squabbling over territory, fighting noisily and splashily with metallic cries. Presenting the bare, whitish forehead shield to a rival is part of the threat display, its effect heightened by fluffing out feathers (though it is the chick that is really 'bald as a coot', with its pinkish bare head). Coots build a large nest of reeds and often flock after breeding. Busy birds, they are seen jumping up to dive down for submerged plants, and will sometimes graze on land.

BRACKEN *Pteridium aquilinum* The fresh, young, green fronds of bracken are now starting to unfurl, thrusting up from the far-spreading rhizomes underground. This fern is now common everywhere (except on limestone and chalk); it requires a rather damp soil, but one which is not too wet. In the hills it usually marks land that has been abandoned. Here, in the past, it was cleared from even poor pastures, for it is poisonous to livestock if eaten in quantity. The spore cases ripen in July, and by October the fronds are dying and turn golden.

LINNET *Acanthis cannabina* 700,000 pairs resident. Although heard in all months (apart from December, perhaps), the linnet is now in full song. This song consists of snatches of informal twittering and cheerful notes. This bird often feeds in restless flocks even when breeding, and its song is not territory-linked. A patch of gorse is a favourite place for nesting, often in small colonies. Some British linnet flocks will begin to move to Iberia in August, when European cousins come to Britain. In February, though, the birds will return to their favourite gorse and bramble patches.

BROOM *Cytisus scoparius* A relative of gorse (but without its spines), this plant is now in showy bloom (May–June). The flowers, though scentless, attract insects to the pollen, and they have a 'trigger' which sprays visitors.

GREEN HAIRSTREAK *Callophrys rubi* Now on the wing, and continuing to fly into June, this butterfly weaves acrobatically and loops the loop. It is our only truly green butterfly, albeit only the undersides of the wings are green (the upper surface is brown). The female often chooses broom or gorse on which to lay her eggs (or bilberry in the north). It will winter as a chrysalis (unlike other hairstreaks, which winter as eggs).

COMMON BUTTERWORT *Pinguicula vulgaris* This, like the sundew, is a carnivorous plant of peaty wet heaths and marshes (though it does not grow on the bog itself). Insects stick to the sappy leaves and their soft parts are then digested for their minerals.

FOX MOTH *Macrothylacia rubi* A common moth of moors and heaths, the male is seen flying on warm, sunny days in May and June, with a wildly erratic flight. The caterpillars feed on heather or bilberry, and spin a longish brown cocoon, often found empty.

MOUNTAIN AVENS *Dryas octopetala* This beautiful little shrub is now in flower (May–July) on turfy ledges in mountainous areas where the soil is somewhat limy, but it also grows at sea level in the north of Scotland (for the same reasons as thrift).

GREEN TIGER BEETLE *Cicindela campestris* On sunny days, this insect is now seen flying or running swiftly over heaths and other dry places. Its grub will choose a patch of bare ground in which to dig itself a burrow up to 1 ft deep; there it will wait with its head and large jaws blocking the hole, ready to take wandering ants and other insect prey.

ROWAN (or MOUNTAIN ASH) *Sorbus aucuparia* Also known as 'summer's pride', the rowan is now in full blossom (May–June) alongside the pale green foliage (in autumn, the leaves will redden, and the ripe, bright-red September berries will be eagerly taken by birds). Able to withstand deep frosts, the rowan is found in a wide variety of places and soils. It is often the last tree on the way to the summit of a mountain, growing from a crack in the rocks or over a stream, out of range of the ever-hungry sheep.

NIGHTJAR *Caprimulgus europaeus* 2000 pairs visit from May to October. This bird is now quite rare, its heathland habitat much reduced in recent times, although it will also nest in young plantations and open woodland. It spends the day quietly, camouflaged against the litter on the ground. Like the bat, it becomes active at dusk to hunt moths, when it may now be seen in twisting, erratic flight. (Holiday-makers in the Mediterranean can watch it feasting on moths attracted by street lights.) This bird's song consists of an unusual, rattle-like churring of two notes repeated, which it begins to voice sharply at sunset.

PAINTED LADY *Cynthia cardui* The arrival of a migrant butterfly is a poignant sign of incoming summer, and although it may be seen as early as March, the painted lady can now be expected, aided by southerly winds (it is likely to be seen first along southern coasts, resting and feeding). The scale of its migration was only recently discovered: its homeland is in North Africa, and each year variable numbers make the hazardous journey to Britain. May's arrivals are quite likely to breed, and will be seen courting on hilltops and other high ground. The eggs are laid on thistles, and the resulting flying adults are seen in August and September. However, none survive the first frosts of winter.

GREAT NORTHERN DIVER *Gavia immer* This bird usually winters around our coasts from October to May, but a few may remain to summer on lakes in the north and west of Scotland, where they may perhaps breed. Thus, there is a chance of seeing them now in handsome breeding plumage and to hear their eerie wailing echo back from the mountainsides. However, in May these birds may also be seen in passage up the English Channel, to the delight of southern twitchers.

BURNET ROSE *Rosa pimpinellifolia* A very spiny rose (its stems also bear stiff bristles), this is now seen in flower (May–July) on coastal dunes and limy hills, suckering to give widespread bushes. The hips ripen to purple-black in autumn.

COMMON SKATE *Raja batis* The empty capsules (known as 'mermaid's purses') which held the eggs of the skate are often found washed up from May onwards. When first laid, these are attached to seaweed fronds with long threads for anchorage; the young hatch after two to five months, depending on the sea temperature.

HEART URCHIN *Echinocardium cordatum* Burrowing into sand just around and below the low-tide mark, these heart-shaped urchins feed on detritus on the sand's surface. Fishing lore has it that they burrow deeper before storms. The dead, empty 'test' is often found as a 'sea potato', blowing along the beach.

NATTERJACK TOAD *Bufo calamita* Sadly, this toad can now only be seen in a few places in Britain, restricted mainly to nature reserves on sand-dune systems and heathy ground on the coasts of East Anglia, Lancashire and Cumbria. It tunnels in this soft soil, emerging to feed at night. Breeding (accompanied by loud croaking) is now taking place in May, and may continue into June or July. The eggs are shed and fertilized in shallow water, being laid in strings wrapped around plants. After about two months' development, the young toadlets will leave the water, still under ½ in. long, and they will not be fully grown for four to five years.

KIDNEY VETCH (or LADY'S FINGERS) *Anthyllis vulneraria* A handsome member of the pea family, this is now coming into flower on sea cliffs in the south-west. It also flowers on mountainsides, and inland on chalky dry soils (May–September). These latter plants have yellow flowers, but the coastal ones may be extremely beautiful with additional colours, such as bright-red, purple or cream flowers.

CLOUDED YELLOW *Colias croceus* This migrant butterfly reaches us from southern France from late spring onwards. If the first arrival is early enough, there is a chance of two broods during the summer, so that many of these attractive butterflies are seen on the wing in September. The females will lay their eggs on red clover, but bird's-foot-trefoil and some other pea flowers may also be chosen.

FULMAR *Fulmarus glacialis* 400,000 pairs resident. These birds are now seen wheeling against their breeding cliffs around most of Britain. Their's is a true success story, for 100 years ago the only British colony was on the island of St Kilda; today, their numbers speak for themselves. Presumably these birds are now exploiting a new food source—perhaps the offal thrown overboard from modern fishing fleets. They will haunt their breeding sites in all months, except possibly September and October. However, close contact with fulmars is to be avoided—they repel intruders with a jet of stinking liquid.

JUNE

This is the month of long days. Hereford, for example, has an average day length of nearly 17 hours, twice the December figure, while to the north of Scotland the nights can remain twilit. The longest day, at the midsummer solstice, falls on or around 21 June, while Midsummer's Day, a quarter-day for rent and other farming calculations, is 24 June. 'High summer' now begins, running from 18 June to 9 September.

With long hours of daylight and the sun high in the sky, light receipts are now high; in the south-east, they are as much as five times their December level. Plant productivity is also at a high, boosted by the generally warm weather.

The pretty sequences of flowers continue along the hedges, but a sombre note is cast

A pair of fox cubs. They grow rapidly, and after a couple of months the blue eyes they were born with have become amber and their coats have begun to turn reddish. They are now at a very playful stage.

when disease strikes an elm. These trees were all but wiped out a few decades ago, but sizeable young trees are now again to be seen. However, when the foliage browns and withers in June, this is an indication that the fungus spores of 'Dutch elm disease', carried to it by the bark beetle in spring, have now grown to block the sap tubes of the tree.

Hay is made in June in the south, whereas in the north haymaking is often delayed until July. Hay fever, an allergic response to pollen, also reaches its peak for the human population in June. Despite this, to bury your face in a sweet handful of June grass is to savour summer's goodness. The fragrance is yielded by coumarin, an oil, and is noticeably stronger when the stalks are drying after the hay has been cut.

June is a fragrant month. Honeysuckle may be recognized a hundred yards away on a tranquil dewy evening. These warm evenings also bring out many nocturnal insects. Throughout Britain, the ghost moth now flits back and forth over a grassy spot, attracting his mate with this pendulous flight. In England, its pure white wings give it a ghostly effect in the dusk, but in the Shetlands, where the June nights are too light for this to have an effect, a local race flies with darker wings.

By midsummer, bird song is slackening. Although swifts are barely settled in, the nightingale is rarely heard after the second week in June. The burden of breeding is now over for many species. Some, however, will continue to lay and rear new broods until the autumn.

On or about 16 June the new coarse fishing season opens, after a three-month break to enable the fish to breed. Up to three million people enjoy fishing, although most of what they catch is returned to the water.

Little remains of the old pagan rituals associated with Midsummer's Eve, once a potent date. Many of these involved bonfires, it seems, and keeping watch. But the white-robed modern druids who solemnly attend Stonehenge to welcome the dawn are the fruit of romantic Victorian imagination rather than a relic of prehistoric times when these megaliths were first raised, aligned on the year's solar axes.

There are, perhaps, truer echoes of that distant past and the spiritual link between man and nature to be found in such things as the 'Midsummer Cushion', described by John Clare. Clare, a peasant poet born in 1793, wrote of cutting a patch of flowery midsummer turf and nailing it on the cottage door in celebration (and for good luck).

June's clear sun shining on the green countryside can create some of the most enjoyable weather in the world. With long hours of daylight and the sun high in the sky, light receipts in the south-east are five times their December level. Plant productivity is at a high and the grain fields please the farmer.

HIGH SUMMER

The June sun is powerfully high in the sky in the northern hemisphere. The great areas of high pressure, known generally as the Azores high, are now at their most northerly position, and release lesser progeny which move slowly to the north-east, perhaps crossing western and southern Britain in due course. The air moving from the still-cool sea on to warmer land creates little cloud, and clear days can allow the land to be really warmed up in the sunshine.

On average, June is the sunniest month, and is the least cloudy by day and by night. Average monthly sunshine is around 230 hours in Falmouth, 200 hours in Cambridge, but also 180 hours in Aberdeen—all four times their respective January totals. The daily average at Kew is over seven hours, the highest of the year. However, cooler spells with calm clear nights in the early days of the month may still give frosts; there were six ground frosts at Kew in June 1971, with ten recorded at Exeter.

One feature of June may be the return of wet weather from westerly directions after the past month or so. These spells are sometimes called the 'European monsoon' when they end an easterly warm spell.

However, fine spells are likely in June, and on a long run of years, the days between 18 and 22 June are quite hot and dry, especially in the south. As usual, such a spell of fine weather brings with it the threat of massive cumulonimbus clouds and thunderstorms. These are quite likely during this month, but June 1970 was exceptional with thunder in England for 21 days.

Overall, June is like many months, being notable for its marked regional differences. Now it is the onset of high summer in the south, marked by spells of hot weather which leave the north lagging behind.

Thunder can be heard at any time of year, but June's powerful sun can certainly trigger thunderstorms. For those whose skin tingles and who become edgy during thunder, be assured that such a reaction seems common in the animal world. Even the industrious ant reacts to static electricity before deciding to launch its mating swarms, and there is some evidence that birds delay long flights if thunder is imminent. The map shows the average number of days with thunder heard per year.

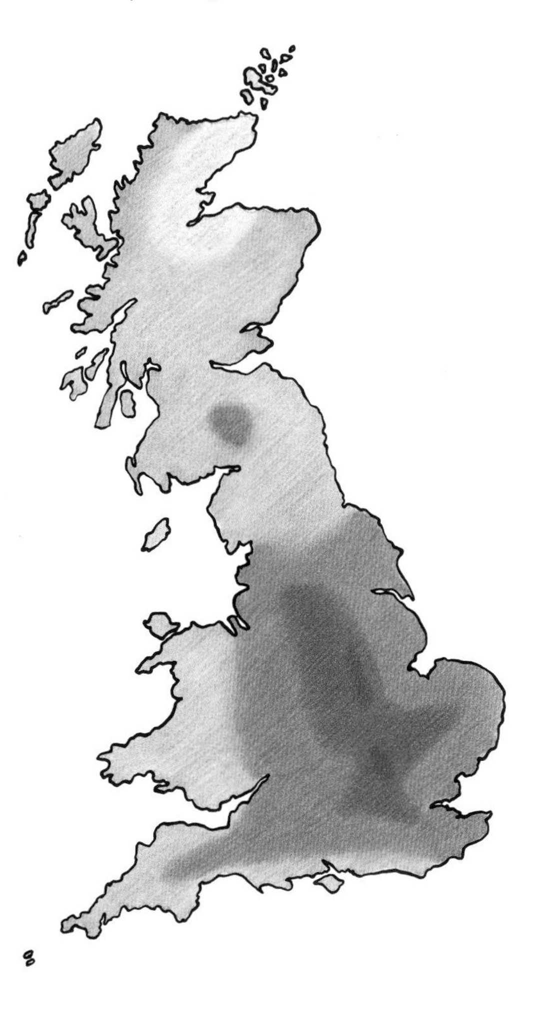

Over 20 days
15–20 days
10–15 days
4–10 days
Under 4 days

THUNDERSTORMS

Thunderstorms may develop from some thick clouds such as altocumulus, but they are usually associated with cumulonimbus, those tall cloud castles which are a frequent part of the summer scene. Indeed, the ice forming at more than $3\frac{1}{2}$ miles high in the upper regions of these clouds has an important role to play in their genesis.

On hot, damp days, very vigorous currents of warm air rise from the land, condensing into puffy cumulus clouds, and may continue their climb to create cumulonimbus clouds, tall enough for ice crystals to form. The turbulent friction among the water and supercooled droplets and these ice crystals making up the cloud creates electrical charges. Overall, the cloud becomes negative at its foot, positive at its head. The ground is also positively charged, and when the potential difference between it and the negative base of the cloud is great enough, a spark jumps the gap—a flash of lightning, often more than a mile long. Sometimes the flash leaps the charged areas between clouds; when obscured, these flashes are seen as sheet lightning.

The flash violently heats the air along its path, which expands at supersonic speed,

The forked nature of lightning strike is shown clearly in this night-time photograph.

producing a clap of thunder that echoes back from other clouds and hills. The light reaches us almost instantaneously; the sound takes five seconds to travel a mile—which yields an easy way of estimating the distance to the lightning flash. Solitary, sentinel trees are sometimes struck by lightning, the bark scarred and perhaps set on fire. Towers and steeples are usually fitted with conductors to earth the stroke safely.

Ball lightning, a glowing globe of light perhaps a foot across, is very rare. Seeming to drift with the wind, its cause is unknown. Another phenomenon, St Elmo's fire is a slight, hazy discharge from such things as steeple wind vanes and lightning conductors.

Although thunder is more likely to occur in summer, it may be heard at any time of the year. Winter thunder, perhaps in mild spells with air moving swiftly in from the ocean, is often limited to single claps. Thunder is heard in Edinburgh on around eight days a year, but for 10–15 days over much of England towards the south and east, and even more than 20 days in some areas.

Thunderstorms often let loose showers of hailstones to cover the ground. These have a curious origin. When an ice crystal falls within the warmer, lower part of the cloud, it collects small water droplets which splash around its surface and freeze, giving a thin layer of clear ice. This young hailstone may then be caught by an upcurrent and carried to the top of the cloud. Here it is so cold that the supercooled droplets in its path instantly freeze to it, trapping small air spaces and giving a frosty layer. If and when the hailstone falls, another layer of clear ice is added, and so on. When this 'onion' becomes too heavy to be kept aloft by the upcurrents (which may reach 90 ft per second), it falls as a hailstone.

Westerly or northerly airstreams may bring hail showers in the spring, but these are usually not true 'onion' hailstones but pure white snow pellets, easily crushed between the fingers, or harder clear ice pellets.

Unlike raindrops, which have a maximum size beyond which they break up, hailstones can be quite large—the British record is 5 oz in weight, falling in Horsham, West Sussex, in September 1958. Heavy hail can damage plants, and the damage is particularly noticeable in fields of tall, standing corn just before the summer harvest. Wildlife may also be injured by hail showers.

WEATHER SENSITIVE

Bottom left Lesser celandines with their bright-yellow flowers fully opened; on dull days, these flowers will close (**bottom right**).

Below A pair of ringlet butterflies are seen here mating. Unlike other butterflies, this species is often seen on the wing in drizzle.

In past centuries, those about to start haymaking on a fine June day anxiously kept an ear open for the rooks. Noisy cawing by these birds was believed to give advance warning of rain—and a sudden downpour would ruin the newly-cut hay. The alarm could also be sounded by bees lingering within a stone's throw of their hives, swallows skimming low over the river, or leaves sighing in a breeze in a wood—in the 'quiet before the storm'.

Such weather lore was largely an oral tradition, of sightings amassed over centuries and coincidences remembered. Although many weather superstitions were bizarre and unlikely (can New Year's Day presage a windy summer simply because it falls on a Monday?), wildlife sightings do tend to reflect weather—if not of the future, at least of the present.

This is certainly true of plants. The daisy is seen to open in bright light, and close if the day turns gloomy; hence its name, 'day's eye'. But it is responding to subtler cues—the petals open when the air temperature is between 11°C and 14°C, *and* when the air is not too damp, with a relative humidity of between 64 and 80 per cent. If the humidity rises, the flowers close.

Humidity, which can dramatically increase before dull, glowering clouds bring rain, influences many plant forecasters, affecting the turgidity of certain cells at the roots of the petals. For that most classic of weather forecasters, the scarlet pimpernel, the crucial relative humidity which affects its petals is also 80 per cent. As an augur of wet weather, though, it does not do too well, as rain follows its closure on less than one in five days. But if this pimpernel remains open, dry weather is 80 per cent certain. The white hedgerow trumpets of hedge bindweed also close before rain, while mushrooms thrive in humid conditions, and a dawn before a damp September day can see caps scattered across old pastures.

High humidity also seems to affect the turgor and rigidity of the leaf stalks of the poplar, lime and sycamore. Although no rigorous tests have been done, these stalks do seem to bend more easily in the breezes which often come before showers, fluttering the pale undersides of their leaves.

Two hoary but widely-held beliefs are, however, definitely not proven. Pine cones do not reliably close before rain. And it needs not a taste of rain but more like a fog with 100 per cent humidity to dampen dry seaweed enough to make it limp.

Some plants react to wind rather than humidity, such as the windflower. It flutters in breezes which sweep the wood, often in advance of rain. In addition, clover closes its leaves in gusty winds.

As for plants, so too for animals—but for rather different reasons. Rove beetles race and ruby-tailed wasps scuttle only in sunshine on dry days. A sudden downpour of rain could harm them severely, as it would many small insects. Most butterflies fly only on dry, especially sunny, days. At rest they can be seen angling their wings to control heat gain, as they usually need some sunshine to augment their slender energy reserves. One notable exception, though, is the ringlet butterfly, which can be seen on the wing around bushes and in woodland glades in light rain.

Bird behaviour certainly reflects the annual almanac of climate, and it can also reflect the shorter, current spell of weather. Birds often fall silent before a storm. Pheasants are late to roost in fine weather, plovers fly higher, and skylarks sing high in the sunshine (in fog they will perhaps sing from a fence). There is also plenty of rook lore—for example, these birds will remain by their nests on a morning heavy with the prospect of rain. In spite of old beliefs, though, they do not build nests higher in fine years—they sensibly and simply choose the stronger branches at their traditional rookeries. But why they should choose to 'tumble' in autumn, flying aerobatics, is not at all clear.

Swallows will fly high on fine evenings, presaging a clear, dry day for the morrow, for aphids and other flying insects are carried aloft by the rising air currents usually present in settled warm weather.

For much the same reason as the lofty swallows, another sign of a forthcoming good day might be a spider near the centre of her web, expecting increased insect traffic. Or that web itself may be the clue, as they are not spun on rainy, windy mornings. (Some orb-web spiders consume the old web and spin anew each day.)

Frogs seem to croak louder before rain—perhaps the increased humidity encourages them into voice. But is it true that 'the busy heving of moules declareth rain'? And do cows lie down before rain? Certainly neither are proven, yet a countryside walk would be far less fun without such entertaining possibilities to put to the test.

The ruby-tailed wasp is to be seen only in bright sunshine, and when seen it is extremely active, searching for the nests of other wasps and bees, on which it is parasitic.

Far left Responding to the cues given by temperature and humidity, the familiar daisy tends to close if the day becomes gloomy; however, it will again open if the day brightens and warms (**left**).

HAYMAKING AND SHEARING

The hay harvest is one of the oldest of all, yet it too is now mechanized. After being left to lie on the ground, drying in the sun, the loose hay is baled. It will then be put under a roofed shelter.

At this time of year, working capital is heavily tied up in livestock or in the grain crop growing in the fields. So, in need of extra cash flow, some farmers resort to pick-your-owns. These have become very popular over recent years, and this is their busy season. The strawberries are now plump, but they will have needed a bit of rain as well as sun to fill them out. Some offer raspberries too, though these do better with a cooler summer, hence the major commercial fields are in Tayside in Scotland.

June is the haymaking month. The old, traditional hay meadows were situated alongside rivers, because grass grows better in damp soils. The animals were allowed into the meadows for an early bite in spring, and the fields were then shut up until the haymaking. Meanwhile, plenty of wild flowers had time to bloom; in May and early June an old-time meadow was a natural garden. Then, after the hay had been sweatily scythed, stooked and stacked, the animals were again allowed in to graze the aftermath.

Today's haymaking is not such hard work, but it takes just as much skill to judge the best day for it—it is a matter of timing, like many other things in farming. The hay on sown ley fields is usually best cut before Midsummer's Day, or a bit later for meadows with mixes of wild grasses (in the north, the haymaking may be in July, anyway). Beyond these dates, the living grass begins to put its energy into seed and its leaves lose their goodness. (The wheat, also of the grass family, is beginning to come into ear in June; the early barley was in ear in May.)

Haymaking means hay-drying. When the sweet grass is cut, it holds 80 per cent moisture which must be lowered to 25 per cent for storage. The grass is cut long with mowers, some of which crimp the grass, bruising or 'conditioning' it to help the moisture escape.

After the cut, it is left to dry; a repeat run with the tractor and hay-tedder (rather like a food mixer) fluffs it up, stirring it into swathes, with rows running up the field. These may be turned twice more with a swathe-turner which simply turns the hay over, damp bottom to the sun, without shaking it up too much, for as they dry the grass stems become fragile. After about three days, the hay is dry enough to be baled. This can be done by a standard farm baler drawn by the tractor, which delivers blocks of hay that are not too large to be handled and can be piled under cover easily. Quite often nowadays, the hay (and straw) is baled into a giant half-ton roll which can only be handled by a tractor.

In the past, of course, all these jobs were

done laboriously by hand with hayfork, cart and horse, with the whole village taking part. Now, as then, the weather is critical—however, nowadays hay can be cut in damp weather and dried out with a fan heater in the barn. But this is very expensive and is only sensible as a last resort, as the aim is always a cheap crop.

Hay is not always a planned harvest, but if it was a good year for grass and the farmer already has enough silage, hay can always be sold on for a good price—for those Sunday afternoon ponies, perhaps. Hill farms will buy it because it can be carted from the barn to be fed to livestock in the snow, something which cannot easily be done with silage.

In late June, the grass is being nudged by the calendar to divert its effort from leaf to seed. Milk yields may start to drop as a result, and even a spread of fertilizer will not help. However, to make up for this, there may be some grazing from the aftermath of the early silage; incidentally, it was essential to fertilize this after cutting, to encourage the new growth.

New potatoes are now ready in most parts of Britain and sprouts will be planted out. Many of the year's selling lambs will also be ready. But the other highlight of the month is sheep-shearing. On lowland farms, wool may only bring in a sixth of the income gained from the meat, but on hill farms wool may be worth half the income.

Sheep-shearing is a back-breaking job. In the upland areas, neighbours may often help each other, but elsewhere shearing gangs are usually hired. The animal has first to be cleaned up (sometimes even washed beforehand, for clean fleeces bring a better price), and then held so that it cannot struggle and its skin is taut. A skilled shearer can often manage one sheep every two minutes, the fleece being removed in one piece with electric clippers.

The yield can be anything from 2–4 lb of wool to more than 10 lb for a longwool breed. Different wools suit different purposes. Mountain and moor sheep, such as the hardy Dalesbred and Scottish Blackface, have a coarse but springy fleece suitable for carpets, whereas grass hill sheep, such as the Cheviot, have a rather finer fleece. The finest knitware wools come from lowland stock; in the past, down breeds, the Southdown for example, were famous for their fine knitting wool, while the heavy-fleeced longwools, such as the Cotswold, produced large amounts of wool.

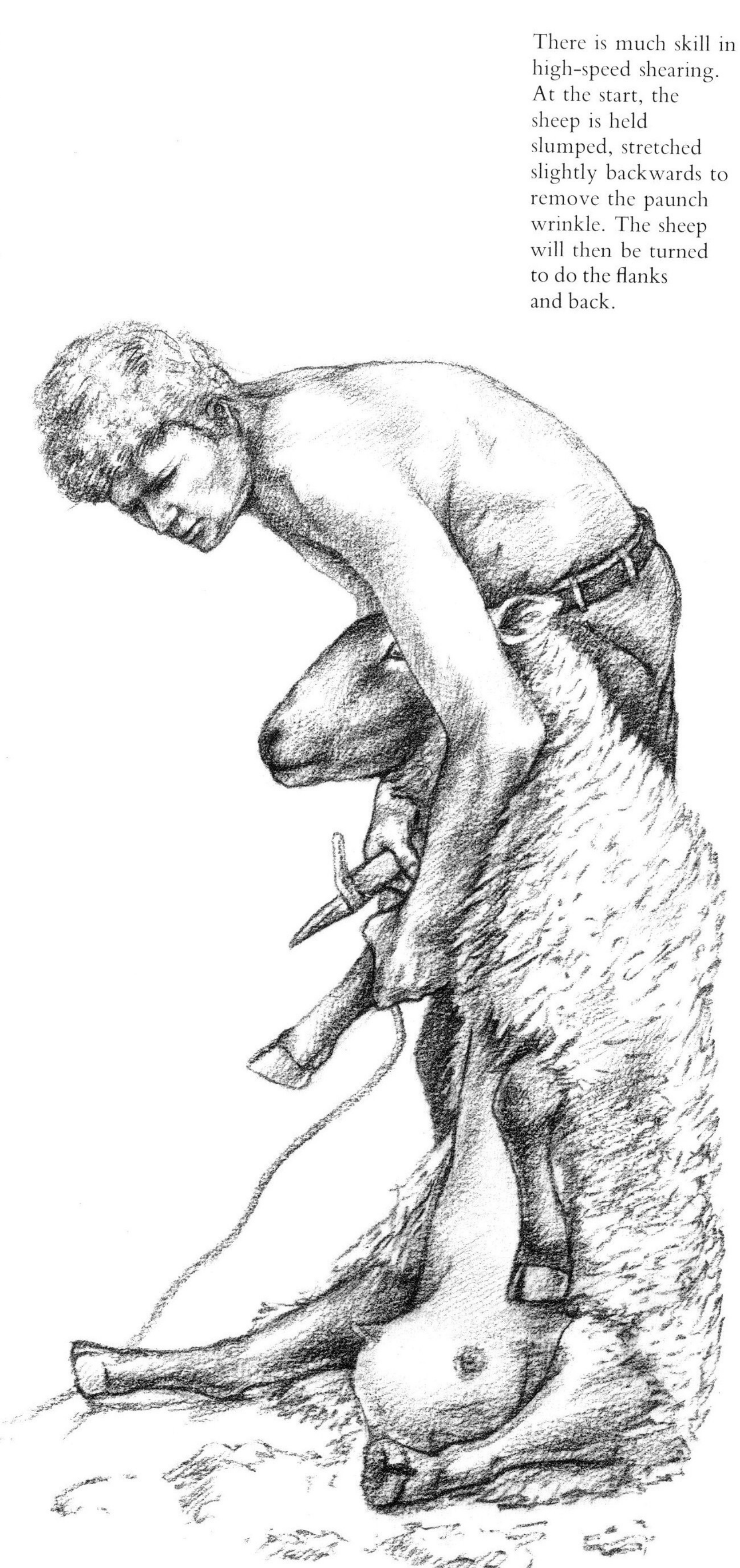

There is much skill in high-speed shearing. At the start, the sheep is held slumped, stretched slightly backwards to remove the paunch wrinkle. The sheep will then be turned to do the flanks and back.

THE NORFOLK BROADS

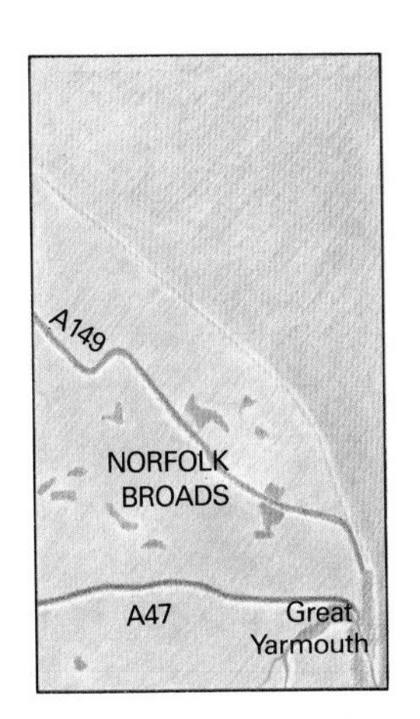

The Norfolk Broads lie on the flood plains of several rivers which converge at Great Yarmouth. Owing to its unique character, this area is of National Park status in all but name.

June is one of the best months to visit the Broads. It is a relic landscape. In the distant past, wide swampy wetlands covered large parts of the lowland river basins. They were bountiful in fish and wildfowl, but this was not enough to protect them from drainage, both in Roman times and later, when the monasteries put in hand a great deal of land reclamation. In the course of time, too, lakes naturally fill with silt and rotting vegetation, eventually drying up—and the same happens even more rapidly with small ponds. So a wetland wilderness is a prize in our cultivated countryside.

Something of this ancient habitat can still be seen in the Norfolk Broads. Paradoxically, these Broads are themselves man-made. By origin they are medieval peat diggings which became flooded by the nearby rivers and reverted to nature. Although they have become a favourite holiday area, the handful of Broads which remain free of the wash of boats and the clamour of summer visitors give us a fascinating glimpse of those past ages, when 'the haunt of coot and heron' was a literal backwater.

In these undisturbed Broads, dense beds of reeds surround shallow, crystal-clear lagoons. Water-lilies jostle for space on the water's surface; moorhens tread daintily on the floating leaves, while exotic great crested grebes paddle nearby. Noisy coots and shyer teals feast on the seeds of water plants, and magnificent Norfolk dragonflies, coloured head to tail with patches of emerald green, patrol the surface. In June, the equally-rare swallowtail butterfly flickers among the host of insects on the wing in the sunshine.

From the reeds comes the churring of warblers as they build their nests and attend to the demands of their broods. Bearded reedlings, small long-tailed birds, fly low over the reeds; as is so often the case with many Broadland species, they are only infrequently seen elsewhere. Further off, a bittern booms like a foghorn. But all seem to draw breath as the hunting harrier glides low across the scene. Only the teeming fish remain unaware of the presence of this aerial threat; they face hazards enough from the voracious pike of these waters.

Fenland surrounds the lagoons and reed-beds. Here, on the marshy ground, grow tussocks of sedge, backed by a dense woodland of low trees and shrubs, alders and willows, known as 'carr' or 'fenwood'. The damp ground is littered with rotting stumps and alight with vivid mosses and ferns. Straggling bindweed festoons the branches like lianas in a tropical forest, and there are tangles of guelder rose.

It is this natural succession from open water through reedbeds to carr woodland which makes the Broads so interesting to the naturalist. But, even here, what we see is not entirely untouched by man.

Indeed, these Broads remain open water partly because the tawny winter reeds have for centuries been cut for thatching—even some local churches are thatched. The local saw sedge is used for ridging the thatched roofs. Where it is cut, or the fen opens out for other reasons, lush meadows are found, with meadowsweet, yellow wild iris, purple loosestrife and pink hemp agrimony blooming in profusion, each in their own season. There are wild orchids, too.

January and February can be austere months here. The Broads are exposed to biting easterly winds blowing unimpeded across the North Sea. Frost decks the dead reeds, while ice encrusts the sedge tussocks. Colour is muted, focused in the broken 'brandy bottles' (the seedcases of the yellow water-lily), the sturdy brown bulrush or the purpled twigs of the alder. For the bird-watcher, however, winter rivals summer with its visiting flights of Bewick's and whooper swans, and flocks of wigeons and other waterfowl.

The swallowtail (*Papilio machaon*) is our largest butterfly, on the wing from late May into June, and perhaps again in late August. The females choose only the sturdiest plants of milk parsley (not a common plant) for their egg-laying, which limits their range. Indeed, they only breed in the Broads nowadays.

BRITAIN'S WETLANDS
Some of these are nature reserves and open to the public by permit only, but their birdlife can still be seen from the paths alongside:
1 Insh Marsh, Spey Valley, Highland. This tract of wetland along the River Spey forms the largest area of natural fen in northern Britain.
2 Washington Waterfowl Park, Tyne and Wear.
3 Hornsea Mere, Humberside.
4 Sandbach Flashes, Cheshire.
5 Kingsbury Water Park, Warwickshire (near Tamworth, Staffordshire).
6 Crmlyn Bog, near Swansea, Glamorgan.
7 Wicken Fen, near Ely, Cambridgeshire.
8 Rye House Marsh, near Hoddesdon, Hertfordshire.
9 Stodmarsh, near Canterbury, Kent. Its birds match those of the Norfolk Broads.
10 Thatcham Reedbeds, near Newbury, Berkshire.
11 Radipole Lake, near Weymouth, Dorset.
12 Slapton Ley, near Dartmouth, Devon.
***Norfolk Broads**.

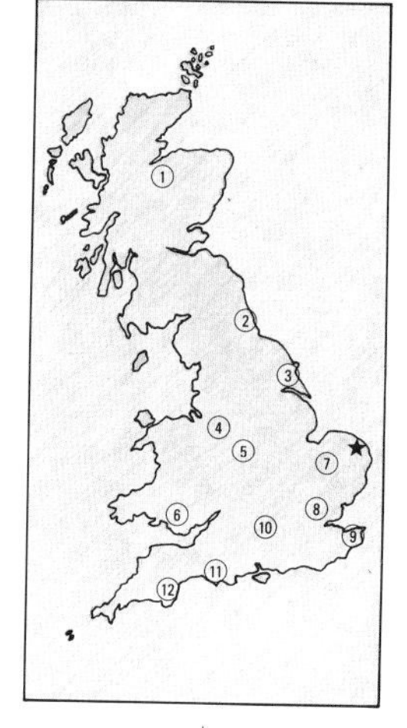

This is Calthorpe Broad, enclosed and unpolluted—showing the Broads as they once were. The water below the water-lilies is crystal clear and bursting with aquatic life.

FALLOW DEER *Dama dama* This is the noble animal of deer parks, but wild herds have long been established in the New Forest and elsewhere in England (and parts of Scotland and Wales, though not so widely). Feeding usually at dawn and dusk, they may now be seen resting among the fading bluebells. The males cast their antlers in April, becoming secretive while the new ones were growing, but by mid-June most fallow deer are in their summer coats, with broad-bladed antlers (which the does lack). Fawns are born at this time, and will soon be seen with their mothers. The rut takes place in October and November, when the master bucks lay claim to traditional rutting stands where they fray the bark of saplings to mark territory and attack rival males.

FOXGLOVE *Digitalis purpurea* The attractive foxglove is now in flower (June–August). A biennial, it spent the winter as a low rosette of leaves before growing its erect stem of flowers, which open in sequence from the bottom of the stem upwards. Later in the summer, a few flowers may still hang on at the top of the stem, with the seed capsules below. After producing plentiful small seeds, the plant then dies. Its name perhaps comes from 'folk's glove', a corruption of the Anglo-Saxon word 'gliew', which was the name of a musical instrument with bells.

SPOTTED FLYCATCHER *Muscicapa striata* 200,000 pairs visit. The adult has, in fact, a streaked breast. Perching in a clearing or at the edge of a wood, it will 'flycatch' with twisting sorties, returning to the same post each time.

COMMON TWAYBLADE *Listera ovata* This orchid is now seen flowering (June–July) in woodland as well as on open grassland (although it may be nibbled down by fallow deer in woods).

PEPPERED MOTH *Biston betularia* Flying in May and June, the peppered moth habitually rests well camouflaged against lichen-covered bark. In response to pollution, a dark (melanic) form first evolved in smoky industrial Victorian towns, where the trees were covered with soot.

WOODY NIGHTSHADE (or BITTERSWEET) *Solanum dulcamara* Though now in flower (June–September), this plant is more noticeable in autumn when carrying brilliant-red berries. It is found scrambling over other plants in woods, hedges and scrub.

SILVER-WASHED FRITILLARY *Argynnis paphia* Seen on the wing now, this butterfly often soars in majestic flight. In general, woodland fritillaries lay their eggs on violets; however, this species chooses not the plant itself, but the crevices in the bark of a nearby oak tree. After the caterpillars hatch, they soon (in August) enter hibernation until March, when they will reappear, crawling down the trunk to feed on the violets.

STAG BEETLE *Lucanus cervus* The male's fearsome 'jaws' are merely a sexual symbol. A male will rear up and open them, but they can impart only a gentle nip. Seen in the south on warm dusks from May to July, pesticides and the lack of rotting tree stumps (in which their grubs live for many years) have led to a decline.

HONEYSUCKLE *Lonicera periclymenum* Flowering from June to September, the honeysuckle's nectar can be tasted at the foot of the flower tubes (the flowers darken after pollination). Its perfume now fills the air, carrying further on still, humid evenings. It is early into leaf, and there is another burst of flowering in September, when the woody twining stems are already bearing bright-red berries from earlier flowers.

SPARROWHAWK *Accipiter nisus* 15,000 pairs resident. The female is browner and larger than the gunmetal-backed male. Now at the nest, a secretive time, this bird may be glimpsed flickering among the treetops or along a hedge, taking small birds by surprise; it can also outfly its victim, matching every twist and turn. The prey is plucked before eating, often at a site which becomes littered with feathers. In courtship, the pairs are more visible, soaring high above their territories. However, in autumn they cover wider tracts of countryside as the shorter days limit their hunting time.

ELDER *Sambucus nigra* Although the may blossom is now fading along the lanes, the hedges are quickly replenished with tiers of pungent white elder flowers (June–July). Attracting hosts of insects on warm days, the elder is a pioneer shrub, being seeded on to new soil when birds void the pips after eating its berries, which ripen in August and September. But rabbits dislike its bark and ignore it, so elder can mark their burrows.

STARLING *Sturnus vulgaris* 4,000,000+ pairs resident, with numbers swelled by continental arrivals in the autumn. Young starlings are now the noisiest birds, harassing the parents while feeding on grassy fields and lawns. Excellent mimics, starlings have an amusing repertoire of notes. Later in the year, family groups will unite in feeding flocks, which each evening join up with others to roost, often in cities, which can be 2–3°C warmer at night. Come the morning, they again disperse into feeding parties to scrounge in the suburbs and beyond—a reverse rush-hour.

QUAKING GRASS *Briza media* Elegantly waving in the breeze in many open habitats, ranging from meadows to chalk downland, this plant is now in flower. However, we are probably seeing several different races of quaking grass, each one adapted to its local microclimate.

FRAGRANT ORCHID *Gymnadenia conopsea* Now seen in flower (June–July) in many kinds of grassy places, it has a pronounced scent on warm humid days. Wild orchids are at their peak in June. Weather apart, their young growth relies on a soil fungus, which partly explains their generous presence in some places (and years) but not in others.

MEADOW GRASSHOPPER *Chorthippus parallelus* Common in grassy places, it utters a short, chatty, chirping song. Grasshoppers are first heard in late June, coming into full song in July—a song produced by rubbing a file on the inside of the hind legs against the forewings. They sing and reply to each other in chorus, and in warm sunshine will be seen hopping and flying busily.

COMMON BLUE *Polyommatus icarus* A double-brooded butterfly, the common blue is on the wing from May to June, and again in late August (the eggs are laid on bird's-foot-trefoil in many grassy habitats). Though widespread, it is rarely seen in large numbers. Other blues can be seen in colonies, but will still be restricted to the habitat where their caterpillar's foodplant grows. (Note that blue females are brownish in colour.)

PIPISTRELLE BAT *Pipistrellus pipistrellus* Britain's smallest but most numerous bat is now seen weaving patterns against the sky, 20 minutes after sunset. In June, the mothers are at their nursery roosts (often in large buildings). Bats rely on warm, dry weather to catch as many as 3000 flying insects a night, in order to lay up fat reserves for hibernation. The loss of grassy meadows and other insect habitats has caused their decline.

SKYLARK *Alauda arvensis* 2,000,000 pairs resident, but some leave in autumn to be replaced by continental arrivals; the reverse occurs in spring. The skylark now sings strongly over open downs, hills, fields and sand dunes, hovering high above the ground (higher in warm weather than cold). On misty or foul days, it may sing from a fence or even from a grass tussock. And although the skylark sings most notably from February to mid-July, with a marked resumption in October, it may be heard in all months of the year. Like plovers and thrushes, it is mobile during spells of winter cold.

DOG ROSE *Rosa canina* Flowering in hedgerows and on commons and downs (June–July), its delicate pink blooms are followed by red hips a month later. These hips are generally ignored by birds; however, mice will eat the pips, but voles will only take the flesh.

COMMON WILD THYME *Thymus praecox* Found in many dry habitats, the pretty trails of stems and rose-purple flower heads may now be seen (May–August). This species of thyme has only lightly scented leaves, but one sniff can still evoke memories of hot downs, shimmering in the sun.

YELLOW WATER-LILY *Nuphar lutea* and WHITE WATER-LILY *Nymphaea alba* Summer pools are brightened when these water-lilies flower (June–August). They may be seen together (on Scottish lochans, perhaps), with the yellow growing nearer the shore. The white's flowers open towards midday, but they close and partly sink when evening comes. The leaves are anchored to a rootstock in the mud (to which the plants die down in winter). While all leaves of the white water-lily float, some of the yellow's leaves remain submerged. The fruit of the yellow water-lily is the green 'brandy bottle', seen in August.

PERCH *Perca fluviatilis* Perch are predatory fish that hunt in shoals, which become smaller numerically as the fish grow older. They may be cannibalistic until over 5 in. long. These fish spawn from April to June in the shallows.

WATER-PLANTAIN *Alisma plantago-aquatica* This is a quite common plant of watersides or muddy shallows. It flowers from June to August—the petals of the small flowers open after noon, but shut again by the end of the day. (Conversely, a close relation with narrower leaves, which often grows alongside, flowers in the morning.)

PURPLE LOOSESTRIFE *Lythrum salicaria* Its handsome flower spikes are now on display in damp places (June–August). There are three types of flower, differing in the lengths of pollen stamens and styles (to which the pollen sticks), which elaborately guarantee cross-pollination. For example, one plant will have flowers with short styles but medium and long stamens; another will have medium-length styles, and short and long stamens; long-styled flowers have short and medium stamens.

YELLOW WAGTAIL *Motacilla flava* 100,000 pairs visit. Though from a distance perhaps mistaken for an escaped canary, this bird (visiting from April to October) is now often seen snapping up midsummer's abundant flies from around the feet of cattle in streamside meadows—and only a distant view is likely, for it is a shy bird, very difficult to approach.

PUSS MOTH *Cerura vinula* A large number of moths, including the puss moth, rely on the foliage of willows, poplars and sallows of damp places on which to lay their eggs. This large furry moth, which is widespread in Britain in May and June, has a bizarre-looking caterpillar, seen in July and August; this is heavily disguised by its markings, and will rear into a threatening display if frightened, lashing its red 'tails' at predators.

CHUB *Leuciscus cephalus* A popular angling fish, the chub has a liking for clean water and is mainly a river fish. Spawning occurs between May and June. The summer will see shoals of young, but the older fish are solitary, favouring their own deep pools where they will also be found during the coming winter.

MEADOWSWEET *Filipendula ulmaria* Now in flower (June–September), the heavy, lingering scent of meadowsweet helps to make June one of the most pungent months of the year. Its name, however, comes from its use in olden days as a sweetener of mead, the drink made of fermented honey. It is a plant found in many damp places.

MUTE SWAN *Cygnus olor* 6000 pairs breed, plus 12,000 non-breeding birds. Large, graceful and seen everywhere, this is the one bird species that everyone can put a name to. It builds its large nest usually in April, and family parties which include the greyish cygnets are now seen. By custom, swans on the River Thames below Henley are registered at an annual 'swan-upping' in the third week of July—unless they have a bill notched to show possession by a London Livery Company, they belong to the Crown. Mute swans have complicated posturings, used during courtship earlier in the year and for aggression (when, for example, the neck is drawn back and the wings arched out). They dredge the river bottom for weeds and other food, and are hazarded when they take up discarded lead fishing weights. Signs of lead poisoning are lethargy and a slack neck. They are generally mute, though they will grunt and hiss; their most characteristic sound is the throb of their wings when flying.

GOLDEN-RINGED DRAGONFLY *Cordulegaster boltonii* After the lingering spring, the mountain rivers and tarns now throb with insect life. Watch for this handsome hawker dragonfly, which may attend its territory along a mountain stream not only by day but also during these light summer nights. After mating, the female may often be seen hovering over the water, pushing her eggs into the mud below.

TORMENTIL *Potentilla erecta* Its yellow flowers (June–September) brighten heathlands and similar places with rather acid soil (it avoids chalky soil). The petals close in wet weather and at night. (Tormentil always has four petals; if five are seen, then the plant is one of the cinquefoils.)

LONG-EARED OWL *Asio otus* 3000 pairs resident in many areas, but less so to the south-west of the Midlands. It has the archetypal 'wise old owl' tufts. These are not ears, but are probably a threat or simply part of its sexual display. Strictly nocturnal, it is most likely to be seen 'frozen' with tufts raised against intruders in conifer plantations and other woodlands. It may be heard from early spring onwards, uttering a thrice-repeated, long-drawn 'oooo'.

STONECHAT *Saxicola torquata* 20,000 pairs resident. Although once seen in all counties, it is now mainly limited to those towards the coast, where areas of heath or heath-like habitat are still extensive (it is rather more widespread in winter). Its double notes (one sharp, the other throaty and deeper), which sound like pebbles being struck together, are still heard, though the main period of its scrappy song is earlier in the year.

LARGE HEATH *Coenonympha tullia* This butterfly is unusual in being seen only to the north of Shropshire and North Wales, not in the south. (Presumably, like the mountain ringlet, it is a relic of the waning Ice Age.) It also varies in colour: the darkest subspecies, with the clearest eyespots, is seen to the south of its range. Zigzagging across boggy ground, the large heath flies from June to July, up to 2000 ft on the hillsides; its eggs are laid on upland sedges.

SUNDEW *Drosera rotundifolia* The sundew is now in flower (June–August) on the bog surface. The peat below can supply it with few nutrients; instead, the plant gains nourishment by catching and digesting up to 2000 insects a summer. The plant's leaves are covered with red hairs, glistening with droplets—midges are attracted by these apparent drops of water, but learn to their cost that they are sticky. Once stuck, they are enfolded by other hairs and the leaf also curls over; the hapless prey is then digested by enzymes exuded by leaf cells. The lethal droplets resemble drops of dew, hence the plant's name.

WHINCHAT *Saxicola rubetra* 20,000 pairs visit. This bird arrives late in April, travelling from as far south as Angola, and chooses much the same gorsy habitat as the resident stonechat. Although they look similar, the whinchat starts singing a month later, and will continue into August. The song is rather pleasant, if hurried, with rich, sweet notes. The birds return to Africa in September.

CROSS-LEAVED HEATH (or BOG HEATHER) *Erica tetralix* This plant may now come into flower (June–September), starting somewhat in advance of its relatives. On close examination, different kinds of 'heather' can be identified, which give an interesting insight into their ecology. This particular species, identified by its four-leaved 'whorls' up the stems, likes wet ground and so is commonly found in low-lying hollows on moors or heaths, where it often grows with tussocks of purple moor-grass. In contrast, bell heather (*E. cinerea*) and ling or heather (*Calluna vulgaris*) pick out rather drier ground, thus avoiding competition.

MOUNTAIN RINGLET *Erebia epiphron* On the wing from late June into July, the mountain ringlet is only found in the Lake District above 1800 ft, and in parts of Scotland above 1500 ft. It is a good example of a species which has had its range reduced by climatic changes: spreading north as the Ice Age waned, its open habitat was later overwhelmed by forest on low ground. This butterfly lays its eggs on mat-grass.

COMMON SEAL *Phoca vitulina* One of the highlights of June in the Wash is the birth of common seal pups. These quiet animals favour sheltered waters up the eastern coast to Northumberland, and on the east and west coasts of Scotland. The date of pupping varies by region, and the pups will swim from birth. After breeding, common seals become more widespread. They have loose colonies, and while one bull may watch while the others rest, there is no territorial battling. They like to 'haul out' on sandbanks or weedy rocks when the tide ebbs, leaving to feed again when the tide comes in. In 1988, seals began to suffer from a virulent disease akin to dog distemper; it is not yet clear how this has affected numbers.

MANX SHEARWATER *Puffinus puffinus* 200,000 pairs visit. Arriving in March and leaving again in October, this bird (the scientific name given is correct!) is now nesting, not only on the Isle of Man as its name would suggest, but also on many other islands off the west coast. The nest is in a burrow on the cliff top. Nights in the colonies are noisy, for the parents usually leave the chicks during the day in order to feed far out to sea, returning just before midnight.

RED VALERIAN *Centranthus ruber* This is now in flower (June–August), colonizing rocks and walls, especially in south-western coastal areas.

YELLOW HORNED POPPY *Glaucium flavum* Its flowers can now be seen on coastal shingle banks (June–September). Like many seaside plants, it has waxy leaves to prevent excessive water loss on the quick-draining habitat. Later on, the curving seed capsules may grow to as much as 1 ft long.

EDIBLE CRAB *Cancer pagurus* Although shop crabs will have been fished from deep water (and peak catches are in May and June), at this time of year small youngsters, too small for eating, may be found under rocks at the low-tide mark. They can be recognized by their pinkish colour and the shape of the shell. They will migrate to deeper water in autumn, and spawn in December.

ROCK DOVE *Columba livia* 100,000 pairs resident. Holiday-makers visiting remote cliffs at such places as Berry Head in Devon, Bempton Cliffs in Humberside, and Orkney may be surprised to see 'town pigeons' nesting. These birds are in fact rock doves, ancestors of today's feral pigeons. They were probably introduced in Roman times, for if food is available they can breed at any time of year, and the tender young 'squabs' helped relieve the dreary winter diet of olden times. They continued to be kept in manorial dovecots until quite recently. Over the centuries, however, they escaped to live free in towns and cities, where many still sport rock dove plumage.

SHORE CRAB *Carcinus maenas* Remarkably well adapted to the changing seashore habitat, this is the crab most likely to be glimpsed in a rock pool, or out of the water, rushing back to a rock crevice or scuttling away across mud at low tide. Patchy when young, the adults (up to 4 in. across) are dark green.

TREE MALLOW *Lavatera arborea* This plant is now in flower (June–September) on south-western coasts.

COMMON SHRIMP *Crangon vulgaris* With a flatter body than the prawn, shrimps can be up to 3 in. long. They spend the daylight hours buried in the sand-flats or pools on the lower shore, and emerge to scavenge at night. Well camouflaged, they can adapt their colour to the sandy background. By this time in summer, they will be moving into estuaries from more open sand-flats.

GANNET *Sula bassana* 120,000 pairs resident. This bird is now nesting in large colonies or 'gannetries' on offshore islands and certain coastal sites. The nests (foul affairs of seaweed glued with droppings) are neatly spaced out. The gannetry is always a lively place, with continual traffic. Fish are caught by plunging dives made from as high as 90 ft above the sea. The juveniles are dark grey, gradually lightening as they mature over a few years. Once breeding is over, the adults disperse, and though still fishing inshore in August, they generally winter in warmer southerly waters.

JULY

Charles II wittily described the English summer as 'three fine days and a thunderstorm', and this can certainly be evidenced in July. But there may also be spells of uncomfortable, sweltering heat. The rich, swift Perseid shower of meteors crosses the night skies between 1 and 18 August.

The 'dog-days' are reckoned to set in on 3 July, lasting until 11 August. In old almanacs they were days of sultry heat and flies, named after Sirius, the Dog Star.

Thunderstorms and showers are likely, but not consistent rain. 'St Swithun's Day if you bring rain, for 40 days it will remain', ran the old adage; the day falls on 15 July. Medieval forecasters held such saints' days to be of great significance, but although St Swithun's Day is still remembered, this example of ancient weather lore has long since been proved to be unreliable. (Strangely, though, it *did* rain for more than a month without cease after the bones of St Swithun were reinterred at Winchester in July AD 971.)

The foliage of woods and hedgerows is now in its deep summer green, the vivid tint of spring having since darkened. The green colouring matter is chlorophyll, with whose aid plants synthesize carbohydrates, namely sugars, from soil water sucked up by their roots and carbon dioxide from the air.

On the lower boughs in the deep shade beneath the woodland canopy, the leaves of hazel, oak and sycamore are now sometimes seen to be enlarged in response to the dim light reaching them. In a typical wood, this may be a fraction of the light in the open. The leaves of true shade plants, however, are not enlarged to increase their vital photosynthesis. Instead they *reduce* it, by having fewer leaf pores for gas exchange with the air around. Geared to lower productivity, for them there is no benefit to be gained from growing in open sunshine.

A common darter dragonfly. July is a good month for seeing these 'birdwatcher's insects'. This one is resting on heather; moors and heaths often make good dragonfly habitats.

July is the month of 'cherry ripe', and by its end a start can be made collecting honey. In the countryside generally, plant production is going into seed and berry rather than into new growth. The swelling heads of grain please the farmer's eye—indeed, the first grain harvest of winter-sown barley is in July, its gold contrasting with the still-green wheat.

The cattle cast short shadows in the height of summer. The stone walls and bright whitewashed houses are clues that this is a Lakeland scene, and up in the northern hills the farmer's diary is likely to be somewhat behind those in the south. We can see that some of the fields have only recently been shaved bare by the silage cut (in the south this is first cut in May). The cattle here are Friesians, popular for their high milk yields.

On hot days, birds may sometimes be seen panting with open beaks, losing heat in the same way as a dog, by breathing out and evaporating moist air. Sometimes they perch with feathers raised, to allow air to reach the skin. In really hot sunshine, blackbirds are prone to sunbathe, lounging sideways with feathers raised akimbo to let the sun get to the skin. This may ease the bites of ticks which usually infest the skin beneath the feathers.

With breeding generally over, and in many cases the year's crop of youngsters all but indistinguishable from their parents, the adult birds may now begin to moult. They have to replace worn flight and other feathers for the coming migration flights and the hazardous months of winter which lie ahead. The mallard drake is a notable example; he is usually now seen in 'eclipse' plumage.

Birds are at risk from predators at this time, and begin now to fall silent, the territorial song which would mark their presence suspended. Perhaps, at the end of the month, there may still be a solitary blackbird or thrush singing, with wood-pigeons still cooing, sparrows cheeping and swifts still screaming overhead. But this is about the only time of year when the robin is tardy into song. This general silence can underline the brooding quality of these dog-days.

THE DOG-DAYS

July expects to see warm, sultry weather. High temperatures may be registered everywhere, although the south-to-north temperature gradient, that was in evidence as early as April, is well marked. Mean temperatures are now 6°C higher in the north and 8°C higher in the south than in April.

There is a twist to the map, however, for the highest mean daily temperatures usually occur in the Thames basin and sometimes also around the Solent, in Hampshire. The highest temperatures also tend to occur inland rather than on the coasts, and are usually reached two to three hours past midday.

The weather overall is usually more unsettled than in June. Westerlies often prevail, bringing air that has spent much time over the Atlantic, but there are fewer gales in July (and June) than in other months. Although the streams of tropical and polar air are closer in temperature than in winter, thus generating less-marked depressions along their common front, frontal clouds and rain are still produced and may be slow-moving.

As an example, a very hot day can come about when an anticyclone has moved from the south-west across Britain to centre itself over the North Sea. Western Scotland receives warm, damp air from the south-west, but for the rest of Britain the high brings in a light wind from the south-east, giving clear skies and high temperatures. The highest may be reached when tropical continental air from the Sahara arrives from across a warm European mainland.

It can be hazy as well as hot, although the air reaching us from France is much less polluted than that which arrives on a more northerly east wind from industrial Germany and Poland. In fact, the haze from smoke and pollution, downwind from our own cities, is often very noticeable in summer.

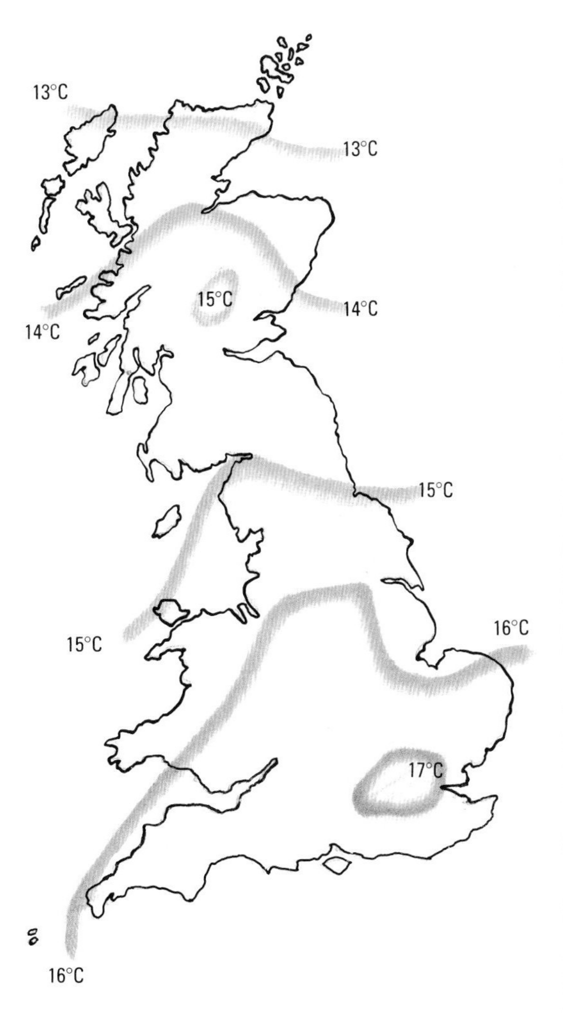

Here we show the average July isotherms (reduced to sea level) for comparison with those of January (see page 14). You will notice that the balance of influence has now swung around, with the Atlantic Ocean no longer such an exaggerated source of warmth. This has meant that the isotherms, rather than running from warmer west to colder east as they did during January, now tend to run from warmer south to colder north.

STRANGE SIGHTINGS

Ragged patches in the crops, caused by squalls or short sharp showers of rain or hail, are quite common sightings, but each year 50 'crop circles' are reported, and many more presumably go unnoticed. These are flattened circles, neatly rounded and from 10–100 ft across. No tracks lead to them through the untouched standing corn, and they are too tidy to be caused by rampaging hares or rabbits. So how did they get there?

The current theory is that they are the result of freaks in local weather. They are seen near hills. When wind meets an obstacle, it divides to flow around each side, uniting again when past. The airstreams usually join smoothly past a hill, but sometimes they do not, in which case the stronger gust on one side could cause the air to spin in a sudden whirlwind, rather like the eddies which swirl around loose leaves in a winter wood (or the familiar whirlpool of water past a boulder in a stream).

These swirls of air last only for a few seconds, but as they sink they flatten the crop below. They may also occur in winter, but they are usually only noticed in July and the other summer months when the corn is standing tall.

Did a spacecraft land here? These are classic examples of crop circles—and a possible explanation for their formation is given in the main text below.

True whirlwinds are not all that uncommon in Britain, with perhaps one a month being sighted. They are very much smaller and less powerful than the famous prairie tornadoes of the United States, which may have a diameter of between 150 and 600 ft and cause great damage, but our British whirlwinds are very exciting nevertheless.

They are twisting whirls of air which move across country, and because of the dust, leaves and other loose objects they suck up along the way, they are seen as dark ropes snaking down from the clouds. Sometimes they appear as small waterspouts on lakes or on the sea—several were seen on the English Channel in 1974. Occasionally, looser 'dust devils' (or 'water devils') are seen; these whirr up from the ground (or lake surface), but last for only a short time.

The reason why such whirlwinds make an appearance is not clearly understood. They can occur at any time of the year and are often seen with thunderstorms; it is possible that a strong updraught of air needs to start rotating to set them off, and these are commonly found below cumulonimbus clouds. (Local tornadoes, however, must not be confused with the vast cyclical tropical storms—the hurricanes of the West Indies, the cyclones of the Indian Ocean and the typhoons of the Pacific.)

From time to time, weather evidences itself in extraordinary ways. When a whirlwind passes over a pond, fish may be deposited far away when it collapses. After a summer storm in 1987, hundreds of small pink frogs were found hopping along the streets of Cirencester, Gloucestershire. It seems that they were airlifted from the Sahara, by courtesy of violent hot updraughts which became incorporated into north-flowing airstreams. These reached Britain, and the frogs fell in the ensuing stormy rains.

The aurora borealis, or northern lights, are atmospheric sightings of a completely different kind. They are a feature of the Arctic but are often seen in Scotland, and occasionally (in spring 1989, for example) in the south of Britain as well.

They are caused by magnetic storms high in the atmosphere, and often coincide with sunspot eruptions. Splendidly coloured arcs, curtains and rays appear in the night sky, most commonly yellow-green but sometimes with reds, blues, greys and violets, set handsomely against the velvet black.

SUMMER DANGERS

It is nature's paradox that summer, while for most of us a time of warmth and relaxation, is for much of our birdlife a period of greatest stress. Mortality may match that of winter, and it is during the months of summer and autumn that the size of next year's population is decided. Surprisingly, the coming winter, unless exceptionally severe, will have less effect on overall numbers.

As already seen, the amount of food available in spring is reflected in the timing and size of a bird's egg clutch. For the great tit, as many as ten or more eggs may be laid in a brood, but incubation only begins when the last is laid. This means that all will hatch at about the same time, and the nestlings will be equally clamorous for food. Caterpillar food is usually abundant and few nestlings starve; indeed, they may even be able to lay up fat reserves to help them through the coming months. When they eventually leave the nest, the parents will continue to feed them for a couple of weeks, after which they are left to forage for themselves.

By July, though, that spring larder is bare, the few remaining caterpillars having since pupated and now difficult to find. Less-nourishing spiders may need to be included on the menu. As a result, there is a very high mortality among the year's young in these first free months, so much so that perhaps only two out of the original ten chicks survive. This is an excellent example of the fit of wildlife to its habitat—for next year's population is unlikely to boom to exceed the food available.

A tawny owl with its prey; as with many predatory birds, egg-laying will be curtailed if food is at all scarce.

Even stronger curbs come into play if, by chance, that first brood of great tits is destroyed by a marauding jay, weasel or squirrel. A new nest site is chosen and the hen will lay again, but now the peak of the larder may be past. This time, however, it seems that incubation begins as soon as an egg is laid. Hence, the nest contains chicks of different ages, and the oldest and largest will grab the food first. These are quite likely to live, but their younger, weaker brethren will starve if the caterpillar supply falters. In this way, at least some of the race survives.

This stepped pattern of incubation seems to be adopted by some birds of prey. If hunting is good, the whole brood survives, but if poor, at least the first birds hatched will have a sporting chance.

On the grouse moors, the keepers are now anxiously estimating numbers in preparation for the August shoots. The year's populations tend to fluctuate, with the periodic declines being known as 'grouse disease'. The cause was originally thought to be a parasitic worm, but recent research has shown that more complicated factors are involved in deciding the population levels of this game bird.

The male bird's territory is crucial. After some half-hearted attempts to establish territory in the autumn, quickly abandoned in snowy times, the males take it up again in February. Pairs are formed and those without land have to scavenge on sparse open grazings where they are poorly camouflaged against predators.

Food is again the key in the occupied territories. The better-fed females gain adequate supplies, laying larger clutches of eggs, but if the year's heather is poor, infertility can result and the weakened birds are less able to fight off parasite attacks.

Although the total size of the population is

thus determined by the fierce territorial land-holding of the males, there is again an immense death toll among the juvenile birds. As many as 50 per cent of those hatched die by the end of July; unlike tits, these young have to find their own food from hatching, eating insects for protein at first and then heather shoots. This means there is a low proportion of young birds to old in poor years, with a subsequent drop in population the following year. Shooting, of course, depletes total numbers, but it seems only to accelerate a natural pattern, not introduce a new one. At heart, the numbers rely on the territorial holdings of the cock birds.

Such checks and balances lie behind the numbers of birds we see. Even good weather can affect a population. For example, a drought in summer can bake the soil and put young blackbirds at risk (thrushes, which feed on snails, are not so affected). Woodland blackbirds, though, having large areas of damp leaf litter to pick through, can survive drought better than those living in gardens.

This balance of numbers against food is found everywhere in nature. Short-tailed voles sometimes have local population explosions, which immediately attract short-eared owls and other predators to plunder the natural food store.

A short-eared owl hunting short-tailed voles over open ground, its sensitive ears alert for the slightest rustling in the grass below. Its eggs are laid at two-day intervals.

A pair of grouse in their heather domain. The size of the population is largely regulated by the number of good territories available for the males.

This must have been a good hunting year for the parent kestrels, for here we have a large and well-fed brood. Kestrels have adopted motorway verges and similar grassy areas, where they can often be seen hovering, searching the ground below for evidence of mice and voles.

BARLEY FOR THE ANIMALS

Between the haymaking in June and the wheat harvest in August, July traditionally used to be a quiet month. Today, though, it is busy. The wheat is now past the threat of mildew, but aphids can be a nuisance and need spraying. A second crop of silage may be cut later this month, when the stocking of the milking herd in its fields may also need adjusting and the paddocks enlarged as the grass begins to slacken.

Modern crops, such as oilseed rape, are harvested in July. This particular crop is cut and left to dry before being taken up by the combine harvester (if the pods are too ripe they release and scatter the seed). Oilseed rape is commonly planted as a break crop for wheat, and it can be almost as profitable. Its seeds are crushed to yield an oil with many uses, from lubrication to food (it is edible).

Grass seed is also a modern July harvest, to be used for seeding the future grass ley fields. It can be quite a gamble, for if the seed is of poor quality, the field is a complete write-off—and the chances of both silage and hay will have been lost.

Barley is another crop harvested in July. Winter barley, sown in the autumn, is now ready. It is a fairly modern crop—previously only spring-sown barley varieties were used, to be harvested in August. The look of the barley fields changes as the harvest month approaches. The heads, once held as proudly upright as the wheat, droop and nod, while the sun catches the long hairs of the 'beard', giving the field a muted, natural sparkle.

Some British barley goes for malting, to be used in brewing—but large quantities also go for animal feed. So, on a mixed farm with both arable and livestock, the barley harvest may be taken straight into the storage silos.

Part of the farm's barley may be kept in store for the pigs. The pigsty was an important part of the traditional farmyard, but not so many farms keep them in use today.

Unlike wheat straw, barley straw is palatable and nutritious, and may be baled to be fed along with silage. Grain barley can also feed poultry, pigs and cattle in the form of concentrates.

There is a market for free-range eggs, from birds allowed out to roam over grassland each day, and for barn eggs, from birds kept in light, airy sheds lined with straw. Commercially, most eggs come from birds reared in totally unnatural wire cages under controlled conditions. Those destined for the table are usually reared also in closed sheds, but may live on straw.

Similarly, market pigs are mainly kept in an intensive unit nowadays, which is rarely part of the normal farm. Food and temperature are carefully calculated and controlled to bring these animals to sales weight in the quickest time possible. A pork pig reaches about 11 stone (the equivalent of about 70 kilos), whereas a bacon pig will weigh more. Heavier pigs with coarser meat are destined for pies and sausages.

Although a few farms still have the traditional pigsty, consisting of an individual hut and yard, rather like a zoo pen, the days are now gone when every farm (and cottage) had a pig or two. Many areas even had their own local breed—the Gloucester Old Spots, for example, was reared on windfalls in the orchards. Most pigs today, though, are of the long-backed, flop-eared Landrace breed, reared mainly for bacon.

In recent years, many farmers have opted for the odd field of 'pigloos'. These are individual dwellings, each 'owned' by a mated sow, and are usually in the form of curved corrugated-iron 'tents'. The animals look happy enough, scratching the field bare with their scavenging, but the piglets are destined to be sold on for fattening in the intensive sheds. Pigloo pigs seen over the hedge are often 'blue crosses'; this means that they are of Landrace blood, but have a grey patched skin.

The specialist pig and poultry units are an easily-recognized part of the countryside, consisting of long, low sheds with a feed hopper at the end and few, if any, windows. However, the slurry of dung and waste liquors is expensive to get rid of, and very often a pig unit manager will offer this by-product free (and may spread it also) to dispose of it—but as it is raw stuff, it will taint the soil.

Back on the fields, the farmer keeps a watch for wheat diseases, which can strike havoc even this late in the year. One in particular, known as 'take all', is very damaging—with only a month to go to harvest, the head turns white and the grains do not finish. Sultry weather often aids disease; it certainly increases the chances of potato blight, and if it is thundery the potato crop will perhaps be sprayed as a precaution.

It is in such weather that flies are a terrible nuisance to cattle, though in the past they were more serious. One of the worst was the warble fly, which is not so common nowadays, although it is still compulsory to treat cattle against it. It lays its eggs on the legs of the cattle in June and July, and the grubs eat their way under the skin, moving to the cow's back to cause a swelling, or warble, with a pore to the air. The irritation to the animal is immense, and the hide is also ruined.

Barley is often the modern farm's first harvest of the year. It is Britain's biggest cereal crop, with almost twice the acreage of wheat. Its straw may also be kept to be fed to livestock.

BRAUNTON BURROWS

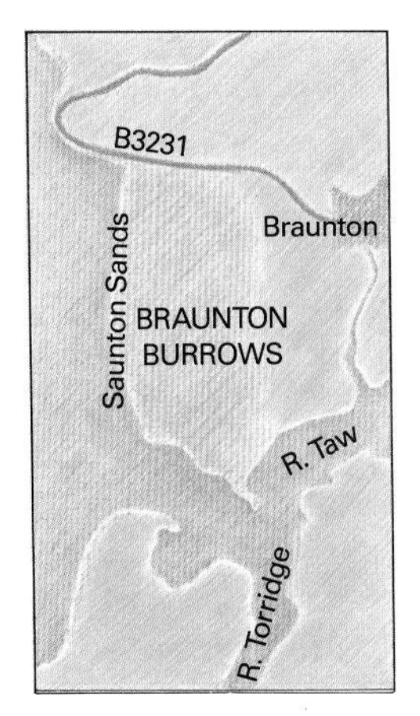

The Braunton Burrows nature reserve, near Barnstable, Devon, totals some 1500 acres. However, some parts of it lie within military zones and there is no access to these areas when red flags are flying.

Sandy beaches are scattered along the length of our coastline. The sand itself consists of grains of quartz or flint and other minerals, together with fragments of seashells which may be present in large amounts. Clearly, for the beach to form at all and not be scoured away, the power of the restless sea must be muted. In some places, currents and tides combine to create beaches which run for many miles along open coasts, whereas elsewhere, in rocky areas, the beach is snugly tucked within the embrace of a bay. Even so, there is usually a considerable difference in its depth, profile and texture in winter and in summer.

The sea's might lies in the fast incoming 'swash' of the waves, which carries sand and shingle with it. The weaker 'backwash' can move the lighter sand grains, but not the larger pebbles. These remain, especially in the wilder winter, to create a 'storm ridge' along the back of the beach.

Open sandy beaches usually form at right angles to the prevailing winds and waves, and this is clearly seen at Saunton Sands, Devon. At low tide, the Atlantic rollers break far out and the flat sand seems to stretch endlessly to the horizon. There is considerable life in this sand, but most of it is hidden; only the strand-line carries the clues in the shape of empty shells of crabs, vacant hard 'tests' of burying heart urchins, and shells of cockles, tellins and razor shells, mixed with seaweeds torn from rocks miles away up the coast.

At the back of this beach, the never-ending breeze blows the dry sand inland to create Braunton Burrows, one of the finest sand-dune systems in Europe, which is now colourful with many wild flowers. The whistling sand builds up in the sheltered, lee side of any small obstacle, and in time forms a small hump of dune. This 'young' dune is shifting, scarred by wind, but where marram grass can extend its mesh of underground rhizomes, it begins to become stabilized. Here also may grow sea bindweed, rare sea stock and sea holly, one of Britain's most beautiful wild flowers. Like its namesake, the sea holly has spiny, thick-skinned leaves, a strategy to cut down water loss in this quickly draining habitat. The roots of these plants also serve to bind the sand.

The dune system is thus ceaselessly being built up by the wind on its seaward side. Behind the first ramparts of newly-fixed dunes roll other, older dunes. The new dunes are still largely bare and sandy-yellow in colour, but nutrients are being added by the decay of the pioneering plants and in time a thin soil is created, especially in the hollows or 'slacks' between the banks.

The younger slacks become covered with a carpet of ground lichens and mosses, and scattered with scented wild thyme, blue viper's-bugloss and many other flowers. As the soil deepens, shrubs take root, with scatters of wild privet and tangled brambles in the older slacks. Privet prefers lime in the soil, provided here by the shelly sand below. Where sand is lacking in shell fragments, the soil tends to be acidic, and here heather may grow on the back dunes.

Though they may be just past their peak now, wild orchids add their own exotic presence, especially in the damper slacks. These wet areas may have pools, where wildfowl choose to nest. Elsewhere, the open habitat welcomes skylarks and meadow pipits; stonechats, partridges, ringed plovers and shelducks are also typical—these last often nest in old rabbit burrows. Sand dunes make ideal rabbit country and in Braunton they have created many finely nibbled turfs from the natural flowery meadows.

Braunton is a fine natural garden, but if by chance the fragile surface is broken, for instance when a path is overused, the wind quickly punches the breach into a blow-out of loose sand, and the slow process of colonization has to begin all over again.

The rhizomes of marram grass (*Ammophila arenaria*) form a dense mesh which stabilizes the shifting sand and allows other plants to root; its leaves are rolled inwards to cut down water loss. Sandhill snails (*Theba pisana*) are often seen clustered on such plant stems, waiting for rain, whereupon they become active.

BRITAIN'S SAND DUNES
Other sand-dune systems worth visiting (although access to some parts may be restricted):
1 **Aberlady Bay**, Lothian.
2 **Lindisfarne**, (Holy Island), near Berwick upon Tweed, Northumberland. The lime-rich sands encourage a variety of plants to grow.
3 **South Walney**, near Barrow in Furness, Cumbria.
4 **Ainsdale on Sea**, near Southport, Lancashire.
5 **Newborough Warren**, Anglesey.
6 **Kenfig**, near Porthcawl, Mid Glamorgan.
7 **Gibraltar Point**, near Skegness, Lincolnshire.
8 **North Norfolk coast**. Classic sand-dune systems at Blakeney Point and Scolt Head Island.
9 **Winterton Dunes**, near Great Yarmouth, Norfolk.
10 **Berrow Dunes**, near Burnham on Sea, Somerset.
11 **Dawlish Warren**, Dawlish, Devon.
12 **Studland Bay**, Dorset.
***Braunton Burrows**, near Barnstaple, Devon.

Here we see part of the youngest section of the sand-dune systems at Braunton Burrows—marram grass is only just beginning to colonize and 'fix' the deep sweeps of loose sand.

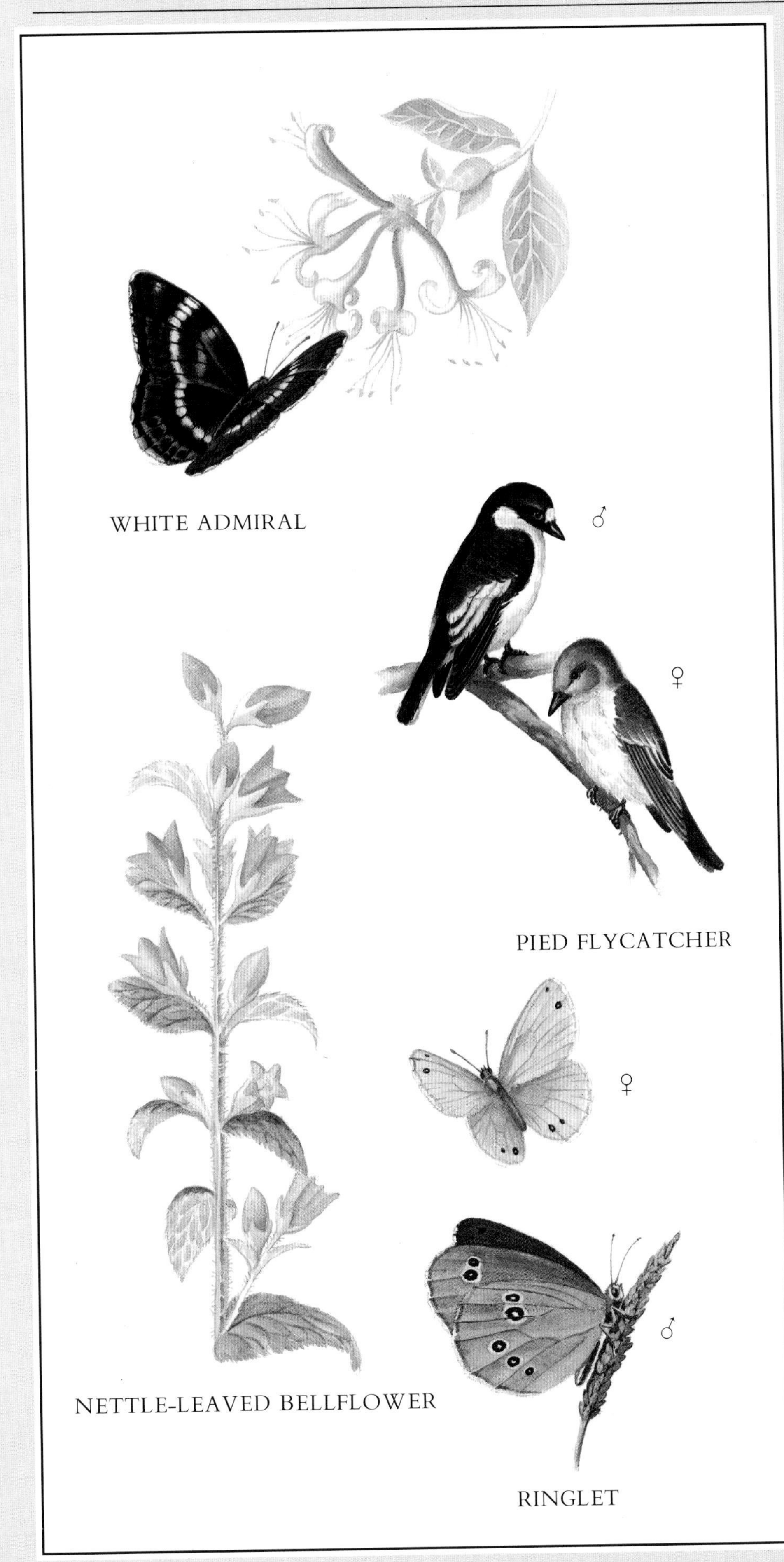

WHITE ADMIRAL *Ladoga camilla* In this sultry month, and into the next, watch out for the handsome white admiral, flying with grace across the glades of old oak woods in the south (but not the south-west). It is attracted to bramble blossom in shady nooks, but when perched the black-and-white wing pattern breaks up its outline, making it hard to pick out in the dappled light. The eggs are laid on straggling, long-limbed honeysuckle in the shade (plants in sunlight are rejected). Its caterpillar overwinters in a tent of nibbled leaf, feeding again on awakening, until June when it pupates.

PIED FLYCATCHER *Ficedula hypoleuca* 50,000 pairs visit from April to October. This is one of the last of our summer visitors to arrive, yet now, not long after, it seems to disappear. With the young now fledged from the nest hole, it is ready to moult and is skulking in the woodland canopy. (Most birds are now approaching moulting and are shy—the woods may thus be at their quietest in July, with little bird song to be heard.) Once moulting is over, these flycatchers will move to Iberia to lay up fat stores en route to tropical Africa. They are typical of the rather open, hillside oak woods of Wales, northern England and northern Scotland. Perching on a tree stump, they will flicker off after insects, before flying back to a different post—but they will also feed from the foliage. Their song includes a pleasant, descending trill.

NETTLE-LEAVED BELLFLOWER *Campanula trachelium* Seen flowering in woods on limy soils (July–September), this plant was once known as the 'Canterbury bell', for it was abundant on the Kentish chalk (today's garden flower of that name comes from Italy, however). A handsome tall plant (up to 3 ft high), its flowers are often clustered like bells in a belfry.

RINGLET *Aphantopus hyperantus* This butterfly likes overhung glades and other shady places where lush grass grows, on which it chooses to lay its eggs. It is now on the wing over most of Britain, continuing into August. The ringlet is one of the few butterflies to fly on dull or even drizzly days.

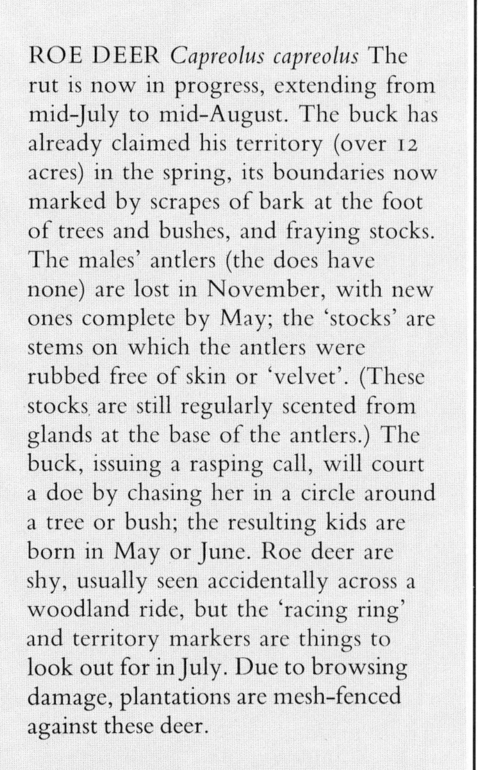

ROE DEER *Capreolus capreolus* The rut is now in progress, extending from mid-July to mid-August. The buck has already claimed his territory (over 12 acres) in the spring, its boundaries now marked by scrapes of bark at the foot of trees and bushes, and fraying stocks. The males' antlers (the does have none) are lost in November, with new ones complete by May; the 'stocks' are stems on which the antlers were rubbed free of skin or 'velvet'. (These stocks are still regularly scented from glands at the base of the antlers.) The buck, issuing a rasping call, will court a doe by chasing her in a circle around a tree or bush; the resulting kids are born in May or June. Roe deer are shy, usually seen accidentally across a woodland ride, but the 'racing ring' and territory markers are things to look out for in July. Due to browsing damage, plantations are mesh-fenced against these deer.

ROSEBAY WILLOWHERB *Epilobium angustifolium* Although familiar on waste ground in towns (in fact, during World War 2, it was one of the first plants to colonize newly-bombed sites), it may also be seen in woods, perhaps growing in the tractor-torn ground of recently-felled clearings. Woodland may even have been its original natural habitat, occupying ground cleared by fires started by lightning.

LARGE SKIPPER *Ochlodes venata* Skippers are moth-like butterflies, with an active darting flight and plumpish bodies; when basking, they may raise their forewings. This member of the clan flies from June to August in grassy places, including sunny glades.

GOLDEN-ROD *Solidago virgaurea* While the bellflower blooms in woods with limy soil, the golden-rod signposts acid soil in the woodlands in which it flowers (July–September).

HORNET *Vespa crabro* The hornet is the largest member of the wasp family in Britain. However, it has an ill-merited reputation; it is far less angry than common wasps. Rather rare, it is likely to be seen in old woodlands with ancient hollowed trees, in which it will nest. As with other wasps, only the queen survives the winter.

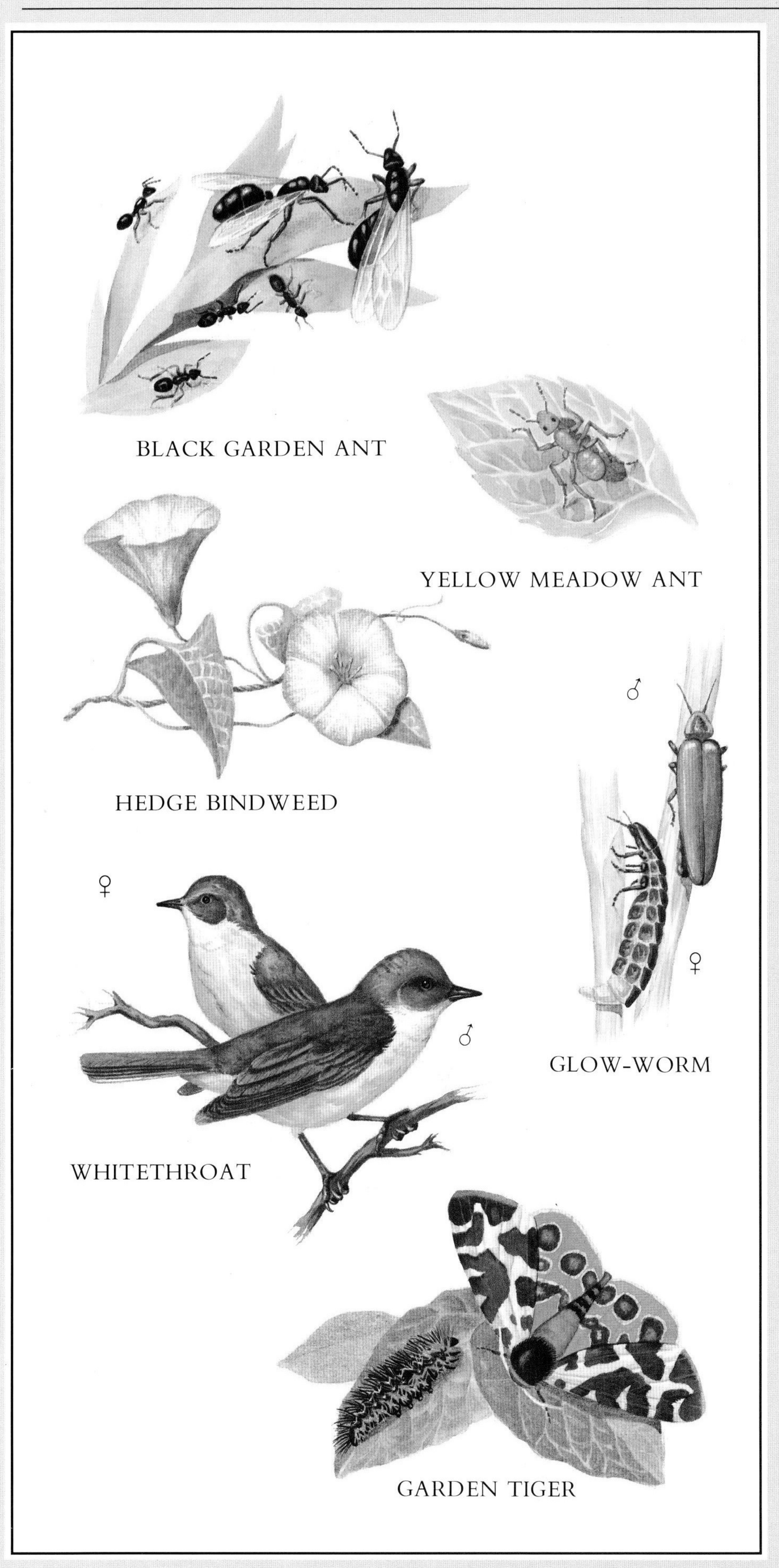

BLACK GARDEN ANT

YELLOW MEADOW ANT

HEDGE BINDWEED

GLOW-WORM

WHITETHROAT

GARDEN TIGER

BLACK GARDEN ANT *Lasius niger* Colonies of these ants, over a wide area, are reputed to 'read' the weather (reacting not only to temperature, but also to static electricity perhaps). They will swarm simultaneously on settled days in July and other summer months. This is a marriage flight, with the winged males and females (queens) mating in mid-air. The male then dies and the female either returns to her home nest beneath a stone to commence egg-laying, or starts a new colony elsewhere. Her eggs mainly hatch sterile females: the workers.

YELLOW MEADOW ANT *Lasius flavus* The ant-hills of old pastures are created by these ants, which may swarm at the same time as black garden ants.

HEDGE BINDWEED *Calystegia sepium* The handsome white trumpets of this plant are now seen (July–October) where it climbs among the hedgerows. The flowers stay open after dark, and sometimes never close during these light summer nights; they may attract moths.

GLOW-WORM *Lampyris noctiluca* A species of beetle, the female produces the cold, steady glow to attract the night-flying males. The light may now be seen (and from afar) on dry, grassy banks in limestone or chalk countryside where snails (on which the glow-worms feed) are plentiful.

WHITETHROAT *Sylvia communis* 400,000 pairs visit from April to September. This bird can still be heard at the start of July, voicing rather hurried three-second bursts of shrill warble, repeated ten or more times a minute. It was once the commonest of the migrant warblers, but numbers crashed in 1970, and by 1974 only a sixth of previous numbers visited; the cause was drought in the wintering grounds south of the Sahara. In spring, the cock sings while on a hesitant, 'dancing' display flight up and down from as high as 30 ft.

GARDEN TIGER *Arctia caja* This moth often comes to lighted windows in July. Its caterpillars are the familiar 'woolly bears' seen crossing garden paths in the summer months.

COMMON LIME *Tilia* x *europaea*
In July, the lime now comes into drooping clusters of heady blossom, attracting bees and hover-flies (it seems that bumble-bees may become 'drunk' on the nectar, as they are sometimes found on the ground below). This is a favourite tree of parks and roadsides, even if often infested with aphids, which exude honeydew on to the cars parked beneath! It is a hybrid between our native small- and large-leaved limes. (The former is found only in ancient woodlands; its leaves are only $1\frac{1}{2}$–$2\frac{1}{2}$ in. long, as compared with $2\frac{1}{2}$–4 in. for the hybrid lime, and with tufts of reddish hairs between the leaf veins.)

MEADOW BROWN *Maniola jurtina*
With its eyespots, this is a typical 'brown' butterfly, seen enjoying the July heat, mating, and laying its eggs on grasses. It may never leave its home field.

SPEAR THISTLE *Cirsium vulgare*
Many thistles now come into flower (July–October); this species is often seen on roadsides. As a group, thistles provide nectar, attracting bees and butterflies (including the painted lady).

ICHNEUMON FLY *Ophion luteus*
The ichneumons are parasites, using their long ovipositor (not a sting) to lay eggs inside caterpillars and grubs. They are most usually seen at lighted windows in summer (and spring).

BARN OWL *Tyto alba* 5000 pairs resident (except in north Scotland). The long, eerie shriek of this bird is sadly less common nowadays. It hunts over a small area of four square miles, so clearance of the old mixed countryside has been damaging; another cause of its decline is the build-up of pesticides in the food chain. It nests in large cavities, such as hollow trees, and old barns often had a round hole high at one end to invite these owls in to deal with the vermin. In the words of Gilbert White, it hunts by 'beating the fields like a setter dog', starting just on sunset when the mice begin to run (July, with its long dusks, is a good month to see it). However, it may begin to breed and screech its territorial call as early as February in some years.

MALLARD *Anas platyrhynchos*
40,000+ pairs resident (but 500,000 are also bred and released for wildfowlers). The mallard is one of our most familiar wild birds, yet few people notice the changes now taking place, for the male (drake) is assuming 'eclipse' plumage, beginning to resemble the drabber duck, except for his yellow bill. While feathers are being moulted and renewed, the drakes seek safer waters, and it will not be until October that their fine colouring is again generally seen. Prior to this, the spring courtship was lively to watch, with several drakes surrounding a duck and competing for her attention with bill-dipping, tail-raising and other displays. The first ducklings were seen in May, but now in July these may match their parents for size. This is a dabbling duck: it feeds from the surface, up-ending to strain mud and water, filling its belly with seeds and small invertebrates.

ARROWHEAD *Sagittaria sagittifolia*
Our aquatic plants were once land-based, having adapted their leaves to suit new surroundings. This plant, now in flower at the water's edge (July–August), has *three* kinds of leaves: aerial arrowheads, rounded floaters, and long, narrow, submerged leaves.

CRAYFISH *Astacus pallipes* Rather like a small lobster, the crayfish is a denizen of chalk streams and other lime-rich waters. Retiring by day, it may now be seen crawling slowly in July's long dusks.

CANADA GOOSE *Branta canadensis*
30,000 pairs resident. Introduced to decorate parks, this large bird can now be found wild, mainly south of the Scottish border. Usually seen grazing grass near inland waters, it will probably choose quiet, safe waters now for its moult. When disturbed, and in flight, it 'honks' loudly.

GNATS and MOSQUITOES (Family Culicidae) Closely related, these are members of the same family of flies. They are now frequently seen, with fragile legs and narrow wings. However, not all suck blood; the common gnat, *Culex pipiens*, takes the blood of birds, but never that of man. All have aquatic larvae.

WATER (or DAUBENTON'S) BAT *Myotis daubentoni* All bats are now rare, and occasional glimpses are the most that we can expect. This bat is likely to be seen on a summer's dusk, fluttering close to the surface of quiet, wooded waters, catching the dancing mayflies and even small surface fish.

KINGFISHER *Alcedo atthis* 5000 pairs resident, mainly south of Scotland. This bird, seen as a shy flash of exotic colour, relies on steep rough banks in which to burrow to make a rat-proof nest, and so suffers from river engineering work. Usually feeding by diving down from a perch over the water, the birds swallow their fishy prey head first, after beating them to flatten their spines. Kingfishers suffer greatly in cold winters when the streams freeze over.

COMMON HAWKER *Aeshna juncea* Many hawker dragonflies are now on the wing, rather later than their damselfly cousins. They have the habit of patrolling a pond, or even a woodland glade (they may be seen far from water). Rivals of their own kind are chased off, with torn wings resulting from aerial battles, while smaller, flying fry are caught and eaten. The larval stage is an equally fierce aquatic 'nymph'. Just before dawn in July, when fully grown, the nymph climbs up a stem, out of the water. There it pauses, its breathing pattern changing; the skin then splits, and the adult slowly pulls itself out, pumping blood into its wings to extend them. Once these are dry and tested, the hawker is able to fly.

HIMALAYAN BALSAM *Impatiens glandulifera* Seen now in flower (July–October), this plant flourishes even on the banks of polluted waters, perhaps because it can cope where others fail. The seed pods of balsams will 'pop' open explosively when ripe.

REED WARBLER *Acrocephalus scirpaceus* 40,000 pairs visit from April to October. The churring song of this bird is often heard from dense waterside cover; nearby, it will have slung its nest between reed stems. Unlike sedge warblers, these birds do not put on fat for migration, but stop to feed in Iberia en route to Africa.

BELL HEATHER *Erica cinerea* and LING (or HEATHER) *Calluna vulgaris* Although the moors attain their full heathery glory in August, these two species are now coming into flower (July–September), the former preferring somewhat drier ground (and so perhaps to be found along the better path). A mycorrhiza (a fungal association) helps them grow on these poor, acid soils by supplying nutrients. Ling's small leaves overlap in four rows; those of bell heather are in whorls of three (but whorls of shoots also look rather like leaves). During winter, large patches of heather will be burned on grouse moors; new shoots then grow to feed the birds, while the unburned tussocks give them shelter (this 'muirburn' creates a mosaic on the moor).

SILVER-STUDDED BLUE *Plebejus argus* On the wing in July and August at many heathy areas in the south, this butterfly lays its eggs on heather and gorse.

GREYLAG GOOSE *Anser anser* 100,000 birds. Scottish moors set with lochans are its natural breeding ground, heather and moss being the materials for the nests. But it may now also be seen far south, at flooded gravel pits. Its stock gave us farmyard geese—the resemblance is still strong, not only in appearance but also in their honking and cackling. These birds are now assembling to moult, accompanied by their young. In the wild, greylags mate for life, and greet each other with ritual postures at every meeting. Family parties will stay together for the winter, the young birds leaving the parents in spring.

HIVE (or HONEY) BEE *Apis mellifera* The bees now busy at the heather may fly here from hives several miles away, though in summer hives are often placed on remote moors, for heather honey is prized. However, they may be making 'beelines' from a 'wild' colony: when a new queen is about to hatch and the hive is overcrowded, the old queen will leave, taking a whirling swarm of many thousands of bees with her—and here on the hills, it may well be that she will evade recapture and start her own wild colony.

RED SQUIRREL *Sciurus vulgaris* This is our native squirrel, seen now in its brightest chestnut coat, with thin tail hairs and perhaps sparse ear tufts (it will moult in autumn to grow a long silky winter coat, with brownish-grey back, bushier tail and long ear tufts). Most likely to be seen shortly after a calm sunny dawn, this squirrel is located from afar by the noisy chewing of fir cones, but it is shy and will quickly hide on the opposite side of a trunk. It may now be active for 17 hours a day (compared with eight hours in winter). The red squirrel is found in mixed woodland, but mainly in old Scots pine woods; however, it has declined in central and southern Britain, perhaps following population crashes when seed harvests failed (the grey squirrel is then quick to take its place and prevent recolonization). The red squirrel makes a compact drey of interwoven twigs lined with grass, often about 20 ft from the ground, between the trunk and a side branch. It does not hibernate and is often seen in winter (though not in wet weather).

GRAYLING *Hipparchia semele* A strong, fast flier, this butterfly can be seen on dry grasslands and heaths in July and August. It spends much time on the ground, but is often unnoticed as it angles its wings to the sun so that very little shadow is cast. When approached, it instantly flies up, planes some yards away, then lands and again becomes 'invisible'.

HAREBELL *Campanula rotundifolia* This, the 'Scottish bluebell', flowers in dry grassland and heaths throughout Britain (July–September), although it is localized in the south-west.

TREE PIPIT *Anthus trivialis* Much like the meadow pipit, this bird (visiting from April to September) chooses open countryside scattered with trees or bushes for perching, so look for it now in young conifer plantations.

ANTLER MOTH *Cerapteryx graminis* Its caterpillars feed on grass, and they can appear, from time to time, in vast numbers on the high northern moors. This moth is on the wing throughout Britain in July and August.

SEA HOLLY *Eryngium maritimum* Many wild flowers are now to be seen on the coast, and the sea holly is one of the most beautiful (July–September). It is an umbellifer, related to cow parsley. It grows on quick-draining shingle or sandy beaches and dunes, and has waxy, spiny leaves to reduce water loss.

AVOCET *Recurvirostra avosetta* 200 pairs resident. Strictly protected, avocets breed at a few coastal sites in East Anglia, notably Havergate Island, Suffolk, where they can now be watched from hides. Here the water level is artificially maintained to suit them. They feed by sweeping their upturned bills from side to side in the water to sift out small invertebrates. After breeding, avocets become mobile and can be seen wintering in estuaries in milder south Devon, for example. They can be rather noisy birds.

PILOT WHALE *Globicephala melaena* As with other whales, this is most likely to be seen, but never regularly, off the Shetlands in July and August, usually in schools up to a score strong. Pilot whales are still, sadly, slaughtered in the Faroes, driven ashore by a line of boats to be killed on the beach. They are sometimes stranded on our coasts—in Britain, by ancient custom, stranded whales become 'royal fish', the property of the sovereign.

SEA ASTER *Aster tripolium* Like a fleshy-leaved garden Michaelmas daisy, the sea aster brightens the salt marshes and sea cliffs from now until autumn. Usually the flowers have both central yellow disc florets and surrounding purple ray florets, but some plants are ray-less.

COMMON STARFISH *Asterias rubens* In some years, summer storms wash thousands of small starfish up along east-coast beaches. This reddish-brown starfish spends its time low on the shore. Unlike others, it does not burrow, but moves slowly across the sand, keeping a foothold with sucker-like 'tube feet'. With their aid, its arms can grasp a bivalve shell and slowly force it open. And as it can extrude its stomach through its central mouth to begin digestion inside its prey's body, it will also attack sea snails.

COMMON BRITTLESTAR *Ophiothrix fragilis* Though clearly related to starfish, the brittlestar crawls along the shore with sinuous movements of its five spiny arms. Brittlestars are most commonly discovered under rocks and stones low down on the shore.

MACKEREL *Scomber scombrus* This is now the peak of the inshore mackerel season, and they can be found (often in large shoals) all round the coast of Britain in these summer months. Fishing for them with a line from boat or beach forms part of many a happy holiday memory. Mackerel began arriving in May and June when the coastal waters warmed up (a sea temperature of 15°C seems to be the trigger), and they will stay until September or October (perhaps even later). They then swim off to find warmer waters or may descend to the seabed, where sluggishly (with food being scarce) they virtually 'hibernate' until the spring.

SEA-LAVENDER *Limonium vulgare* Wild flowers often chart different zones of the salt marsh, reflecting the regularity of tidal coverage. The sea-lavender is now in flower (July–August), rather closer inshore than the sea aster's zone. (Rock sea-lavender, *L. binervosum*, a rather similar relation, grows on cliffs and other drier coastal habitats.)

GREAT SKUA *Stercorarius skua* 2500 pairs visit. Breeding in the far north, mainly in the Shetlands where it is known as the 'bonxie', this bird arrives in May to nest in moorland not too far from the sea. This powerfully-beaked bird is a bullying pirate, pure and simple, and is now at its boldest. It will hurl itself at the head of any intruder—bird, sheep or man. Skuas prey on all cliff birds, taking their eggs and young, and even harass returning parents so that in panic they disgorge their food, which is caught up by the skua. They will also take puffins, blinded by the harsh new light, on the way out of their burrows, and will even turn cannibal if another skua is injured. (Always an exciting sight, there is often a notable passage of pomarine skuas, *S. pomarinus*, off Beachy Head in May.)

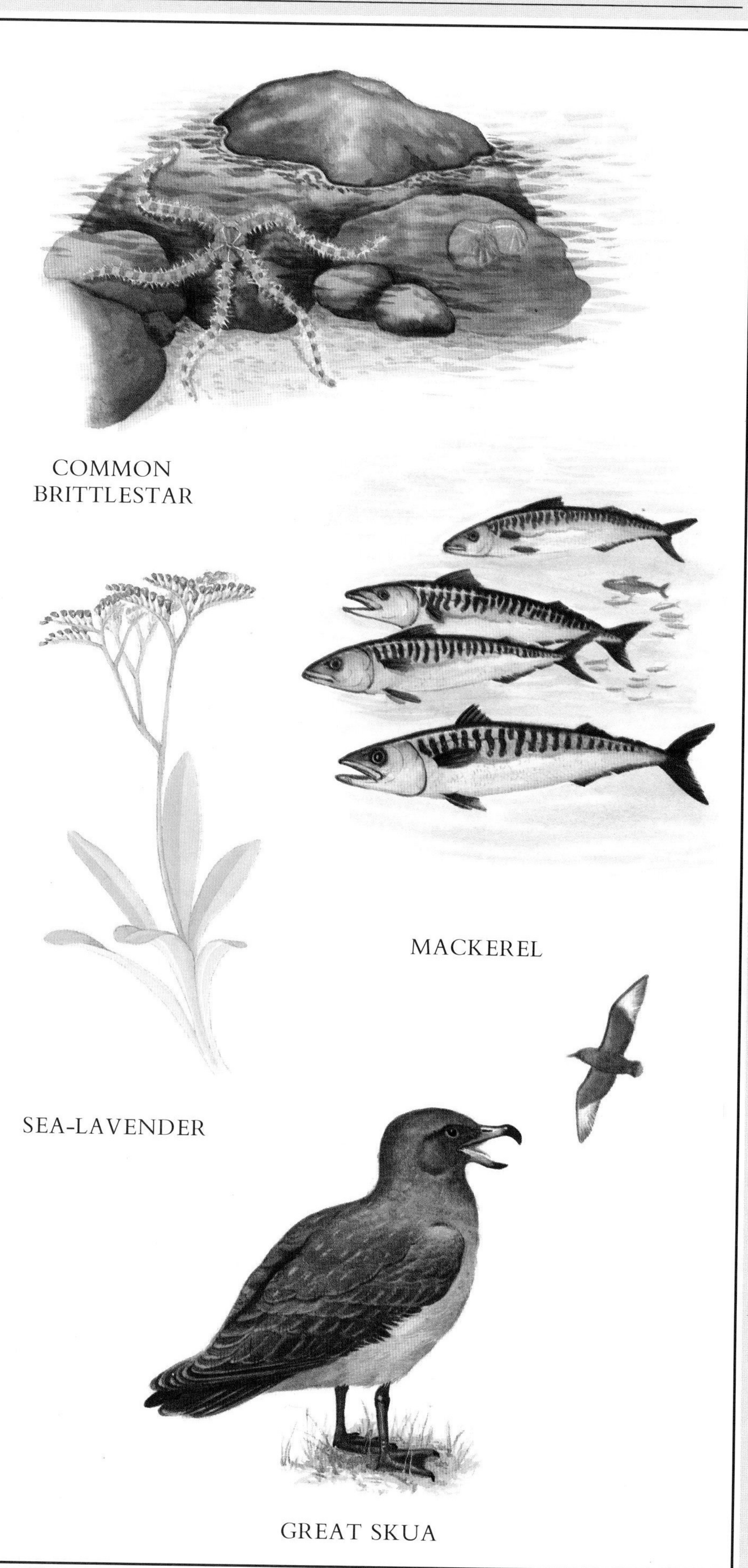

COMMON BRITTLESTAR

MACKEREL

SEA-LAVENDER

GREAT SKUA

AUGUST

In this, the traditional month for the harvest, the skies may be rather variable. Indeed, August can be quite a wet month, and is less likely to have long spells of sunny holiday weather than July. The moors are now deeply purpled with flowering heather at its peak, while on 12 August, 'the Glorious Twelfth', the grouse shooting season begins. However, morning mists across the meadows, ripening hazel nuts in the lanes, and the first ripe blackberries all presage the coming of autumn.

Clues that August is past the peak of summer are everywhere to be seen—in the ripening berries and seeds, the congregating clans of house martins and swallows, and other pre-migration stirrings of the birds. Interesting sightings are made at reservoirs, estuaries and other ornithological magnets. But even among the blackbirds and other birds which do not migrate, there is a great loosening of the territorial ties.

Of bird song itself, that of the robin tends to strengthen late in the month, though sounding rather wistful and lacking the boldness of spring. This bird is the most reliable of our songsters—territory is held all year round, and so the song is heard for most of the year. The wren and the dunnock may also be heard again in August.

August is, of course, the traditional harvest month, and it was mainly for this reason, rather than for any weather considerations, that it became the main school holiday month also. In the past, the village children were recruited to help with the harvest—even the youngest child could play a useful role in keeping the pigeons and crows away from the gleanings—and the first general Education Acts of Victorian times, providing primary school education for all, took account of this.

Sea holly pioneering on to a sandy beach. It is one of our most handsome wild flowers; the flowers brighten in hue as the month progresses.

For those lucky to visit them, the moors are at the peak of their beauty in August, with the purple heather rolling like a sea under clear blue skies. Normally the sky is rather pale with dust at this time, but the frequent rain of the hills can clear the air.

Rainbows are created by simple optics. The raindrops act as prisms—they absorb the sunlight but reflect it back out, splitting it into its elements on the way. The

total effect of this is an arc of colours, the blue below the red. Obviously, rainbows can only be seen with the sun low and at one's back, and secondary rainbows may sometimes be seen above the first, with the colours reversed. Moon rainbows are also possible, but are much fainter.

As suits a holiday month, the coast is often sunnier than inland in August, especially in the south. East-coast resorts also live up to their bracing reputation, with a brisk sea breeze common in August. The land heats up faster than the sea; thus, in sunshine, warmed and lighter air rises over the land, drawing in air from the sea. This breeze is noticed first in the late morning, becoming strongest in mid-afternoon, and dying away again during the early evening. In the old days, the coastal smacks took advantage of this phenomenon—they set out before dawn on a land breeze, fished, and then caught the sea breeze back again, to sell gloriously fresh fish for high tea.

The rising air over the land is also much appreciated by swifts for its reliable lift. The birds travel long distances to take advantage of and feed in such favourable natural weather conditions as this. They will also follow the 'streets' of warm air, which give lines of cumulus clouds inland.

The harvest is itself a sign that the peak of summer is past, and plant energies are going into seed rather than leaf. This field of barley, with the heads now tumbling, is well on the way to ripening. It is a northerly field, for the barley would most likely have already been taken in further towards the south.

SULTRY PERIODS

July's weather may continue into August, becoming rather unsettled compared with June, but it is often a wetter and cloudier month. The period of the sultry, uncomfortable dog-days can linger from July and continue past the first week of August, but as in July, westerly depressions may bring spells of dull, rainy weather especially to the north and west, although these lows may have dried out by the time they reach easterly areas.

The temperature of the surface layers of the sea around Britain is now at its highest; the average may be 17°C in the English Channel, for example, although shallow, sheltered bays and estuaries can be much higher, the water being warmed by the wide mud-flats or sand exposed to the sun at low tide.

The air can be quite humid, and this tends to keep the nights warm in August, at least in southerly areas. But the nights are lengthening quite noticeably now, and in Scotland there may already be an autumnal feel to the evenings before the end of the month, with valley temperatures down to freezing, especially if the air has swung around to arrive from the north or north-east.

In the high Pennines, farmers consider that the grazing season is over at the end of this month. The grass continues to grow, and will do so for another month, but the soil is now becoming much wetter and the grass is liable to poaching by the animals in many fields.

Overall, August is quite a wet month. Central and south-east England receive 9–11 per cent of the year's rainfall, compared with 8 per cent in September. However, this may not be lengthy spells of rain to ruin a holiday, because the tendency is for short, heavy thundery showers at this time of year, which quickly pass.

August in Britain is not guaranteed to be either the sunniest or the warmest month of the year. It was, however, the harvest month when the dates of school holidays were settled in Victorian times—children out of school could help, if only by scurrying back and forth with fresh jugs of tea, or gleaning the cut stubble for dropped grains. This map shows the average number of days per year with more than nine hours of bright sunshine; the amount of sunshine also reflects the geography to some extent.

Over 60 days
50–60 days
40–50 days
30–40 days
Under 30 days

FINE DAYS AND DEWY NIGHTS

An anticyclone, or high-pressure area, is a large mass of sinking air. It is generally drier and more settled than a depression, and its pressure differences are slight over a large area, hence winds are light. In summer it can give blue skies, for clouds usually form where warm air rises and cools, though not all fine summer days rely on this genesis.

In winter, an anticyclone can again give cloudless skies, which may be accompanied by biting cold. Alternatively, it may mean a spell of dull quiet weather with low cloud, because a widespread temperature inversion is created. Ground warmed by the sun warms the air above it, which then rises, cooling as it does so. But when air is compressed, it also warms, and if the sinking, compressing air of the anticyclone is warmer than the air rising from the ground, it will block it. Cooler air is thus trapped below warm, and clouds may form along this 'inversion'.

Dews are an indication of warm summer days to follow, for they are common in the clear calm nights typical of anticyclonic weather—'Dew at night, the day will be bright'. They are likely in August and may benefit smaller plants in dry weather, although little dew falls if the ground is very

A dew-pond on the chalk downlands of Sussex. Although some dew-ponds date from recent times, others are thought to be of quite considerable age.

dry. The reason for this will become clear.

As we have already seen, warm air can hold more water vapour than cold, so that as it cools it is likely to reach a temperature at which it is saturated: its dewpoint. A further fall will mean that droplets of water will appear, seen as cloud in the sky or as fog or mist at ground level. Dew is formed in much the same way.

On a clear calm evening after a sunny day, the warmed ground surface cools by radiating heat up and away. At the same time, some of its dampness evaporates into the air alongside to mix with the vapour already held by the air. This air also chills, and if there is no strong breeze to mix it with higher layers, it can reach its dewpoint, whereupon it has to release some of its moisture. Dew 'falls', not in the way of rain, but by condensing from the air nearest the ground. In fact, our heaviest dews come in September, when the ground is really damp from the rain that fell in August.

Although summer dews dry out a couple of hours after sunrise, with the new dew rarely falling until half an hour before sunset even in very moist air, in winter the dew may not dry out in the daytime at all. In very cold winter spells, dew can even be deposited as feathery hoar frost.

Dew falls more easily on grass. Bare soil cools slowly, for the warmth it loses is replenished from below. The top of the lawn, though, is insulated from this heat store by the blanket of still air held by its stems and leaves. Being cooler, dew is thus more likely to fall on a lawn, and even more so on long grass.

On the high, dry chalk downlands, 'dew-ponds' were important sources of water for sheep and shepherd alike. They are saucer-like depressions, perhaps 20 ft across and originally lined with straw topped with trodden clay (concrete is used nowadays). This is impervious and also acts as an insulator against the warmth of the soil. It collects rain, but damp, cooling air also releases its dew on to the cold surface of the clay or pool. However, they were cannier than that in olden times. . . . After a quiet warm day, as the air cools it becomes denser and sinks. There can therefore be a noticeable, if slight, breeze down some hillsides at dusk. For this reason, dew-ponds were often made in a shallow gully just below the brow of the down, so that a continuous flow of sinking moisture-laden air passed over, replenishing them more generously than the normal fall of dew.

THE ROCKY SHORE

Under the hot August sun, the rock pool glistens like a jewel on the shore. It is a new world. But the pool is not simply a guarded refuge for ocean life when the tide is out, for conditions are harsh and often extreme within its confines.

With a strong breeze on a sunny day, evaporation makes a shallow pool highly salty. However, the tide sluicing in can reduce that salinity back to the ocean level in a few seconds, while heavy showers of rain running off the surrounding rocks can quickly dilute a small pool almost to fresh water, creating a serious hazard for animals and plants adapted to life in the sea. The water can also become quite warm under the midday sun in August. Earlier in the year, the sea is usually at its coldest in March, but on winter nights the pool becomes bitterly cold, and it may even freeze.

A subtler threat is posed by the respiration of the animals and seaweeds living in the pool. They all consume oxygen from the water, giving out carbon dioxide. Plants can balance the supply by taking in carbon dioxide for photosynthesis and releasing oxygen, but only in daylight. At night, the oxygen of a small pool may become depleted and the accumulating carbon dioxide can turn the water dangerously acidic.

A shore crab feeding on mussels. Ill-warned of the danger, these molluscs gape open when covered by the tide, making them easy prey for crabs.

The length of time for which the pool holds its own identity depends on its height up the shore. The tides run twice a day, but rise highest and reach lowest in the monthly 'spring' tides (unconnected to the season), and move least in the 'neaps'. A pool at the top of the shore may be uncovered for much of the month.

An exotic ark of animals seeks refuge in these rock pools. Some, such as the beadlet sea anemone seen high up on the shore, are resident all year round. Despite appearances to the contrary, they are of course animals, and are armed with stinging cells at the base of their tentacles. These serve the same purpose as a spider's web, immobilizing hapless victims, even small fish that come too close. Others, such as winkles, are grazers. These and other shellfish can be distinguished not only by their shell shape and colour, but also by their position on the shore, for this reflects the amount of time they are able to withstand exposure to the air when the tide ebbs.

Prawns leave the deeper sea for rock pools in spring, and often choose those quite high up the shore. Being transparent, they are difficult to see. In summer the females may be seen 'in berry', carrying pale clusters of eggs. Lobsters, too, may visit the sheltered summer pools at the foot of the shore.

Shore crabs remain on the shore all year; their relatives, the edible crabs, which can be recognized by their more rounded shape, are sometimes seen in pools on the lower shore in summer. The sea hare, a slug-like creature, is also a summer visitor, come to graze on the green seaweeds.

Blennies are common rock-pool fish. From April to June, they may be joined by 15-spined sticklebacks, especially in weedy rock pools. The normally green male takes on a bluish tint and builds and guards a nest of seaweed containing the young—behaviour similar to that of his red-bellied cousin, the three-spined stickleback, more often seen in inland streams and ponds. The summer pools may also contain young lumpsucker fish. Looking rather like tadpoles, they attach themselves to rocks in the swirling waters with a belly sucker.

Seaweeds festoon the rocks and often invade the pool. While many are a dullish green in colour, some display vivid hues. Bright green weeds inhabit many of the higher pools in summer; these may often dry out and the weeds are bleached white. Some small red weeds can vary from deep red to pale yellow, depending on their exposure to the bleaching sunshine. Changes of this kind are about the only colour changes to be seen on the shore; there are none of the massed seasonal foliage changes of the plants growing on land, though there are subtle seasonal differences to be noticed with some of the species.

The edible carragheen, a red seaweed, is at its best in midsummer. However, it is weakened by producing spores, and the autumn gales frequently wreak havoc on its carpets across the rocks lower down on the shore. It seems to show a seasonal movement of a kind.

Many of the smaller seaweeds are quite short-lived, lasting perhaps less than a year. Their spores are carried by the sea to all parts of the shore, and they grow where conditions suit them. Thus, some of those vivid green weeds, which can almost fill the pools higher up the shore in summer, are found restricted to the lower shore in winter. In winter, the sea is usually warmer than the air, and these weeds can only grow where the tide exposes them for the shortest time. Alternatively, in winter some threadlike red weeds move via their spores higher up the shore, seeming to require exposure to all the light they can get.

A blenny lies still in the rock pool, very well camouflaged against the green and limy red seaweeds and the chequered shadows cast by the sunshine.

Unlike the beadlet anemone, this opelet or 'snakelocks' anemone is unable to withdraw its tentacles fully, and so seeks some protection from the waves; it is usually found in cracks in the bottom of rock pools.

At low tide, seaweeds on the rocks at the foot of the shore are uncovered. Other species, which cannot survive exposure to the drying wind, can also be seen in the tidal channels. Here the long strings of thong weed can be seen, its pliability allowing it to move with the swirls of water and so escape damage.

HARVEST SCIENCE

By now, the lambs will have been weaned from their mothers' milk and be flocked separately. Between 14 June and 5 September, all sheep must be immersed in antibiotic liquid against scab, a skin disease. They hate this dipping process—this year's lambs on their first run are the only ones to take it quietly.

Wheat, probably the most profitable crop on British arable farms, is harvested now. Spring barley may also be harvested from August through to September, but a farm will plan to stagger its sowing (and hence its harvesting) in the same way as it does its calving and lambing, in order to spread the work load—and improve the chances in the annual gamble with the British summer.

The state of the grain in the ear is crucial. The traditional method of testing it was to bite it, judging its state from the texture, but a modern electronic moisture meter is more reliable. The grain must be fairly dry with a moisture content of below 16 per cent to take safely into store, otherwise it will rot. It can be harvested 'greener' and dried with a fan drier, but this adds to the cost and dents the profits. The grain may also char in the heat and be useless for malting if it is barley; nor is seed corn likely to germinate after such treatment.

A warm spell before harvest may give grain with only 12 per cent moisture. On the other hand, a few gloomy weeks can give 25 per cent by the time the normal date is reached. If the wet continues, the grain, particularly wheat, may sprout while it is still in the ear.

Another hazard is a thunderstorm bringing a heavy shower of rain or hail to flatten or 'lay' the crop. Much grain will therefore be lost when harvesting time arrives.

Drying out is a natural process and is part of the rhythm of seed production. If a dew or light rain falls on an already self-dried crop, there is little harm done—half an hour's morning sunshine can put all to rights again. But nature gives only a couple of days' grace between the crop that is ideally ripe and one in which deterioration is already beginning to affect the unharvested heads.

The situation can change by the hour—and starting from the minute the dew has dried off the crop in the sun, the combine harvester may be at work late into the evening, Saturdays and Sundays and the bank holiday at the end of the month included.

Larger farms may possess their own

With the weather right and the grain ready, taking in the wheat harvest can be a day-long activity. Wheat straw is less nutritious than barley, but some may be baled for litter.

combine harvesters—only they can afford to have so much capital locked up for such infrequent use. Smaller farms will hire theirs, or hire a harvesting gang; this is another factor in timing the sowing date earlier in the year. Such things as increasing the spread of fertilizer in earlier months now pay off—or may not, since although more fertilizer means higher yields, it also delays the ripening of the grain.

Combine harvesters, as their name suggests, carry out what were once several separate operations. In the old days, the standing corn was cut at its foot with a sickle or scythe, the cut stalks being bundled into sheaves which were loosely stacked together in 'stooks' to dry out further. The sheaves were then carted to the barn to be stored until winter, when they were threshed.

Threshing was a long dusty job, hated by all. The sheaves were pitchforked down on to the hard-surfaced threshing floor in the centre of the barn, between the facing pairs of doors at each side. Here they were bashed with flails, which were simply strips of wood nailed to leather belts. This process separated the grain from the chaff. Then the mix was winnowed—that is, the doors of the barn were opened wide on both sides to let the breeze through, while the threshed grain was tossed into the air, allowing the light chaff to be blown away. The grain was then swept up and taken to be stored in the granary, which was raised on toadstool-shaped supports to keep out rats and mice. The straw was stored at the opposite end of the barn, to be used to litter the animal pens.

The farmyard barn was cleverly built for its job. It often had a small window high up on one side—an open invitation to a barn owl to take up residence and keep down the vermin.

In the past, the harvest involved the whole village; women and children helped stook the sheaves and afterwards glean the fields for fallen grain. But today's combine harvester does all these jobs in one pass of the field. It cuts the corn, taking it in stalk and all; internal gadgetry shakes the grain loose, blows away the chaff, and ejects the spent straw. From time to time, a trailer will be pulled up alongside to receive a deep load of grain, piped from the combine's belly. If too damp, its first stop may be at the fan drier in the barn. A baler will later be brought in to collect up the loose straw left on the field, or it will simply be burned where it lies.

THE NORTH YORK MOORS

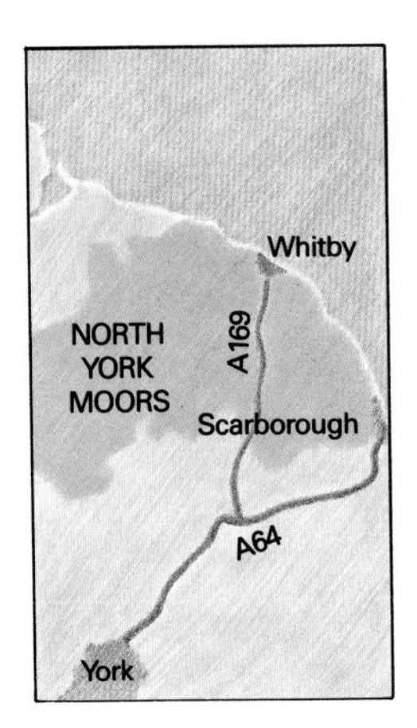

The North York Moors National Park encloses England's largest area of heather moorland; the Park itself covers about 345,000 acres. It is a highly varied area, however, and as well as heather moors there are many examples of woodland, while lakes and rivers give added interest.

From afar, a moor seems to be a dull wilderness; it lacks even the picturesque crags of the mountains. Yet it is a detailed and intricate habitat. Furthermore, man has played a part in its creation.

At the end of the Ice Age, along with the lowlands, Britain's moorlands became tree-covered to 2000 ft. Early settlers gradually cleared them for (and by) grazing, though occasionally a tree can be found growing, somehow safe from the teeth of the sheep, which is a pointer to those now-distant times. By and large, though, grazing kept the moors clear, aided by climatic changes which increased the amount of rain falling on high ground. The soil's goodness was thus leached out and the acid bite given by the grits and other hard hill rocks intensified.

Hardy heather and bilberry can grow in these bleak areas, for their roots house fungal threads which help them gain nutrients. But even they cannot survive in waterlogged soil, and so the wetter areas become the home of springy bogs. Bog mosses can flourish in cool wet climates, surviving on slight nutrients, and will soak up the rain like a sponge, growing to clothe hollows and inch up hillsides. They fill the ditches of some of the side roads on the North York Moors. Below the vivid green of the bog surface, the dead mosses lie largely unrotted in the airless acid conditions, yielding spongy peat.

Changes in local conditions create a mosaic across the moor. Bog survives in places, picked out from afar by the white dancing heads of cotton-grass which can grow on this wet substrate. Alongside, where the peat has dried out and the mosses have died, heather will grow. This dry peat with its heather cap can also be seen along roadsides.

The North York Moors, in fact, consist mainly of dryish peat today, and they carry England's largest expanse of heather moorland. Here the flowers are at their best in August, when their massed purple ranks create one of Europe's grandest botanical spectacles. Bilberry and perhaps some bracken, growing on quickly draining slopes, also vary the pattern, and there is usually plenty of grass, even on 'heather' moors.

The seemingly featureless bog also offers botanical variety, but it is a very delicate habitat, easily damaged by treading, and care must be taken when viewing it. Cranberry throws threadlike stems across the surface, barely noticed until its berries ripen from August onwards, while on many moorland bogs, small rosettes of sundew may be seen on the surface.

There is plenty of insect life associated with moors and bogs. (Enough, certainly, in Scotland and other places, to make a nightmare of summer camping—and force the red deer up to higher ground—although not all of these insects bite.) Bumble-bees, and other mining bees and wasps, dig into dry peat. However, the honey bees which hum around the heather usually come from hives taken to the moor's edge in spring (though there are also wild colonies). There are many spiders, and green grasshoppers are often heard, with a fast ticking song. Adders may also be found, but they are rarely dangerous, retiring when footsteps approach.

Dunlins, golden plovers and curlews breed on these moors, and in August the curlew's haunting call may still be heard, although waders in general tend to leave their summering grounds promptly after breeding. Merlins are sometimes seen hunting meadow pipits and other small birds, while an occasional peregrine may attack the grouse.

These moors are managed for grouse, and the shooting butts, where the grouse-shooters hide, can be seen. Grouse need old tussocks of heather for shelter, but feed on the tender green shoots of the younger plants. To obtain this mixture, grouse moors are often regularly fired in swathes—a distinctive sign of man's hand on this apparent wilderness.

Only 400 pairs of hen harriers (*Circus cyaneus*) breed in Britain, traditionally on moors and marshes (but now sometimes in young plantations also). Harriers have a low, slow, hunting glide, zigzagging into the wind, while searching avidly for prey scuffling in the shelter of the plants below.

BRITAIN'S MOORLANDS
Scotland and Wales have moors aplenty, so here are listed some of the finest moorlands in England, plus (for those in the south and south-east) a number of heaths:

1 Harbottle Crags, near Holystone, Northumberland.
2 Haworth Moor, south-west of Keighley, West Yorkshire.
3 Cannock Chase, near Stafford, Staffordshire.
4 The Long Mynd, Church Stretton, Shropshire.
5 Breckland, near Thetford, Norfolk.
6 Frensham Country Park, near Farnham, Surrey.
7 Ashdown Forest, near Crowborough, East Sussex.
8 New Forest, Hampshire. Fine stretches of heather.
9 Hartland Moor, Isle of Purbeck, and other Dorset heaths.
10 Exmoor, Devon.
11 Dartmoor, Devon.
12 Bodmin Moor, Cornwall.
13 The Lizard Peninsula, Cornwall.
***North York Moors**, North Yorkshire.

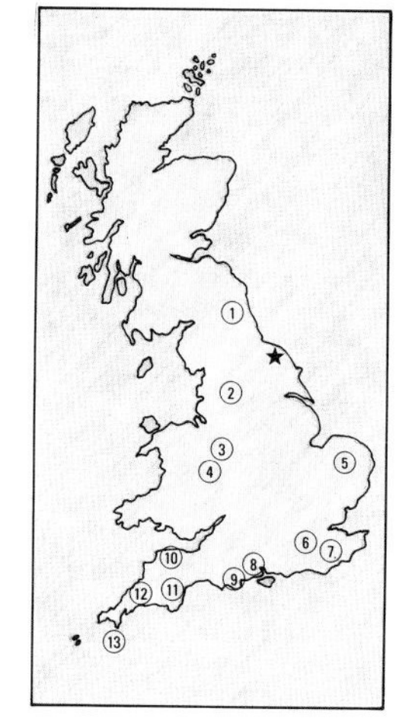

Although the North York Moors carry the largest expanses of heather moorland in England, by no means all of the area is moorland, as we see here.

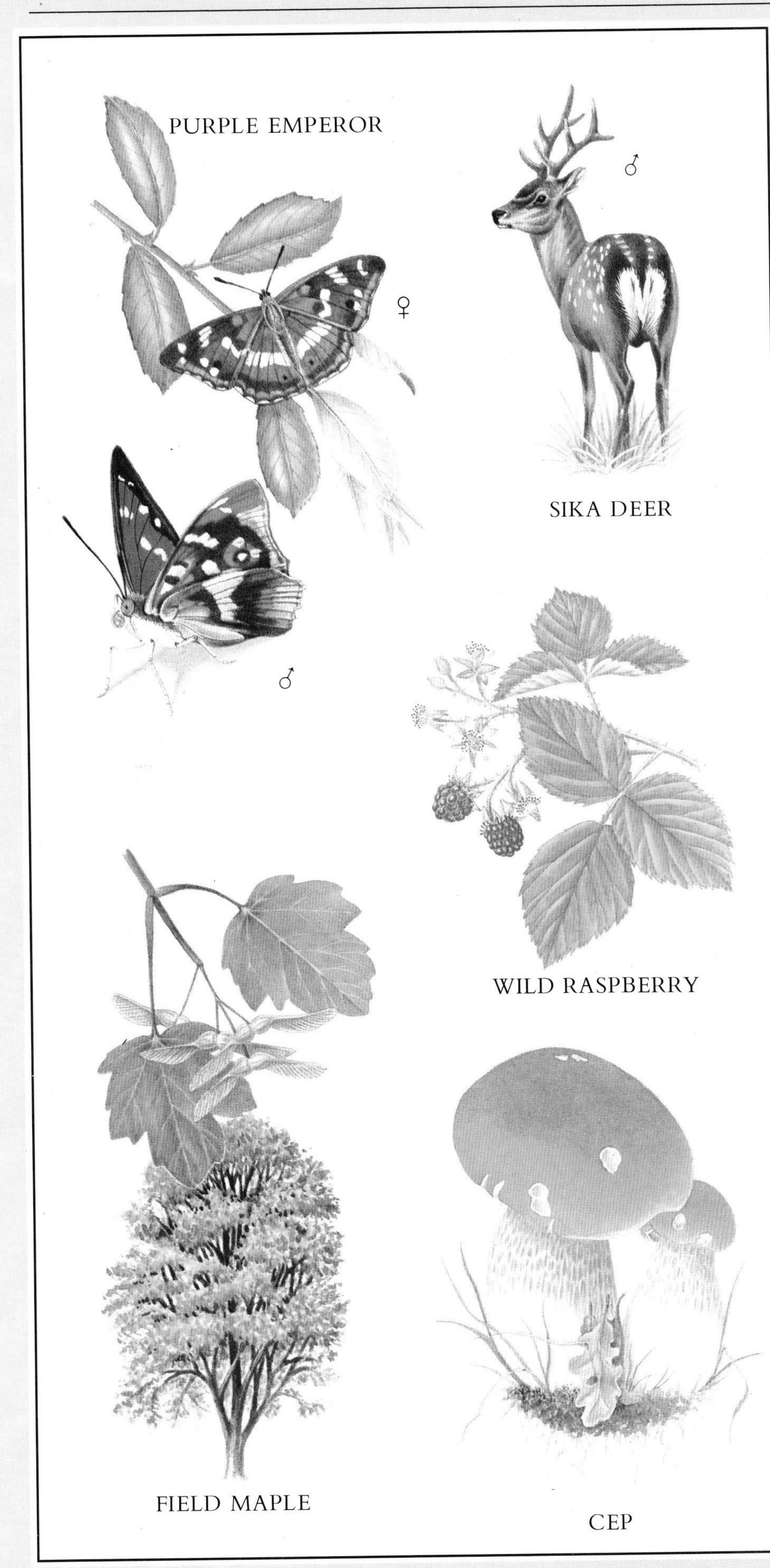

PURPLE EMPEROR *Apatura iris* A sign of high summer in the sultry wood is the sight of a majestic purple emperor on the wing (July–August). The females are seen soaring and gliding between the trees; the males may be enticed down to sip the juices of decaying carrion, but often station themselves at canopy height, around a 'master' tree. There is an ecological reason for this: the females lay their eggs on sallow bushes, one at a time over a very wide area. If there was not some deep instinct to congregate, mating would be hard to achieve.

SIKA DEER *Cervus nippon* Closely related to our larger native red deer (with which they may interbreed), sika deer were introduced in 1860 to a few deer parks, from whence some escaped. They are now established in parts of Dorset and the New Forest, as well as a few places further north and in Scotland. In August, the stags are seen with their antlers still in velvet; this will be shed by early September before the rut, which begins at the end of the month. During the rut, the stag's territory is marked with thrashed bushes and frayed tree bark, and fights between rivals for the harems of hinds are common. The calves are born in May and June.

WILD RASPBERRY *Rubus idaeus* Found growing wild in wet, rocky woods and heaths, this plant will now be bearing fruit, very much like the garden raspberry—in fact, cultivated varieties were bred from this native shrub. (A rather similar plant, the stone bramble, *R. saxatilis*, is found only in the north; its fruit has fewer and larger segments.)

FIELD MAPLE *Acer campestre* A native tree found in woods and hedgerows south of Cumbria, this is often smaller than the sycamore. Seen now, the fruit pairs carry their wings in a straight line (the sycamore's are ranged at an angle). In the autumn, the foliage of the field maple can flame yellow.

CEP *Boletus edulis* Lest we forget that the year is ageing, we now see the first autumnal fungi. Cep is a prized species, considered by French chefs to be the tastiest edible fungus.

SYCAMORE *Acer pseudoplatanus* Though widespread, this is not a native species, but was introduced hundreds of years ago. Widely planted for ornament and shelter (its resistance to exposure has made it a favourite tree for sheltering farms on the high moors), the sycamore has also been so successful in gaining new ground with its winged seeds that it is now found in many different habitats. At this time of year, its leaves are often blotched with black 'tar spot' disease, though this seems less marked in areas of high air pollution! Its winged fruits are now developing; these will be hard and ripe by October.

PURPLE HAIRSTREAK *Quercusia quercus* This small butterfly is likely to be seen only through binoculars; it flies in the canopy of oak woodland in July and August.

COMMON DOG VIOLET *Viola riviniana* The derogatory name 'dog' was often given to any flower which does not have a scent. (Botanically, however, that description includes many habitat-localized violets.) This species is seen in woods, hedgerows and some grasslands—one oddity is that, after flowering in the spring (March–May), it may now again be seen in flower (August–October), though perhaps lacking petals. These second, summer blooms are self-fertilizing.

MERVEILLE-DU-JOUR *Griposia aprilina* Perhaps hard to spot, for its greenish wings expertly camouflage it against the lichen-covered bark, this handsome moth (whose name, when translated, means 'day's wonder') is now worth looking for, flying from August to October, mainly around oak trees.

DEATH CAP *Amanita phalloides* An extremely poisonous fungus (the damaged liver is already beyond cure once the symptoms of illness develop), the death cap may already be seen in beech and oak woods. It may be thought to resemble a mushroom, but remember its woodland habitat, and note its whitish gills and the 'cup' at the base of the stalk, a remnant of a membrane which ruptured as the fungus enlarged.

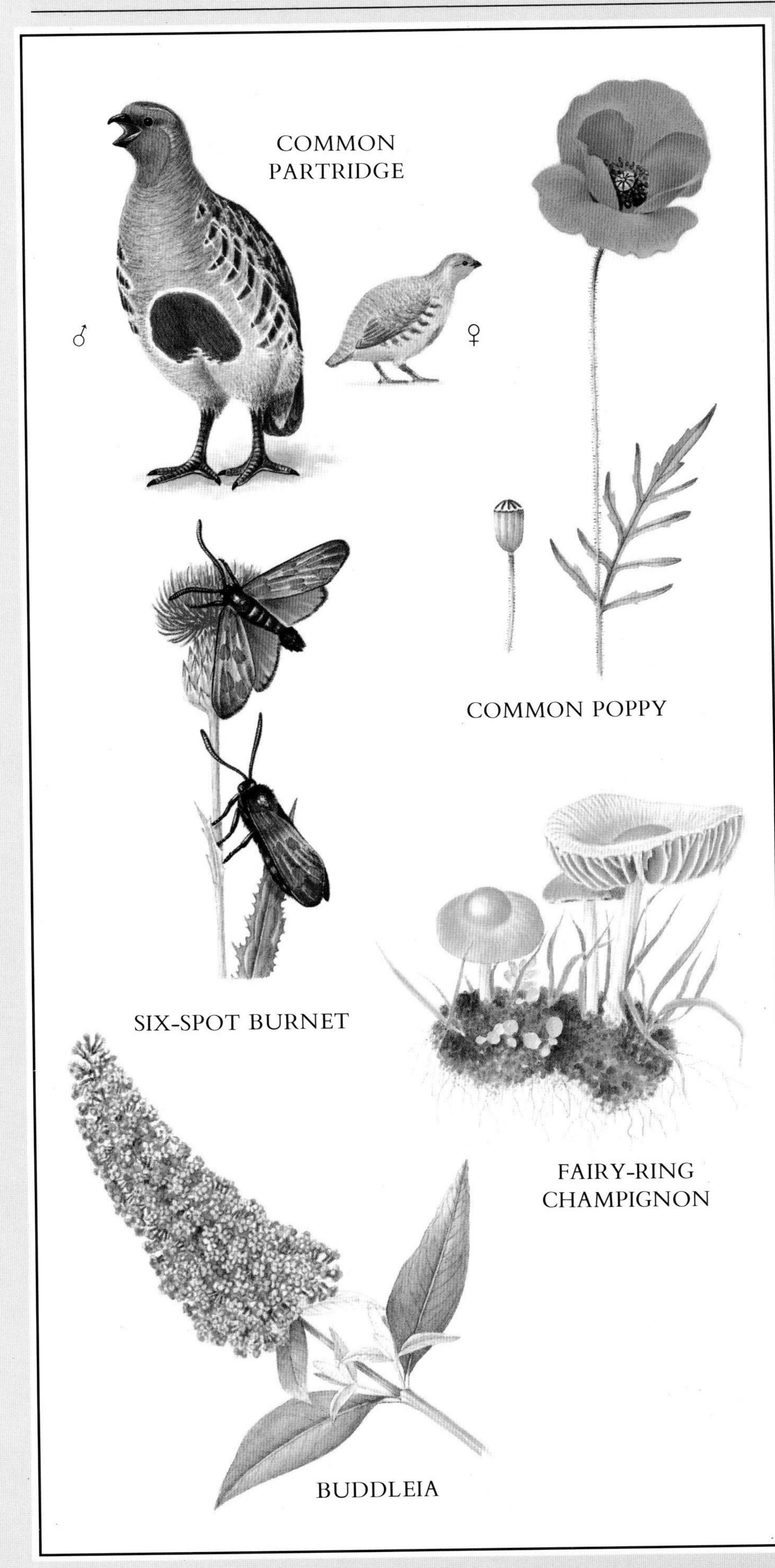

COMMON (or GREY) PARTRIDGE *Perdix perdix* 200,000 pairs resident. Between now and January, when the cocks become territorial, this game bird is seen in family flocks or 'coveys'. The shooting season stretches from the beginning of September to the end of January; the birds take explosive flight when disturbed (with an alarmed 'krikrik' cry). Numbers have fallen in recent years, but not simply from shooting. The young birds seen in May require a high-protein insect diet, gleaned from long grass—modern ploughing and spraying up to the hedge robs them of this. However, the Game Conservancy has found that numbers can be boosted (and those of wild flowers and butterflies) by leaving a strip around the field unsprayed, with no noticeable effect on crop yields. Ground roosting, these birds avoid winter frost pockets.

COMMON (or FIELD) POPPY *Papaver rhoeas* This is now coming into head, although many flowers are still seen (continuing well into autumn). The seed pods scatter vast quantities of seed, which can remain dormant until deep ploughing brings them to the surface.

SIX-SPOT BURNET *Zygaena filipendulae* A day-flying moth, widespread over much of Britain, the 'six-spot' is our most common species of burnet; it is found in grassy, flowery places, and is now perhaps at the thistle heads.

FAIRY-RING CHAMPIGNON *Marasmius oreades* Often clearly seen on garden lawns and other grassy places, this fungus feeds on organic matter in the soil, releasing nitrates which promote a lush, green growth of grass. The first patch extends into a circle as the fungus grows; the 'mushrooms' appear at the pioneering edge.

BUDDLEIA (or BUTTERFLY BUSH) *Buddleia davidii* Now in flower (June–September), the buddleia shrub attracts peacock, tortoiseshell and red admiral butterflies, as well as hover-flies. It was introduced here from China at the end of the last century, and has now spread over much of the country, growing remarkably well on waste ground.

SMALL WHITE *Pieris rapae* Passing winter as a chrysalis, the ubiquitous small white is on the wing in April; the first of the new broods appears in July, with another overlapping it and flying now in August and September. This butterfly has a smooth green caterpillar, seen on plants of the cabbage family.

GARDEN (or CROSS) SPIDER *Araneus diadematus* There are many web-spinning spiders: the garden spider spins a familiar web, with a radiating 'catching spiral' which is coated with adhesive gum. After waiting in cover, the spider will quickly rush down to swaddle any insect that has become stuck. A web is worth inspecting in detail, for there are a number of variations between species: for example, the web of *Meta segmentata* (another orb-web spider) lacks the central platform; there are also differences in the way the webs are angled. Spiders usually continue being active until November, spinning an egg cocoon before themselves succumbing to the ageing year.

AUTUMN HAWKBIT *Leontodon autumnalis* One of the daisy family, this plant's name reminds us that the seasons are swiftly rushing by. The first flowers were seen in June, but this plant will continue flowering on many grasslands well into October.

RED-LEGGED PARTRIDGE *Alectoris rufa* 100,000 pairs resident. Found south of the Lancashire–Yorkshire border, these birds often occur in more open areas than the grey partridge. Although it tends to scuttle into cover rather than fly up, this bird has been introduced to improve sporting stocks, and in some areas outnumbers the grey. The red-legged partridge lays two clutches of eggs.

GREAT GREEN BUSH CRICKET *Tettigonia viridissima* Commonly known as 'long-horned grasshoppers', bush crickets have long 'feelers', and the female has a curved ovipositor (not a sting). This species is seen in hedgerows and other cover in the south of England, and its almost ceaseless 'song' is heard on warm nights from now until October. It preys on other insects.

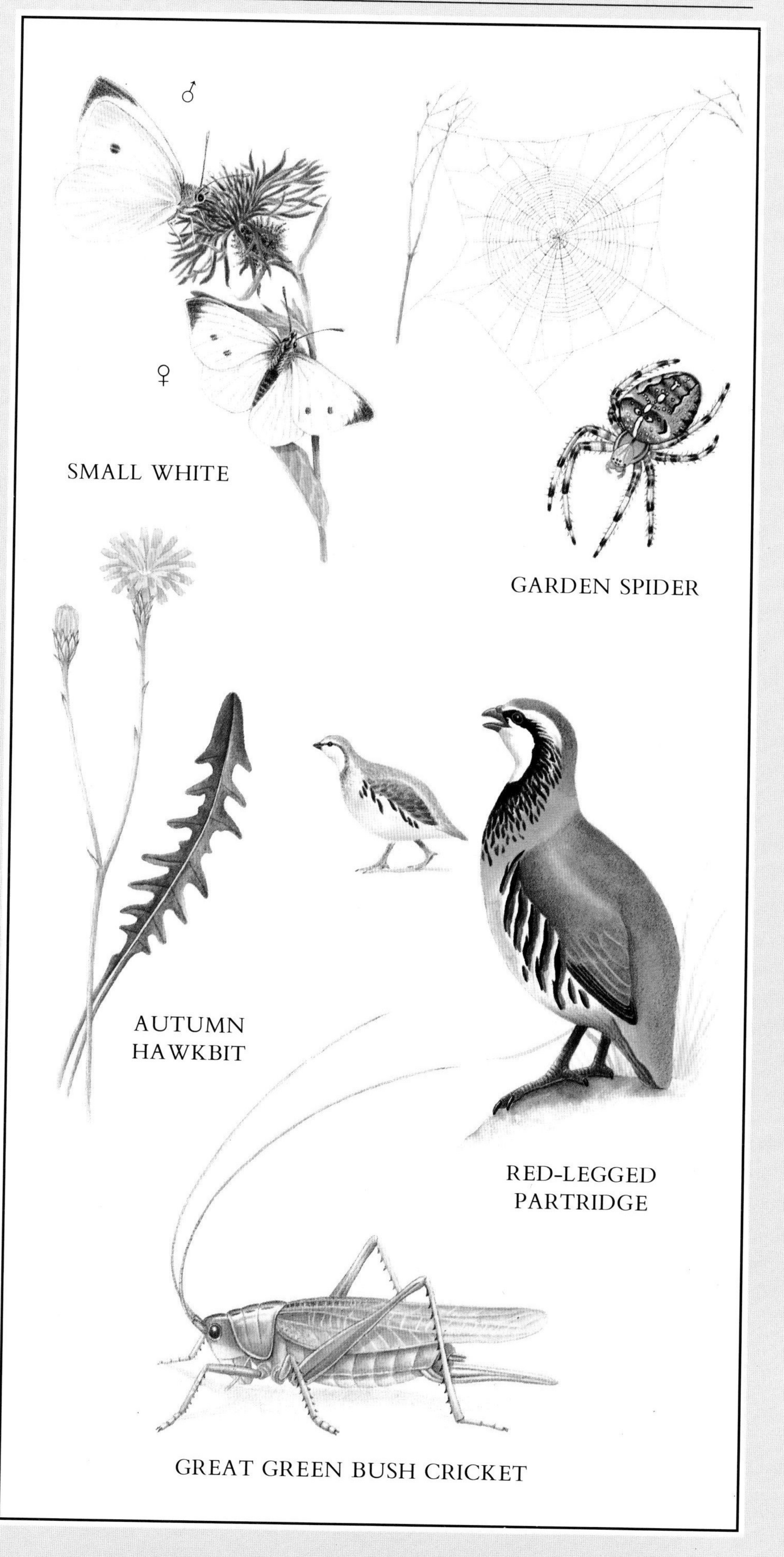

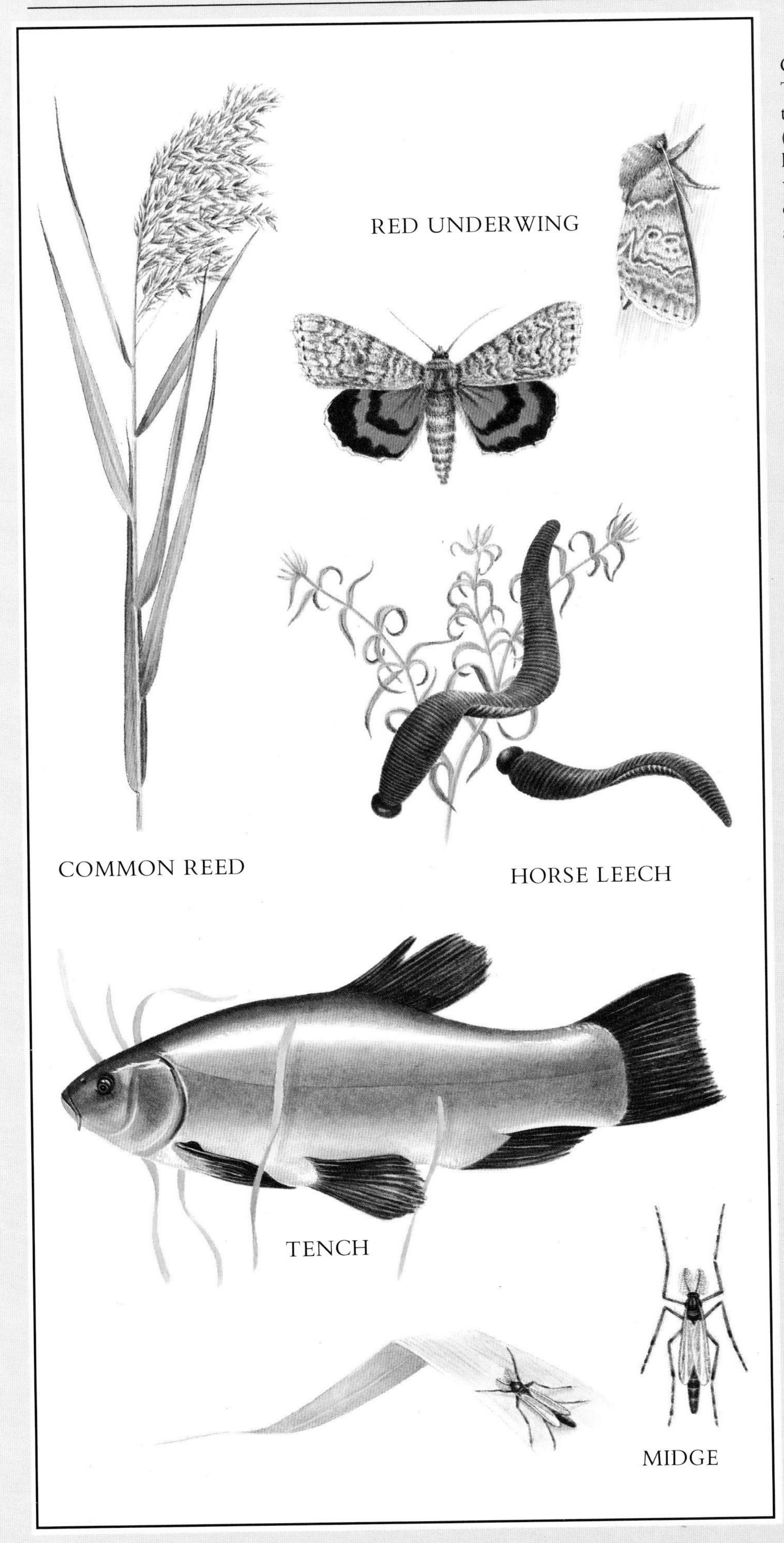

COMMON REED *Phragmites australis* Those who visit fenland will now see the common reed coming into flower (late August–October), bearing a handsome, rather purplish plume. This will gradually become lighter and droop gracefully to one side. In the autumn, this flower head loosens into a mass of silky down, which disperses in the wind, carrying the seeds often quite far away. It spreads also by underwater stems to create dense reedbeds in shallow, still water. Used for thatching, the reed stems are cut during the winter months, when the leaves have withered. The common reed is a very successful plant, found from the northern latitudes down to the tropics.

RED UNDERWING *Catocala nupta* This often comes to lighted windows in August and September. A large handsome moth, it quickly darts away when disturbed, flashing its bright underwings. On landing, it suddenly seems to disappear when its wings are folded, confusing any would-be predators. Its eggs are laid on willows and poplars.

HORSE LEECH *Haemopis sanguisuga* Leeches are generally parasites, sucking the blood of fish, water birds and even snails. The horse leech is our largest, growing up to 1 ft long, and may be seen swimming elegantly through the water. It has abandoned blood-sucking and preys on insect larvae and worms, sometimes coming out of the water to do so. (The medicinal leech, *Hirudo medicinalis*, used in olden days to 'bleed' patients, is now rare.)

TENCH *Tinca tinca* Although this fish spawns most usually in June or July, it may still be doing so in August; if so, it will be seen moving restlessly in the shallows of ponds and lakes.

MIDGE *Chironomus plumosus* Not all midges bite, and this is one of the non-biting species. It is seen swarming in August and many other months, dancing over bushes or water as dusk sets in. Performing in this way, the males attract females with their display, who are then mated in mid-air. Its larvae are the 'bloodworms', bright-red with haemoglobin, seen in streams, ditches and ponds.

ROACH *Rutilus rutilus* Found over much of Britain, except the south-west, west Wales and northern Scotland, the roach inhabits slow-moving or still, muddy waters in lowland areas, and is even able to tolerate some pollution of the water. It spawns around the end of May, accompanied by shoaling and splashing in the shallows. At this time of year, it will still be feeding, but, as with many other fish, it tends to fast during the cold winter months.

WATER SPIDER *Argyroneta aquatica* Pirate spiders may walk the surface of a pond, but this one lives underwater, while still breathing air. When submerged, it has a silvery appearance, due to air trapped by its abdominal hairs. Its brood chamber is an underwater woven 'bell', attached to waterweeds, which also appears silvery as it is filled with air. Insect larvae and small crustaceans form its prey.

LARGE MARSH GRASSHOPPER *Stethophyma grossum* There are likely to be other lesser cousins in marshy places, but it is worth looking out for this, our largest grasshopper. Its distribution is somewhat restricted, though, for it is scattered mainly in wet boggy areas across the south (the New Forest is a good place to find it). The short, slow ticking song, which is now heard, is unmistakable; it also leaps prodigiously.

LITTLE RINGED PLOVER *Charadrius dubius* 500 pairs visit. Fifty years ago, this bird was rarely seen in Britain, and then only on migration. But it began nesting on the shingle 'beaches' of flooded gravel pits. This visitor arrives in April and remains until September, so it is still to be seen and is worth looking for. It makes a charming sight, darting about while it feeds.

HORSEFLY *Chrysops relictus* This species, which has the iridescent eyes of many of its clan, patrols marshy ground and attacks with a low hum. (Some horseflies, known as 'clegs', attack silently, unnoticed until the bite stings.) Only the females feed on blood (the males are nectar feeders). Horseflies are on the wing throughout the summer.

RED GROUSE

HARE'S TAIL COTTON-GRASS

FLY AGARIC

BILBERRY

HARD FERN

RED GROUSE *Lagopus lagopus* 200,000 pairs resident. The grouse-shooting season lasts from 12 August, 'the Glorious Twelfth', until 10 December. Much moorland is devoted to this game bird, and grouse moors are regularly burned to diversify the cover. With a territorial 'go-beck' call and a cackling alarm when starting from underfoot, it takes up territory in autumn with gliding and flapping displays. Grazing the heather, it may remain on high moors in bleak winters, though perhaps moving to local snow-free areas. By February, though, the male will spend all day on his domain, and the pair will stay together until breeding is over. Numbers fluctuate, but shooting is only one factor; males unable to hold a nourishing territory will weaken and fall prey to disease and predators. A mixed habitat of dense heather for cover and young heather for food supports higher numbers.

HARE'S TAIL COTTON-GRASS *Eriophorum vaginatum* Many northern moorlands are speckled with the white heads of this plant—which is in fact not a grass, but a sedge. The white tufts, held one to a stem, are downy seed heads. (A close relation, the common cotton-grass, *E. angustifolium*, has from two to seven heads per stem.)

FLY AGARIC *Amanita muscaria* This handsome fungus is now seen in birch and pine woods (its feeding threads form an association with the roots of these two trees). A pointer to autumn, it will be seen until November.

BILBERRY *Vaccinium myrtillus* Also known as the 'whortleberry' or 'blaeberry' in Scotland, the bilberry is found growing among the heather on moors and often also on southern heaths (in fact, it is only absent from the Shires and eastern England). Some high moors even merit the description 'bilberry moor'. It flowered from April to June, and is now in fruit; the berries are edible raw, but taste better when cooked.

HARD FERN *Blechnum spicant* As an indicator of acid soils, the hard fern is a good guide, found on moors and heaths. The erect fertile fronds are carrying ripe spore cases in August.

CRANBERRY *Vaccinium oxycoccos* This small plant is now coming into fruit—these are the rather spotted berries from which the jelly to accompany meats is made. It has slight stems which trail across the surface of the bog, and somewhat inconspicuous flowers (June–August). The cranberry is found on boggy moorland mainly in the north and west.

SCOTCH ARGUS *Erebia aethiops* As its name would suggest, this butterfly is found in Scotland. Seen now on the wing (July–August), the Scotch argus belongs to a group confined to alpine and sub-arctic habitats. It has a slow fluttering flight, and if clouds hide the sun, it will drop to the cover of the grass. Its eggs are in fact laid on moorland grass, and ten months are spent as a caterpillar in these cold, bleak surroundings.

DARTMOOR PONY *Equus* (domestic) The foals were born earlier in the year, and in autumn the annual round-ups or 'drifts' will take place, with most of the foals being sold. Others are branded and ear-tagged, and then released to rejoin the adults. In winter they are rarely fed, but despite the weather remain healthy and free of disease (their thick winter coats start to grow now in August). The Dartmoor pony is an animal in tune with its environment.

PURPLE MOOR-GRASS *Molinia caerulea* Growing in dense tussocks on wetter areas of moorland, this is also seen on wet heathland. Later into flower than most other grasses, its panicles are now seen in August and September, and are often markedly purple. In the coming winter months, its leaves will wither and curl.

MERLIN *Falco columbarius* 500 pairs resident. This small raptor is still seen on the moors in August, preying on small birds which it takes with fast, acrobatic flight. Its victims are often taken to a plucking site, such as a rock or post, especially if destined for its chicks. Earlier, on arrival on the moors in spring, the male displayed by short flights from perch to perch. But in the coming autumn months, merlins usually forsake the moorlands for lower, open countryside.

CHOUGH *Pyrrhocorax pyrrhocorax* 200 pairs resident. Found mainly in coastal west Wales, a party of choughs may be a prized holiday sighting. This bird has an unusual, downcurved bill, with which it probes the soil for worms, ants, beetles and other food.

BEADLET ANEMONE *Actinia equina* Though static, anemones are of course animals. This one lives on a diet of small sea creatures stunned by sting cells carried at the base of the tentacles, and then pushed into the central mouth. The beadlet anemone is very common, being found in rock pools, and also on rocks exposed by the tide; here its tentacles are retracted and it becomes a blob of jelly, exposing a rim of blue 'beads', hence its name.

COMMON PORPOISE *Phocoena phocoena* This, the smallest of our whales, approaches the coastline in August and early autumn. Large schools are sometimes seen off the Shetlands, for example, or in a bay or inlet along the Scottish mainland. Here they may stay for a while, waiting for the shoaling of the small fish which they catch. Mating occurs in autumn, when the pairs may be seen swimming close to each other.

COMMON (or MOON) JELLYFISH *Aurelia aurita* Up to about 10 in. across, this is the jellyfish most likely to be found stranded along British shores, on the beach or in rock pools. It can also be glimpsed just below the surface of the sea, quite close inshore, where it will 'swim' through the water by pulsating its bell. Although armed with sting cells which could stun fish, the adult feeds on small organisms in the sea; these adhere to its four tentacle 'arms' and are wafted to its mouth, which lies between them.

HERMIT CRAB *Pagurus bernhardus* With a soft body, the hermit crab has to gain protection from empty shells. It then carries its home with it while foraging; however, when moulting to grow, it has to move house. Sometimes a species of sea anemone takes up station on the shell, benefiting both of them: the sea anemone gives added protection in exchange for food scraps, which are wafted its way by the crab's activity.

COMMON OCTOPUS *Octopus vulgaris* Found in warmer southern coastal waters, this species may not be uncommon after mild winters. Hunting often at night, the eight tentacles are used to catch crabs and other food, then carry the prey to the mouth with its horny beak (large octopuses may also raid crab pots, to the annoyance of fishermen). A bottom dweller, it may lie partly buried and can change colour quite rapidly to merge with its surroundings; it will also eject a cloud of 'ink' to confuse a predatory fish, while it shoots backwards to escape.

PORTUGUESE MAN-OF-WAR *Physalia physalis* Though not a true jellyfish, it looks very similar. From its delicately-coloured float bag hang tentacles armed with stinging cells that can stun fish as large as mackerel. This is a subtropical animal, brought to our coasts by the warm Gulf Stream.

COMMON LOBSTER *Homarus vulgaris* Our largest crustacean usually grows 8–20 in. long, but can be larger. It is commonly found off rocky shores, and is usually fished offshore. In the summer, however, it may come to shallower waters and lurk under rocks at the foot of the shore, or in weedy pools. Blue in colour, it becomes red when boiled. The female is in 'berry' (carrying eggs) every two years. Note the specialized difference between the two ferocious pincers: the smaller one is used for cutting, while the larger claw is for crushing prey.

SNAKELOCKS (or OPELET) ANEMONE *Anemonia sulcata* Unable to withdraw its tentacles to avoid damage when buffeted, this common shore anemone is found in crevices or deep in pools. In the course of an hour or two, it can reproduce by splitting itself into two or more, each part armed with tentacles.

BLUETHROAT *Luscinia svecica* A chance sighting of the bluethroat along eastern coasts is a token of the vast migration movements of birds which have now begun. It breeds in Scandinavia, winters south of the Mediterranean, and may be blown astray by a storm, to come here and rest, feeding on berries.

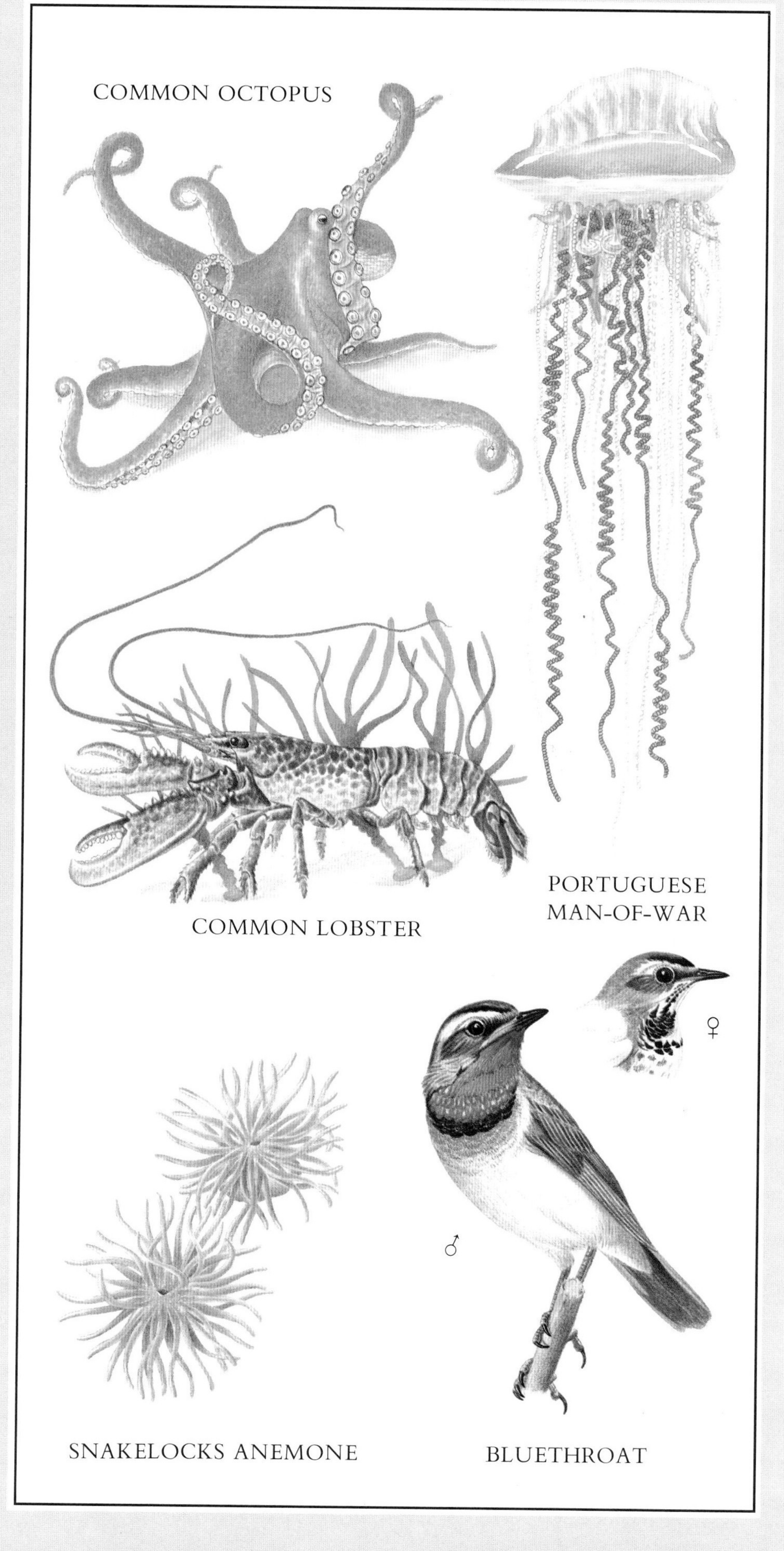

SEPTEMBER

At this time of mellow mists and true fruitfulness, nothing can beat the taste of a September apple straight from the tree, and hedgerow hazel nuts are at their best early in the month. It is also the month of heavy dews, and quick ones. The season 'autumn' runs from 10 September to 19 November.

The autumn equinox falls on 22 or 23 September. The 'harvest moon' is full within two weeks of this date—it rises for several nights in succession at nearly the same time, each day at a point further north along the eastern horizon.

Harvest festivals are also commonly a feature of September. Their origin lies in older celebrations held in August when the last of the harvest was usually gathered in. Corn dollies, formalized dolls woven from the last stalks to be cut, were kept and treasured, to be buried when the ground was ploughed again the following spring. This was clearly a custom of ancient origin, echoing nature's miraculous rebirth.

In Anglo-Saxon almanacs, the days of 20 to 22 September were thought to offer a taste of the weather for the coming three months. If so, and if correct, then these would hopefully include an 'Indian summer' in October, or even November.

A 'second spring' is quite likely in September. The woods now echo with the odd snatch of thrush song, or perhaps even a chiffchaff (these early heralds of true spring are also late to leave and may have a new burst of song in this month). The brimstone butterfly is a possible sighting, as a new generation is on the wing into October. Even dog violets may again be in bloom.

The ivy flowers, which are now beginning to open, attract late butterflies such as this comma, as well as bees and hover-flies.

This second spring is garlanded with the yellow, orange and red of turning leaves which now begin to tint the hedgerows. In place of the predominant whites and yellows of spring, the autumn flowers tend towards the blues and violets of Michaelmas daisies.

Migrant birds are on the move now. Millions of songbirds pass overhead at night; sometimes they can be heard calling, or a flight across the face of the bright harvest moon may give a clue to their numbers.

Hedgehogs seem to be more in evidence now than at other times of the year. As do

wasps; they have been active in the garden all summer, seeking grubs and other insect food for the brood. However, with their life's work nearly done, they develop a crazed taste for the sugary juice of windfalls—or jam.

Partridge shooting begins on 1 September. The traditional ferret season also used to begin now, running until March. These barely domesticated animals could now be released into burrows to chase out the rabbits and then be trusted to re-emerge. (At other times of year, the burrows hold young rabbits, which are rather too easily caught and consumed, thus keeping the ferret below ground.)

For the general farming community, 29 September, Michaelmas, was an important date. It was, and in some places still is, a time of great livestock fairs, especially lowland sheep fairs. There were regional goose fairs too, the birds fat from picking the stubble.

Such fairs were also good opportunities for hiring farm workers. Many farm tenancies ran from Michaelmas, and on this day the farmer hired himself new men if any were needed. Farm labourers would gather to be inspected at these 'hiring fairs', and their skills identified; for example, a carter wore a plaited thong in his hat. Hired for a year, the bargain was struck with a shilling—'earnest money' to be spent 'on the fun of the fair'.

A second spring is quite likely in this month, although the light may be rather hazy and lack the clear-washed clarity of the start of the year. Up in the hills, however, there are usually showers enough to wash it free of dust. The harvest in the hills may well be delayed into September in a late year.

COOL CLEAR NIGHTS

September can provide some lovely periods of quiet sunny weather. If there are westerly or south-westerly breezes, they are not so very cold, and the showers they bring are usually restricted to western counties.

The days are usually rather hazy—the quality of the September sunshine cannot be mistaken for that of any other month—and the air on these days is mild, mellow and fruitful. On higher ground to the north, these sunny spells are a great help to the arable farmer, as the harvest may still need to be taken in.

September can make a better holiday month than July and August, both of which may often be wetter, though this varies from year to year. The first week of September may even be the driest in the year on occasion, and although we tend to associate autumn with damp days, gardeners in south-eastern counties may have to water their dahlias at such times.

There are, however, heavy dews as well as misty mornings. With warm days, clear cool nights, and soil damp from the August rains, the conditions are now ideal for their formation.

In the valley bottoms, reservoirs of cold air collect at night. The air, warmed during the day, begins to cool near the ground as the evening progresses. It becomes denser and sinks down the valley slopes below the warmer air around. These valley inversions are more marked in inland valleys, and are themselves more marked in September than in any other month.

There is also a good chance of frost, and whereas August rarely, if ever, sees frosts in the lowlands, they can often begin now in September. They are more likely to occur in the hills, of course.

It is interesting to look at a map of September's average rainfall expressed as a percentage of the annual average. But bear in mind that even if it begins mild and dry, September often ends in weather tantrums, and can be quite wet. As there are 12 months to the year, it means that an average rainfall per month will be 8.3 per cent of the year's total. Those areas which exceed this average in September, such as the Lake District, tend to be relatively drier in late spring and early summer.

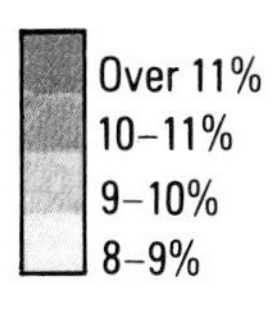

RAIN

Today we have scientific knowledge of the weather. School-children learn of the natural water-cycle which begins when the sun evaporates the surface of oceans and lakes, adding water vapour to the air. Water vapour cannot be seen, but it can be felt if present in high quantities, for the day then feels humid and sticky. This water vapour condenses into small water droplets which can be seen as cloud. From these clouds, the water falls as rain, filling rivers which then run to the sea to replenish it. Where it soaks into the soil, plants absorb it via their roots and later transpire, evaporating water back into the air again. It is a simple enough cycle, but how rain forms is still a partly-unsolved puzzle.

It cannot simply be an extension of the processes which create clouds or fogs. The water droplets which make up these contain only a minute fraction of the water present in a raindrop. If each cloud droplet simply acted as a nucleus on to which more water condensed until a raindrop heavy enough to fall was formed, it would be next month before today's rain fell, so slow is the process!

The explanation probably lies with the fact that as well as water droplets, rain-clouds are cold enough to contain supercooled water

A perfect rainbow arches beyond a solitary rowan tree among the northern hills, indicating the presence of rain.

droplets and small ice crystals, which are light enough to be kept aloft by the air currents. The ice crystals can attach water rather more quickly, by robbing the supercooled droplets, and large crystals grow in half an hour or so to develop into snowflakes. When too large to be supported within the cloud, they fall, melting on the way, to reach us as rain or drizzle. Drizzle drops, a tenth raindrop size, are just too heavy to be kept up.

Rain also (but less frequently) falls from 'warm' clouds, which gather when air rises quickly over hot land surfaces. It is possible that when these contain drops of different sizes, the larger and heavier drops will fall faster, sweeping up the smaller ones in their path; alternatively, they may be lifted through the 'fog' of smaller particles by upcurrents of air. When too large to be supported, they fall, sometimes as heavy showers or 'thundery rain'. Raindrops do not reach the size of hailstones because falling drops of water tend to bulge in at the bottom, and break up into smaller drops.

Some areas of Britain are notoriously wet. The highest annual totals are among the western and north-western hills. These force up into colder regions the air arriving with westerly airstreams—air that is warmish and wet from its long fetch across the Atlantic. Heavy clouds form over these hills, and when cold enough, rain will fall. It is noticeably drier in the lee of such hills.

However, annual averages disguise a monthly pattern that may be rather complicated. For the forecaster, the sea temperature for each month is important, especially in winter when the difference between it and the land is greatest, as this influences the formation of rain-clouds over the land. There is a noticeable slackening in rainfall in February, and March and April are intermediate months. During May and part of June, westerlies are less common, and in these months the Midlands receive more than their monthly average, while the western hills have less. However, summer thunderstorms can distort these averages. (Drought, on the other hand, defined as 15 days without rain, may occur once a year in the south-east, but is rarer to the north and west.)

It must be remembered that although we traditionally total rain by the month, this is more for our own convenience than any other reason. Annual averages are more meaningful.

MIGRANTS ON THE MOVE

In September, the migration of many birds is already well under way. For long centuries, the sudden appearance of swallows and other migrants brought grateful cheer, for these birds were harbingers of summer after winter's deprivations. Their sudden, magical disappearance excited wonderment. Where did they go?

Some believed that they hibernated in the mud of a pond, for the occasional small corpse was found there. The ancient Greeks even went so far as to believe that summer redstarts moulted into the rather similar-looking robins, which visit Greece in winter. Although bird migration gradually became an accepted fact, it was the invention of radar in World War 2 that revealed for the first time its vast scale. The numerous unidentified blips, or 'angels', on the screen were recognized as high-flying bird flocks. Prior to this, these movements could only be estimated from occasional passes seen against the moon (for most small birds migrate over Britain at night). Now we know, for example, that each autumn five billion migrant birds leave Europe and Asia to winter in Africa, south of the Sahara. In Britain, we see 100 species of winter migrants and 50 species of summer visitors.

Out of the breeding season, many birds, from the lapwings of the fields to the blackbirds and blue tits in the garden, make long journeys in search of food. They tend to move towards the milder south-west in harsh weather, while European cousins cross the North Sea to feed in Britain. Milder spells bring about a return to the birds' home area.

Migration, though, is rather different. It is a regular, annual, lengthy movement between quite separate breeding and wintering areas. Food is still the spur, however, and the journeying seems to have originated in the need to supply the chicks with the protein (often from insects) they require when hatched. Primed with this, what begins as a weak, featherless, blind, cold-blooded scrap of life can, within only a few weeks, set off on a home trip of thousands of miles. 'Our' swallows can be viewed as African residents come to feast on the plentiful flying insects produced by the British summer.

Migration is an inbred instinct that cannot be learned, although the weather can vary the actual dates of departure. Small species usually set off in the evening, the darkness protecting them against predators, but overcast weather can cause a delay. They may instinctively wait for a tail wind or other helpful weather, or it may be that the emptying of the larder is the trigger, for in very mild autumns, with plenty of insects still on the wing, some swallows are late in leaving, and may delay even into December.

Even for these swallows, which may be

Below right A migrant clouded yellow seen resting on arrival. The upper surfaces of its wings are a lovely yellow-orange in hue.

Below A flock of geese passing across a full 'harvest moon'. Before the invention of radar, much of the evidence for migration was made up of accidental sightings such as this.

able to feed while flying, success will depend on the stores of body fat accumulated to fuel the flight. A sedge warbler's normal weight is just over a third of an ounce. Some 18 hours and 1000 miles after departure, it will have lost a tenth of an ounce. Even if fat reserves took its start weight to 50 per cent above normal, it will now have to stop and feed in North Africa before facing the 30-hour crossing of the Sahara desert. If its weight drops to a third of an ounce, its metabolism is strained and it will most likely die. However, if fat takes its start weight to twice normal, it may successfully cross the desert without the need to stop and feed.

There is greater instinctive pressure on the spring flight to the breeding grounds. Some wildfowl crossing Britain for the short Icelandic summer have already paired before departure. The return, though, may be leisurely, even delayed, as it often is with swallows and martins. The date of arrival of our first spring visitors is therefore fairly reliable, but their departure less so. Falls of birds are also likely in spring, when overcast weather may suddenly follow fine, making navigation impossible.

Some grazing mammals also migrate. Scottish red deer certainly move down to more sheltered areas in winter, and if our countryside remained unfenced they could well show a further seasonal drift.

Insect migrants can match the birds for interest. Painted lady butterflies come here from breeding grounds in North Africa. They usually arrive in largest numbers from June onwards, their flights aided by the frequent southerly winds of these months. Clouded yellows also fly here from Europe in large numbers in some years, while many strongly flying butterflies, such as the large white, have native British populations swelled by migrants crossing from Europe. The familiar red admiral flies here in spring to breed; its progeny are now to be seen on the autumn buddleia. Moths, too—many hawk-moths cross the North Sea. Some darter dragonflies also fly in.

With some of these insects, the tracks of their autumn flights may show a southerly direction, this perhaps being the start of a return journey. However, the first frosts seem to kill them before they get very far. By migrating here, these species are pushing themselves to their geographical limit, as all living things tend to do.

The red admiral is one of the most familiar of our migrant butterflies.

Bar-tailed godwits active over the saltings. Their nearest breeding grounds are in the open tundras of Scandinavia. Flocks pass through our estuaries and coastal mud-flats in autumn and spring; many birds remain with us for the duration of winter.

OUT WITH THE PLOUGH

As soon as the combine harvester has greedily sucked up all but a few grains of corn, leaving scant pickings for the wood-pigeons, the race is on to prepare the soil for new sowings of winter wheat and barley (unless the field has cannily been undersown with grass for a new ley). Any short-cut to save a day or two is worth considering. The weather is crucial; a period of rain can make the soil unworkable, and if the seed is not sown before the weather worsens, the opportunity is lost until February.

If it is not baled and removed, the spent straw from the harvest can be a problem. Ploughing it in does little to improve the tilth in the short term, and so it is often burned. In September, you will therefore see twisting palls of dark smoke rising high into the sky above fields afire and crackling.

Straw or stubble burning also raises heated arguments. Bylaws offer some control, and the National Farmers Union has its own guidelines—for example: a cleared firebreak of 15 yards, with the 5 yards against the hedges ploughed; burn against the wind; never burn without at least two people to supervise the fire.

The modern plough is then brought in, a foursome set (or more) drawn by the tractor, but still of ancient design. An upright coulter slices straight down into the soil and a ploughshare, following the coulter, cuts a slice of earth ready for a mould-board, which lifts and turns it over. As the soil is always turned to the same side, the tractor works two 'lands', ploughed in reverse directions, to avoid the furrows clashing.

A high proportion of soil can be left unploughed in the corners and when the tractor turns at the hedge, but a modern reversible plough, which can be set to turn the sod either to the left or to the right, avoids this problem. At the hedge it turns, backs and reverses the plough set, before moving back across the field. Incidentally, this reversible plough has been a godsend to wildlife: as it leaves very little soil unploughed, there is no reason to grub the hedge up to provide more space for the turns.

Ploughing has the effect of burying and thus destroying many young weeds, but further work may be necessary. Following the plough come harrows and/or cultivators. When the field is scratched by the rake-like harrow, it encourages weeds to sprout. A second pass a few days later uproots them again to die or be chopped by a pass with the harrow. Ploughing has the advantage of 'pan busting', that is, breaking through the crusty layer that can form below the worked soil, but on well-structured light soils it may not be necessary to plough as the cultivator should be able to do the job.

If the soil is in good heart, minimal cultivation may suffice—the field is sprayed with herbicides to destroy weeds and seeds, and the new seed is planted directly with a seed drill heavy enough to cope with unploughed ground. Some sacks of fertilizer granules are perhaps also drilled in. The soil gains some texture when the roots of the previous crop rot, of course, but it all depends on the type of soil, and no two fields are ever quite the same. In fact, all fields have their own names which may tell of their character: pillpan, for example, hints that when the field gained its name, the pan was granular.

Many dairy cattle are calving at this time of year. They were mated nine months ago, soon after the previous calving, and may have been put to a bull, although artificial insemination is more likely in winter when the cattle are housed.

Milk can only be obtained after calving, and the cow yields for ten months, so this autumn birth is managed with an eye to the winter milk round. To obtain it, the calves are usually separated from their mothers after a week or so, and penned apart to be bucket-fed at first, on milk substitutes and concentrates. But some farms also buy in young calves and delegate one or more of the milking cows to suckle them.

The remaining mothers will be drafted to the milk herd within a few days, going out on the pasture for shortening periods until the low temperatures bring grass growth to an end, at which time they will remain under cover, feeding entirely on silage and hay. Concentrates may be fed in winter to increase the milk yield (and put muscle on the beef cattle) but they are costly, and so again it is a matter of balancing cash in, cash out.

Summer or winter, the cow in milk will have to be milked twice a day. Gone are the days of milkmaids out in the fields. Today's dairy farm has a fully-equipped (often rotary) parlour dealing with many cows at once. The animals are bribed into the stalls with the promise of a tasty bite, then have their udders washed and suction caps attached before the process begins. The milk is then taken away by tanker.

Call a muddy field 'autumn ploughland' and traditional memories are stirred. Even using today's modern machinery, ploughing remains the most evocative of the year's tasks on the farm.

BURNHAM BEECHES

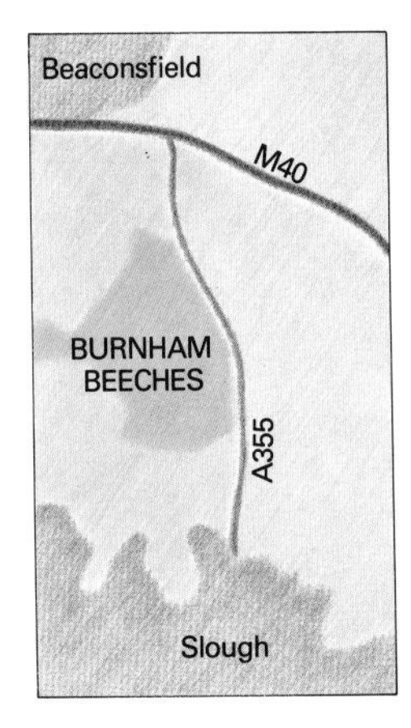

The woodland known as Burnham Beeches, near Beaconsfield, Buckinghamshire, is noted for its gnarled and stunted trees. These were once pollarded (that is, cropped of branches at head height), but since this practice ceased the branches have grown huge. Elsewhere in many parts of the Chilterns, woodlands containing noble tall-trunked beech trees can be found.

The English beech wood is natural architecture. From the tall, smoothly-barked trunks, branches raise the canopy of leaves up to the sky. Its bare floor is shaded and quiet. Indeed, some consider that here was the inspiration for England's glorious Gothic cathedrals—and England's alone, for the evidence of pollen found in old soil layers seems to show that until quite recent times the beech tree was not found growing north of Derby or much into Wales. However, if you visit Burnham Beeches, you will notice that large areas carry ancient pollarded beech trees, some of which are quite gnarled and misshapen.

The beech was one of the last woody species to reach British soil before the English Channel was flooded—one of the last of our native trees. However, it does not set good seed in the north. And although on well-drained ground it can grow to overtop the oak and shade it out, thus creating its own woodlands, it is doubtful that this happened much before man himself started to play a part, clearing woodland and planting anew to suit his needs.

Two centuries ago, the stately beech became a popular ornamental tree as well as a woodland tree, and many groves and clumps were then added to improve the look of country seats. Perhaps some southerly woodlands on the chalklands of southern England have a natural ancestry, but even here the evidence is confused. Some of the famous Chiltern beech woods are known to grow on what used to be open sheep grazings three centuries ago.

The pin-cushion moss (*Leucobryum glaucum*) forms dense, green, cushion-like humps on the beech-wood floor. Also typical of beech woodlands is the porcelain fungus (*Oudemansiella mucida*), otherwise known as the beech-tuft fungus; it often grows high on tree trunks, appearing from late summer to late autumn.

In September, the dense summer foliage which steals the light is still in place in the Chilterns, though here and there a slight browning presages the autumn changes to come. In this shade only the holly, yew and rare spurge laurel can survive—as all three are evergreens, they will be able to catch up on growth in the winter. But there are usually lighter places, marked by a scattering of green dog's mercury, and in an occasional, unexpected shaft of light, wild cherry brightens the wood.

On the beech-wood floor, although the bulk of the crop will not fall until November, the first of this year's beech nuts, or 'mast', lie scattered. These ripen in September and October, and are a very important natural harvest.

In past centuries, this mast fattened the village pigs, when the pasturing, or 'pannage', of swine in autumn woodlands was a jealously protected commons right. Today, however, the mast crop is of greater benefit to a host of bird and animal life. Squirrels and mice feast on it, while mixed flocks of tits and finches come to these beech woods in autumn and winter.

The mast crop fluctuates by the year, with five to ten years between good crops. Such things as a frost-free April and May, when the flowers are seen, obviously play a part, and the ripening is favoured, of course, by warm spells in late summer. Many trees show this fluctuation, even failing completely in some years, and it may be that they exhaust their reserves producing good crops. On the other hand, there is one advantage in that the seed gatherers do not develop too close a dependence on them. If they did, hardly a seed would survive.

The white-rumped brambling, a visitor from Scandinavia, now joins our native birds. This is a true winter visitor in that it does not nest in Britain. Indeed, as the beech wood gives little cover for nesting, its birdlife becomes more interesting for the ornithologist at this time of year. The exception to this is the wood warbler: nesting on the ground and liking an open wood above, the shimmering trill of this bird may echo like a chorister through the empty summer beech wood. By now, though, it has returned to its African wintering grounds.

BRITAIN'S BEECH WOODS
Beech woods are concentrated, by and large, towards the south on limy soils. They are seen at their best at such places as Aston Rowant, Oxfordshire, but beech trees have often been planted:
1 Drum Forest, Crathes, Grampian. Contains beech trees.
2 Argyll Forest Park, Strathclyde.
3 Alkrington Woods, Middleton, Greater Manchester.
4 Sutton Park, Birmingham, West Midlands.
5 Felbrigg Woods, near Cromer, Norfolk.
6 Epping Forest, Essex.
7 Cefn Onn Woodlands, near Caerphilly, Mid Glamorgan.
8 The Cotswolds, Gloucestershire/Avon.
9 Bignor Hill, near Arundel, West Sussex.
10 Box Hill, near Dorking, Surrey.
11 The Hangers at Selborne, Hampshire.
12 New Forest, Hampshire. Among the mixed woodland are stands of beech.
***Burnham Beeches**, Buckinghamshire.

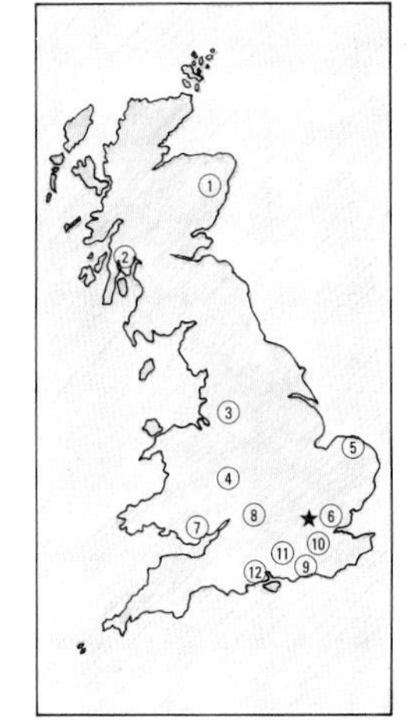

The summer foliage is now just starting to turn towards the colours of autumn here in Burnham Beeches.

CHANTERELLE *Cantharellus cibarius* The breath of the autumn wood is evocative. The first fallen leaves begin to crackle underfoot, and cryptic fungi of all hues are seen. Chanterelle is a classic culinary fungus, now to be seen, mainly in beech woods.

TREE SPARROW *Passer montanus* 250,000 pairs resident. Now coming to roost in open woods, forming perhaps the largest flocks of the year, this bird may also be seen creeping across fields of stubble, searching for spent grain (though today's harvesters leave few gleanings). It is smaller and neater than the house sparrow, and rarely comes to suburban gardens. Earlier in the year, it nested in tree holes.

GUELDER ROSE *Viburnum opulus* Its shiny red berries can now be glimpsed in damp woods and hedgerows. The attractive white blossom is seen from May to July.

MUNTJAC *Muntiacus reevesi* Introduced from China at the start of the century, the muntjac is found in scattered areas in central-southern England. It is not an elegant animal, looking rather pig-like when slipping into the shelter of the underwood. It can be heard barking from afar, very much like a dog. It marks territory by scenting trees, but, unlike other deer, it has no fixed breeding months; fawns can be born at any time of the year. The doe lacks the buck's antlers.

COMMON BEECH *Fagus sylvatica* A native tree, reaching Britain just before the Channel was finally cut after the Ice Age, the beech had little time to spread before man began to change the landscape; beech trees north of Derby have been planted, and some famous Chiltern beech woods now grow on what was open sheep grazing 200 years ago. It flowers from April to May, but most people tend to notice more the fresh green foliage in spring. At this time of year, the mast (seed) is ripening, and in October the leaves will begin turning bright ochre before falling. (However, young beech trees tend to retain their leaves some distance from the ground, for reasons unknown, although it does mean that beech hedges give good winter shelter.)

SWEET CHESTNUT *Castanea sativa* First grown here by the Romans, perhaps for its chestnut flour (a staple food in olden days), this is familiar as an occasional woodland tree, although it is still grown and coppice-cut for fencing in some places in the south. The fruit ripens in September and October, but most shop nuts usually come from southern Europe. Sweet chestnut leaves will start turning yellow, then dark brown, in October.

BADGER *Meles meles* 'Old brock' is a popular animal, yet it is persecuted: illegal badger baiting by dogs still continues, and official gassing was widespread until recently (there is a possibility that badgers may carry bovine tuberculosis). In September, piles of old bedding of bracken and grass may be seen outside active sets (the sows clean out their chambers in autumn and early spring). These sets can be quite old, comprising extensive tunnel systems with many entrances. The badger is one of the few sizeable British wild animals that can easily be observed (foxes are much more wary), and keeping watch at a set is a patient night-time hobby (though in remote areas they may sometimes be seen out in daylight). Clues to badger activity include the animal's network of paths, on which it regularly patrols after dark, and latrine pits and scratched trees near the set. Badgers forage for worms, young rabbits, plant bulbs, etc, but are less active in cold weather (they do not hibernate). The cubs are born in early spring, appearing above ground after a couple of months.

BEEFSTEAK FUNGUS *Fistulina hepatica* This can be a parasitic fungus, its fruiting cap appearing on living oak and sweet chestnut trunks in late summer and autumn.

COMMON HORNBEAM *Carpinus betulus* At first glance, the hornbeam looks rather like a beech tree, but with a fluted trunk. By now, in September, its leaves are often turning yellow.

MILDEWS The newly-shed leaves and twigs that crunch underfoot in the autumn will quickly be attacked by various fungi, including mildews, which impart a whitish bloom to their surfaces.

COMMON HORSE CHESTNUT *Aesculus hippocastanum* Everyone knows the horse chestnut's hard, glossy conkers, which are now ripening—and which are inedible, even to horses. Not a native species (it comes from the Balkans), this is a handsome tree, with exotic white flowers in May. However, its timber is poor, so it is rarely seen in woods, being planted more in parks and gardens, on village greens, and in hedgerows perhaps.

GOLDFINCH *Carduelis carduelis* 300,000 pairs resident, though some move to warmer southern Europe in winter. Small 'charms' are now seen—like other finches, the non-breeding flocks may sometimes consist of only one sex. They pass overhead with a bouncing flight, uttering breezy, tinkling call notes, and feed on the now-ripe seed heads of thistles, ragwort and groundsel, nimbly grasping the swaying stems. Favourite cage birds in the past, their song (heard fully from March to June) is a clear liquid twittering. Orchards (and churchyards) are popular nest sites.

HOUSE SPIDER *Tegenaria gigantea* Seeking water, these spiders now invade the bath, but being web dwellers, their feet lack the adhesive pads of hunting spiders, which would allow them to climb back out again.

BANK VOLE *Clethrionomys glareolus* Often spending its whole life within a 120 ft wide territory, the bank vole creates a network of tunnels through the ground vegetation (and also underground). Active by day as well as at night, it may be seen scuttling out into the open from hidden pathways to win a fallen hazel nut. At night it may also climb for berries (it is largely vegetarian at all times of the year); it often stores food for the coming winter. The bank vole litters in a secluded nest in the tunnel system, the frequency reflecting the year's weather and food available.

CLEMATIS (or OLD MAN'S BEARD) *Clematis vitalba* It flowered earlier (July–August), but is now shaggy with hairy fruit. A good indicator of chalky (limy) soil, it is most noticeable in early winter, whitening leafless hedgerows.

FIELD MUSHROOM *Agaricus campestris* After warm, heavy rain, this is now 'mushrooming' into growth. Far tastier than cultivated mushrooms, it used to be quite common, especially on horse pastures, but is unlikely in today's improved leys.

LARGE WHITE *Pieris brassicae* Earlier on, the plump caterpillars of this well-known butterfly will have made a smelly mess of cabbages. First seen flying in May, another brood is now on the wing (August–October). In addition, from time to time during the summer, migrant butterflies cross over here from Europe. They will overwinter as chrysalides.

COMMON WASP *Vespula vulgaris* These wasps are now at the jam and sappy windfalls. Since spring, worker wasps have been taking caterpillars and other insects for the nest, even expertly butchering flies caught in mid-air. Now, with the job done, they develop a craving for sugar. Later on, the larger queens will be on the wing seeking winter quarters, perhaps coming into houses. The workers, though, die with the frosts.

HEDGEHOG *Erinaceus europaeus* This popular animal seems more in evidence at this time of year, and even late family parties may still be seen. Nocturnal, with a fondness for slugs, it grunts and snorts while looking for them. With hibernation looming, it will now be feeding heavily to lay up fat; it will hibernate at the first frosts in a nest of leaves or grass in cover (leaves provide better weather-proofing), but may sometimes emerge on sunny days to change nests, as footprints in the snow can testify. Contrary to folklore, it does not climb trees to pick apples, though it is attracted by the slugs at the windfalls (it can in fact climb rough stone walls quite well). Hedgehogs will drink a saucer of milk, but it is now believed that this does more harm than good, being difficult for them to digest; it is better to provide tinned dog food.

CLUSTER FLY *Pollenia rudis* These flies are now often seen, clustering on warm walls, from whence they will crawl into crevices (or between roof tiles) to hibernate.

FIELD MUSHROOM

LARGE WHITE

COMMON WASP

HEDGEHOG

CLUSTER FLY

TEAL *Anas crecca* 3500 pairs breed; 200,000 birds in winter. Our breeding teals are now being joined by autumn migrants, some of which will winter here. The close season for wild ducks over water ends at the end of August, so these birds are now game for wildfowlers, who find 'sport' in their quick acceleration from the water and fast low flight, during which they swoop and wheel tantalizingly. They are dabbling ducks, feeding on the surface or up-ending. Those that stay to breed are very secretive in the matter of the nest site (though, prior to this, in early spring, the courtship was a splashy affair, with the drakes challenging each other). Like the mallard, the male takes on duller eclipse plumage for a month or so after breeding.

BLEAK *Alburnus alburnus* A splashing crowd of fish at the surface of the river will probably be the lively bleak (this fast fish is often caught by kingfishers). Keeping near the surface as it does, it is less affected by water pollution than other fish.

ALDER BUCKTHORN *Frangula alnus* This shrub now carries berries, which are unusual in that they ripen from green to red, and then further to black. Found in damp woods (not in Scotland), alder buckthorn is a notable food plant of the brimstone butterfly.

PIKE *Esox lucius* Found throughout Britain, the pike is our largest freshwater fish, growing to over 3 ft long. Despite its size, though, it usually lives quite close to the lake shore in shallowish water, often in a reedy bay. Here it lies still, its greenish-flecked flanks blending into the dappled light. Then, with a rapid flex of its body, it darts out at passing victims, propelled by its powerful tail. Fish are taken, but large pike will also take water voles and small waterfowl. It is seen with its own kind only in spring, when the females come to the weedy shallows to breed, accompanied by the smaller males (the water needs to be more than 6°C in April or May to trigger spawning). The young pike, known as 'jacks', remain close inshore for the first year, often in water no more than 6 in. deep, so now is a good time to see them.

WILD ANGELICA *Angelica sylvestris* An attractive plant, with a hollow stem, this is one of the last of the cow parsley family still to be seen in flower (June–September), in damp places.

CRANE-FLY (or DADDY-LONG-LEGS) *Tipula paludosa* There are nearly 300 different species of crane-flies in Britain; this is one of the most common at this time of year. It takes to the wing at dusk, and often comes to lighted windows. It may occasionally be disturbed from the grass on a walk across a riverside meadow or long grassland. The grubs feed in the soil on the roots of grasses and other plants.

DEVIL'S BIT SCABIOUS *Succisa pratensis* Attracting butterflies and bees to its flowers well into the autumn (June–October), this plant is a good indicator of ancient meadowland.

BARBEL *Barbus barbus* Wintering in large shoals, which may now be assembling, this fish has a liking for clear, fast flows or rough water, such as below a weir. A powerful, fighting fish (much admired by anglers), its shape is an example of environmental adaptation: it is flattened below, the better to lie flat on the gravel, while the water surges past its smooth, curved back. Barbels search for their food with mouth 'feelers'.

LITTLE GREBE (or DABCHICK) *Tachybaptus ruficollis* 10,000 pairs resident. Unlike other grebes, this bird prefers to remain inland in winter; only in really freezing weather will it move to coastal waters. Now, in September, however, it can be seen on many different waters if the shallows have lush vegetation, for it is rarely seen out on open water. In fact, in the breeding season, the only clue to its presence may be its trilling cry, perhaps heard in duet, sounding rather like a horse's whinny but quickly rising and falling in pitch. Strongly territorial, the birds usually keep to themselves, although in good conditions they may nest close together and seem to be a colony. The nest is a floating mass of vegetation. They dive to feed, and will jump up first if there is depth below. (These birds lose their red cheeks in winter.)

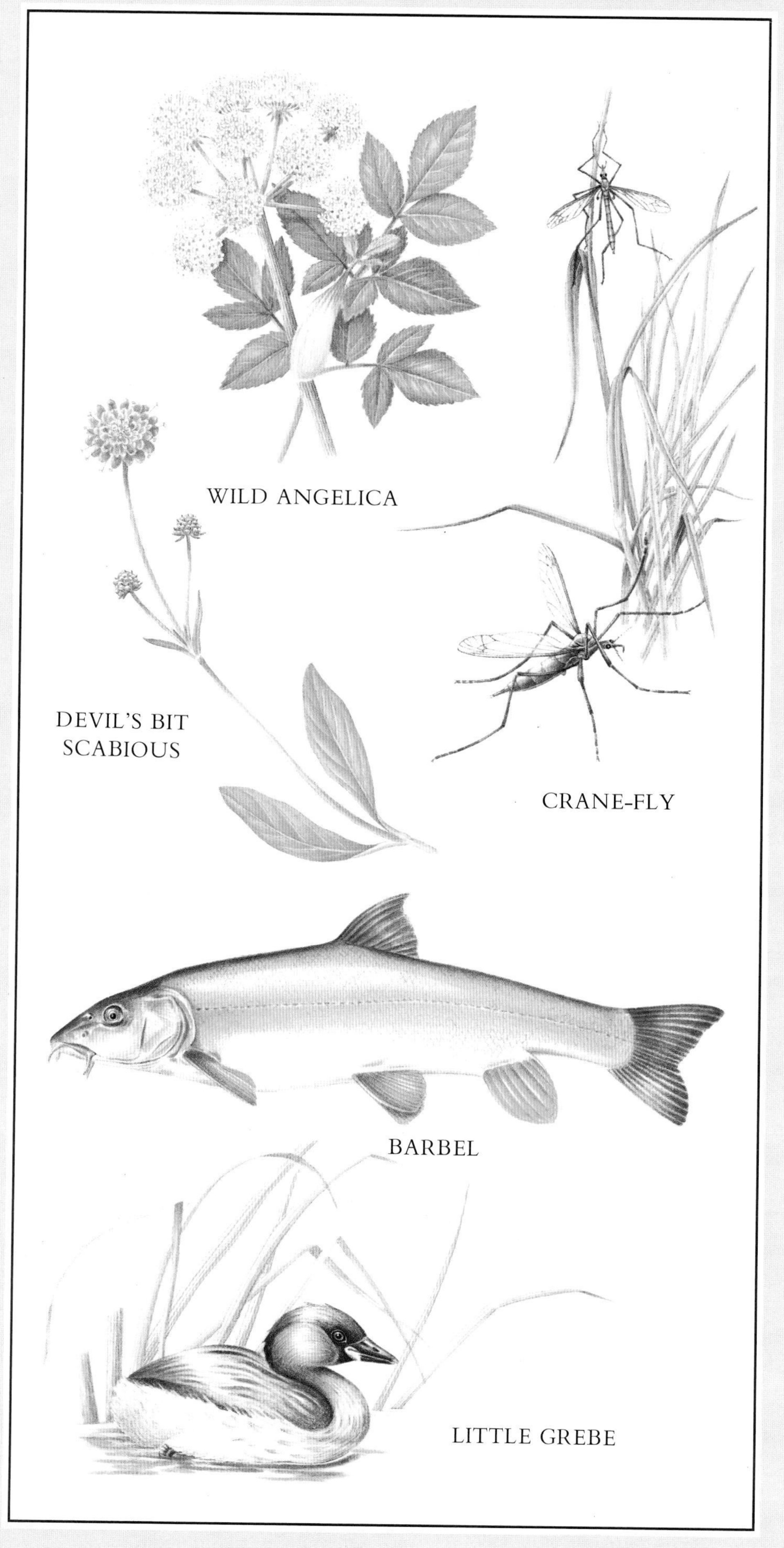

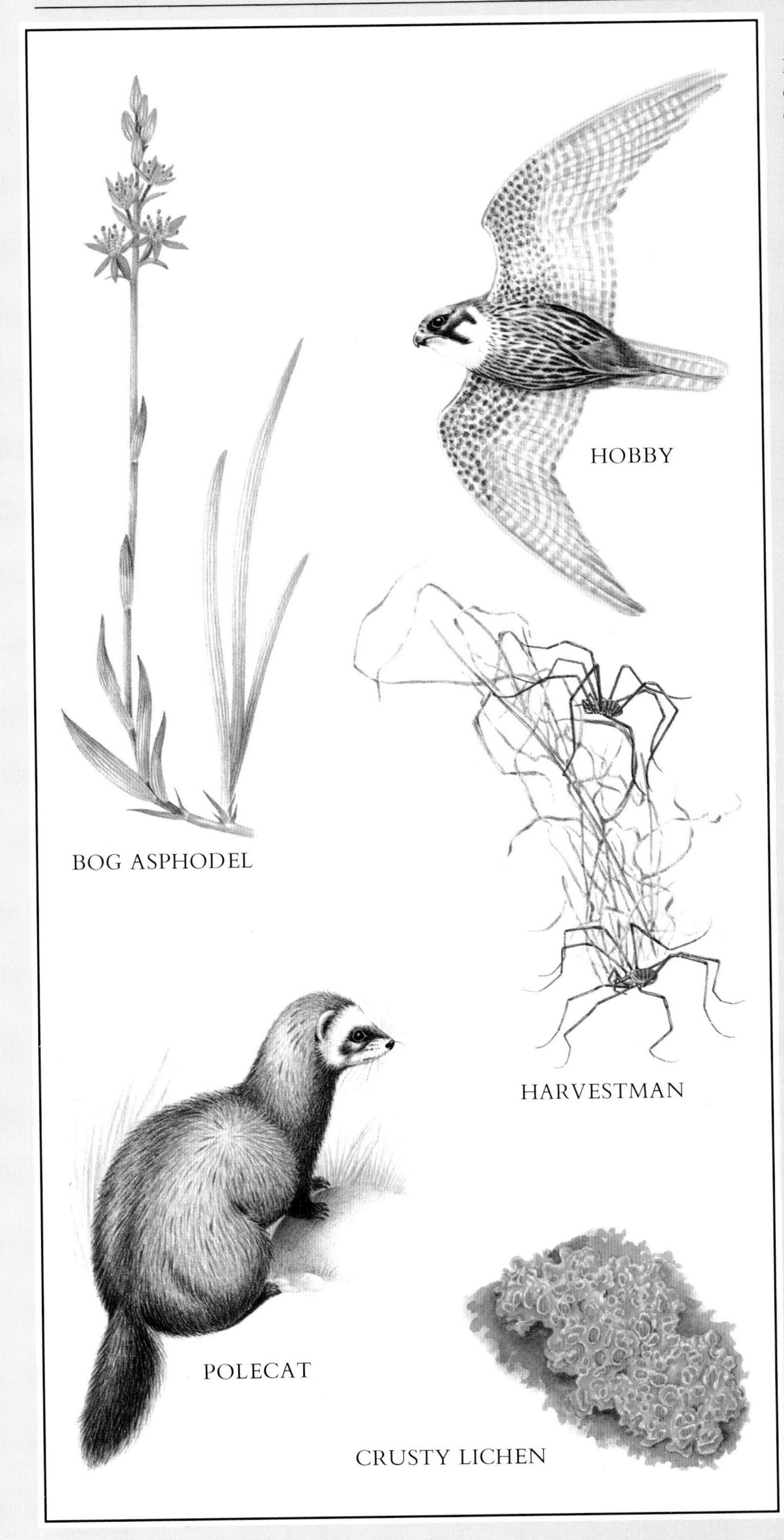

BOG ASPHODEL *Narthecium ossifragum* Exotic colour is given to dour wet moorlands by spreading patches of this plant. After flowering (July–September), the flower stalks become deep orange, and the seed capsules also begin to take on the colour of the rest of the plant.

HOBBY *Falco subbuteo* 500 pairs visit. Arriving first in April to breed, hobbies are now preparing to return south of the Sahara. Although they prefer open country with some trees (heaths are ideal), these rare birds may now be seen elsewhere, perhaps visiting a streamside meadow to take prey. Earlier on, flying insects were caught for the brood, but the adults now take smaller birds on the wing. Pipits, house martins and swallows may all be victims, and with their scything wings, hobbies can even outfly swifts. During the breeding season, dazzling flying displays were seen while the pair cavorted overhead.

HARVESTMAN *Phalangium opilio* Found in many open habitats, most commonly in the autumn, harvestmen are foragers (small living prey may also be taken). Despite their resemblance, these are not true spiders.

POLECAT *Mustela putorius* This animal survives in Wales, its favoured terrain being scrubby thickets or woods, with rocks for a den, but it can also be found quite high on the mountains. It feeds on rabbits, voles and other small animals. Light-coloured ferrets are close relatives which have long been domesticated to help catch rabbits (when released into the burrow, they will drive the rabbits out into waiting nets). Winter is the traditional ferreting season, for then the burrows are less likely to hold young rabbits to keep the hungry ferret below ground. Over the years, escaped ferrets have set up wild colonies and even bred with polecats to give variable coats; these feral animals are known as polecat-ferrets.

CRUSTY LICHEN *Xanthoria parietina* This species is unmistakable, outshining even the brightest of the autumn leaves. It is common in a variety of habitats, including rocks, walls, and even farm roofs.

SNOW BUNTING *Plectrophenax nivalis* 10,000 birds in winter. A few pairs may breed in Scotland, on the mountains, but chiefly these birds are winter visitors between September and April. During the months ahead, they may also be seen in lively flocks feeding on the seashore, filling the air with fluting calls. (In summer, the male's brownish winter plumage will be replaced by striking black-and-white feathers.)

DWARF GORSE *Ulex minor* This low-growing gorse flowers late in the year and is still in bloom (July–September). Though spiny, it can scarcely prick the skin and draw blood. It is found on heathy land in the south-east. (Western gorse, *U. gallii*, grows where dwarf gorse does not, that is, mainly west of a line from Dorchester–Nottingham–Solway. This species does have vicious prickles.)

TUBE-WEB SPIDER *Amaurobius similis* These spiders dwell in crevices in stone walls, in the bark of old pines, and other habitats, spinning bluish silk tunnel webs which entangle the prey. With extra strands being woven each night, the webs grow in size until, by now, they are quite large. It is also at this time of year that mating occurs, and you may see a male paying court by tapping the female's web.

PEREGRINE *Falco peregrinus* 800 pairs resident. This falcon chooses cliff-ledge eyries usually in remote western and northern areas. However, now that breeding is over, there is a chance of seeing it in southern and other areas. Circling high in the sky, this bird's legendary eyesight enables it to spot its prey two miles away. The peregrine positions itself, then folds back its wings and falls out of the sun in a breathtaking 'stoop'. A puff of feathers shows that the attack was successful, the victim's back broken with a blow of talons. Pigeons are the favourite prey, but grouse and larger birds may also be taken. Persecuted for this reason, peregrines also suffered from poisoning by accumulating traces of pesticides which its victims had absorbed when feeding on sprayed grain. Its decline highlighted the problem and DDT was generally banned as a result.

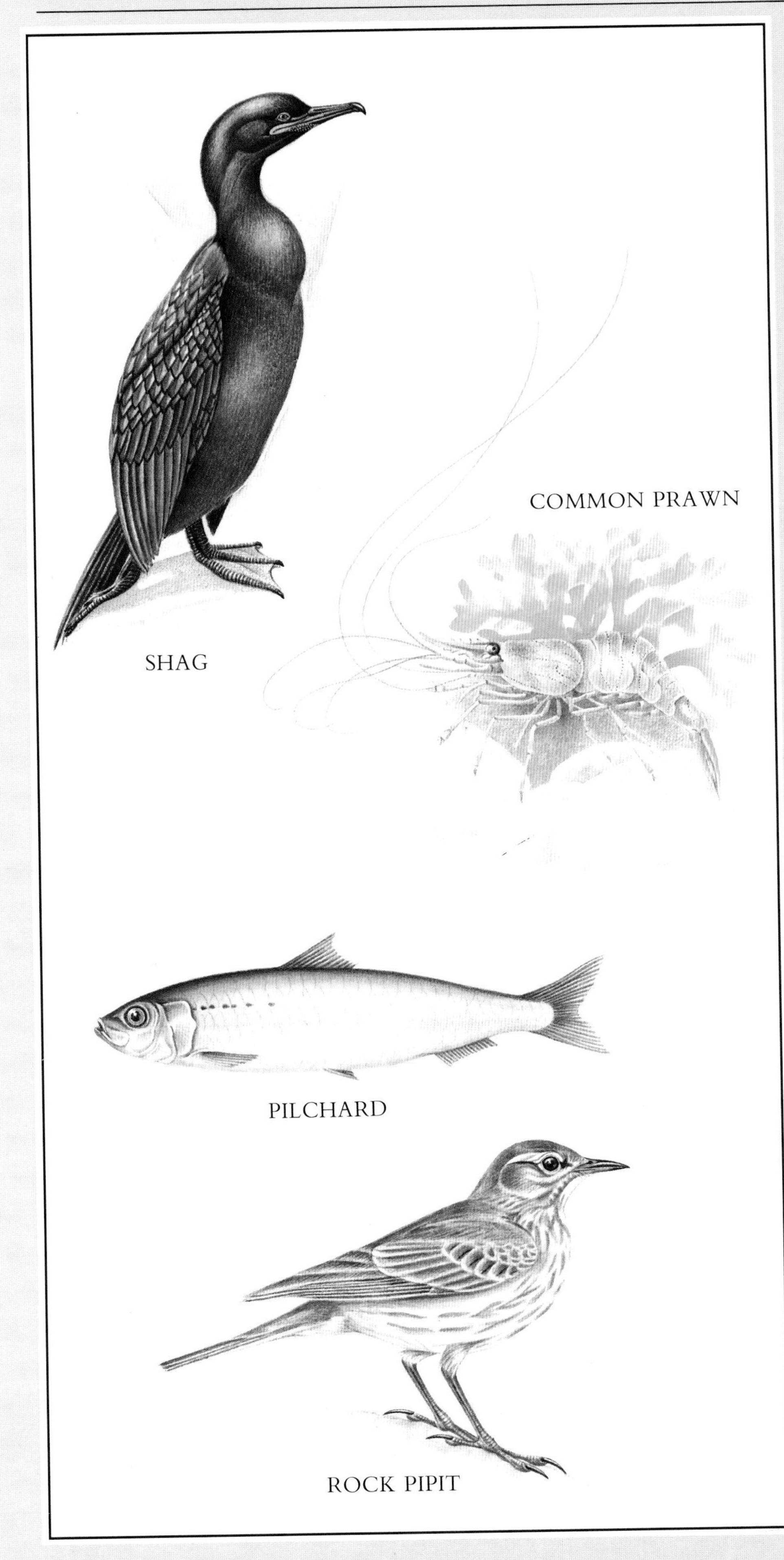

SHAG *Phalacrocorax aristotelis* 28,000 pairs resident. Shags breed mainly on western and Scottish coasts, but at this time of year they may be expected in almost any coastal area, though not inland. (Unlike cormorants, shags will not visit lakes unless driven inland during stormy winter weather.) They are rather slimmer than cormorants, and have a greenish tint when seen in close-up. Both of these species have the quaint habit of spreading their wings to speed drying. Not that they lack waterproofing—this comes not from oil, as many believe, but more from small air bubbles held within the close-knit weave of the feather barbs and barbules. The nest is exceedingly smelly, consisting of a pile of rotting weed and guano on a ledge or in the shelter of a boulder, close to the sea.

COMMON PRAWN *Palaemon serratus* The prawn is now still to be seen in rock pools, its most familiar venue, where it often spends the summer months. It will take to deeper water in winter, returning only when the sea temperature rises. It is most common along western and southern coasts. Points of difference with the shrimp are its 'beak' and two pairs of feelers (the common shrimp has only one pair, and no beak). Prawns walk slowly over the sea bottom, but will quickly flick backwards if alarmed.

PILCHARD *Sardina pilchardus* Cliff-top 'pilchard houses' may still be seen in Cornwall (once the quarters of look-outs for the vast shoals of pilchards that used to sweep past the coast here). Less frequent today, perhaps due to overfishing by factory ships out to sea, these fish may still be shoaling in coastal waters at this time.

ROCK PIPIT *Anthus spinoletta* Although usually remaining on its breeding territories along the rocky shores (where its diet includes many winkles from the weedy rocks), this bird may be seen inland later in winter, coming to watercress beds and old-fashioned sewage farms—in fact, anywhere that insects and other invertebrates can be expected. Such places also attract rock pipits wintering here from abroad. When disturbed, these birds utter a weak cry of alarm. They will nest in a sheltered crevice.

SHANNY (or BLENNY) *Blennius pholis* This small fish, which only grows up to about 5 in. long, is probably the most common fish to dwell on the shore, and is frequently to be seen as the tide retreats, though it is extremely well camouflaged. It inhabits rock pools, usually those on seaweed-covered shores, but also weedy pools alongside breakwaters and such things; it may also be seen at rest out of the water, sheltering like the shore crab under a stone or in a crevice. Shannies can often be seen 'walking' themselves along the sea floor with their forefins.

PURPLE LAVER *Porphyra umbilicalis*, PEPPER DULSE *Laurencia pinnatifida* and CARRAGHEEN (or IRISH MOSS) *Chondrus crispus* In Wales, purple laver is now being collected; known as laver bread, it is fried with bacon. Dulses and carragheen are also edible. These three species are all 'red' seaweeds, their active green chlorophyll masked by pigments which aid photosynthesis in gloomy light. They are most usually found in deep rock pools, or near the foot of the shore, exposed by only some of the month's low tides. On some shores, however, carragheen can be extremely abundant and replace the brown seaweeds.

PUFFIN *Fratercula arctica* 500,000 pairs resident. Mainly found on northern and western coasts, these birds nest, in sometimes large colonies, in cliff-top burrows. These they may dig themselves, or they may commandeer empty rabbit burrows. In any event, offshore islands provide safer sites, free of predatory rats and foxes. The puffin is normally silent, but it may emit a deep growl. Its dramatic bill is clashed with those of rivals in courtship battles, but with special hinges it is really a very sophisticated fishing tool. With it a puffin can poach a shoal of fish (sand eels are favourites)—the bird swims through the shoal, nodding its head from side to side, collecting half a dozen in its beak. In September, puffins will now most probably be leaving their colonies, as they tend to spend their winter months far out to sea. Although these birds are in general decreasing in numbers, some breeding colonies do seem to be keeping up to strength.

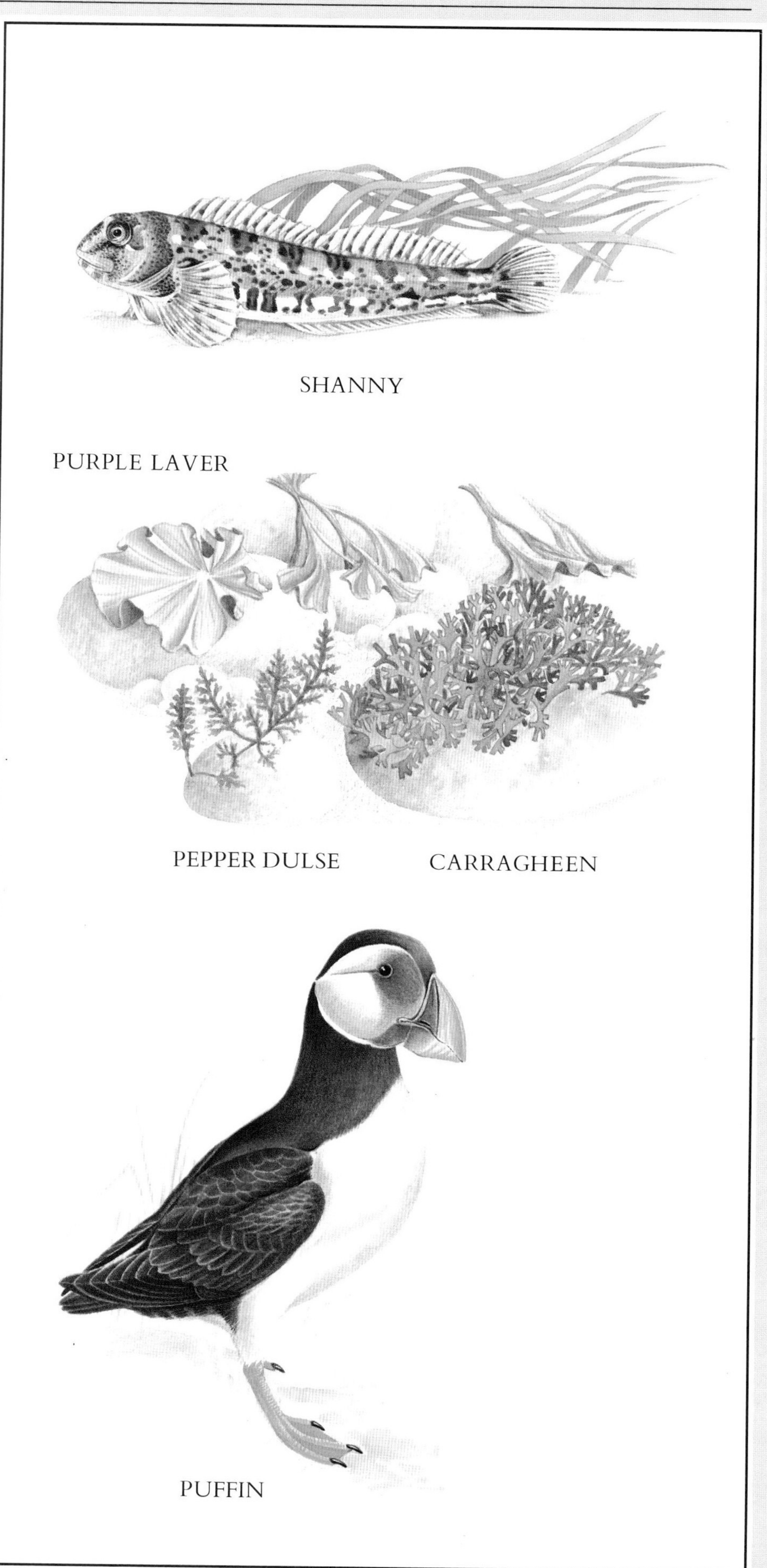

OCTOBER

The difference in the average temperature and hours of sunshine between this month and September is usually greater than for any other pair of months in the calendar. Yet warm days of Indian summers, albeit with frosty nights to follow, are still possible. The clocks are put back an hour on a Sunday in the fourth week, while the smoke of bonfires lingers in valleys. Pheasant shooting begins at the start of the month.

Autumn now has the countryside in its grip. There have already been snatches of colour, with bracken splashed with gold, birch trees more yellow than green, and the horse chestnut also yellowing early. But now, in October, the full glory of the leaf changes decks the woods and hedgerows.

The sap flow to the leaves is cut, but not before the tree has pushed waste products into the leaves, and chemical changes destroy the green chlorophyll and replace it with gaudier pigments. In fact, the brightest flaming colours seem to follow early frosts, which lock the carbohydrates and sugars in the leaves to become the fodder for this chemistry. A spell of warmish quiet weather is then needed, for gusts easily dislodge the leaves once the sap links are cut, and the link is made more fragile in sharp frosts.

Once the leaves have turned, frost can bring them down to pile in drifts across the ground. When fallen, the cells die and oxidation browns the leaf. The best colours are thus to be seen inland, away from the likelihood of coastal gales, perhaps in sheltered valleys. The colours of the Lake District are justly famous, and the south of Britain is normally very colourful.

Red squirrels will raid a heavy acorn crop to build up generous fat reserves. They then survive the winter in good shape and begin breeding early in the spring.

It is arguable which is the most colourful species—some would claim the wild service tree—but it is really the variety which adds enchantment. Even one conifer, the larch, turns. The beech leaf becomes ochre and then bright brown, while some hawthorn leaves turn deep red and the rowan a lighter red. Oak, however, withers without dramatic colour, while ash is liable simply to blacken.

The first severe frosts also decimate the insect populations. Worker wasps die off, and only the queens remain to seek snug hibernation sites, often indoors.

Blackberrying is still possible. There are certainly hundreds of similar 'microspecies' of bramble, each differing slightly in leaf and such things, and time of ripening. However, at about this time the berries tend to become overripe and less tasty.

The blackberries are only part of the natural harvest now being stripped bare by birds, mice, voles and other animals. Blackbirds choose particular hawthorn bushes to raid, working from the top down. Rose-hips, so assiduously collected by school-children in World War 2, to be pulped for their vitamin C content, are left by the birds, but when fallen are taken by mice or voles.

The incoming migrant members of the thrush clan, the redwings and fieldfares, also now arrive, mainly from Scandinavia. Later, in starvation weather, they may come into gardens.

The harvest of fruit and berries marks the end of the natural cycle, and on 31 October falls Halloween, which originally marked a change from the joy of the harvest months to winter ghosts and gloom. The church could hardly ignore so potent a date and switched its focus, turning it into the eve of days dedicated to the saints and the dead—All Saints' Day. Still, the old sinister traditions find echoes today in witch's hats and broomsticks.

Today we take it for granted that autumn colours are a natural wonder to be admired. Yet this was not always so. Our liking for autumn is a legacy of romantic imagination in art and literature over the last 250 years—before this, autumn was a time of misgiving, for the hues augured the onset of winter.

FROSTY MORNINGS

The trend of warmer south to cooler north which set in earlier in the year continues. However, October temperatures are higher than those of April (at the start of summer).

Regions can show great variation. The higher northern hills are often scattered with snow. In extreme years, even low-lying areas in the north may see snow in October, although it is usually limited to the months from November to April.

Some of the southerlies or south-westerlies can bring dull rainy periods, but winds from other directions, such as from the north or north-west, can provide more invigorating brighter days. Generally, there is a noticeable increase in rainfall over the figures recorded for September—a jump from $2\frac{1}{4}$ in. to $2\frac{3}{4}$ in. for the month for a typical inland location.

Many places see frosty patches on the lawn on clear October dawns. On average, in an inland lowland area, a couple of mornings with air frosts may be expected—and usually ground frosts are twice as frequent as air frosts. Frost, though, is always closely related to the lie of the land, and one side of a village may be unlike the other, although these autumn frosts are now rather more widespread than were the last ones in May.

The Arctic is now cooling fast and the temperature difference between its air and that of the Atlantic air it meets along the Arctic polar front becomes very marked. This shows itself in the active depressions and stronger winds which autumn brings.

Towards the end of the month comes the most consistently stormy period of the year, judged over a number of years, but before that, around the middle of the month, a spell of calm, warm, anticyclonic September-like weather may set in—an Indian summer. During such a spell, frosts are more likely.

The onset of autumn is marked by the turning of tree leaves, but grass growth also falters, and hence so does grazing. No year is quite like another, but in this map we see when grazing can be expected to end around the country. The link with temperature is not as direct as it was in spring, when a rise of temperature triggered growth, followed by grazing. Here, at the close of the season, the end of grazing is determined as much by the state of the ground and day-to-day weather as by the last of the grass.

December
November
October
September
End August
August

INDIAN SUMMERS

In the United States, Indian summers are calm, warm spells of weather arriving unseasonally in late autumn. But we in Britain often have something similar, such as in October when an anticyclone brings mellow Septemberish days. This may coincide with St Luke's Day in the middle of the month and be known as 'St Luke's Little Summer'. (Another warm spell, St Martin's Summer, is popularly linked with Martinmas, 11 November, and was mentioned by Shakespeare, while in some years the dog-days, between 3 July and 11 August, are a period of sultry, fly-ridden weather.)

Searching the records over a long run of years, it is possible to discover singularities—that is, spells of weather which tend to be present at the same time each year. Some recorders, for example, detect a stormy spell between 24 November and 14 December—at least, it has appeared in a high proportion of years since 1889. However, the sheer scale of the fluctuations in such measurable things as temperature, rainfall, wind, and the number of storms between one year and another, let alone between one location and another, make these singularities at best possibilities rather than fixtures in the almanac.

An Indian summer brings brilliantly clear skies to this Lake District scene, yet there is a hint of autumn in the browning leaves and bracken.

Dull days tend to get forgotten, but the sunny splendour making the walk to church for harvest festival such a delight that year is long remembered. Memories create a golden age; was the Battle of Britain fought under glorious blue skies to match those of ancient Greece? It does seem that the climate is changing, and some experts agree. A recent study for the EEC predicts that, during the next century, Scotland will become warmer as part of overall climatic changes.

Some people believe that the world's climate is becoming warmer as a result of the 'greenhouse effect'. Carbon dioxide, released by burning coal and oil fuels, acts as an atmospheric blanket, trapping warmth like the glass of a greenhouse. Doubling the quantity of the gas is reckoned to give a rapid temperature rise of between 2°C and 4°C—enough to melt glaciers sufficiently to raise the sea level by 3 ft, flooding much of London and East Anglia.

However, only 12,000 years ago Britain was still in the grip of the Ice Age. The climate has certainly changed since then and may be expected to continue to do so. Analysis of plant pollen preserved in ancient soils shows fluctuation, with some periods becoming wetter, while others were warmer and drier. In Roman times it was warmer than now, but the Plantagenet era saw a deterioration—there was even a 'little ice age' between 1650 and 1720, when alpine glaciers advanced.

Since the last war, commercial vineyards have been established in many southern counties, but in the monastic days of the 14th century they were found as far north as Yorkshire. Safety from spring frosts is crucial for their success, as are hot summers to ripen the grapes.

Internationally, climate is analysed over 30-year periods at least. This is because climate can be regarded as average weather—and an average can disguise wide variations. In 1987, the coldest January on record was followed by the warmest April for a century! The fluctuations in the weather that are remembered so forcibly from one year to the next far outweigh the more gradual, longer-term changes of climate, and a single lifetime is simply not long enough to notice a real climatic change. However, if the man-made greenhouse effect is a reality, this will distort the slower, natural changes that are normally to be expected.

MUSHROOMS AND TOADSTOOLS

In the October wood, footsteps crackle on the fallen litter of twigs and brown leaves. It is taken for granted that these will disappear, preventing the wood from slowly silting up, year by year, to the level of the highest branches with this dead matter.

What we are seeing, in fact, is the efficiency of the destructors. Indeed, there could be no productive life without their unique contribution to the overall picture. Fungi are powerful members of the destructor clan, which also numbers some familiar animals among its members—earthworms and many beetles, slugs and woodlice, as well as minute bacteria and single-celled life forms.

In October there are many fungi, often strange, to be seen in all habitats. There are pastel elf caps and vivid toadstools of evil appearance. Both have spokes of gills hanging below, from which the ripe spores fall. Bracket fungi on a tree trunk have a sponge-like, pore-producing tissue below, whereas stomach fungi, such as the puffballs of sandy places and the earth stars which look like small peeled fruits, produce their spores internally, to be ejected through a mouth when ripe. The morel, which is seen in spring, produces its spores in small pits on its upper surface. Mildews, moulds and rusts are also fungi, members of this large grouping of flowerless plants.

This may be doing them less than justice, though. Fungi are certainly not animals, but some botanists do not consider them as plants either, regarding these organisms instead as a separate living 'kingdom' in their own right. However, their structure *is* comparable to that of plants, although they lack green chlorophyll and must rely on organic matter for nourishment and growth. To reach it they produce their minute spores in millions at a time, and when loosed these drift easily on the wind. This thin soup of spores wafts everywhere, and when a spore lodges on dead matter it puts out feeding threads.

Hidden below the fungus cap of whatever shape or hue stretches a web of these feeding threads. They spread through the soil between the trees, seeking nourishment from the rotting twigs and leaves, or permeate the wood of a fallen bough, or disperse across the pasture to gain nutrients released by the decay

Right Artist's fungus—a bracket fungus parasitic on its host tree (the ivy, by contrast, feeds from its own roots and uses the tree only for support).

Far right The poisonous fly agaric. The fungus cap grows surrounded by 'veils' which tear apart as it enlarges. Fragments of the 'universal veil' remain attached to the red cap. Part-way down the stem hang the remains of the 'partial veil' which separated the gills from the stem.

of dead grass roots and the myriads of dead soil invertebrates.

However, some fungi are parasitic; they attack living tissues. Many bracket fungi are seen on seemingly healthy trees, while the caps of honey fungus clustering at the foot of a tree in autumn are an ominous sight for the gardener or forester, for this potent fungus will not only attack a dead or dying tree, but will also energetically reach across to its healthy neighbours with thin 'bootlace' strands below the soil.

Fungi help to reduce elaborate and sturdy natural structures such as dead timber to their simpler elements. When the fungus itself dies and decays, as all living things must, these elements are released into the soil to fertilize new generations of green plants. Nothing lives in isolation in the natural world, and where fungi attack a fallen branch, alongside them will be other destructors such as beetles, which lay their eggs so that the grubs will eat out tunnels in the timber, and yeasts to ferment the liquors of decay.

It is noticeable that some kinds of toadstool appear only below certain trees. For example, the fly agaric, its red cap dotted with white, is seen below birch and pine trees in the autumn, but not in beech or oak woods. This association is quite interesting, for many fungi have a close relationship with living trees and some other green plants, called a mycorrhiza. It is not a parasitic relationship, although it may have begun as such. The rootlets of the host become wrapped in a white cloak of fungal threads, some of which may actually enter them. There is evidence that the tree or plant benefits from this interaction, for its roots are supplied, by the fungus, with a ready supply of nutrients, while presumably the fungus can take some nutrients from the host.

This could be very useful for the beech trees in a 'hanger', growing on the thin, nutrient-poor soil of a chalk down slope, or a pine tree growing on the acid, impoverished soil of a sandy waste. It could also help young seedlings get away to a good start. In the case of orchids, it does seem that the seedlings rely on partnership with soil fungi, which may explain their generous presence in some years, and their absence in others. Another prized flower, the yellow bird's-nest has quite yellow scale-like leaves, completely lacking green chlorophyll. The plant cannot photosynthesize its own sugars, but with the help of a soil fungus it is able to obtain its food ready-made from decaying leaves. As it does not need sunlight, it can therefore live in the gloom of beech and pine woods, where it is seen flowering from June to August.

Left The porcelain fungus has a translucent cap.

Far left The aptly-named trooping crumble cap festoons a dead, mossy tree stump.

Left The shaggy ink cap, also known as lawyer's wig, is fairly common in a variety of grassy places. As the caps age, they blacken and soften into decay.

FARMERS' SALES

For the livestock farmer, the sales are crucial. A careful and expert eye is needed to ensure that the ewes bought in are sound and healthy, good in foot, tooth and udder.

If any month could be counted as the start of the farming year it is October, with decisions having to be made about what to plant for next spring's rotation crops, and where—although the winter wheat and barley may already be sown by now.

Rotations—taking the plough around the farm, as they used to say—make the best of the soil. Two hundred years ago, under the then-new Norfolk four-course rotation, a field would be ploughed in autumn and sown with wheat. This would be followed by a root crop, such as turnips for sheep grazing, during the coming winter. Next spring the field would be ploughed and spring barley sown. When harvested in August, the field would be left to grass over and perhaps hay would be made in the next year, with ploughing for wheat again that autumn or the following spring.

A modern rotation might be as follows: barley; then to grass when harvested and this grazed by sheep for a year; then ploughed and sown for wheat. In this way, grass breaks in as a pause between the cereal regimes which make greater demands on the soil. Other breaks for spring planting might be potatoes, peas and sugar beet in some areas. Field beans may also be sown, filling the air with a delicious, heavy, sweet scent in June.

October sees great livestock sales. Cattle, especially the year's calves, disperse to farms that are better stocked with fodder for the coming winter. For upland sheep farmers, these sales provide much of the year's income; these farmers also make up their flocks for the coming year at this time.

There are three main types of sheep in Britain. The mountain sheep, such as the Scottish Blackface, Cheviot and Swaledale, can survive out on the northern hills even in winter, while grass hill sheep, such as the Clun Forest, lie between the mountain and lowland breeds in hardiness. The lowland sheep are either shortwools, which include the old Suffolk and other downland breeds, or longwools, such as the Leicester. There are also regular crossbreeds such as the Mule—this is from a Swaledale ewe and Bluefaced Leicester ram. It has its father's Roman nose, and when bred with a lowland ram gives a good lambing rate with quick-growing lambs.

Stratification is at the heart of sheep farming in Britain, when the qualities of the hardiest breeds are added to the more productive lowland breeds. With the poor keep provided by the heather and stringy grass of the hills, the mountain breeds do not produce much milk and usually have only one lamb. But they are hardy—they have to be to survive.

To take just one example: after two or three annual crops of lambs on their birthplace farm, Cheviot ewes may be sold as 'draft' ewes to another hill farmer who will cross them with, say, a Border Leicester ram. The resulting lambs may be 'store'—that is, destined for the butcher—in which case they are known as hogs or hoggets (both male and female) and sold to a lowland farmer for fattening up. Those lambs intended for breeding, however, may be kept for 15 months before also being sold, but in this case as draft animals, to a lowland farm to be mated with a lowland Suffolk ram, for example. The lambs produced in this way fatten well and profitably for the table on these milder lowland pastures.

So, at this time of year in the northern hills, there are great sales of breeding ewes and of store lambs from the Pennine grazings, destined for the lowlands. There may be young mountain ewes being sold to be wintered in the valleys, to be bought back for lambing in the hills in spring. (More usually, however, such sheep will be 'put on tack'—that is, grazed on rented lowland pastures for the winter.) There are no hard and fast rules in all this—and some of those Cheviot ewes, their teeth now rather worn from the harsh grazing of the mountain slopes, may be drafted direct to lowland farms to spend the last two or three years of their lives bringing their hardy background to new crops of lambs.

Towards the end of October, a start will be made on tupping, or putting the ewes to the rams. These favoured animals, pastured on good grass near the farm, are 'raddled', wherein a coloured block of crayon is strapped to the chest, or perhaps the chest is simply daubed with red or blue ochre. The ewes which they mount and service are thus marked with this and can be easily separated out, being penned together to give flocks likely to lamb at the same time, almost five months hence. A ram will serve around 30 to 50 ewes.

Sheep farming in Britain once created considerable wealth, as evidenced by the grandeur of the massive village churches in such prime old wool counties as Suffolk. Local sheep gave their name to the Cotswolds, and in fact many areas had their own breed. Although sheep are no longer as profitable as scientifically-run modern arable farming, they can make a good combination with the plough.

Livestock farmers have to make sharper decisions than most other businessmen. What other manufacturers have to gamble on raw material that can go down with a whole range of ailments and diseases?

RICHMOND PARK

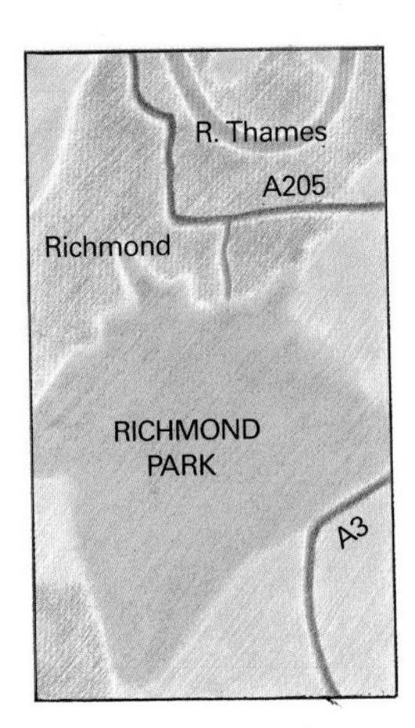

Lying south of the River Thames and Kew Bridge, and closely embraced by the brick and concrete of London's suburbs, Richmond Park remains as a green lung in the city. The sweeps of grassland grazed by the deer are set with ancient oaks and plantations.

Grass puts on lush growth in Britain's damp climate, yet grassland is not a natural form of British vegetation. If left unploughed, ungrazed and to its own devices, nature would scatter bush and tree seeds across it, creating a wood within 50 years.

Open grassland today is familiar in some commons, and in planted ley fields, hay meadows and unploughed pasture fields. Yet in the past, deer parks were also common, and in their heyday, 600 years ago, there were more than 3000 scattered across England, an average of one to every four parishes, and at several hundreds of acres a time, they totalled a large area.

A few survive today, sometimes still being grazed by deer. Originally they were simply deer ranches providing both sport and fresh meat in winter for the magnates and their class. As such, they were usually attached to a castle or grand house, and in the case of Richmond Park, this was royal Richmond Palace, favourite of Queen Elizabeth I but demolished in the early 18th century. Here, in October, both the fallow and red deer are handsome in full antlers, and are in rut.

To keep the deer in, and poachers out (there is an apocryphal story that Shakespeare was caught in Warwickshire's Charlecote Park), deer parks were fenced, most usually atop a specially-dug bank. Around Richmond Park, though, a wall does the job; and it works well to exclude the modern world—only the background hum of London's traffic and the aeroplanes jetting to Heathrow intrude on this archetypal scene.

Many of the proud old oak trees have a neat browse line parallel to the ground where the deer reach up to nibble the leaves. Deer grazing also maintains acres of open turf, although bracken spreads in some places on the acid river-gravel soil (deer find this plant distasteful, as do sheep, and so leave it untouched). Such open grassy 'launds' served for the chase in the traditional deer parks.

These parks often contained patches of woodland, which were sometimes planted and fenced until the trees were tall enough to be safe from the deer. These plantation trees supplied timber, but in such parklands it was also usual to gain supplies of wood from the open trees by pollarding them, that is, cutting the crown of boughs at about 8 ft from the ground. New branches, growing out of reach of the hungry deer, then gradually thickened and were cut again, thus being a useful renewable resource. Pollarding ruins the timber value of a tree, though. Not worth the cost of felling, most of our oldest oak trees are pollards, with their branches now grown to giant size.

While well-managed timber trees offer few holes for nesting owls and woodpeckers, old trees which carry the scars of centuries provide a haven for a wide variety of animal life. They are particularly important for beetles, and if decaying boughs are left to rot on the ground, so much the better. Stag beetles, giants of the British clan, are often found here in June.

In Richmond Park, both red and fallow deer are easily seen. The red deer are native, but it is believed that the fallow were brought here in Roman times. The latter were kept in the medieval deer parks, while the red deer were favoured for the royal hunts of the wilder forests. The rut of both these animals takes place in October. The dominant males mark their territory by thrashing trees and bushes, and fights between master and challengers are common.

The spaciousness of the open deer park captured imaginations two centuries ago, and such places gained a new vogue. Many were landscaped to strengthen the natural look of open lawns and clumped trees. No longer hunted (although in Richmond Park they were being privately shot until 1904), the deer were kept on for ornamental reasons and as natural lawn-mowers.

Red and fallow deer are both to be seen in Richmond Park. Although the red deer (*Cervus elaphus*) is a true native, it is believed that the fallow (*Dama dama*) was introduced in Roman times; it was recorded as well-established in the Domesday Book, and became a favourite for parks—for the hunt and for venison.

BRITAIN'S PARKLANDS

Here are some other parklands and similar areas worth visiting:

1 Galloway Forest Park, near Newton Stewart, Dumfries and Galloway.

2 Chillingham Castle Park, Northumberland. This encloses a race of wild white cattle.

3 Hardwick Hall Country Park, near Sedgefield, Durham.

4 Lyme Park, north of Macclesfield, Cheshire.

5 Charlecote Park, near Stratford upon Avon, Warwickshire. A typical estate deer park, where William Shakespeare went poaching.

6 Hatfield Forest Country Park, near Bishop's Stortford, Essex.

7 Weald Park, Brentwood, Essex.

8 Windsor Great Park, Berkshire.

9 Dynevor Deer Park, Llandeilo, Dyfed.

10 Dyrham Park, north of Bath, Avon. A typical deer park.

11 New Forest, Hampshire.

12 Trelissick, Fal Estuary, south of Truro, Cornwall.

***Richmond Park**, London.

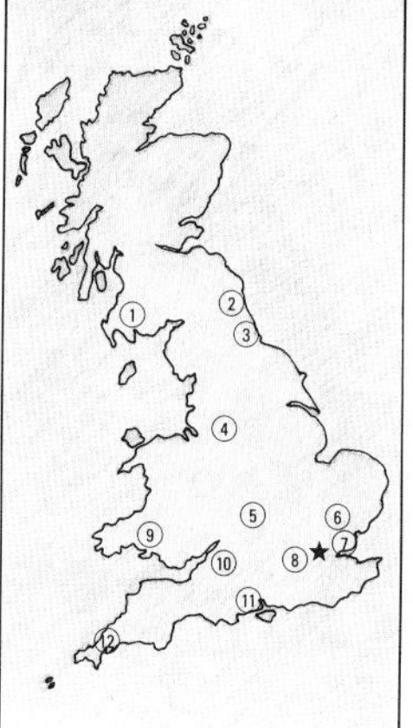

Here we see a red deer stag calling during the rut, while mist wreathes the trees. He is accompanied by his own harem of hinds. Take note of the ever-venturesome starling!

RED DEER *Cervus elaphus* These deer are now in their finest fettle, for it is the time of the rut. They can be seen in many places in England and Scotland, but not Wales. In their Scottish strongholds, they may now be coming down to the lower moors and forests (they will return to the high ground in May, not only to graze the new heather, but also to escape the troublesome flies). Stags and hinds are seen together only at the rut. In September, the stag herds will have dispersed; each male now tries to secure a harem of as many as 20 hinds. The older, larger and stronger stags (with hard antlers fully tined in the sixth year) stake out part of the hinds' territory and deter rivals by thrashing trees, urinating and bellowing. Wallowing in churned peat is also part of the ritual, and wounding tourneys sometimes occur. After rutting, the stags will regroup back on their own territories. By the end of April, the stags will have cast their antlers, and the calves are born in June.

HONEY FUNGUS *Armillaria mellea* This fungus may now be seen as clumps of caps on dead trees, but it will also be condemning those still living: it rots the heartwood. It spreads by spores, but also by long dark strands, or 'rhizomorphs', which reach through the soil.

PHEASANT *Phasianus colchicus* 500,000 'wild' pairs resident (but many more are reared and released). The pheasant is not a native bird, but it has now been established here for hundreds of years. Several varieties of plumage may be seen. It is reared for shooting coverts; its rapid climb when disturbed is regarded as giving good 'sport'. (Its close season ended on 30 September and will begin again on 2 February.) Kale and sweet corn are often planted to give it field cover. However, many evade the table by taking to other copses and woods. Tending to stay in cover on colder winter days, pheasants will often roam further in milder weather.

COMMON EARTH STAR *Geastrum triplex* This fungus develops its unusual shape when its outer skin folds back; it is now worth looking out for, particularly in beech woods.

DEAD MAN'S FINGERS *Xylaria polymorpha* Here is another example of the often bizarre forms taken by fungi (we have around 7000 species in Britain, compared with 1500 seeding plants). Dead man's fingers generally grows in groups on tree stumps, commonly beech, throughout the year.

WOOD-PIGEON *Columba palumbus* 3,000,000 pairs resident. This bird's appetite for sprouts and fodder crops in lean times is voiced as justification when it is decimated in 'rough shooting'. Despite this, it remains a strong element of the countryside with its five-phrase cooing song: 'co-*coo*-coocoo-coo', ending with a 'cuk'. The clap of its wings is an alarm note, heard also in display flights. Parents feed their young on rich 'crop-milk' and so do not have to rely on the early summer flush of insects for body-building protein. It may still be breeding in October or even later, at the end of a season which began in March. Before combine harvesters, there was a breeding peak in September when the gleanings lay scattered in the fields, but in London nowadays (wood-pigeons are also seen in urban areas) the peak is in May.

WOOD (or LONG-TAILED FIELD) MOUSE *Apodemus sylvaticus* Common in woodland and other habitats, the nocturnal wood mouse digs its own burrow system in which it passes the day (and rears its young). In its search for food it will forage widely, and may occasionally be seen bounding over the grass. It will now be storing berries for winter, perhaps using a deserted bird's nest. Numbers may be at a peak now, but this will not simply be due to breeding, for when the territorial boss mice die, several others can invade the best territories.

STOCK DOVE *Columba oenas* 100,000 pairs resident. Similar in appearance to town pigeons, the stock dove may at first escape notice. It is also less fond of human surrounds, preferring instead open country with old trees. Nesting in holes, usually in trees although rabbit holes may also be put to use, the birds feed their young (as do all pigeons) on the 'milk' from their crop lining. Its song is a gruff double 'coo-*coo*'.

DEAD MAN'S FINGERS

WOOD-PIGEON

WOOD MOUSE

STOCK DOVE

IVY *Hedera helix* The familiar evergreen climber is now flowering (September–November), and many bluebottles, drone flies, wasps, bees, butterflies and moths may still visit it on warm sunny days. Note that the flowering stems bear pointed oval leaves (not ivy-shaped ones, which appear only on non-flowering stems). The forthcoming black fruits will be taken by birds in early spring. Ivy has its own root system and only uses a tree, wall or rock face for support; its pliable and probing young stems are covered with sucker-like rootlets.

BULLFINCH *Pyrrhula pyrrhula* 300,000 pairs resident. These handsome birds mate for life and are usually seen in devoted pairs. With their powerful bills, they will now strip and split the 'keys' of ash trees. In spring, they rob the buds of orchards; fruit growers can be licensed to shoot them. However, bullfinches do not breed until the first seeds of the year are available. Orchards most at risk are those with woodland cover nearby, for these are shy, retiring birds.

PIGMY SHREW *Sorex minutus* Our smallest mammal, measuring $2\frac{1}{2}$ in. (head and body), the pigmy shrew forages in the runways of other rodents, more or less continuously, like its cousin the common shrew.

RED ADMIRAL *Vanessa atalanta* This butterfly is now seen feeding on the last flowers or sipping the juice of windfalls. It migrates here from the Mediterranean in spring, and migrants may continue to arrive throughout the summer. These mate, lay their eggs on nettles, and the home-bred generation flies from July to October. However, they cannot survive the frosts to come.

QUAIL *Coturnix coturnix* 100 pairs visit from May to October. Numbers fluctuate but are low, for nesting is abortive when, instead of hay, silage is cut early before the brood is fully fledged (quail are ground nesters). They are also game birds, and many are shot en route to and from Africa. Retiring birds, they are able to slip quickly through the long grass or growing corn, but their presence is revealed by their liquid call, the three-syllable 'whit-whit-whit'.

COMMA *Polygonia c-album* Most common in the south, the second of the year's generations is now on the wing and will fly until hibernation—they are the last to hibernate, usually in bark crevices. They emerge again in warm spells from March onwards, the eggs being laid on nettles; this new brood will fly in July (the butterflies which we now see began flying in late August).

COMMON SHREW *Sorex araneus* Living everywhere, even on mountains (though lack of worms may limit its numbers on acid soils), the common shrew is more often heard than seen, spending much of its time hidden in its tunnels or below cover. Solitary except when mating, it is fiercely territorial, and incomers are met with shrill squeaks. In autumn, the young may dispossess the adults, which often then come to gardens to feed. Almost ceaseless activity day and night sharpens its appetite for insects and snails, and it will quickly lose energy if unfed for a few hours.

PINK-FOOTED GOOSE *Anser brachyrhynchus* 100,000 birds visit. Arriving from Icelandic breeding grounds, this bird is now found in the north and down the east coast as far as north Norfolk. Often the commonest wild goose, it is seen in family parties feeding mainly in stubble and other arable fields, though they roost on mud-flats and other coastal areas. They move from one to the other at dawn and dusk, and on clear moonlit nights (of the kind often met in October), they may delay their return 'flighting' and continue to feed.

YARROW *Achillea millefolium* This strongly scented plant is often still in flower on grassy verges (June–October). Resembling cow parsley, it is in fact one of the daisy family.

EARWIG *Forficula auricularia* The name 'earwig' may derive from this insect's instinctive habit of hiding itself away in any crevice—at this time of year, it may be found deep inside a dead flower head, seeking a possible hibernation den. The female (with less-curved pincers than the male) is a devoted mother, protecting her young until they can fend for themselves.

JACK SNIPE *Lymnocryptes minimus* 20,000 birds visit. One sign of autumn is the first sight of this bird on a waterside meadow. Staying from September to April, the jack (that is, undersized) snipe is dumpier than the larger snipe, with shorter bill and legs. It can also be recognized by its habit of bobbing when feeding. It is an unsociable bird, usually seen singly.

RAINBOW TROUT *Salmo gairdneri* First introduced from North America into English waters for sport in 1880, the rainbow trout now breeds wild in only a few waters, such as the Derbyshire River Wye, despite its ability to tolerate warmer and less-oxygenated water than the native brown trout. The rainbows fished in reservoirs and such places have been reared in hatcheries; it is the fish most commonly bred in fish farms, for it grows quickly and can withstand crowding better than the brown trout.

GREAT POND SNAIL *Limnaea stagnalis* Commonly found in ponds and ditches, it can grow quite a large shell (2 in.). Disliking bright sunshine, there is a good chance of seeing it still active on gloomy October days, breathing from the surface with a simple lung. It will hibernate in the winter. Eggs are laid as a jelly-like mass on the undersides of vegetation.

HERALD MOTH *Scoliopteryx libatrix* This moth, on the wing in autumn prior to hibernation, is interesting in that its resting camouflage of colouring and jagged outline is adapted to the autumn tints of shrivelled leaves. Its eggs are laid on wetland trees—sallows, willows and poplars.

COMMON CARP *Cyprinus carpio* The carp, from eastern Mediterranean lands, first stocked monastery fish ponds hundreds of years ago. The most common form is the fully-scaled king carp (mirror carp have a row of large scales, while the leather carp is almost scaleless). At this time of year, carp are smooth, handsome fish, but with the onset of breeding in May and June, the head of the male will develop small swellings. Breeding is successful only when the water is 18 °C or over. Many of the carp seen and fished will have been stocked.

RIVER SNAIL *Viviparus viviparus* Breathing with gills, this snail may remain active on the riverbed in cold weather. Like seashore winkles, it has a 'lid' to close off its shell. The eggs are retained within its body, so the young are born 'live'.

LITTLE GULL *Larus minutus* Visiting during winter, the little gull, unlike the black-headed gull which it rather resembles, retains a spot on its pate. It has a black head when breeding. This bird feeds in a rather tern-like fashion, beating up and down over the water, before dipping to take a fish. It is now seen on coastal and inland waters in the south and east.

GRAYLING *Thymallus thymallus* Looking quite like a small salmon, but with a rather large back fin, the grayling can compete with trout in cold, well-oxygenated running water, eating the trout's food and (so many claim) tasting better. At this time of year, grayling will be seen in shoals; they separate to spawn from March to May.

WHITE-FRONTED GOOSE *Anser albifrons* 7000 birds visit. Easily identified by the white blaze on its forehead, this bird visits from October to April. Those with rather orange bills seen in western Scotland come from Greenland, while those with pinkish bills at Slimbridge in Gloucestershire, and other sites in England, come from Russia. They graze mainly on open fields and wet pastures, usually in family groups for the pair are strongly linked. If the moon is bright, they will even graze at night. They have a rather high-pitched yodelling call.

CRACK WILLOW *Salix fragilis* Often found growing beside lowland rivers, this is a rather handsome tree, with a green crown and fissured bark. It is frequently late shedding its leaves, and may still be well covered. This willow is commonly pollarded (that is, cut back to the trunk) to grow a new head of shoots, which will thicken into branches. This provides a supply of smallwood, and also prevents the fragile branches breaking (the way that the twigs can be snapped off gives the tree its name).

EXMOOR PONY *Equus* (domestic) One of the key sights of the country year is the annual pony round-up. Exmoor ponies are usually rounded up in October, at which time the year's foals are branded. Small and stocky, they are probably quite true to the original wild type, for these ponies have been living semi-wild and running free on Exmoor since the end of the Ice Age. Belonging to a pony family long inured to arctic conditions, they have a dense, insulating undercoat below the wiry top coat; in fact, so good is this coat that snow often lingers unmelted on their backs.

SMALL COPPER *Lycaena phlaeas* Widely distributed over much of Britain, this brilliantly-coloured little butterfly is a late flier, with broods on the wing from May to the first sharp frosts (usually at the end of October). It flies over heaths and other open ground, and is fiercely territorial.

DARTFORD WARBLER *Sylvia undata* Over 100 pairs resident. Our only warbler resident throughout the year, this bird needs to feed on hibernating insects and spiders, so survival is risky when snow hides the larder—especially as, unlike many birds, it tends not to roam far in its search for food in winter. In addition, its preferred habitat of heathland with gorse and heather has increasingly been cleared in recent decades. In March, it may be heard singing before its warbler cousins arrive, a rather unmusical warble: 'terr-err-tiddle-tiddle-dee'. When disturbed, the bird bouncily flies away, and it keeps its long tail cocked at a jaunty angle when perched.

SOFT RUSH *Juncus effusus* Rushes are frequent members of plant communities of wet moors and hill pastures. This particular species is typical with its sharp, pointed stems, and a panicle of flowers held halfway to their tips.

GROUND LICHEN *Cladonia floerkeana* This species is one of many lichens found on the peaty ground of moors and heaths. The bright-red spore body atop the grey fruiting stalk is particularly noticeable.

BOG MOSS *Sphagnum palustre* In spite of its bad press, a bog is neither smelly nor muddy, but is instead a fragile habitat. It is the creation of bog moss, the floppy stems of which create a living, waterlogged sponge. This moss needs few nutrients to survive—even those which are brought by rain can help. On the rainy hills, bogs may spread to blanket the ground, but they may also form on wet valley gravels, where seepage saturates the soil with acid water. In the acid, airless conditions below the bog surface, the dead vegetation does not rot and so peat forms, in time many feet thick. A bog is often a mosaic of wet bog-moss areas and hummocks of drier peat where heather and bilberry root.

GREATER TUSSOCK SEDGE *Carex paniculata* A sedge is a grass-like plant, but its solid stem is often triangular in cross-section. This species is seen on boggy ground in England and Wales, and often in wet woodlands where it can form large tussocks. It is rare in Scotland.

SHORT-EARED OWL *Asio flammeus* 1000 pairs resident. Breeding mainly in the Welsh hills, the Pennines and Scotland, with a few in the south, this bird becomes more widespread in winter while still keeping to open horizons, such as salt marshes. Seen more often hunting in winter than at other times of the year, especially towards dusk, it will slowly quarter open rough grassland, sometimes hovering, while listening for a rustle in the grass. Normally silent, this owl may scream a warning if the nest, a shallow scrape among the heather, is approached. It also roosts on grass tussocks and other ground vegetation.

COMMON EARTH-BALL *Scleroderma citrinum* A fungus of mossy heathland, this may now be found dried up and empty of its spores. Beetles may occasionally bore into the old fruit bodies of the earth-ball.

PINE MARTEN *Martes martes* Restricted to remote areas, mountains or woods (but not necessarily pine forests), this animal's hunting begins at dusk. With nights now falling earlier, it may be glimpsed bounding lithely across a forest ride.

BASS *Dicentrarchus labrax* This is a prime sporting fish, powerful and elegant. Its prefers warmer waters, and the October run past Portland Bill is a notable autumn run. It feeds on smaller fish, as well as shrimps and crabs.

BRENT GOOSE *Branta bernicla* 50,000 birds visit. Autumn is the time when wild geese wing in, and among them are Brent geese, arriving on southern and eastern coasts. These are largely of the black-bellied race, from Arctic Russia. They feed on eel-grass on the tidal mud-flats, but may also raid fields of young winter barley and wheat. Their voice is a croaking grunt.

KNOT *Calidris canutus* 100,000 birds visit. Large numbers of knots pass Britain on their passage migration flights, and some may remain, usually on estuaries. The name may be a corruption of King Canute (Cnut), for they too defy the tide, roaming the mud for shellfish and worms, and roosting just out of reach of it—but they do have a low 'nut' call. Often seen in large flocks, they fly with spectacular finesse, twisting and turning together so precisely that the flock seems to change colour as dark backs replace white undersides as they wheel.

SEA LETTUCE *Ulva lactuca* This species usually grows lower on the shore than *Enteromorpha*. Green seaweeds such as this are commonly grazed by limpets, and often the only place they can survive is on the limpet shell itself, out of reach!

DUNLIN *Calidris alpina* 4000 pairs breed; 500,000 birds in winter. Though a number breed on moorland in Britain, many more dunlins winter here (they are our most numerous winter wader). They have now recently lost the black belly of their summer plumage. Like knots, they form spectacular wheeling flocks over the saltings and estuaries. When feeding, they scamper across the shore, head down, stitching holes in the mud as they go. They are lightly probing for food; when this is found, the bird will pause to probe deeper. On the breeding moors they are secretive, but with a purring trill that carries through the mists.

SANDERLING *Calidris alba* 10,000 birds visit. This bird may now be seen on passage south, though peak numbers were likely a month or two earlier. Those remaining to winter here are usually seen in small flocks of ten or so. In spring (peaking in May), there will be a return migration north. They are seen scurrying down the beach after the retreating backwash of a wave, pecking up food, then running back as the swash of the next wave approaches, legs as busy as clockwork. Now silvery-grey in colour, their breeding plumage is reddish. If disturbed, these birds will call 'twick-twick' and usually run away rather than taking flight.

GREEN SEAWEED *Enteromorpha* species. Lacking pigments to help their photosynthesis in the gloom underwater, green seaweeds are found in shallow rock pools. This species is found high on the shore in summer, but in the winter months to come, its bright-green fronds may be seen lower on the shore. The sea is warmer than the air in winter, and it is perhaps only in the lower pools that the young plants will find the temperature they need to grow.

BARNACLE GOOSE *Branta leucopsis* 30,000 birds visit. Now arriving on north-western coasts, mainly in west Scotland (from Greenland) and Solway (from Spitzbergen), these geese fly in ragged, yelping flocks and will remain until April, grazing on grass on various coastal pastures. Equally noisy when feeding, they roost on the tidal flats, commuting at dawn and dusk. In deep winter, they must spend the short days grazing, and like other geese they will continue to feed by moonlight. (On Islay, farmers are compensated by the Nature Conservancy Council for the damage done to the pastures, and sometimes shooting licences are issued.) Their name derives from an old belief that they hatch from barnacles.

BALLAN WRASSE *Labrus bergylta* A colourful fish (a few are rather red, though the majority are brownish-green), the ballan wrasse is still fairly common in our coastal waters until November. In winter, it usually retires to deeper water. The young are often seen in rock pools.

NOVEMBER

The season 'early winter' extends from 20 November to 19 January. With our variable weather, one way of determining winter is when the temperature falls below 6°C for long periods and grass ceases to grow. This is a foggy month; nevertheless, there are often clear night skies. Guy Fawkes Night, or Bonfire Night, is on 5 November, and fox hunting begins this month.

The final fall of beech nuts occurs early in November. This mast and the earlier acorn crops were vital in past centuries, being used for the grazing of swine. Once fattened up, the slaughter of these animals traditionally took place on or about Martinmas, 11 November, and their bacon was a staple to be rationed carefully throughout the coming winter.

Although seemingly a dead time, some hint of the coming year is already present. Resident song thrushes reoccupy territories, although they will desert them to find food in the hard days to come. Robins, too, hold territory at this time of year, and sing loudly to reinforce it. Meanwhile, male blackbirds clatter noisily at dusk, proposing themselves for the future breeding territories.

Migration apart, many birds are generally quite mobile in November, shifting ground during the day in response to local weather conditions. This mobility is crucial, for few have fat stocks enough to last more than a few days' hunger, and many have even less. Thus, lapwings will cross counties and flocks of skylarks, a hundred strong, fly here from Scandinavia. These visiting skylarks are silent, but our resident birds, more confident, may well be singing at this time, to be silenced only by bitter or foggy spells.

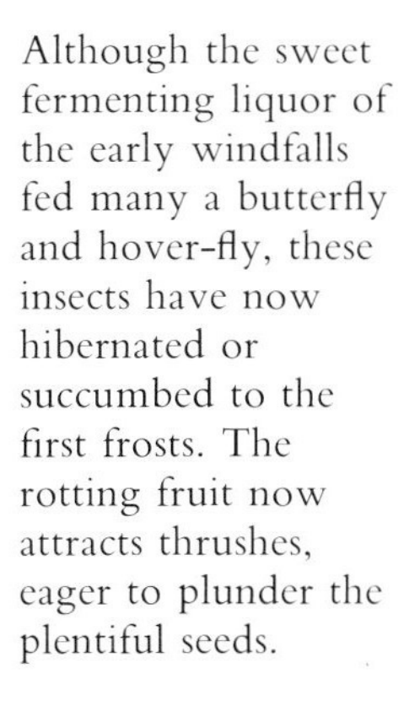

Although the sweet fermenting liquor of the early windfalls fed many a butterfly and hover-fly, these insects have now hibernated or succumbed to the first frosts. The rotting fruit now attracts thrushes, eager to plunder the plentiful seeds.

Rather unusually, swallows may still be seen, and in mild autumns bats will also be apparent, into November and beyond. If so, there must obviously be insect food still on the wing for them; mature insects in flight at this time of year, if not destined to hibernate, will often stay alive until killed by frosts. Grasshoppers are sometimes heard in November, while gnats are reliably late. Winter gnats are also on the wing, sometimes dancing in large swarms at this time of year.

Ptarmigan are now moulting again to

white on Scottish hills, the white feathers being produced, as are white hairs, by lack of pigment. On these hills, and on some English moors, patches of heather will be burned during these winter months to provide the young growth on which the grouse feed. Up on these high wildernesses, the red deer will be more mobile, the flies having died off with the cold, and they will now be stalked and shot; without selective culling they would exhaust the food available.

Culling is also part of the argument for fox hunting which begins on 1 November, extending until mid-April. Without the hunt, the fox population would have to be accurately decimated by shooting or trapping; they are too successful for their own good. Unlike the farmers' packs of the Lake District and other areas, many fox hunts are also grand social occasions. Paradoxically, the still-growing popularity of the sport ensures the survival of wild foxes in Britain.

Guy Fawkes took over the traditions of Celtic bonfires to mark the start of winter. Last century, Guy Fawkes Night was a mischief night, mischief being a very ancient folk tradition. All Saints' Day falls on the first of the month, and All Souls' Day is on the second—both originated with older pagan celebrations.

Most trees lose their remaining leaves as November advances. With links weakened by frost, they are snatched away by gusty winds. Even weak branches may fall, snapped off by the first of autumn's strong gales. However, November still has an autumnal feel rather than a wintry one.

HEAVY RAIN

The Atlantic Ocean has considerable influence on the British climate and its spells of weather, and it is interesting to compare November's seas with those of February. The temperatures off Cornwall, Norfolk, and Wick in north-east Scotland are respectively (November/February): 12.7°C/9°C; 10°C/5.5°C; 10°C/6.6°C.

Although the sea temperature is only part of the picture, we may guess that November is a month with more of an autumnal feel than a wintry one. Snow whitens high ground in Scotland and the Pennines, and perhaps in the higher Welsh hills by mid-November, but the rest of the country has some way to go yet to feel the bite of winter.

Continuing the pattern of October, many westerly and south-westerly gales lash the cliffs and bring heavy rain to the country beyond. This wet lessens to the east in the lee of the western hills, and in the Midlands conditions may be good for fog to form. As the sun is weak, these fogs may be rather slow to clear away.

The chance of a really warm day is not as good as in October, although severe cold is unlikely in November. As with any month, though, aberrations can be expected. A historically famous one was the strong 'Protestant Wind' which, in November 1688, blew the ships of William of Orange from Holland to Torbay in Devon (somewhat west of his intended destination of Bexhill, East Sussex); here he landed on what is now Guy Fawkes Day to dispossess Catholic James II.

Another feature of November is that the days are now so cool, while the rain is so heavy, that evaporation from the ground is slow, if at all. Many fields remain noticeably damp, and will do so until March (although, of course, modern field drainage helps them dry out towards the end of the winter).

Thick fogs frequently cause havoc on the roads in November (although, of course, fogs can form in any month). This map shows the average number of days each year that thick fog awaits the waking world—this is defined as the number of days when the visibility is less than 200 yards at 9 am. From these figures, it is clear that those commuting to work in our major cities stand a good chance of being seriously affected by fog on many mornings each year.

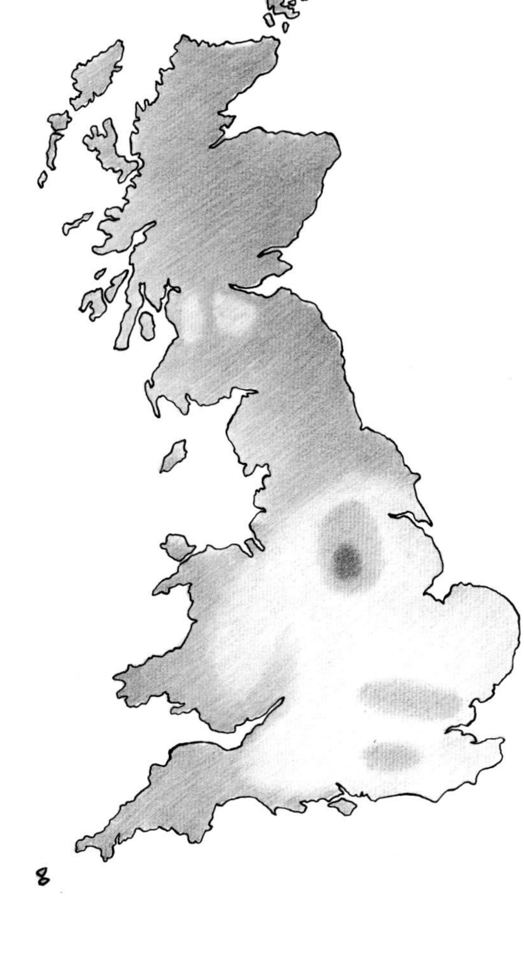

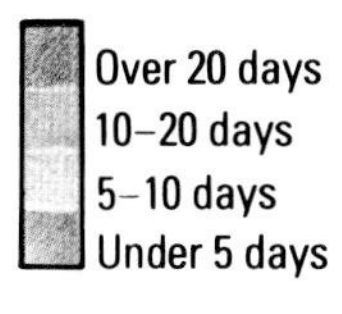

FOG AND MIST

The rains of autumn, the weakening sun and the lengthening nights conspire together to create mists and fogs. These are rather similar, and a mist is likely to be seen as a step in the creation of a fog. Both are a suspension of small water droplets, those of mist being smaller and fewer than those of fog.

Mists and fogs form for much the same reasons as dew. On a still evening, damp ground loses its heat to the sky. Some of its water evaporates and the air just above the soil becomes saturated so that when it cools, the expelled droplets fall as dew. If there is a slight stirring of the air, however, moisture is carried up from the ground layers and condensation occurs in the air above. Mist and then fog forms. In hilly areas it can present a delightful prospect, a white sea filling the vale below. Valley fogs of this kind can be quite deep—most are between 50 ft and 300 ft. Fog may also be long-lasting, as the winter sun cannot heat the ground sufficiently to set warm air rising to stir things up.

Hill fogs are, in effect, low clouds; their moisture condenses when damp warm air is moved up to cooler regions to cross the high ground. Visibility is often less than 300 ft.

Officially, a 'fog' cuts visibility to less than

An early morning mist in late autumn is slow to dissipate among the now-bare deciduous trees.

1100 yards (1000 metres) and affects airports, while 'thick fog' in the forecasts means visibility cut to 200 yards or less. Visibility can be well over 1000 yards in a 'mist'. However, when people talk about 'mist patches' in which visibility is limited, they are referring to small patches of fog. This can be localized in pockets, where its formation is guaranteed by the local geography of slopes and surfaces. On motorways, these pockets are sometimes marked by the sudden eruption of a length of overhead lights.

Mists and fogs are seen mainly in valleys and lowlands in early winter. But something similar is created when mild moist air rolls across thawing snow, resulting in a rather raw fog. Sea fogs form in much the same way, when warm moist air crosses a colder sea and condenses. Many summer holidays on the east coast are spoilt by sea fogs, when east winds bring warm continental air across the North Sea. However, these 'haars' (see page 94) can be avoided by driving inland, where glorious sunshine is often found, part of the same weather system.

Smog is simply a combination of smoke and fog. This dirty fog is particularly hazardous under a temperature inversion, which puts a lid over the area. Thankfully, London's pea-soupers are a thing of the past—smoke pollution control has eliminated them. However, even now, smogs can restrict the daylight reaching industrial towns.

Many plant leaves become bedecked by drops of water in a fog. This is not dew but water sucked up from the roots, which is slow to evaporate in the damp air. Lady's mantle is notable here.

Fog affects the movements of animals, especially birds. Hunting birds cannot see their prey, while starlings come to roost a couple of hours earlier on foggy winter evenings, and gulls remain on shore since both fishing and navigation are more difficult. When courting, black grouse call more loudly when fog rolls through the pine woods, and other birds, realizing they are unseen, possibly do the same.

Certainly, fog poses hazards to birds on the wing and many are found dead or injured as a result of collision, but it may not have much effect on migration since the sky is usually clear above the bank of fog. Quite often, though, the cliffs of Dover hold ranks of birds in foggy weather, waiting for clearance before crossing the Channel.

CASTING SEEDS

Few plump heavy acorns can now be found lying beneath the oak. It is also noticeable that young oak saplings are seldom seen growing beneath the canopy of an oak tree, where they could be expected to get away to a good start in the sheltered surroundings. Yet ash will happily sprout here.

By and large, our native trees prefer to germinate, and their seedlings will only flourish in sunny clearings, or under the lighter shade of another species of tree, perhaps. Some species are more demanding than others, and of these the silver birch is much the most light-demanding. It will not grow under other trees, but it casts a light shade and oak will grow under it. Ash also casts a light shade, and oak may be found growing under it, whereas the densely-leaved beech is happy to grow slowly under oak.

Birch trees make good pioneers when woodland is colonizing open ground. Their myriads of small winged seeds ripen in September to be spread far afield by the autumn's gales. Ash seeds are also helicoptered by wind to germinate thickly even in shady places, although they will demand more light later on. Animals can help this distribution by collecting the seeds and dropping some of them, or by leaving their buried caches unclaimed.

It is noticeable at this time of year that the dangling ash keys are rarely taken. Not all birds find them objectionable, though, and bullfinches will eat them. However, when plump acorns fall to the ground in the shade below the oak, animals are relied upon to remove them to a new site.

At the end of the last Ice Age, Britain was largely open, waiting to be colonized by plants and trees from the warmer south. Yet pollen preserved in ancient soils shows that oaks were already growing at Loch Maree in Scotland 9000 years ago—a very rapid spread north, at an average rate of 600 ft a year.

In autumn, the grey squirrel may be observed successfully spreading acorns. This squirrel is a hoarder and buries small caches of nuts when they are abundant, choosing featureless open ground. However, this animal has only helped the spread of the oak in recent years, for the grey squirrel was only introduced to this country from America a century ago. This squirrel seems to have no clear memory of the exact locations of its hoards, but digs at random while foraging. The chances of acorns being abandoned to germinate are therefore high.

Below right A single rosebay willowherb plant produces vast numbers of seeds to drift far afield on the wind. Although by origin a woodland species, this plant is often seen on waste ground and roadsides as a result of its excellent seed-dispersal abilities.

Below Many animals exploit autumn's larder. Observe here how skilfully the dormouse grasps the swaying bramble stem in its quest for berries.

Perhaps birds were more important in the spread of the oak, for some birds also cache acorns. Jays are well known for this and seem to have a better memory than the squirrels; in fact their scientific name, *Garrulus glandarius*, translates as 'noisy bird fond of acorns'.

However, the seed crop will in turn also affect animal populations. The birds and other animals that rely on tree seeds have plenty in some years, scarcity in others. Good beech mast crops are five to ten years apart, while heavy acorn crops are two to four years apart. Scots pine similarly produces a good crop of cones and seed only every two to three years. The good years will obviously be marked with greater activity in the woods—for example, wood-pigeons may stay in the woodlands and only be rarely seen out on the grain fields.

A good autumn with plentiful acorns and beech mast will clearly help many bird species from tits and chaffinches to jays. They will lay up good fat reserves and be better able to survive the winter ahead. With some specialized feeders, however, the variability of such seed crops dictates some unusual and adaptable behaviour.

The crossbill is one example. These birds feed on pine seeds, prising open the cones with their unusual bills. The seeds are ripe early in the year, and so these birds are early nesters as a result. In a good food year, many young crossbills are successfully fledged, but for this to happen a copious supply is needed, for the parents may have to collect up to 100,000 conifer seeds. However, the resulting swollen population may thus be faced with hunger the following year when the crop falters.

Rather oddly, when animals bury the tree seeds they may (if not reclaimed) help them on their way to germination. Many trees drop seeds which are in a dormant state, and are not ready to germinate the next spring. However, this dormancy is often broken if the seed is buried immediately; the chances of germination the first spring are then quite good, and almost certain during the second. Of course, the buried seeds may be eaten by mice.

All in all, land left to its own devices to revert back to nature will usually become woodland within about 50 years.

Birds are effective distributors of seeds; this song thrush will later wipe its bill against a branch to free it of adhering seeds, while any thickly-walled pips that are eaten are likely to be voided undamaged several miles away.

The spear thistle is a very common plant of roadsides, waste ground and grasslands as well as open woodlands. Its plentiful seeds waft far on the wind to enable it to colonize new sites.

CATTLE UNDER COVER

If the weather allows, the tractor remains busy in the fields in November. Indeed, in a dry autumn, winter wheat and barley can be sown right up to Christmas. But it is more likely that the soil is now too wet and sticky to work. If work is attempted and a soil with quite a bit of clay becomes compacted, it could take a year or two to correct this damage.

The fields already sown will be sprouting green—they look like fields of grass. If the month is mild, the growth may be tall; consequently, there is a danger of frost attack. In the past, sheep were often let in to graze the field down, although this is not so popular today as there is a danger of their hooves causing damage. They may also be let on to the cattle pastures, to nibble them down to a close-knit turf that is better able to withstand the killing frosts later on.

Where the sheep can still scavenge a bite, the cattle cannot, and although the cattle summer can be extended by strip-grazing kale or leafy root crops, the animals are most likely to be under cover now. On average, they will be winter feeding for 180 days of the year, but this figure is nearer 200 in the north. (On the northern lowland pastures, where dairy herds do less well, beef cattle may spend most of the winter out at a low stocking rate, being fed hay in the fields in addition to the grazing.)

There are various ways of stalling the cows and the fattening beef bullocks and heifers. Usually they are housed under one roof, with the silage clamp at one end. They will stand on straw, into which the dung will be trodden. Yeasts and bacteria in the dung are thus activated, and the messy mixture becomes 'muck', a very beneficial organic manure. This can be dispersed over the resting pastures with a 'muck spreader'—a tractor trailer with rotating arms—or ploughed into the arable fields.

Alternatively, the cattle may be 'bedded' on slatted floors so that the dung and urine drop through to accumulate as liquid slurry. Being raw, this tends to poison the field, tainting the grass, but it is expensive to dispose of. Or the animals may be on concrete flooring. This can be cosier than it looks. The open central floor is surrounded by cubicles with insulated floors, in which the cattle choose to lie to chew the cud (being insulated, the floors are warmer). As they cannot back into a cubicle, the dung collects on the central area, from whence it can be shovelled up. This dung can also be spread on the fields, but is not as good as muck—yet a cow can produce 6 tons of the stuff in the course of a winter!

The autumn calving cows will be giving good yields of milk at this time, each day consuming around 45 lb of silage or 20 lb of hay. They will also be fed 12 lb or so of concentrates (4 lb to each gallon of milk they produce). There is tasty variety in this—crushed barley perhaps, with added vitamins and minerals, linseed-oil cake, occasionally some turnip, and chopped barley straw for roughage. In return, a cow gratefully produces about 3 gallons of milk a day. However, the spring calvers will now be drying off in preparation for the coming births. The cattle will also receive injections against worm and warble.

With the harvest in and the autumn stock sales over, it is a good time to analyse the feed and adjust it. As well as the cows, the farm may be housing beef cattle to be fed on barley. Nevertheless, it could be a good time to sell off some of the home-produced barley stored in the farm's silos, if it is surplus to requirements. Feed barley can fetch a good price in November.

Many farmers follow the hounds. But it is in the northern hills that hunting is most closely linked with farming. There is little doubt that foxes will take lambs, and up here lambs may be the farm's sole source of income. Therefore, the farmers' packs of such places as the Lake District always get a good turn-out from local folk to follow the hunt. This is John Peel's old domain, his 'coat so grey' being made of undyed local wool. And here the hunt is followed on foot, as John Peel himself did, although it is quite difficult to keep up with the hounds coursing the fells.

Horses are a feature of today's countryside, and a growing part of it. Land devoted to horse grazing may now total over 150,000 acres. They are kept principally for recreation—for hacking, competitions and hunting—although, on a few farms, heavy horses such as the Suffolk are seen as pets, or a hobby. These traditional breeds once pulled the plough and other farm equipment, the jobs now done by the tractor. It is partly for the purpose of feeding horses that hay is made and oats are sown.

The bulk of the cattle are now likely to be under cover. Large livestock sheds are a familiar part of the countryside today, but on many farms you will still find the traditional farmyard buildings in use.

GRAFHAM WATER

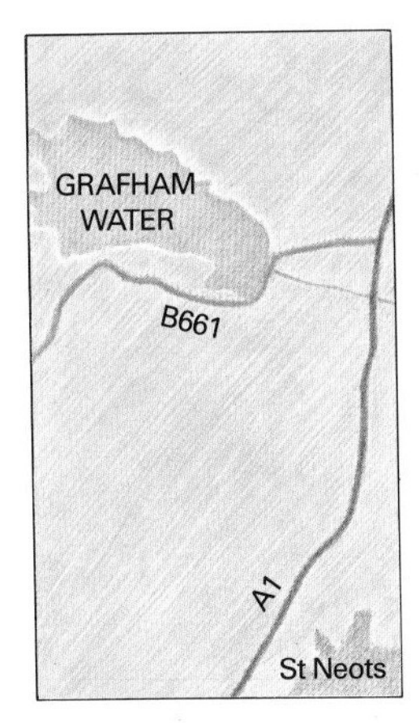

The Grafham Water reservoir in Cambridgeshire is some 1570 acres in extent when full. There are sanctuary areas and hides for birdwatching, as well as nature trails. In addition to this, other areas are popular for boating and fishing. Surprisingly, all these different uses manage to co-exist quite happily.

Waterworks of one kind or another are part of the modern world. Victorian reservoirs have retaining walls of architectural quality to match the best industrial architecture, while London has giant storage reservoirs holding up to 8000 million gallons of Thames and canal water. Even picturesque Thirlmere in the Lake District is not natural, but a valley dammed in Victorian times to supply Manchester with pure drinking water.

Today's reservoirs are frequently sited in open countryside. Grafham Water in Cambridgeshire is typical of them; officially opened in 1966, it laps up to fields on its shoreline. But it is also typical in the great interest of its birdlife, so much so that in 1986 it received the official accolade of registration as an SSSI, a 'Site of Special Scientific Interest', joining a very select club indeed.

Most of the wildfowl congregate at the western end where 375 acres have been set aside, free from disturbance from anglers and boats. However, the birds can regularly be seen over the main body of the water.

Grafham is especially busy in winter. Great crested grebes are sometimes to be seen by the hundred on the deep water by the dam, with perhaps over 2000 coots. Ducks are its main attraction, though, with mallards 1500 strong, and teals and wigeons, the latter sometimes feeding on the fields alongside.

Grafham provides plentiful shallow water along its shoreline for the dabbling ducks, which feed by up-ending from the surface, whereas in other deeper, sloping reservoirs they may have to adopt the habits of diving ducks. There are also plenty of these to be seen here; tufted ducks are the commonest diving duck, with up to 2000 at a time—about 1 per cent of Britain's population. With them are smaller numbers of pochards, goosanders and goldeneyes.

Hard weather is always an exciting time for the reservoir birdwatcher, for smaller ponds ice over, forcing their waterfowl to move out. Many move to the coast when the freeze comes, but some species prefer to stay by fresh water and so visit these reservoirs and larger lakes which are kept free of ice by the waves thrown up by the winds scudding across the surface. In such weather, the waterfowl take avoiding action, seeking shelter, while some crowd together in 'rafts' facing the wind.

Alternatively, Grafham may also attract birds from the coast when the ocean is stormy. Bewick's swans, scaups, eiders, smews and others visit, with occasionally even a cormorant to be seen (unlike the shag which does not come inland). Here on Grafham, the cormorant fishes the trout which stock the waters.

Spring and autumn see numerous bird movements, and at these times Grafham is visited by many migrating waders. These birds literally drop in to rest and feed along the shorelines of the lagoons. Real rarities such as ospreys, avocets and phalaropes are also sometimes seen.

Summer, too, is of interest. The great crested grebes perform their curious courtship, and a few of the ducks and waders may stay to nest while their companions leave. Redshanks, lapwings, and ringed and little ringed plovers also nest here, being joined by terns, normally considered birds of the coast alone. About 200 mute swans will gather here to moult when the time comes.

Such lowland refuges were not uncommon in the past, when our river systems were flanked by countless miles of wet wilderness. A reservoir not only offers a variety of birdlife, but also interesting insights into its adaptability. Although, by and large, birds have rigid lifestyles, they are also opportunists, and population pressures will force them to try all new options open to them. In this way, they have adopted modern reservoirs, while the now-familiar 'garden' birds are yet another example of this form of conquest of new opportunities.

Up to 10,000 goldeneyes (*Bucephala clangula*) winter on our waters; they are often seen diving for food, and when spring approaches the males throng around a duck, throwing back their heads. However, only 260 pairs of gadwalls (*Anas strepera*) breed here, though more than 2000 birds stay for the winter.

BRITAIN'S RESERVOIRS AND LAKES

Other reservoirs and lakes noted for attracting wintering birds are as follows:

1 Loch Leven, south of Perth, Tayside. This large, shallow loch holds the largest number of breeding ducks in Britain.
2 Kielder Water, Northumberland.
3 Derwent Reservoir, Tyne and Wear.
4 Fairburn Ings, near Castleford, West Yorkshire. Mining subsidence created these flooded lakes.
5 Kingsbury Water Park, Warwickshire.
6 Abberton Reservoir, near Colchester, Essex.
7 Lake Vyrnwy, near Welshpool, Powys.
8 Bewl Bridge Reservoir, near Hawkhurst, East Sussex.
9 Chew Valley Lake, south of Bristol, Avon.
10 Tring Reservoirs, Hertfordshire.
11 Staines Reservoirs, Surrey.
12 Sutton Bingham Reservoir, near Yeovil, Somerset.
★Grafham Water, Cambridgeshire.

Rafts of waterfowl are often to be seen on Grafham Water, particularly through the winter months.

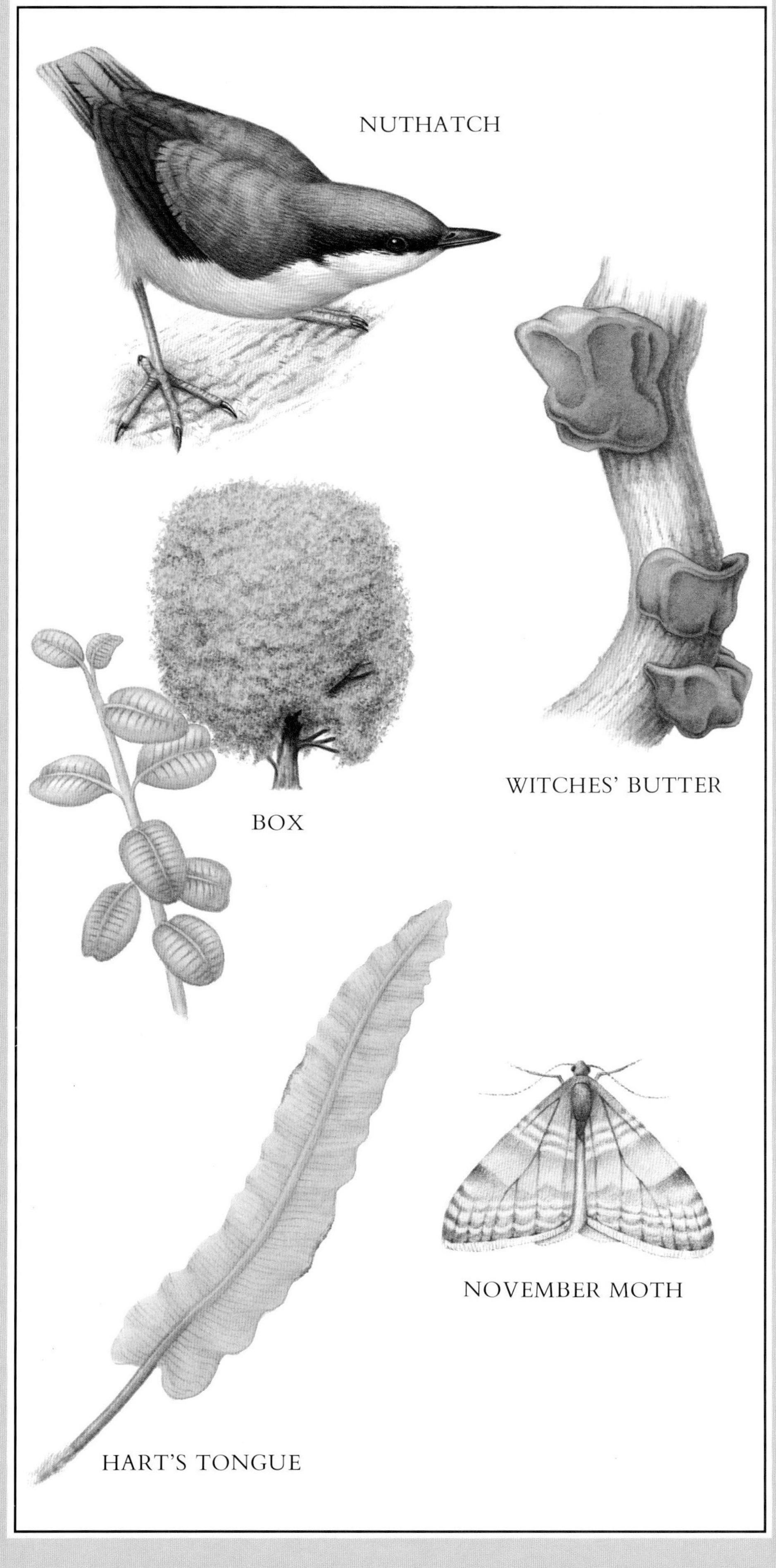

NUTHATCH *Sitta europaea* 50,000 pairs resident. In the silence of the empty November wood, the nuthatch can frequently be heard hammering away for the kernel of a nut which it has jammed into a bark crevice. Hazel nuts, beech mast and acorns are all collected, but it will also eat insects from the bark. The only bird to be seen climbing a tree trunk both up and down (pointing head first) in search of insects, the handsome nuthatch is found mainly in southern Britain and in Wales. Its nest is a hole, whose entrance is narrowed with mud to deter larger birds. It has a loud trilling whistle, plus a loud metallic 'twit' and other calls, usually heard from early January into the breeding season, though some birds may still be heard now in November.

WITCHES' BUTTER *Exidia glandulosa* This fungus is seen in winter months, on rotting boughs upon the woodland floor.

BOX *Buxus sempervirens* With deciduous trees now quickly shedding the last remnants of their summer foliage, the box notably retains its leaves, which are pleasantly scented when crushed. Although box varieties are most familiar from garden hedges, it is a native species, growing as a shrub or low tree, but confined to only a few sites on chalk or limy soils in southern England (Box Hill in Surrey is a well-known place where wild box may be seen). Like the yew, it casts a very dense shade, thus killing other tree seedlings which might have grown to overtop it.

HART'S TONGUE *Asplenium scolopendrium* Except for the Scottish mountains, this fern is seen in many different habitats everywhere, including rocks and walls. Although dead fronds may be seen at this time of year, it is still a very handsome plant, being largely an evergreen.

NOVEMBER MOTH *Epirrita dilutata* A very common moth on the wing at this time of year, this species flies mainly at night (and is usually one of those caught in the bright beam of car headlights). It may sometimes also be seen in flight during the dull November days.

YELLOW-NECKED MOUSE *Apodemus flavicollis* A species introduced into Britain, the yellow-necked mouse now has a patchy distribution in south-eastern counties and the Welsh borders (in some years and places it seems quite common). During this month, it may venture into garden sheds, or even houses, seeking cosy quarters for the winter. A nocturnal animal, little is known about it, but it seems as agile, and with much the same feeding habits, as the slightly smaller wood mouse.

COMMON POLYPODY *Polypodium vulgare* This evergreen fern can be seen throughout Britain. Although it will grow in the soil, it is as often, if not more frequently, found growing off the ground on the tops of walls, or on tree trunks and rocks. Hence, it does better in the wetter west, where the copious rains ensure that its roots do not dry out, as well as bringing slight traces of nutrients to enrich its site.

WOOD BLEWIT *Lepista nudum* In spite of its ominous bluish or violet colouring, this is an edible fungus found in beech woods or mixed woodland at this time of year. 'Blewits' (of which this is but one species) are named after this tingé, and were once commonly sold for cooking.

CHERRY LAUREL *Prunus laurocerasus* An introduced evergreen garden shrub, the cherry laurel can quickly seed itself elsewhere if given the chance. If left unclipped, it carries loose candles of white marzipan-scented flowers (April–June), and the berries begin to ripen earlier in the autumn—there may still be a few left, but only a few, for they are very popular with birds.

TREECREEPER *Certhia familiaris* 200,000 pairs resident. This bird may be seen climbing jerkily in spirals up a tree trunk, picking spiders and insects from the bark with its thin bill, while using its tail as a prop. On reaching the top of the trunk, it flies down to the base of a neighbouring tree to start all over again. Its call is shrill, with its song a hastening series of 'see-see' notes. It nests in a tree hole or simply sheltered behind a flap of bark.

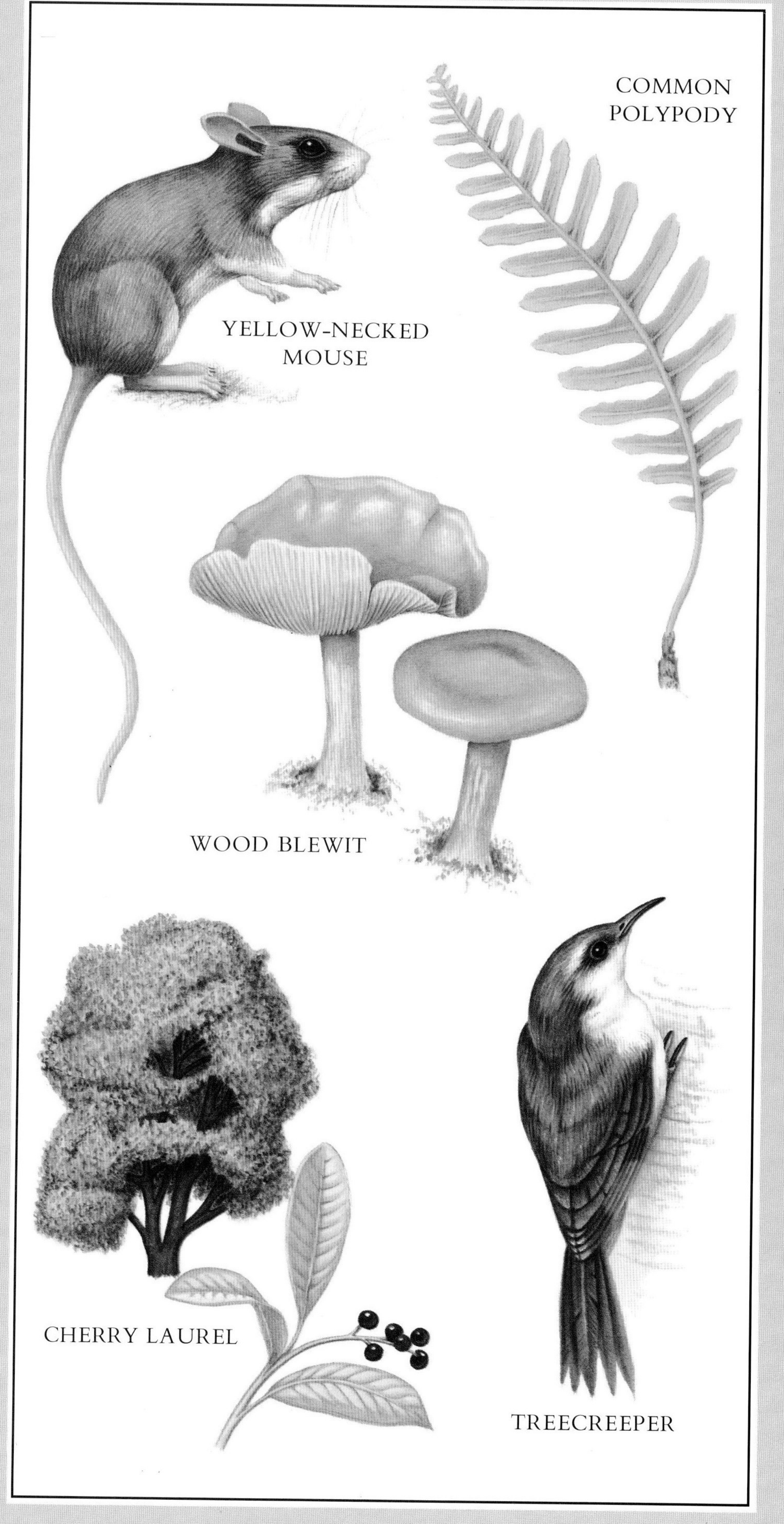

COMMON (or GARDEN) SNAIL *Helix aspersa* While doing the last bits of gardening for the year, this handsome snail is often discovered hibernating under stones or logs, clustered with its fellows; it is also common in hedgerows. During the summer months, it keeps a secure retreat from which it issues forth each night in search of succulent leaves, travelling fair distances before dawn and leaving a slime trail across flagstones as evidence of its passage. After mutual courtship (snails are hermaphroditic), eggs are laid in the soil which later hatch into small snails, complete with minute shells.

HOUSE SPARROW *Passer domesticus* 3,500,000 pairs resident. This is more a bird of town and village than the open countryside. In mild years its breeding can be extended, even into this month. With chirruping calls, but no real song, it makes a fair din at all times of the year, but it is possibly noisiest in spring when, after making the nest, the cock sparrow advertises it by chirping ceaselessly from close by. The cocks are also noisy when displaying, belligerently circling each other. The untidy nest is in a hole of some kind or hidden behind ivy.

EAR FUNGUS *Auricularia auricula-judae* This fleshy fungus is noticeable on the bare boughs of elders at this time of year, until the frosts strike.

MAGPIE *Pica pica* 200,000+ pairs resident. The magpie is found everywhere in Britain, except in the Scottish Highlands. Its rounded, domed nest can now be seen in the bare branches—and it will keep its shape throughout the winter. At this time of year, magpies may be seen in groups, but usually they remain in pairs. Wary pairs, too, for this bird is difficult to approach. They utter noisy cackling calls, and are often seen at roadsides, picking at small corpses squashed by cars. Scavenging apart, they are pirates of songbirds' nests in spring and summer, regularly stealing eggs and nestlings in spite of the loud scolding of the parents. They will not attack pigeons and other larger birds, but as magpies patrol their territory once every six hours or so, they often find these birds' eggs left unguarded.

COLLARED (or RING) DOVE *Streptopelia decaocto* 40,000 pairs resident. This bird has dramatically expanded its range since first nesting here in 1955. Suburban gardens, with trees for nesting plus bird-tables providing plentiful food scraps, are a favourite habitat. It is also seen on farmland, and may now be found picking over the unploughed stubble. It has a pleasing, if monotonous, three-note 'coo-cooo-coo' call.

GREAT GREY SLUG *Limax maximus* This is the largest of the 23 species of slugs found in Britain. A slug is basically a shell-less snail; however, without a water-retaining shell, it needs a more humid lair. It is now found hibernating, often in groups.

PIED WAGTAIL *Motacilla alba yarrellii* 300,000 pairs resident. With flicking tail and undulating flight (and a 'chizzuck' call), the pied wagtail is a familiar bird in villages, and even towns. It is attracted by the winging insects of watersides, which are caught not far from the ground, often with running dashes, but it will also feed elsewhere. It has the reputation for choosing quaint nest sites—in unused farm machinery, for example. In bleak winter weather, it may choose equally unusual communal roosts, packing together in large numbers in greenhouses and other snug places.

BANDED (or GROVE) SNAIL *Cepaea nemoralis* Seen along hedges, as well as in grassy places and woods, this snail is a favourite of the song thrush, and its shattered shells are often found around that bird's 'anvil'. The shells are variable in colour and pattern.

BROWN RAT *Rattus norvegicus* Now that food is running short in the fields, the heavy-bodied brown rat may be returning to farmstead and village. It is also regularly found in a variety of other habitats, including town sewers, cellars, rubbish tips, canal banks (it can swim well) and roadside lay-bys. Although mainly active by night, it is often glimpsed during the day. This rodent digs burrow systems in which to rear its young (and will take over rabbit warrens); breeding reflects the availability of food, and females may have up to five litters a year.

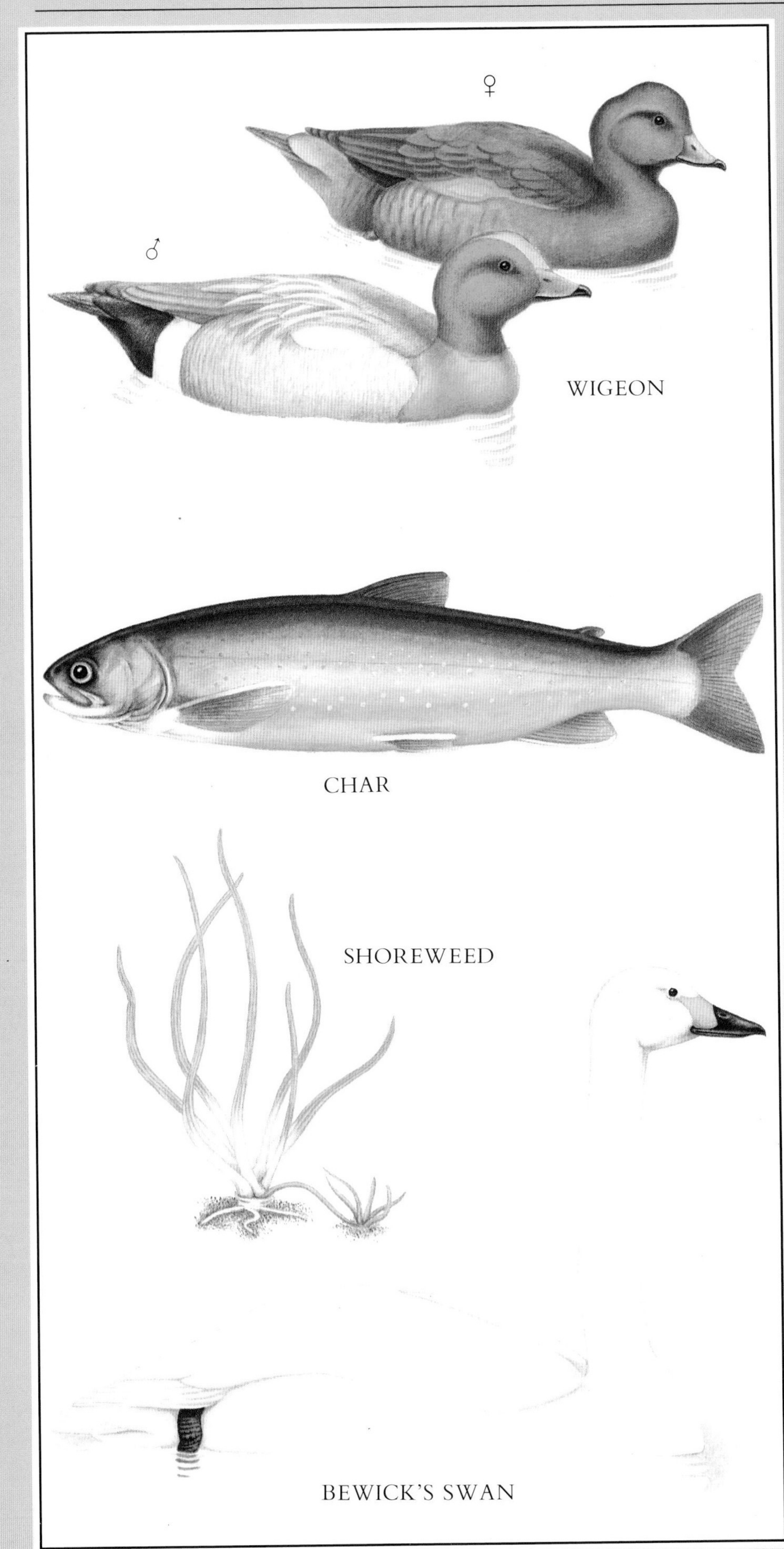

WIGEON *Anas penelope* 200,000 birds in winter. In November, our resident wigeons, which breed mainly in the north alongside freshwater streams and lakes, are being joined by incoming migrants, flying in large numbers in V-formations. Now seen resting in large flocks on open waters, wigeons are unusual among ducks for grazing, goose-like, on grass, although they will also feed from the surface, dabbling down for waterweeds.

CHAR *Salvelinus alpinus* This fish is found in lake colonies, and as it does not move far into the rivers, these colonies may have been in separate existence since the end of the Ice Age, 12,000 years ago (fish of one water even show slight differences to those of another, lending weight to this belief). They stay in deep water except when coming to the surface in the evening to feed on other fish fry. Generally, they spawn in almost ice-cold water, within the months of November to March—and will now slowly migrate to the shallower margins, even a little way up the filler streams, so there is a good chance of seeing them.

SHOREWEED *Littorella uniflora* Forming tufts in the shallows of mountain lakes in Wales and the north, shoreweed is sometimes exposed in summer when the water level drops, but is now covered in winter, perhaps creating a submerged sward if the spot is protected from waves. Its small, barish flowers are seen from June to August.

BEWICK'S SWAN *Cygnus bewickii* 5000 birds visit. Goose-like skeins of Bewick's swans may now be winging their way in from the Arctic, yelping like a pack of hounds. They go to various lakes and other freshwater sites scattered around Britain, but there are sizeable populations in the Ouse Washes, and at the Wildfowl Trust reserve at Slimbridge, Gloucestershire. It seems that several years' progeny remain together in small family flocks, and they may faithfully return to the same site winter after winter (the record at Slimbridge is 23 years). Individual birds can often be easily identified, because each has its own pattern of yellow on the bill.

VENDACE *Coregonus vandesius* Even more restricted than the char, the vendace is found in only a few deep waters in the Lake District and Scotland. It, too, spawns close inshore in the cold months.

WHOOPER SWAN *Cygnus cygnus* 2500 birds visit. This bird began arriving a month or so ago, mainly in northern Britain. The visiting flocks tend to split up, but can still remain fairly sizeable. Family parties, though, usually graze together, often on fields of stubble. Highly vocal, especially when in flight, whooper swans have a far-reaching trumpeting call—hence the suitability of their name. But unlike the semi-domesticated mute swan, both whooper and Bewick's swans have relatively quiet wingbeats. These visitors will return to the Arctic in April, though a small number may remain behind to breed.

COMMON QUILLWORT *Isoetes lacustris* An aquatic plant growing close to the edges of stony tarns and lakes in the mountains, quillwort lives totally submerged at a deeper level than shoreweed, and so is relatively unaffected by the waves thrown up by strong winter gales.

GREAT DIVING BEETLE *Dytiscus marginalis* This is a ferocious species of insect, as the adults and larvae are both capable of giving intruding fingers a sharp nip. The adult male has smoother wing-cases than the female, but both adults have distinctive yellow undersides. The beetles are active throughout the year, and may often be noticed when coming up for air—they float to the surface, tail first, and remain there for some time, filling their breathing tubes.

SWAN MUSSEL *Anodonta cygnea* The largest of our freshwater bivalves, the swan mussel is often to be seen, despite living in the bottom mud or gravel of hard-water streams and pools, as it always keeps part of its shell exposed. The shell is held ajar, with the edges of the siphons perhaps visible; these suck water past the gills, which strain out food particles. It is a good idea to introduce swan mussels into garden pools, as they are excellent at keeping the water clean.

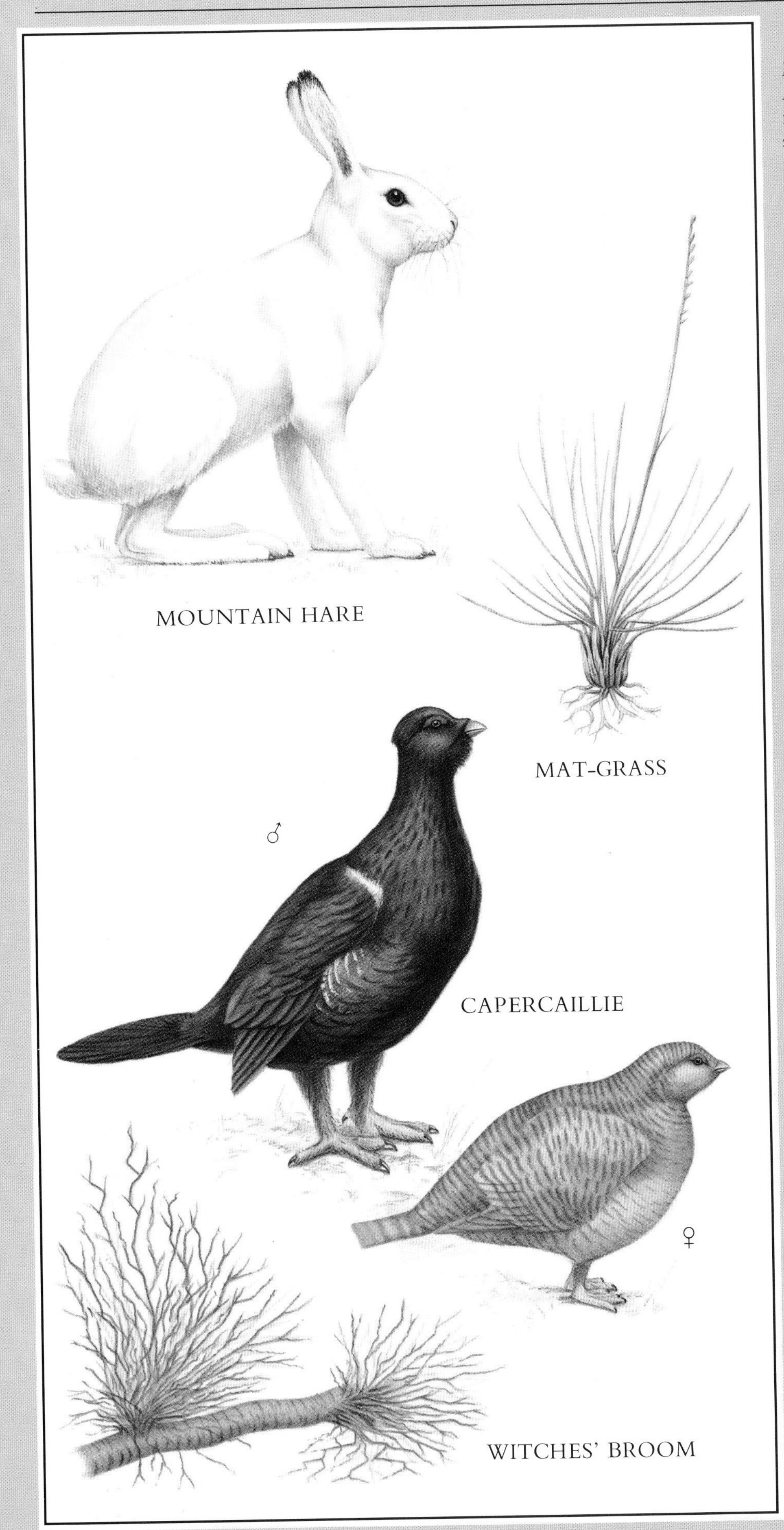

MOUNTAIN (or BLUE) HARE *Lepus timidus* The mountain hare is mainly found 1000–3000 ft up the slopes of the Scottish Highlands, where rocks amidst the heather offer security from buzzards and eagles, but there are also small populations in North Wales and the Peak District. With occasional snow flurries now whitening the high moors and mountains, this hare is now in its winter coat. It is most likely to be full white in the Scottish Highlands, but even here the colour may be patchy, as it is elsewhere (the coat often has a rather bluish tinge given by the underfur). In spring it is brown again, and there is another moult later to a shorter coat; however, throughout these changes, the tail remains white and the ear tips dark. Most of the day is spent in a 'form'—a regular hollow in the ground or nibbled from the heather. Feeding begins at dusk, and paths are nibbled out across bilberry, heather and grass. There are two or three litters a year.

MAT-GRASS *Nardus stricta* The wiry tussocks of mat-grass are easily recognized: greyish-green in summer, but dying and whitish in winter. Sheep do not eat its bristly leaves, so it may create vast areas of 'grass moor' on drier areas in the hills.

CAPERCAILLIE *Tetrao urogallus* 5000 pairs resident perhaps. Now found only in the Scottish Highlands, at the approach of winter this turkey-like bird prefers the forests in which it breeds (it feeds on pine shoots), but in late summer it is often seen out on the open heather. Clearance of the pine forests and shooting had eliminated it 200 years ago—the birds we see today have been reintroduced. It has an extraordinary courtship display, which may be seen as early as late December in mild weather. With tail spread peacock-fashion, throat feathers fluffed out and head raised, it emits a slow series of clicking calls which hasten to become a rattle, accompanied by short jumping flights. Territorially proud, the capercaillie will even attack human intruders.

WITCHES' BROOM These bunchy outgrowths, now clearly visible on the leafless branches of birches, are a form of plant gall, caused by fungus attack.

TINDER (or HOOF) FUNGUS *Fomes fomentarius* This may now be seen on birch trees in the Scottish Highlands. In the days before matches, flammable 'tinder' was used to catch the spark from struck flint—and dry tinder fungus, soaked in saltpetre, was counted the best.

FIELD (or SHORT-TAILED) VOLE *Microtus agrestis* Found throughout Britain, from valleys to moorlands as high as 3000 ft, the field vole will noisily defend its territory against rivals. It nests beneath a grassy tussock, log or other shelter, but now that the tussocks are collapsing with the onset of winter, its hidden network of runways from the nest may become exposed. A vegetarian, it likes the more succulent grass stems, but will even nibble bark if hungry. In favourable circumstances, its numbers can swell to as many as 500 an acre. These 'vole years' have a knock-on effect, for owls and other predators can also breed strongly. Then the vole population slumps (perhaps the stresses of overpopulation also reduce breeding), and will remain low until the next boom, which may occur within three to five years.

RAZOR-STROP FUNGUS *Piptoporus betulinus* The fine corky flesh of this birch-tree fungus was ideal for honing a fine, sharp edge on old-fashioned, cut-throat razors.

PTARMIGAN *Lagopus mutus* 10,000 pairs resident. This relative of the grouse is found only on the high mountains of the Scottish Highlands, which can remain snow-covered for many months. It changes its plumage to suit the changing scene. Towards the end of August it is assuming the mottled grey of eclipse; this will then become the white winter coat, with its feathered feet making good snow-shoes; in summer, the upper parts are a mottled darkish brown, with white belly, throat and wingtips. Its breeding depends not so much on the summer weather (which is usually bleak at these heights), but on the snow-melt in late May or June, at which time the territorial skirmishes are seen. The diet of the ptarmigan includes the shoots of heather, bilberry and other mountain plants.

BAR-TAILED GODWIT *Limosa lapponica* 30,000 birds in winter. This visitor, now grouping on various coastal feeding grounds, will stay for the winter, its numbers swelled by migrants on passage elsewhere. In fact, some non-breeding birds may even stay for the summer. This bird feeds in flocks, probing the exposed sandy mud with its bill—the touch of a hidden shellfish or worm will send it spinning around, digging deeper to secure its prey. 'Wik' and 'kirrick' calls are heard in flight.

COMMON LIMPET *Patella vulgata* Closely related to sea snails (in evolutionary terms, its shell represents the end of the coiled shell), the limpet spends the daylight hours, when the tide is out, lying sedentary, tightly clasping the rock. To prevent desiccation, the fit needs to be close, and so the shell edge either grows to match the rock surface or grinds a ring into it. At other times (if not too stormy), the limpet moves away from its base, grazing the young seaweeds. It cleans the surrounding rock, leaving patches totally bare of weed. After grazing, the limpet must return to its home site, but if knocked off the rock, without a guide back, it is doomed.

CHANNELLED WRACK *Pelvetia canaliculata* Many brown seaweeds are left exposed for hours when the tide is out, and the amount of desiccation they can withstand 'zones' them down the beach. Channelled wrack is found at the top of the shore, regularly exposed for several whole days each month, at which time it becomes black and brittle. Its fronds curl lengthwise, presumably to protect it from extreme drying-out.

BLADDER WRACK *Fucus vesiculosus* Occupying the middle shore, this brown seaweed has paired bladders (float chambers) to lift its fronds when the tide is in. These fronds also bear dimpled spore sacs.

BLACK-TAILED GODWIT *Limosa limosa* 4000 birds in winter. Passage migrants and winter visitors now join the residents (which breed on the Ouse Washes and by the Solway). With longer legs than its bar-tailed cousin, this bird feeds in the shallows.

PURPLE SANDPIPER *Calidris maritima* 15,000 birds visit. This bird, now seen at rocky winter coasts, prefers tumbled weedy rocks, where it forages a diet of winkles and other shellfish at the water's edge. Here it is often unnoticed, so well is it camouflaged. It is also a quiet bird (though with a piping alarm call).

OARWEED *Laminaria digitata* This is exposed only at the lowest low tides (the 'spring tides') of the month. Seaweeds do not have roots, but a leathery 'holdfast' attaches them to rocks or stones. Oarweed is frequently washed ashore by winter storms, and the holdfast can then be inspected. Small limpets and other animals can often be found claiming protection within the fist of the holdfast.

SLIPPER LIMPET *Crepidula fornicata* Introduced from North America, this has since spread, becoming a pest of oyster beds. It settles in chains, changing its sex—the oldest limpets (underneath) are female, while the youngsters atop them are male. The empty shells are often found washed up on stormy winter beaches.

BEAN GOOSE *Anser fabalis* 200 birds visit. Wintering in East Anglia, Northumberland and south-west Scotland, this relatively quiet goose is closely related to the pink-footed goose, but, unlike its cousin, this bird regularly feeds on pastureland. It is a 'grey goose' (as are greylag, white-fronted and pink-footed geese), with a typically fast flight despite heavy wingbeats. It flies in V-formation on migration, but this may break up when landing, and the bean geese 'whiffle' down in disorder. All grey geese swim well. (Brent, barnacle and Canada geese are 'black geese', with a dark crown.)

SUGAR KELP (or SEA BELT) *Laminaria saccharina* Washed ashore, this has long been a favourite seaweed for amateur weather prediction. It is no real guide, however.

WHITING *Merlangius merlangus* A familiar fishmonger's fish, the whiting comes inshore in winter and is often caught by beach anglers. It feeds on sand eels, sprats and shrimps.

DECEMBER

The shortest day of the year is on or about 22 December, the winter solstice, when the sun is furthest from the equator in the southern hemisphere. Although this can be regarded as a turning point in the year, true winter is yet to come; December is noted for being stormy rather than cold. Christmas falls on the 25th, of course, with Boxing Day on the 26th.

In old farming communities, the Twelve Days of Christmas beginning on 25 December were believed to forecast the weather of the coming year. And although spring may be just around the corner in the south-west, as determined by the appearance of some flowers, the rest of the country steels itself for the onslaught of winter to come.

The Glastonbury thorn is a subspecies of the hedgerow hawthorn, and in popular lore was believed to have grown from the staff of Joseph of Arimathea when he visited Britain. It flowers at variable times in winter, often on Christmas Day. When the calendar was changed in 1752, and 11 days were lost, people crowded at Glastonbury to see what the thorn would do. It waited until 5 January to flower! Cuttings have since been taken and it now grows in various other places.

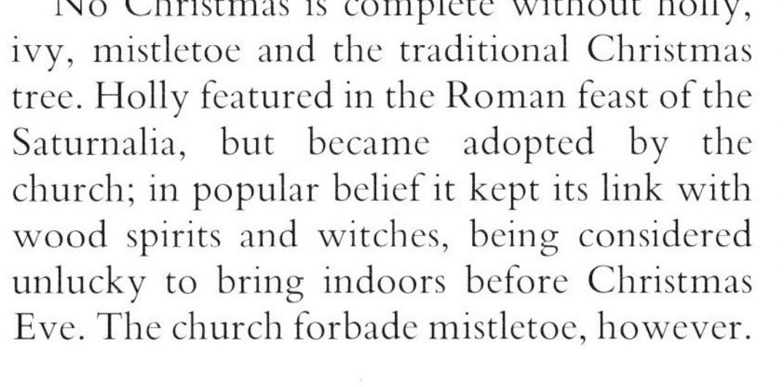

No Christmas is complete without holly, ivy, mistletoe and the traditional Christmas tree. Holly featured in the Roman feast of the Saturnalia, but became adopted by the church; in popular belief it kept its link with wood spirits and witches, being considered unlucky to bring indoors before Christmas Eve. The church forbade mistletoe, however. With a golden sickle, the Celtic druids cut it from a sacred oak, to be used for divination. Mistletoe was also linked with fertility, and the practice of kissing below it is perhaps a last echo of this.

Although there are references to Christmas trees in the streets of medieval London, the custom of bringing the tree (the Norway spruce) into the house and decorating it is German in origin, introduced by Queen Victoria's spouse, Prince Albert, in 1847.

Fire played an important part in many ancient ceremonies, and Christians adopted the yule log, to burn in every hearth. The log was not brought in until Christmas Eve,

The scarlet berries of holly persist all winter, seemingly ignored by the birds. Not all trees carry berries, though, for the male and female flowers are often held on different trees.

However high the summits, Scotland's heights are often known as 'hills' rather than mountains. Here they carry the first heavy snowfalls of the year. December's landscapes such as this have a muted glory; here the dark-brown heather patterns the paler fawn of the grass slopes, while conifers rank sombre green—even the abandoned dwelling has a muted mystery in this wintry setting.

and once lit, the fire was not allowed to die out until the log was reduced to ash. Other traditions had unusual origins: the chariot of the Norse god Odin became a sledge, while St Nicholas became Father Christmas!

The Twelve Days of Christmas were always a time of eating and merriment and a direct descendant of the Saturnalia. In old times, it was very much a last chance for feasting before the rigours that lay ahead. Boar's head, beef or goose were traditional English dishes (turkeys only appeared on the British scene in the 16th century), with mutton or haggis in Scotland. And in Scotland, many ancient English Christmas customs have become linked with Hogmanay, New Year's Eve.

Robins are now in striking song. In many areas, both they and wrens were hunted through the woods on Boxing Day.

Hunting of some kind is still a strong element, with Boxing Day meets in pursuit of the fox or Boxing Day shoots among neighbouring farmers and landowners.

New Year's Eve has its own customs, which are stronger in Scotland than the rest of Britain. In both, the 'first-footer' superstition is widespread, in which it is believed that luck is brought in when a man or lad brings bread, salt and coal into the house.

ONSET OF WINTER

Inland, December is usually the cloudiest month, offering least sunshine. The coasts, though, do have brighter skies, perhaps even during stormy spells.

Again, it is the Atlantic Ocean which is having the greatest influence on the weather pattern. It is still relatively warm, enough to delay the onset of cold along western coasts. In fact, in the extreme south-west, horticulturalists can count the growing season as extending through to 8 January, although for Cornish farmers the grazing season ends early in December.

This oceanic influence is a stormy one, and December is perhaps the stormiest month of the year on western coasts affected by deep Atlantic depressions. These bring gales and heavy rain—the moist air flooding in can give vast rainfalls when pushed up and cooled over some mountain areas. Snow is likely to the north and it is much colder in Scotland.

Fogs and frosts are possible when pressure rises inland during anticyclonic spells and winds drop, for the lowest temperatures come with calm, clear nights. In fact, the lowest temperatures of the year are registered on such nights in December, January and February, when the ground is snow-covered and continental Arctic air has arrived.

It usually snows when the air temperature lies between −2°C and 2°C. (The expression 'too cold to snow' has some justification, as very cold air may be too dry to offer much precipitation.) As for the chance of a white Christmas, this is obviously more likely for high villages and farms, for hills favour snow as they do rain. For the rest, the chances really rely on the weather patterns on the run-up to Christmas Day. Although the 1920s and 1930s were not snowy decades, the next three were. More recently, however, snow in December has been generally infrequent.

Snow at Christmas is usually welcome, but often unpredictable. Over a range of years, however, it is possible to show the likelihood of snow occurring at least at some time during the winter months. Thus, the map shows the average number of days per year with snow lying on the ground as dawn breaks. The effect of high ground is very apparent from the distribution of these figures.

Over 40 days
30–40 days
20–30 days
10–20 days
Under 10 days

SNOW

When snow falls in the British lowlands, it usually melts on reaching the warm ground or stays for only a short while. In the Midlands, for example, it snows on average up to 20 days a year, but the snow rarely lies on the ground outside the period December to March, and during these months it may lie on ten or more mornings in all. The north-east often sees heavier lowland falls, but nowhere is quite free from the risk of a deep snow. Wind can increase the danger—snow of 5 in. deep can quickly drift to imperil wildlife, sheep, and motorists, who are frequently left stranded, unprepared for such an occurrence, until rescued by a clearing snow-plough.

Height also increases the chance of heavy snow, for if the air temperature is a rainy 4°C on the valley fields, it is likely to be 0°C and snowing at 2000 ft. In the Midlands and Wales, for every 330 ft gain in height, five more days of snow can be expected. In northern Scotland, though, the figure is 17 days per 330 ft.

Snowflakes have a wonderfully delicate natural beauty, with an infinite variety of branching patterns. If the air is cold enough, clouds hold supercooled water-vapour drop-

Above The wind has blown the snow into miniature patterned 'dunes'. At the edge of the field the snow has drifted deep, to endanger the mice, voles and other wildlife of the hedgerow. Compacted snow such as this is slow to melt.

Above left A typical snow scene, with rime also clothing the tree branches.

lets and small ice crystals—these droplets freeze on to the crystals to build up into flakes. 'Cold weather' snow is dry and powdery, but when the flakes fall through air which is slightly warmer than 0°C, some melting and adhesion of separate flakes occurs, and they become larger and thicker. (During the summer months, many clouds high above us contain ice crystals and snowflakes, but these melt long before reaching the ground, to fall as rain.)

For wildlife, snow can be a serious hazard. It can quickly cover favourite feeding grounds and cause severe hardship to small birds which normally only have fat reserves to last a night or two. However, pheasants in the lowlands and ptarmigan on the hills are able to scrape away snow to feed, as can deer and badgers.

Snow may also bring surprising benefits. Consisting mainly of trapped and still air (12 in. of snow melt to give only 1 in. of water), snow is an excellent insulator. If the air above a foot of snow drops to −10°C, the soil surface may still be unfrozen. Thus, if snow falls before frost strikes, it can protect young green shoots from frostbite. At the same time, it allows worms to continue their activities near the top of the soil. It will also keep many a small animal snug in its burrow, and mountain sheep can survive burial for many hours if they are able to breathe.

The pure whiteness of snow reflects back 85 per cent of the sunlight to create an eye-aching glare. It also reflects back the larger part of the warm element in the sun's radiation. In other words, it is not sunshine which melts snow, but rather a spell of warm air or falling rain. If unfrozen, the soil will also give off warmth to melt the snow from below. However, turf insulates the snow from this direction, which explains why slight snowfalls tend to lie on the garden lawn but not on flowerbeds.

On days when the air temperature is just at freezing, even the slight warmth given off by the living needles of conifers can melt the snow sitting on branches. In addition, large stones act as hot-water bottles, soaking up the warmth of the sun's radiation and reissuing it to melt the snow lying against them. In the months to come, these first patches of snow-melt will be very important for the ptarmigan and meadow pipits on the hillsides, for in such places food plants start to grow and the first insects begin to emerge.

BEATING THE COLD

We have our Christmas dinner in the artificial microclimate of a heated room, heated not to warm us but to prevent the loss of body warmth, which occurs quickly in cold surroundings. Clothes are an insulation against this heat loss, as are fur and feathers for wildlife.

Feathers give a misleading impression of the size of a bird: many have tiny bodies. A smaller body has a higher proportion of skin to bulk than a large one, and as warmth is lost from the skin, it loses warmth more readily. To ease their plight, many small birds adopt odd roosting behaviour on very cold nights.

Pied wagtails roost together in scores when they can gain access to sheltered places such as greenhouses. This close proximity means that less heat is lost by individuals in a crowd than alone and exposed, at least for those on the inside. Sparrows may perch nudging each other near a street light, a source of warmth. Starlings will roost crowded together in thousands—and are canny enough to prefer cities where the air is warmed both by the buildings and by the traffic in the streets. But the oddest roosting is perhaps that of tiny wrens, which in bitter spells often congregate, neatly arranged in layers, in such places as nest boxes. Here they really are creating a larger 'body' with less surface area to radiate warmth away. The risk, of course, is that the inner birds may smother. As a result of their susceptibility to cold, the British wren population tends to fluctuate violently, dropping sharply in harsh winters.

The solitary winter nest of this dormouse has been opened to show it curled in its typical hibernating posture with head bent, and eyes and mouth tightly closed.

Small birds fluff up their feathers in bitter cold, and mammals can raise their fur to deepen the layer of trapped still air, the insulating factor. Dartmoor ponies grow thicker, shaggy winter coats. Goose pimples are our own attempt to erect hairs that evolution shed long ago; and shivering increases heat production by the muscles. A layer of fat below the skin also helps insulation—the solution adopted by seals and whales. However, many mammals do as we do, and retire to a warmer microclimate, namely a burrow in the ground, venturing outside only when driven by hunger.

We see only the frozen surface of the ground and assume that the frost bites deep. Soil, however, is a good insulator owing to its myriad small air spaces. Insulation is added by turf atop the soil, and if it snows so much the better, for a foot of freshly fallen snow can keep the soil from freezing even when the air temperature drops to -10°C. This may aid not only worms, which otherwise tunnel deeper in cold weather, but also those early spring flowers.

Among the many chambers of a rabbit warren, the deepest are occupied only in very cold weather, while the sets of badgers would only be worth tenanting for generation after generation if they were reliably snug. The chambers have a reasonably steady regime; they may vary between 12°C in summer and 7°C in winter.

In cold spells, tits and some other birds can apparently reduce their body temperature and become torpid until daybreak. Cold-blooded mackerel may do much the same, but for a longer period. When the sea cools in November, they may swim to the seabed and sluggishly remain there until spring.

True hibernators adopt a very special strategy to beat the cold, and they also require a snug hideaway to safeguard them from predators. Mammals need a store of body fat to slowly 'burn' while they are unconscious. The heart slows (to one beat every 12 seconds in the dormouse), hence circulation is very sluggish and breathing barely detectable. But hibernation can be broken. Hedgehogs appear and bats are sometimes seen on the wing on warm winter days—this may be extremely hazardous, though, for they waste their precious fat reserves which cannot be restored as there is no food available.

The hedgehog makes a hibernation bed usually of a deep pile of leaves or grass, well insulated from the air. There is an advantage in this, for only a really long spell of warmth will reach the dormant animal—it is unlikely to be awakened by odd warm days. At temperatures of between 7°C and 12°C, a dormouse will awake to feed every evening in the winter months, while at 4°C and below, it will hibernate without a break from September to March. Squirrels, however, merely doze, waking to feed at intervals.

Cold-blooded animals, such as frogs and snakes, also hibernate, while many insects hibernate as adults, although hibernation can be broken—for example, a disturbed peacock butterfly may take to the wing at this time. Insects in general, with their complicated life-cycle, may overwinter at other stages—as egg, grub or caterpillar, or as resting pupa or adult—with only slight protection in a crack of bark and similar places. Though becoming deeply chilled, the body cells of these invertebrates seem to contain some natural anti-freeze, for the freezing process does not rupture their tissues.

A hedgehog hibernating in a nest of leaves. Hedgehogs are quite likely to wake in warmer spells and perhaps change nests.

A great tit fluffing up its feathers in extreme cold to deepen the insulating layer of still air and prevent its body losing warmth.

In common with many mammals, Dartmoor ponies tend to grow a thicker, warmer coat to help see them through the winter. They start to grow it in August and it will remain until May.

HEDGING AND DITCHING

Fat-stock shows are held in December, up and down Britain, the best-known pair being the Edinburgh Show and London's Royal Smithfield Show (now held at Earls Court). They are a clue that December can be a rather quiet month for the farmer. The displays and the talk are more about machinery than animals, however.

There are one or two tasks to be attended to at this time. The autumn calving cows may now have to be served if this has not already been done. It will be the first time for the heifers, now aged between 18 and 24 months. At this time of year, they will be artificially inseminated rather than being served by a bull. The yards will be cleaned out and the calves weighed to check growth.

Snow can now begin to make life difficult for the hill farmer. Quite probably many of his breeding ewes will be in rented, lower and sheltered fields. But many could be open flocking, wandering their familiar fells for forage. They will need some hay—not only hay to keep alive, but also to begin building up their body reserves for lambing; to this end, they will also soon start being fed rations of compound feed. There is quite a difference between these hardy scavengers and lowland down sheep, which are noticeably lazier and will crowd round the empty trough rather than search the field for a bite here and there.

It is a good month for maintenance. There will be ditching to be done, making sure that the soil will be satisfactorily dry in the spring. For although wheat and barley are grasses, which normally like wet conditions, they are Mediterranean by origin, introduced by our first farmers, and thus prefer dry soil. (Oats, however, are less particular.)

Most probably the arable fields are already lined below ground with networks of pipes to dry the soil. Clear ditches are needed to collect the water from the outfalls of these systems and carry it off to the nearest stream. Ditching can mean anything from work for a couple of men with spades to contractors' gangs armed with hydraulic shovels. Contractors will also be called in to lay any new pipes—nowadays these are often made from plastic rather than pottery. Sometimes a network of mole drains is dug above the pipes—though short-lived, these are easily made by drawing a bullet-shaped 'mole' through the soil.

Wood is sawn for logs, and for fencing the paddocks and other areas. Hedging may be another task. Hedges can be trimmed by hand using a sharp-edged slasher, a billhook, or by using a tractor-powered flail or cutter. They can be trimmed into various cross-sections, square or triangular.

Alternatively, an old hedge may be laid or layered. This is a living tradition, seen in many places, especially where the hedge encloses grazing, for a well-laid hedge is animal-proof. If left to itself, a hedge grows tall and tends to develop a gappy bottom, but trimming can help to thicken the bottom. However, there is a saying that anything sheep can see through, they will get through—but a laid hedge should remain stock-proof for 20 years, needing only the occasional trim.

The hedge is first cleaned up, the climbers cut back. Work then starts on the pleachers, the line of strong upright branches which will be the skeleton of the new hedge. They are each cut with an angled slice near their foot, through the hardwood but leaving a strip of

bark unsevered. The pleacher is then bent over, hinged by this strip of living bark. Sap still reaches it, and in time it throws up new branches from its prone position, which thicken to create a dense barrier. A final stage may be to tighten the line of pleachers with a row of stakes, joined by a twisted binding or 'heathering' of string or hazel shoots, or the briar stems cleared earlier.

Counties each had, and may still have, their own pattern. A Midlands bullock hedge, enclosing the beef pastures, has the brushy twigs of the pleachers all facing into the field to deter the steers. Welsh sheep hedges have brushy ends on both sides.

Hedging is a skill. It may be tackled by someone on the farm, though not the stockman, of course, for he is always busy. Or a professional pair of gangers could be called in. The cost is about the same as barbed-wire fencing, but better for wildlife.

At last, it is Christmas. There may be a few farm geese to pluck and truss, but all too soon it is over—and someone still has to milk the dairy herd twice a day. But on an arable farm, with Christmas Day, Boxing Day and New Year's Day all public holidays, and perhaps some days still owing from the annual four weeks' leave for the men, it might be sensible to close down for a fortnight.

Ditches are needed to carry off the water from the drains in the fields; they also keep the farm tracks dry and usable. Hedging is another important job: a countryman tightens up a laid hedge with a row of stakes—by the time the stakes have rotted, the hedge will have grown into itself.

GRIZEDALE FOREST

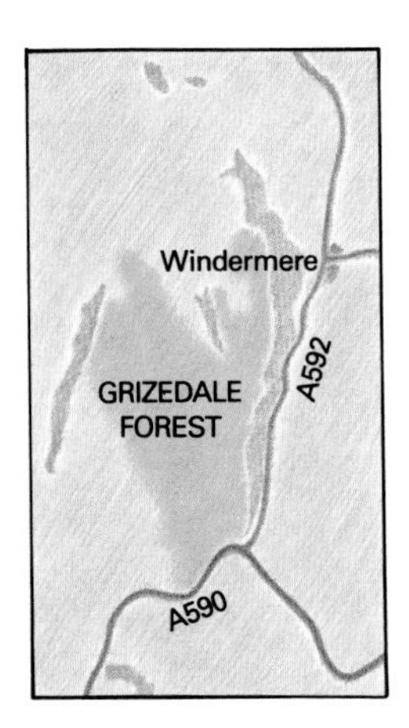

Bounded to the east by Lake Windermere and to the west by Coniston Water, Grizedale Forest comprises one of the larger blocks of modern tree planting in the Lake District. Concerts and other activities are often staged at the Forest Centre.

Some three centuries ago, the diarist John Evelyn considered that Britain 'had better be without gold than without timber'. A timber shortage meant that the Royal Navy was threatened. Partly due to his blandishments, many royal forests were planted for timber, and society also began to plant up their inherited deer parks and other holdings.

In those days, they planted mainly native oak or beech and other hardwoods, the soil dictating the choice. However, in this century conifer plantations, which give a quicker return on capital, have become common enough to make up around three-quarters of our woodland. The close-ranked rows of these evergreens, usually foreign species, now march on the poor acid soils of once-open fells and commons, but have also replaced the oaks and native woodlands of the richer vales.

Grizedale Forest, lying within the Lake District National Park, is well worth a visit. The fells and distant peaks can be glimpsed capped with snow at this time of year, seen from the many access rides and firebreaks which divide its compartments. On many large plantations these carry trees of different ages, giving some variety to the scene. Visual variety is also added when contours are followed and blocks of different species are merged, which is now common practice.

On a crisp winter day, Grizedale Forest has a distinct character all of its own; not quite barren wilderness, certainly not diverse and varied, but of interest, nevertheless. Extra entertainment is given by the 'Sculptures in the Forest', created in wood by different artists and encountered unexpectedly along the rides—bridges, forts, and rows of poles.

Of course, wildlife does not care about aesthetics or interesting walks. Food and shelter are its concerns, and here an alien wood such as Grizedale is a poor second to a native oak wood. Not only does the latter supply much more of a range of insects and other food for birds, but also a greater variety of nest sites to suit the birds' exacting, if instinctive, demands.

In such winter plantations, small parties of goldcrests may sometimes be heard, though rarely seen as they flit in the foliage above. They may join with parties of tits, such as coal tits, which use their long slender beaks to probe hibernating insects from flakes of bark or cones. Apart from these, many species use the densely-ranked conifers for winter roosts, not only crows, wood-pigeons and other common birds, but also charms of goldfinches. The deep shelter of the conifer plantation also attracts deer; the tracks of roe deer are often seen in the snow of the rides and the fields alongside when they need to leave the plantation's seclusion to feed.

Paradoxically, the recently-planted compartments of a plantation may see a succession of ground nesters such as meadow pipits, which like the low rough cover of the young trees and the grass tussocks between them. These also attract voles, which in their turn may bring in kestrels and buzzards. Later, when the conifers form shoulder-high dense scrub, songbirds such as blackbirds and warblers may nest. Thereafter, however, the trunks of the conifers are 'brashed' or cleared of side branches to stimulate tall growth, and only canopy-nesting birds such as crows and wood-pigeons are likely to be attracted.

Although the Scots pine is frequently seen in conifer plantations, and in some places old stands are seen, it reaches its full natural potential only in the Black Wood of Rannoch and other remaining fragments of the ancient Scottish pine forests. They are living museums, relic fragments of the forests which covered much of Britain before being invaded by the oaks. These woods have an open feel to them. Below the widely-spaced trees—and these each have their own shape and age (quite unlike a plantation)—is a thick, tangled, low undergrowth of heather, bilberry and sometimes juniper.

Around 500,000 goldcrests (*Regulus regulus*) breed in our conifer woodlands. Although they are more usually heard than seen (for they are active in the treetops), there is perhaps a better chance of seeing these tiny birds at this time of year when in bitter times they take to roaming, often through other woods.

BRITAIN'S CONIFER PLANTATIONS
Plantation areas which may be visited include:
1 Kyle of Sutherland, Highland.
2 The Queen Elizabeth Forest Park, Central.
3 Argyll Forest Park, Strathclyde. Bordered by sea water along half its boundary, this was Britain's first forest park; it showed how commercial forestry can be combined with wildlife and recreation.
4 Galloway Forest Park, Dumfries and Galloway.
5 Kielder Forest, Northumberland. This is Europe's largest man-made forest.
6 Delamere Forest, Cheshire.
7 Gwydyr Forest, Betws-y-coed, Gwynedd.
8 Ystwyth Forest, Dyfed.
9 Thetford Chase, Breckland, Norfolk.
10 Maulden Wood, Luton, Bedfordshire.
11 New Forest, Hampshire.
12 Isle of Purbeck, Dorset.
***Grizedale Forest**, Cumbria.

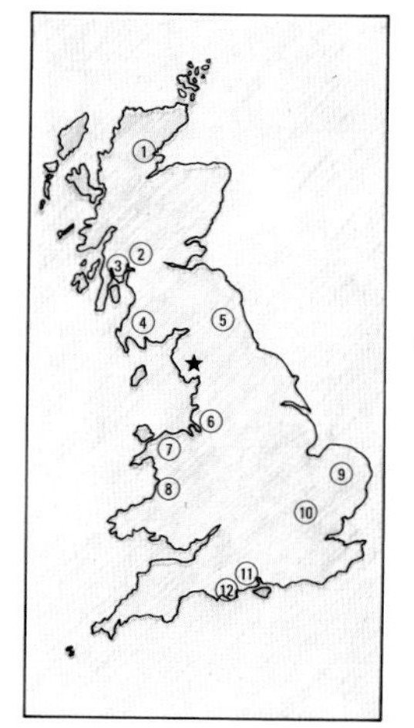

Grizedale Forest lies within the Lake District National Park, pictured here with the Lakeland hills beyond. Among the ranked green of the evergreen conifers, it is possible to spot isolated compartments of larch—a deciduous conifer.

MISTLETOE *Viscum album* Playing an important part in the Christmas festivities, mistletoe flowers early in the year (February–April), and is now carrying sticky berries (November and December). Despite having green leaves, it is a semi-parasite, feeding on the sap of the host tree. Although traditionally linked with oak, it is rarely seen on this tree, occurring most commonly on apple, poplar and lime.

ROBIN *Erithacus rubecula* 3,500,000 pairs resident. Now, when bird song is least, these birds often sing a sweet liquid song, for they hold territory all year round. Indeed, the autumn song (after a pause for moulting in July or August) may be the finest of the year. In reasonable weather, no robin will bear another on its own land until February, when the females abandon their holdings and trespass on to the males' until accepted. However, in bleak spells, hunger may result in the breakdown of boundaries. Robins are cheerily tame (and may even be trained to come indoors in winter), and this, too, is deeply instinctive. They have the habit of picking over soil disturbed by other animals, such as moles (which also live in woodland) and badgers. From here it is a short step to perching on the garden spade. Robins begin to breed early, from March onwards, and the nest is in any handy hole (old tins are sometimes used), and it is often found inside a garden shed.

COMMON YEW *Taxus baccata* Growing in beech woods, and perhaps forming woods of its own, this native conifer is also frequently planted. According to legend, the yew sheltered the first missionaries to Britain, hence the reason it was planted near many churches, as a symbol of faith. Its rugged trunk, with rotted heartwood, may give a false impression of age. The berries (in fact, the swollen scales of a cone) are still seen in December, but beware: the pips (and leaves) are extremely poisonous.

OYSTER FUNGUS *Pleurotus ostreatus* This is now seen on or near tree roots, especially those of beech. Apart from 'mushrooms', this is about the only other fungus cultivated (not collected) for the kitchen.

COMMON HOLLY *Ilex aquifolium* A native tree or shrub, the holly is more common towards the west of Britain. Not all carry the ripe red berries, though, for male and female flowers (May–August) are usually carried on different trees. Birds such as blackbirds seem to leave the berries until last, and in mild winters they may remain on the tree until the spring. The leaves are waxily shiny to reduce water loss (hence they do not droop when cut for decorations), but only those towards the ground are spiny—this may perhaps be a defence against grazing animals (in olden days, the top foliage was cut for iron rations to feed to the cattle in winter). The leaves are held for about four years, then drop.

WINTER MOTH *Operophtera brumata* One of the few insects now on the wing, the winter moth is often seen caught in the bright beam of car headlights and coming to lighted windows. The male flies, but the female is wingless. She makes her way up the bark to lay her eggs in the unopened buds, including those of orchard trees (an old-fashioned remedy was to fasten a sticky band around the tree trunk).

NORWAY SPRUCE *Picea abies* This plantation tree is cropped for timber and for the traditional Christmas tree (the sitka spruce would be far too prickly). Its leathery cones are ripe in late autumn.

LODGEPOLE PINE *Pinus contorta* var. *latifolia* Another common plantation tree, this pine's cones have a longish prickle.

WREN *Troglodytes troglodytes* 3,000,000 pairs resident. Small, dumpy and brown, with sharply cocked tail, the wren is seen in almost every kind of habitat (even moorland) if there is enough cover. It will quickly slip out into the open with a fast-whirring flight, sing loudly, and then slip back again. And it does have a very loud, sweet torrent of a warble, heard at all times of the year. Being so small and therefore greatly at risk from chill, hard winters cause massive mortality among wrens. Communal roosting is common, with many birds cramming together for warmth.

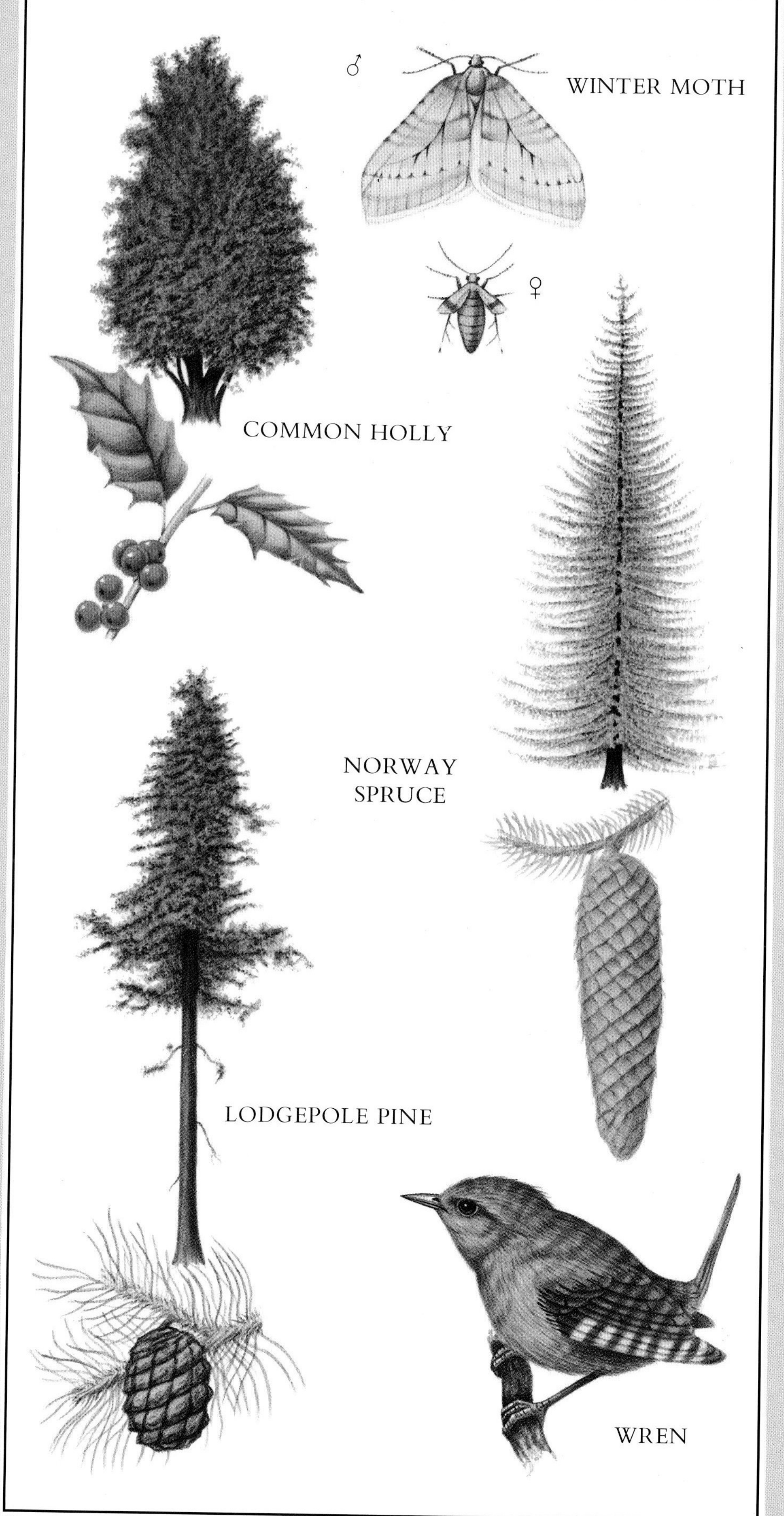

REDWING

DAISY

SONG THRUSH

RED CAMPION

REDWING *Turdus iliacus* 500,000 birds visit (but numbers vary each year). The arrival date of this winter visitor is fairly regular—an average first sighting in Surrey is 5 October, for example. (They will leave again in April, though some have nested in northern Scotland.) On calm nights, flocks of redwings are sometimes heard far overhead, calling with a lisping cry. They are now seen settled in, feeding on the ground, but they will later eat hedgerow haws if forced to by starvation. Really harsh weather can bring them to suburban gardens. In February, they may break into bars of a warbling subsong, but they are usually gone before beginning to sing more fully.

DAISY *Bellis perennis* This familiar plant is often still in flower, although its main period is earlier (March–October). In bad weather, and at dusk, its petals close—hence its name: 'day's eye'.

SONG THRUSH *Turdus philomelos* 1,500,000 pairs resident. This bird's song is on a par with those of its cousins, the blackbird and mistle thrush, but is perhaps more easily recognized. 'Summer is coming, summer is coming, I know it, I know it, I know it'—Tennyson tried to put the song into words, and although he failed, he did catch its rhythm. With such an identifiable song, this bird seems commoner than it really is. The full song is heard even now from time to time, but will pick up in spring. This thrush is also known for its 'anvil'—it collects snails, bringing them to a chosen spot, and hammers the shells against stone or ground until they shatter. The snails are then wiped on the ground before eating. In winter, these thrushes will also take berries (including yew berries, which blackbirds ignore). The nest in a bush is mud-lined, with the sky-blue eggs often clearly visible.

RED CAMPION *Silene dioica* Though the main flowering period for the red campion is from March to October, it is also regularly still in flower in December. It may cross with its cousin the white campion, producing a plant with pink flowers as a result, and (unusually) this flower is also fertile.

FIELDFARE *Turdus pilaris* 500,000 birds visit. Fieldfares are much noisier than redwings, chuckling harshly as they form loose flocks feeding in pastures. They raid hedges when winter begins to bite and will tolerate other birds—except redwings! When spring brings milder weather, they change habits and join the lapwings in the meadows.

GREENFINCH *Carduelis chloris* 800,000 pairs resident. This attractive bird regularly visits gardens in winter, but we rarely see the same individual twice. As with many species, the winter population roams widely during the day, responding to weather and food. It nests in rather open wooded areas (the woodland edge rather than the wood itself), and in spring the male will tour his territory with tail and wings spread in a bat-like fashion, engaging in a fluttery, 'butterfly' display over the trees. The song is a repeated series of phrases, some twittering, other liquid. It also has an odd, nasal drawling note.

DANDELION *Taraxacum officinale* Opening gladly to the sun, even now, the dandelion is mainly seen at other times of the year (March–October). It has a peak in May when it gilds the fields before the buttercups, but it may often still be in flower in winter. One reason is, perhaps, that the plant known as 'dandelion' is really a host of closely-similar microspecies with slightly different habits. Microspecies often set seed without fertilization. Dandelion seeds float away from the familiar puffballs on the wind.

COMMON FIELD SPEEDWELL *Veronica persica* Unlike the other 'weeds' regularly seen in flower at this time, this is an *annual* plant; it flowers from January to December.

LITTLE OWL *Athene noctua* 7000 pairs resident. Found in England and Wales, the little owl is more a bird of parkland or park-like woods, with old trees providing nest holes. Though seen quite often in daylight, perched or flying (with an undulating flight rather like that of a woodpecker), it usually hunts at dusk and dawn. Its diet consists mainly of insects (and it will take young birds when it can).

SMEW *Mergus albellus* 300 birds visit. Arriving in November, this winter visitor from northern Scandinavia and Russia can now be seen on reservoirs and lakes, mainly around London. The drake is unmistakable with his handsome black-and-white plumage and black eye-patch. The smew is a 'sawbill', with the edges of its beak armed with studs to grasp the fish which it finds on short, shallow dives.

WILD MINK *Mustela vison* Preferring darkness or poor light for hunting, the mink is quite likely to be active on dim December days. First farmed in Britain for its fur in 1929 (it is a North American species), mink have been escaping to live wild in many parts of Britain ever since. It is an agile predator, and a serious pest on nature reserves, killing water birds as large as geese and ducks, and nestlings too. Fish do not escape either, for it is an excellent swimmer. Like the otter, it leaves waterside droppings, but these are foul-smelling (unlike the otter's).

GOOSANDER *Mergus merganser* 1000 pairs breed; 5000 birds in winter. This bird breeds around lakes in Scotland and the north, often high up in the hills, and is one of the few ducks that will nest in trees. Now, in December, numbers are also seen on southern reservoirs and other waters.

CADDIS FLY LARVAE These larvae can be seen crawling over stones on the stream bed or lake bottom, protected by a portable 'home', usually tubular in shape, made up of sand grains, leaf patches or other material. The adults are on the wing in the summer. Britain's largest caddis fly is *Phryganea grandis*.

COMMON GULL *Larus canus* 30,000 pairs breed; 600,000 birds in winter. Although resembling a small herring gull, in winter this bird has dusky streaking on its head (which is white in summer). Despite its name, though, it is not a very common gull except in northern Scotland, where it nests on marshy ground around inland lochs or along the coast. However, with winter visitors swelling numbers, it may now be seen everywhere, sometimes following the plough or feeding on the grass of playing fields.

HARVEST MOUSE *Micromys minutus* With the foliage now withered in winter, the grass balls of this retiring animal's nursery nests are disclosed attached to stalks in rank grass along a verge or motorway, or alongside water—and very often in reedbeds, despite the water below. In winter, though, it nests in a ground burrow. The harvest mouse is a confident climber, its prehensile tail grasping plant stalks for security. Although it gains its name from the cornfield, modern farming has more or less eliminated it from that habitat.

BEARDED REEDLING (or BEARDED TIT) *Panurus biarmicus* 600 pairs resident. Found mainly in reedbeds in East Anglia and along the south coast, this bird becomes more widespread in winter when searching for food. However, with a sufficient area of reeds, it may choose to spend all of its life among them, feeding on insects in summer and seeds in winter. Even when hidden, its clear chinking calls can be easily heard. The nest is built at the base of the reeds.

FRESHWATER SHRIMP *Gammarus pulex* This is not a true shrimp, but is related to seashore sandhoppers. It is found in daylight beneath stones and leaves, but when disturbed it rapidly heads for new cover.

WATER SHREW *Neomys fodiens* An animal with a liking for watercress beds, the water shrew has home tunnels which often open at the water's edge. From this base it tours its territory, which can extend for 300 ft or more, with both water and land reaches. As it does not hibernate through winter, the water shrew must hunt by day and night, needing to take the equivalent of its own weight in food each day to fuel its small body.

SHOVELER *Anas clypeata* 500 pairs breed; 10,000 birds in winter. The large, spade-like bill of this bird is unmistakable—it is fringed with fine 'teeth' through which vast amounts of water are strained for small shellfish, seeds and other food. For this reason, the shoveler prefers marshy shallows which have plenty of mud for sifting. Winter migrants will leave in March.

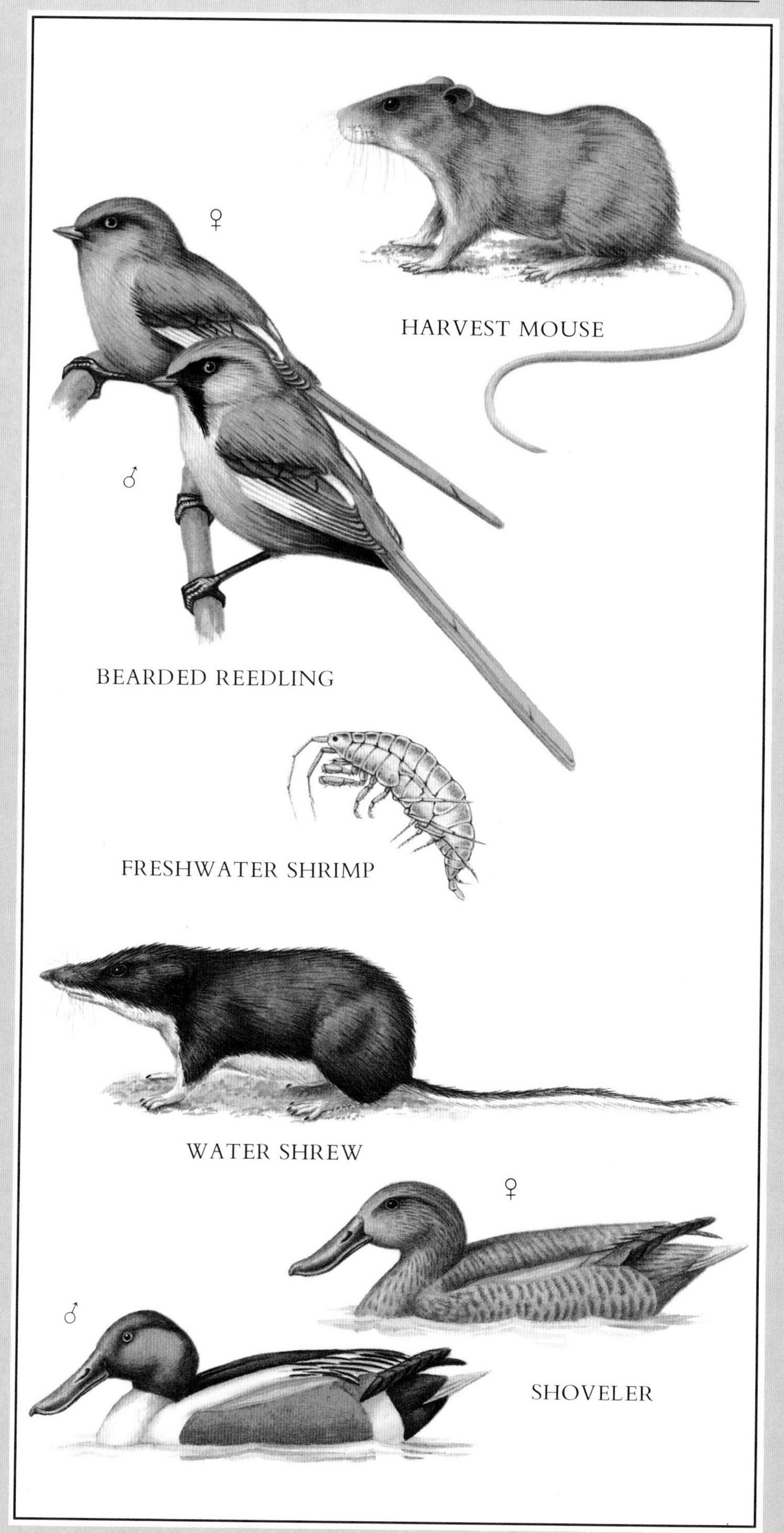

CRESTED TIT

SITKA SPRUCE

REINDEER MOSS

BLACK GROUSE

CRESTED TIT *Parus cristatus* 900 pairs resident. Found only in Scotland, this bird may be seen in old pine woods, especially those in the Spey Valley. With few insects still active at this time of year, it must winkle out hibernating invertebrates from deep between the pine needles or within cracks in the bark. In the course of its search for food, the crested tit may be seen moving along the trunk in the same manner as the treecreeper. Icing of the branches in winter puts this tit at risk, a danger magnified by the fact that it is rather sedentary and will not move far elsewhere to feed. Although it also feeds on birch and alder if mixed with Scots pine, it has not exploited the new conifer plantations elsewhere in Britain.

SITKA SPRUCE *Picea sitchensis* This favourite plantation tree (a native of western North America, introduced to Britain in the 1830s) can thrive on wet ground. It may be recognized by its very sharp needles.

REINDEER MOSS *Cladonia rangiferina* Despite its name, reindeer moss is in fact a tall ground lichen, growing up to 8 in., found on mountains in Scotland and Wales. In the Arctic regions, it is a favourite food of reindeer, forming a major part of their diet.

BLACK GROUSE *Lyrurus tetrix* 10,000 pairs resident. Found in Scotland, Wales, northern England and Exmoor, this bird's preferred habitat seems to be on the fringes of moorland, in woods or fields, rather than on the open ground. Unlike red grouse, these birds do not pair, but meet to mate at communal displays. These 'leks' take place at traditional sites, usually early in the morning. The males each hold territory at the site, and will confront each other, fanning their tails, drooping their wings, and giving voice to weird bubbling and cooing notes and hisses. When one bird yields, the winner takes on another, often jumping into the air. This display also attracts the hen bird, who wanders between the males, before crouching to offer herself to the victor. At all other times of the year, these birds live apart, and the males play no part in rearing the chicks.

HIGHLAND CATTLE *Bos* (domestic) These hardy animals overwinter out of doors (although extra feed may be given). With a double-thickness coat, they can survive both the long Highland winter and the wet of other months. Their coats were originally black (as may sometimes still be seen); however, breeders have favoured the more-familiar reddish coat. They are beef stock, and may calve as early as January in some years.

BUZZARD *Buteo buteo* 8000 pairs resident. Due to persecution, the buzzard is now a bird of remote areas, found mainly in western and northern Britain. In September, it will have begun reappearing over nearby farmed countryside, but now in winter hunger may impel it to range further afield. Called 'the poor man's eagle', it is usually seen circling effortlessly or gliding with wings held slightly back. When soaring, it holds its wings outstretched with the primary feathers spread like fingers to clutch the rising air thermals, watching all the while for rabbits and other prey or carrion. It is most active at those times of day when the thermals are strongest, usually mid-morning to mid-afternoon, but it will also hunt from a perch in woodland. Its mewing cry is instantly recognizable. In the breeding season, the pair will circle their territory, diving at each other from time to time. The nest, a bulky affair of sticks, is set in a tree or on a cliff ledge.

COMMON JUNIPER *Juniperus communis* One of our three native conifers, this can be a shrub (on chalk soils in the south) or a small tree (on moors in the north). On sea cliffs or mountains, it may grow almost flat to the ground. The 'berries' (cones, in fact) are green in the first year, ripening to blue-black. They are often taken by birds in hard weather.

FIRECREST *Regulus ignicapillus* Particularly attracted to Norway spruce, this bird may now occasionally be seen with tits, foraging in conifer and other woods in southern Britain. Among the dense foliage, the only clue to its presence may be the sound of its high-pitched 'zit' calls. It is mainly a winter visitor, although some have been known to nest.

HIGHLAND CATTLE

BUZZARD

COMMON JUNIPER

FIRECREST

TURNSTONE *Arenaria interpres*
Variable numbers pass through on migration on their way to and from the Arctic, and perhaps some 25,000 may winter here. Its dark winter plumage makes the turnstone well hidden on the seaweed-covered rocks, where it flips over weeds and pebbles looking for sandhoppers and other food. But when it takes to flight, uttering a sharp twittering call, its white underside flashes brightly. Unlike other waders, it remains on the shore even in storms. (Indeed, in olden days, when there could be up to 2000 wrecks a year around our coasts, it was considered a bird of ill omen, being the first to flock to a drowned corpse washed in by the waves.)

LESSER SPOTTED DOGFISH
Scyliorhinus canicula Quite common around rocky shores, the dogfish is sometimes caught by inshore fishermen. Its egg-cases are the 'mermaid's purses' frequently found washed ashore (as are those of the skate); the corner threads are used to anchor them to fronds of seaweed.

EIDER *Somateria mollissima* 15,000 pairs breed; 70,000 birds in winter. These ducks breed along the Scottish coast (and beside lakes and rivers), but they are also seen further south in winter, the drakes particularly noticeable against the gunmetal sea. They are very much at home in rough inshore waters, diving or up-ending for mussels and other shellfish. 'Eiderdown', used for stuffing bed coverings, is the soft, highly-insulating breast plumage plucked by the female to be used for lining her nest, which is built among the rocks on cliff turf and other places. Artificial sites are provided for them in Scandinavia for the sake of the down, which is collected once breeding is over. The drake has a crooning call, the duck a contrastingly harsh cry.

GLAUCOUS GULL *Larus hyperboreus*
100+ birds visit. This infrequent visitor is most often seen in severe winters. Almost the same size as the great black-backed gull, this bird is also something of a pirate. It has a greyish-blue back, similar in colour to the 'bloom' on sloe berries (the meaning of the word 'glaucous').

GREY SEAL *Halichoerus grypus* The cows gather to give birth at noisy 'rookeries' on rocky shores, sometimes in large numbers (around 900 assemble at the Farne Islands, for example; it is not yet known how the virus epidemic which first struck in 1988 has affected numbers). Pupping may occur in late August or September in southerly areas, such as the Scillies, but perhaps not until November or December in the north. The young pups remain on the noisy nursery beaches while their mothers feed out to sea, returning only infrequently to suckle them. Mortality is quite high in these early days. The bulls also now crowd on rocks nearby, for mating takes place soon after the birth of the pups. In spring, they will again come inshore, to moult.

LITTLE AUK *Plautus alle* In its habit of wintering in flocks well out to sea, the little auk is typical of many sea birds. However, very stormy weather may bring 'wrecks' of these birds inshore, and in an average winter some are usually blown inland—a surprising sighting on the winter fields.

BLACK-THROATED DIVER *Gavia arctica* 150 pairs resident. During the breeding season, in Scotland, the hills surrounding the chosen lochs echo with this bird's wailing cry. Forsaking their nesting grounds soon afterwards, they may now be seen (in less-striking winter plumage) in many coastal areas.

LUGWORM *Arenicola marina* This is a familiar fishing bait, and its casts are often seen dotted across the muddy sand at low tide. A shallow hollow near the cast marks the head end of the buried U-shaped tube in which it lives, where sand is taken in at its head to be expelled at its tail. Lugworms do not leave their burrows, which they make only slowly and with some effort. Their reddish colour is given by haemoglobin, which stores oxygen so they can survive the stagnant water of their burrows when the tide is out.

RED-BREASTED MERGANSER *Mergus serrator* 1000 pairs breed; 9000 birds in winter. This bird breeds mainly in the north, in sheltered sites near coastal and inland waters, but it may now be seen wintering in southern estuaries.

INDEX